SOUTHWEST

PUEBLOAN RUINS
of the SOUTHWEST

ARTHUR H. ROHN AND WILLIAM M. FERGUSON

University of New Mexico Press ■ Albuquerque

15 14 13 12 11 10   2 3 4 5 6 7

LIBRARY OF CONGRESS CATALOGING-IN-PUBLICATION DATA

Rohn, Arthur H., 1929–
    Puebloan ruins of the Southwest / Arthur H. Rohn,
        William M. Ferguson.
            p. cm.
    Includes bibliographical references and index.
    ISBN-13 978-0-8263-3969-0 (cloth : alk. paper)
    ISBN-10 0-8263-3969-7 (cloth. : alk. paper)
    ISBN-13 978-0-8263-3970-6 (pbk : alk. paper)
    ISBN-10 0-8263-3970-0 (pbk. : alk. paper)

    1. Pueblo Indians—History.
    2. Pueblo Indians—Antiquities.
    3. Southwest, New—Antiquities.
    I. Ferguson, William M. II. Title.
E99.P9R634 2006
978.9004'974—dc22
                                                2005020759

DESIGN AND COMPOSITION: *Mina Yamashita*

Contents

List of Illustrations

Preface

Various students of Southwestern culture history have argued that many ideas and practices have diffused out of Mesoamerica to influence the development of Puebloan culture through time. While there is very little secure evidence for such influences other than agricultural plants, ceramics, and trade, we can see Mesoamerican inspiration in the creation of this book.

The passion of two Kansas lawyers (and politicians) for Mayan archaeology led them to fly their private airplanes during weekends and other days off over the jungles of the Yucatán Peninsula and adjacent areas of Belize, Chiapas, and Guatemala in order to photograph from the air the spectacular ruined cities of the ancient Maya. The resulting photographs then inspired William M. Ferguson and John Q. Royce to produce two books featuring their photographs and studies: *Maya Ruins of Mexico in Color* and *Maya Ruins in Central America in Color*, both published by the University of Oklahoma Press.

Inspired by those two books, Ferguson looked in new directions, and his publisher at the time, Luther Wilson, suggested he employ his talents, especially for both aerial and ground photography, on the ancient ruins of the Colorado Plateau. At that point, Ferguson enlisted the help of lifetime professional Southwestern archaeologist Art Rohn, and the two began an intensive accumulation of information and photographs that ultimately led to publication of

Anasazi Ruins of the Southwest in Color by the University of New Mexico Press. This current volume is a revision of that first work.

The purpose of this book has always been to offer the general public a complete and informative picture of Puebloan culture from its prehistoric beginnings through roughly twenty-five hundred years of growth and change ending in the culture of the modern-day Pueblo Indians of New Mexico and Arizona, from Taos in the northeast along the Rio Grande Valley to Isleta, then westward through Acoma and Zuni to the Hopi Pueblos. We have combined color aerial and ground photographs, maps, settlement plans, drawings, and charts with detailed descriptions of ruins, artifacts, and historical developments to make this picture both thorough and easily understood.

We have tried to emphasize as much as possible those ruins that are open to the public and that either may actually be visited or at least viewed from nearby. Even though we have omitted many excavated and published ruins because they cannot be visited, those covered here provide a complete picture of the history and culture of the prehistoric and historic Puebloan peoples of the American Southwest.

The original version of the book would not have been possible without the full cooperation and assistance of the United States National Park Service and particularly Robert C. Heider, superintendent, and Allen S. Bohnert of Mesa Verde National Park; William R. Germeraad, superintendent of Canyon de Chelly National Monument; John Hunter, superintendent, Kevin McKibben, Chris Judson, and Sari Stein of Bandelier National Monument; Walter P. Harriman, former superintendent, and Tom Vaughn, superintendent of Chaco Culture National Historical Park, and W. James Judge, chief of the Division of Cultural Research; John Loleit of the Navajo National Monument; and Susie Schofield of Salinas Pueblo Missions National Monument.

Most of the aerial photographs in this book involved the team of Ferguson flying the plane and maneuvering it expertly into just the right positions with Rohn dangling several cameras around his neck and trying to avoid getting airsick. Many of the ground photographs involved arranging special trips and often hiking into somewhat remote areas. Bill Ferguson took the vast majority of the photographs, but about one-sixth of them have been contributed by Art Rohn, who also rendered the settlement plans of Lowry, Yellow Jacket, the Hovenweep ruin groups, and the Salinas pueblo layouts.

Special thanks also go to Richard B. Woodbury, who reviewed the text for the first edition and offered numerous helpful suggestions; to Ethne Barnes, who offered editorial comments on the draft revision and

who contributed two photographs; to John Q. Royce, who doubled as pilot and aerial photographer; and to Lovinia A. Villarreal, who helped take a number of the aerial photographs (noted in captions) and who served as cataloger for the more than four thousand photographs and negatives from which the vast majority of illustrations have been taken. Joan Foth contributed a painting and several drawings, and Lisa Ferguson added several additional drawings, both artists providing views the camera lens could not show (also noted in captions). Michael Brack produced the seventeen colored maps, three ruin plans, and one sketch. The Center for Desert Archaeology in Tucson graciously allowed Michael to use their computer software to develop the maps. The National Geographic Society gave permission for use of one of their paintings and a graphic reconstruction.

While many individuals have had some role in producing this book, any shortcomings in this work can only be attributed to the authors themselves.

—Arthur H. Rohn
Tucson, Arizona

CHAPTER ONE

Introduction

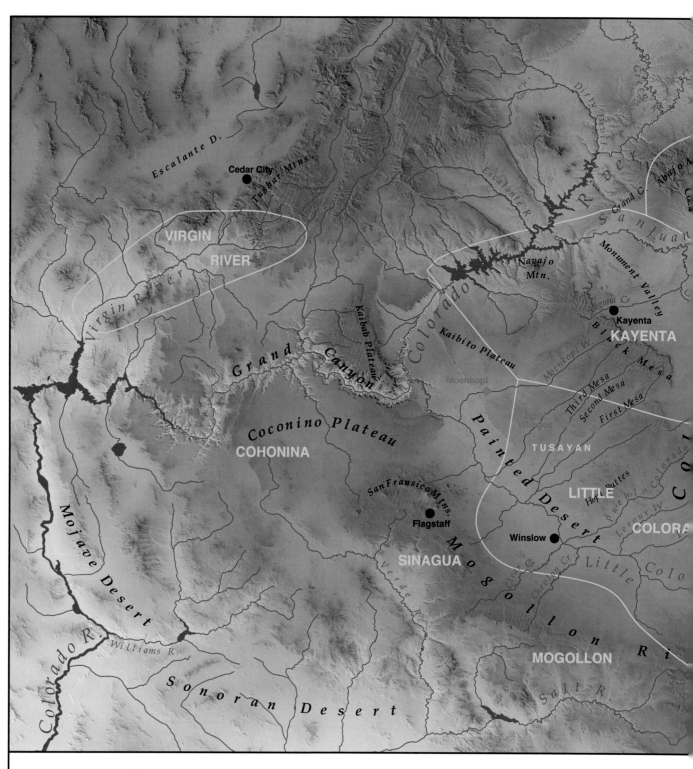

Key

● **Modern City**

◆ **Modern Pueblo**

⬡ **Regional Limit**

1-1. Pueblo-land, the regions occupied by the prehistoric Puebloan people from about A.D. 700 to the arrival of the Spaniards.

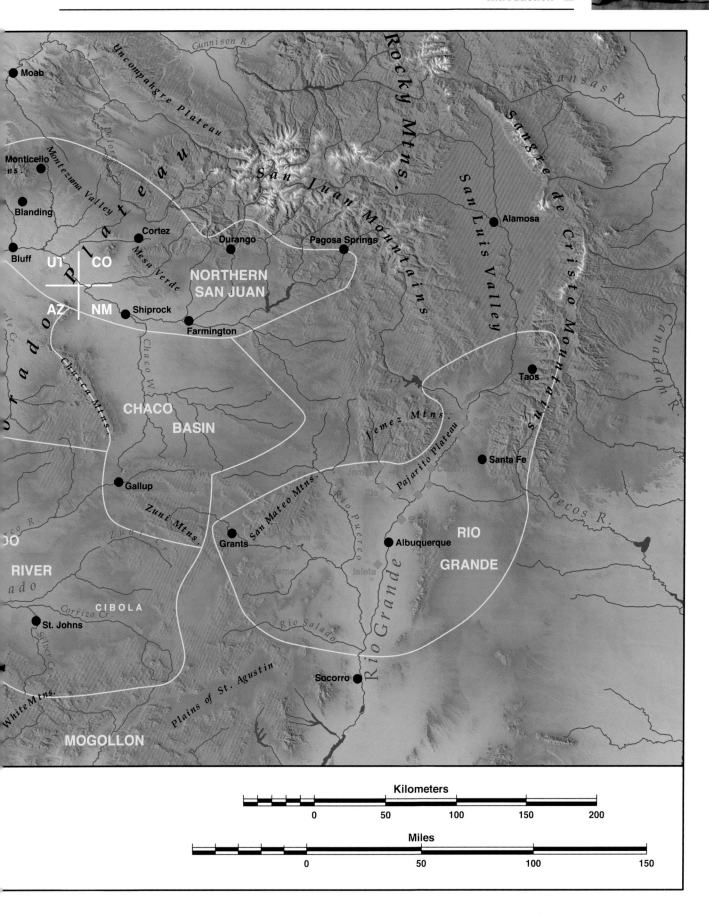

Kilometers

0   50   100   150   200

Miles

0   50   100   150

The Ancient Puebloans

Archaeologists and anthropologists refer to the prehistoric Indians who inhabited the Four Corners area of southeastern Utah, northeastern Arizona, southwestern Colorado, and northwestern New Mexico for over two thousand years from about 700 B.C. until the Spaniards arrived in the Southwest in A.D. 1540 as ancestors of the historically known Pueblos. The prehistoric Puebloan people descended from older hunting and gathering peoples, and they appear to reflect a fusion of Shoshonean speakers from the Great Basin and Tanoan speakers from the western Great Plains with indigenous Zunian and Keresan speakers.

Once in the Four Corners area, these linguistically diverse peoples developed a remarkably common culture that evolved into the historic pattern of the Pueblo Indians of Arizona and New Mexico. For most of their known prehistory, the ancient Puebloan occupation centered in the drainages of the San Juan and Little Colorado rivers.

The distant ancestors of these and all other pre-Columbian peoples of the western hemisphere originally came from Asia across a land bridge that once connected eastern Siberia with Alaska in the region of the Bering Strait and extended southward into the Bering Sea. Huge Ice Age glaciers that covered major portions of northern Europe and North America between roughly 25,000 and 10,000 B.C. had trapped so much water that sea levels dropped enough to create this bridge of dry land. Perhaps several migrations of these ancient peoples ultimately spread throughout North, Central, and South America.

Prehistoric Pueblo-land covered most of the Colorado Plateau, an elevated geographic area bounded by the Rocky Mountains on the north and east, by the Colorado River on the northwest, and by the Mogollon Rim on the south (fig. 1-1). At various times during their history, the Puebloans expanded westward into the Grand Canyon and Virgin River in southwestern Utah and northward across the Colorado River into the Escalante River drainage and the Kaiparowits Plateau of southern Utah. During the Great Migrations from the late 1100s until about 1300, the Puebloan people completely abandoned the San Juan River drainage while expanding to the east of the Continental Divide into the valley of the Rio Grande ranging from Taos to Socorro, New Mexico.

Prior to the Great Migrations, the Puebloans occupied four main regions:

(1) Northern San Juan. This region includes the portions of southwestern Colorado, southeastern Utah, and far northwestern New Mexico lying north of the San Juan River. The San Juan River has its headwaters in the high, rugged San Juan Mountains near Pagosa Springs, Colorado, from whence it flows southwesterly past Farmington, New Mexico, and then northwesterly into southeastern Utah where it joins the Colorado River at Lake Powell. This region encompasses Chimney Rock, Aztec Ruins, Mesa Verde and the Ute Mountain Tribal Park, Hovenweep, Montezuma Valley sites, and numerous sites in southeastern Utah.

(2) Chaco Basin. The Chaco Canyon ruins lie in the center of the Chaco Basin of northwestern New Mexico. This Puebloan region includes the area drained by the Chaco River, bounded on the east by the Continental Divide, on the west by the Chuska Mountains, on the north by the San Juan River, and on the south by the drainage divide around Crownpoint. Besides the Chaco Canyon ruins, numerous so-called Chacoan outliers include Salmon Ruin, Pueblo Pintado, and others.

(3) Kayenta. This region, named after the town of Kayenta, Arizona, includes the territory west of the Lukachukai-Chuska Mountains, south of the Colorado and San Juan rivers in Utah, east of the Grand Canyon, and north of the Hopi Mesas. Major Kayenta sites may be visited at Betatakin and Keet Seel in the Navajo National Monument, in Canyon de Chelly, and at the Grand Canyon.

(4) Little Colorado River Valley. This region includes the Zuni River and other upper tributaries to the Little Colorado River beginning at the Continental Divide east of Zuni, New Mexico, extending northwestward from Springerville to Winslow, Arizona, and then northward past the western flank of Black Mesa to include the Hopi Mesas. This region covers Atsinna at El Morro, Village of the Great Kivas, Hawikuh, Puerco Pueblo Ruin, the Homol'ovi Ruin cluster, and Wupatki. Several early scholars have referred to the eastern Zuni territory as "Cibola" and the western Hopi territory as "Tusayán."

By the end of Pueblo III around A.D. 1300, the Puebloans had migrated from the Kayenta, Northern San Juan, and Chaco regions to the Little Colorado River Valley and to the Rio Grande Valley in New Mexico. The succeeding Pueblo IV Puebloans settled in two districts in the Rio Grande Valley, one to the north and the other to the south of modern-day Albuquerque. Some Puebloans had colonized these districts during Pueblo III, and even as early as Pueblo II, but the Great Migrations out of the Chaco Basin and the Northern San Juan more fully populated the valley during Pueblo IV.

Archaeologists have recognized five distinguishing—signature—qualities that identify prehistoric

1-2. A masonry Pueblo III kiva in Step House at Mesa Verde showing its ventilator opening, draft deflector, and fire pit. Its dome-shaped cribbed roof rested on top of stone pilasters rising from the circular banquette. A ladder through a hatchway in the roof provided access.

UNIT PUEBLO

1-3. The unit pueblo formed the standard module for construction of villages and pueblos from the mid-700s to after 1300. This habitation unit contained storage and living rooms, a pithouse or kiva beneath the courtyard, and a trash dump, all aligned from north to south.

1-4. Three distinctive styles of Puebloan pottery: a gray corrugated-surface cooking and storage jar, a seed jar with black geometric designs painted on its polished white surface, and a polychrome bowl decorated in red and black paints on an orange background. All three vessels belong to Kayenta Pueblo III ceramic style (specimens from the collections of the Arizona State Museum).

1-5. Late Pueblo II burial from the Ewing Site, Yellow Jacket district, Colorado.

Puebloan culture. First, the kiva (fig. 1-2), a generally circular underground structure used for kin-group gatherings, belongs exclusively to the Puebloan culture. No other cultural group employs such a structure. Second, the residential building unit (fig. 1-3), consisting of a room block of two to twelve rooms fronted by an outdoor plaza or work space containing a kiva or a pithouse, formed a modular unit of standardized design that could either stand alone as a "unit pueblo" or be multiplied to form larger settlements, whether in the cliffs or in the open. Each residence unit probably housed an extended family.

The third cultural element can be seen in the idealized north-south orientation for both kivas and residence units. Kivas and/or pithouses most often lay south of the room blocks and directed their axial features toward the south. Distinctive gray and white pottery comprises the fourth distinctive feature. Balanced geometric painted designs decorated the white wares, while the gray utility vessels often displayed corrugated exteriors resulting from the practice of not smoothing over the exterior surfaces of the coils (fig. 1-4). Less commonly, some potters produced two-color or multicolored pottery on a red base. The Puebloans fired both wares in nonoxidizing atmospheres (in fires that restricted the supply of oxygen) to produce the distinctive colors. Richard St. John, a professor of ceramics from Wichita State University, has been able to recreate these firing conditions and duplicate the Puebloan colors.

Fifth, the prehistoric Puebloans in all areas buried their dead with legs flexed against the chest, lying on one side, with the heads oriented directionally—often toward a solstice sunrise—or parallel to the contour if on a steep slope (fig. 1-5).

While exceptions to each of these characteristics may be found in any one site, the cluster of traits occurs only in Puebloan culture and nowhere else. Neighboring cultures may show influences from one or more of these qualities, but they never seem to duplicate them precisely.

Chronology Building

Archaeology in the American Southwest has benefited greatly from three major conditions. The arid climate plus extremely dry conditions found in caves and rock shelters have often preserved many usually perishable materials such as items of clothing and wooden construction materials. Secondly, the obvious continuity from prehistoric culture and peoples to their modern descendants permits projections to be made backward in time from observable practices in the present. Finally, the invention of tree-ring dating, or dendrochronology, has made available to Southwestern researchers one of the most accurate methods for dating events in prehistoric times.

While studying the relationship between sun spot activity and climatic changes on earth, the astronomer Andrew E. Douglass discovered how the annual growth rings in certain trees quite accurately reflected patterns of rainfall. This allowed Douglass to track such rainfall patterns backward in time far beyond the availability of weather records. By correlating the growth ring patterns seen in living trees with patterns found in timbers cut in the past, he was able to extend his climatic record even farther back in time. Hence, he soon sought the well-preserved timbers found in archaeological ruins in the Four Corners.

In collaboration with Southwestern archaeologists, Douglass began to assign dates to prehistoric timbers. The archaeologists then found they could assign these dates to past events, such as the construction of buildings and parts of buildings such as individual rooms. By careful analysis of the prehistoric beam samples together with rigorous interpretation, many events could be dated to a single calendar year, and in the very best of cases, to a particular season of the year.

As dendrochronology has developed over the many years since Douglass applied his concepts, the process and interpretative principles have been greatly refined. When an ancient beam specimen is analyzed, the last recognizable growth ring indicates a live tree during that year. Should bark be adhering to this outermost ring, or traces of bark-eating beetles be present, or if the ring continues unbroken around the beam's circumference, the analyst can infer the once living tree had been cut down during that year (a cutting date). Without such conditions, it may be impossible to gauge whether some outer rings have been lost and how many might have been lost. Consequently, not all reported tree-ring dates possess the same degree of accuracy, and careful interpretation must intervene.

Interpretations of tree-ring dates must recognize several cautions. The dendrochronologist can tell when a tree still lived and when it probably died, presumably caused by someone cutting it down. He cannot tell us when it became part of a roof. We must infer that by its context within a building and among other dated timbers. Several identical dates from a single roof most probably date that roof's construction. When one date predates others in the same roof, we must suspect the earlier date represents a reused timber or collected dead wood. And we have considerable evidence that the Puebloans reused both salvageable timbers, building stones, and other materials.

When done properly, the interpretation of tree-ring dates can place construction of prehistoric building units within very narrow time frames. It becomes much more difficult to date times when people abandoned these same building units. Still, dendrochronology provides the most accurate dating procedure other than complete and accurate written records.

Unfortunately, tree-ring dating cannot be applied to all prehistoric situations. New advances have expanded the technique beyond the reaches of the

Colorado Plateau, to include virtually all the Southwest from the Wyoming border into northern Mexico. Separate chronologies have now been developed in parts of Europe and the Middle East with a very active laboratory in Turkey. In Pueblo-land, the chronology now reaches back in time over two thousand years to 322 B.C. For earlier times, Southwestern archaeologists have had to depend on radiocarbon dating, a much less precise technique. By measuring the amounts of a radioactive carbon isotope remaining in once living plant or animal tissues, approximations of the time frame during which the original organism died can be determined. This kind of dating has been most useful for Basket Maker and older materials.

The habits of human beings constantly change or modify the ways they make and use things in their daily lives. We can all recognize changing styles of clothing, automobiles, and other items of our material culture as reflections of particular time periods in our recent history. In this same way, archaeologists have arranged sequences of changes in pottery making and decoration among the Puebloans. Where tree-ring dates can be applied to these ceramic styles, the pottery styles then can also provide absolute time frames for events for which neither tree-ring nor radiocarbon dates are available. Through the combined use of these major chronological techniques, Southwestern archaeologists have been able to construct the Puebloan culture history presented in this book (fig. 1-6).

Archaeologist A. V. Kidder has applied the name "Anasazi" to this distinctive cultural pattern. Because this word translates literally from the Navajo language as "enemy ancestors," we have elected to employ the terms "Puebloan" and "Pueblo" as the labels for both the prehistoric people and their modern-day Pueblo Indian descendants of the Southwest. Kidder also led the 1927 Pecos Conference to agree on a chronological framework for describing Puebloan evolution according to three Basket Maker and six Pueblo stages. The

1-6.

PUEBLOAN CHRONOLOGY

	Revised (this book) Pecos Classification	Roberts's Terminology
1900	Pueblo VI	
1800		
1700	Pueblo V	Historic Pueblo
1600		
1540		
1500	Pueblo IV	Regressive Pueblo
1400		
1300		
1200	Pueblo III	Great Pueblo
1100		
1000	Pueblo II	Developmental Pueblo
900		
800	Pueblo I	
700		
600	Basket Maker III	Modified Basket Maker
500		
400		
300		
200		Basket Maker
100		
A.D.		
0		
B.C.	Basket Maker II	
100		
200		
300		
400		
500		
600		
700		
800		
	Oshara (Basket Maker I ?)	

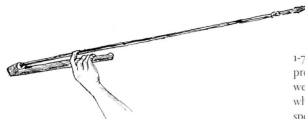

1-7. Basket Maker II Puebloans and their Archaic Desert Culture predecessors employed the atlatl (throwing board) and dart for a hunting weapon. They held the atlatl in the hand to add an extension to the arm, which would then impart greater velocity when throwing the dart or spear. (Drawing by Joan Foth.)

stages of Puebloan cultural development did not run concurrently in all regions.

BASKET MAKER I. Because in 1927 the earliest known Basket Maker remains seemed too well developed to have lacked any preceding inspirations, and because no one at that time could identify an antecedent, this first Basket Maker stage was set aside as a hypothetical beginning for the sequence. Today, archaeologists recognize the Archaic Oshara Tradition as the most likely ancestor of Basket Maker culture. The Oshara Tradition represents a long-term development in the northern Southwest between about 5500 and 700 B.C., probably culminating in the Basket Maker culture. These people hunted animals and gathered plant foods utilizing stone projectile points, chipped stone implements, stone grinding tools, and hearths. Excavations of the Desha Complex of the Oshara Tradition in south-central Utah and north-central Arizona revealed open-twined sandals and one-rod foundation interlocking stitch basketry.

BASKET MAKER II (ca. 700 B.C. to A.D. 450). These preceramic people take their name from the large quantity of baskets found in cave sites in the Four Corners. They often lived under rock overhangs, but in some areas they did build circular pithouses. They combined hunting game and gathering wild seeds with gardening of maize and squash. They hunted with atlatls or spear throwers (fig. 1-7) and darts, they carefully chipped dart points, knives, and drills from stone, and they wove baskets and other items such as sandals, aprons, bags, and robes. Frank H. H. Roberts prefers to label this stage simply as "Basket Maker" because of the lack of any recognizable Basket Maker I. Roberts also suggested the following Basket Maker III stage be labeled "Modified Basket Maker." We will employ Roberts's terms interchangeably with those of the Pecos Classification.

BASKET MAKER III (ca. A.D. 450 to 700–750). Sites of this stage may be found all over Pueblo-land (fig. 1-8). Modifications on preceding Basket Maker culture include villages of substantial four-post roof-supported pithouses, the earliest Puebloan pottery, the bow and arrow replacing the atlatl and dart, domesticated turkeys, a developing agriculture, and some large structures that develop later into great kivas.

The Basket Maker III people lived a more sedentary lifestyle than their predecessors. In addition to the wild plant foods (piñon nuts, juniper berries, yucca fruit, rice grass, pigweed, acorns, and sunflower seeds), they grew corn and squash, while adding domesticated beans to their diet. They traded for pottery, turquoise jewelry, and marine shells from as far away as the Pacific coast and the Sea of Cortés.

PUEBLO I (A.D. 700–750 to 900). The term "Pueblo" derives from the Spanish word for "town" or "village" that they applied to the sedentary Indians they found living in villages. Of course, these Pueblos had descended from the pre-Spanish Puebloan people.

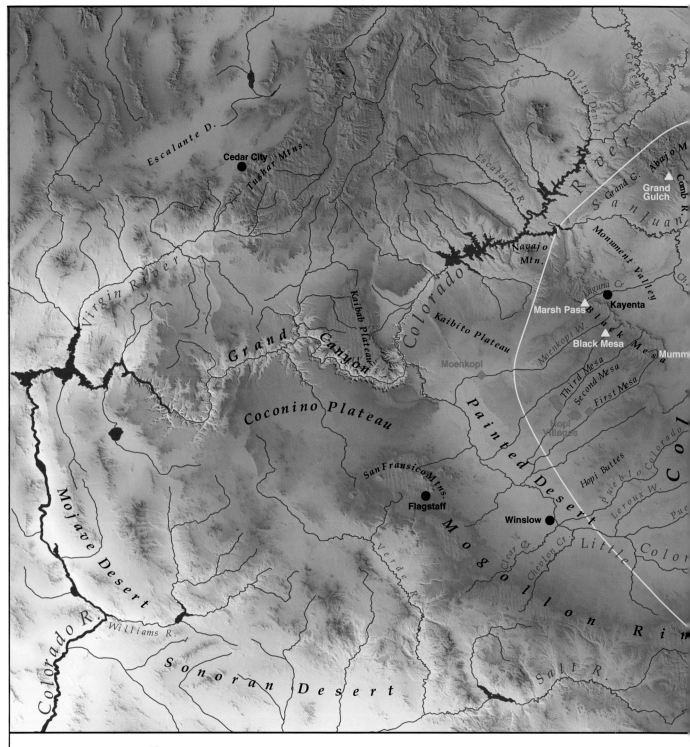

Key

● **Modern City**

◆ **Modern Pueblo**

▲ **Basket Maker II/III Site**

⬡ **Regional Limit**

1-8. The Basket Maker II and III stages began around 700 B.C. and lasted for more than one thousand years. Relatively few of these earliest Puebloan sites have been found. Examples may be seen by visitors to Canyon de Chelly National Monument and Mesa Verde National Park.

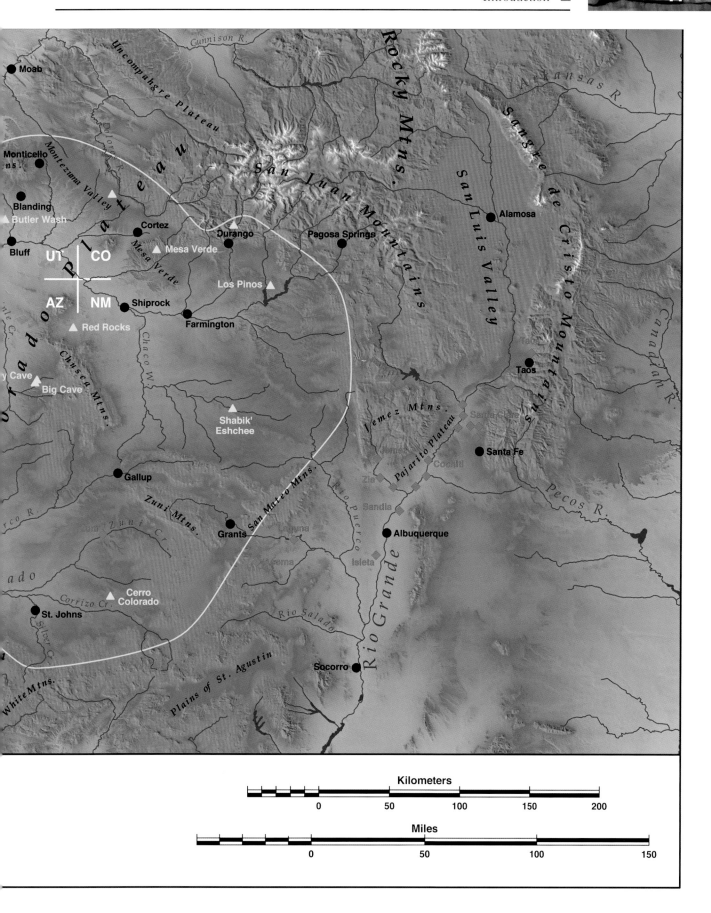

Kilometers

0   50   100   150   200

Miles

0   50   100   150

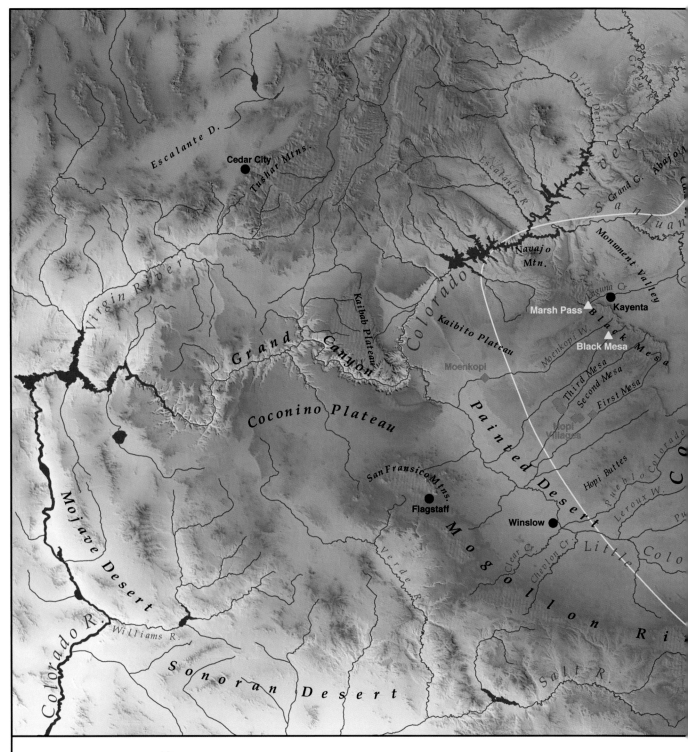

Key

- ● Modern City
- ◆ Modern Pueblo
- ▲ Pueblo I Site
- ⬡ Regional Limit

1-9. Regions occupied by the Puebloans during Pueblo I (700–750 to 900).

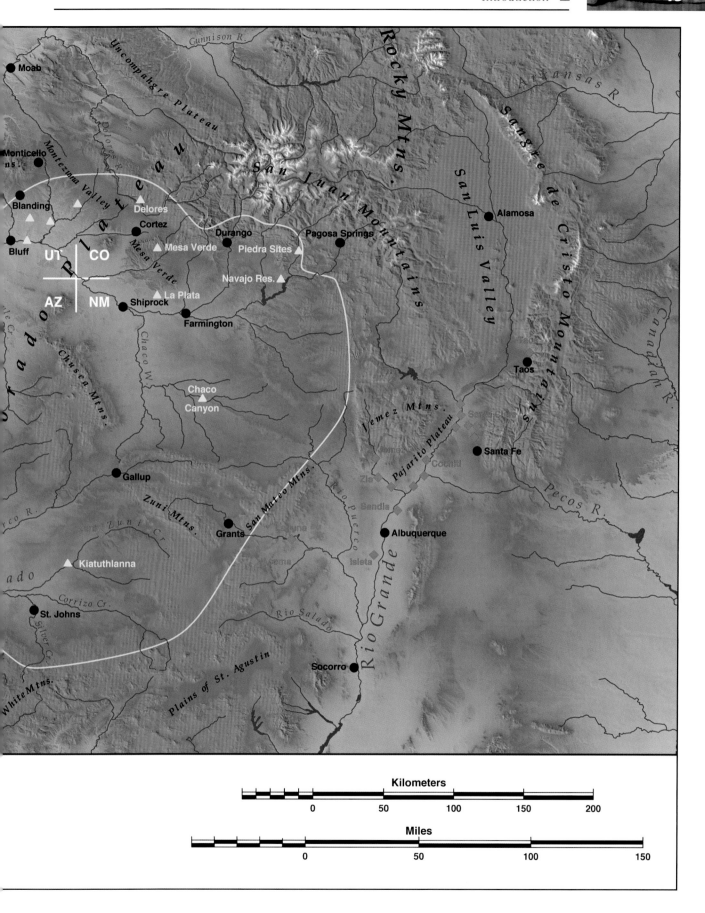

Kilometers

| 0 | 50 | 100 | 150 | 200 |

Miles

| 0 | 50 | 100 | 150 |

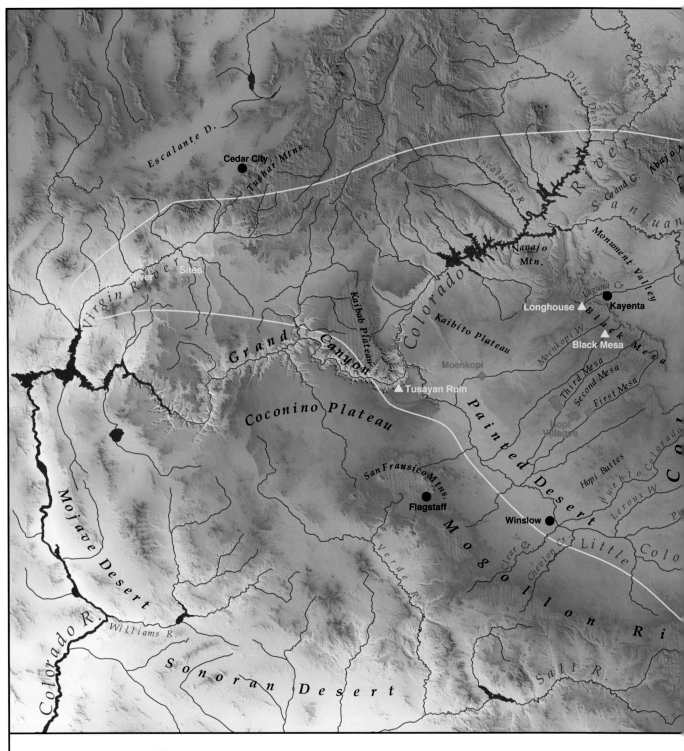

Key

- ● Modern City
- ◆ Modern Pueblo
- △ Pueblo II Site
- ◇ Regional Limit

1-10. Pueblo II occupation limits (900 to 1070 or 1100).

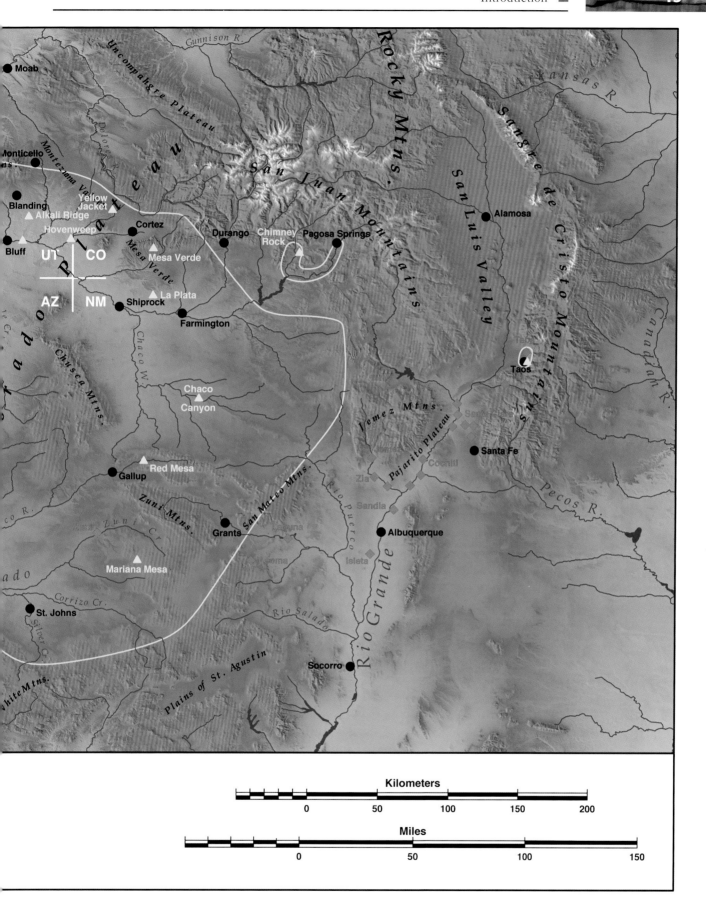

Kilometers

0   50   100   150   200

Miles

0   50   100   150

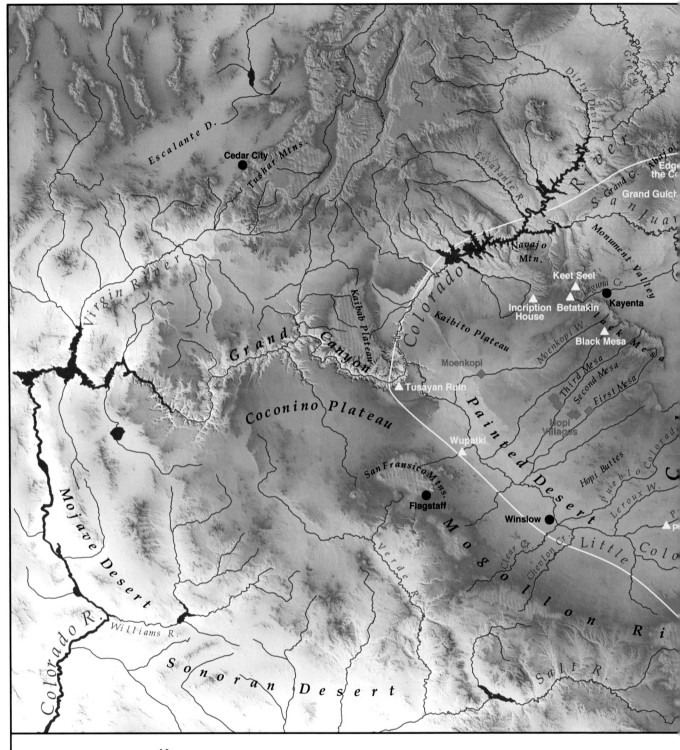

Key

- ● **Modern City**
- ◆ **Modern Pueblo**
- ▲ **Pueblo III Site**
- **Regional Limit**

1-11. Pueblo III occupation zones (1070 or 1100 to 1300). Most sites open to the public represent Pueblo III.

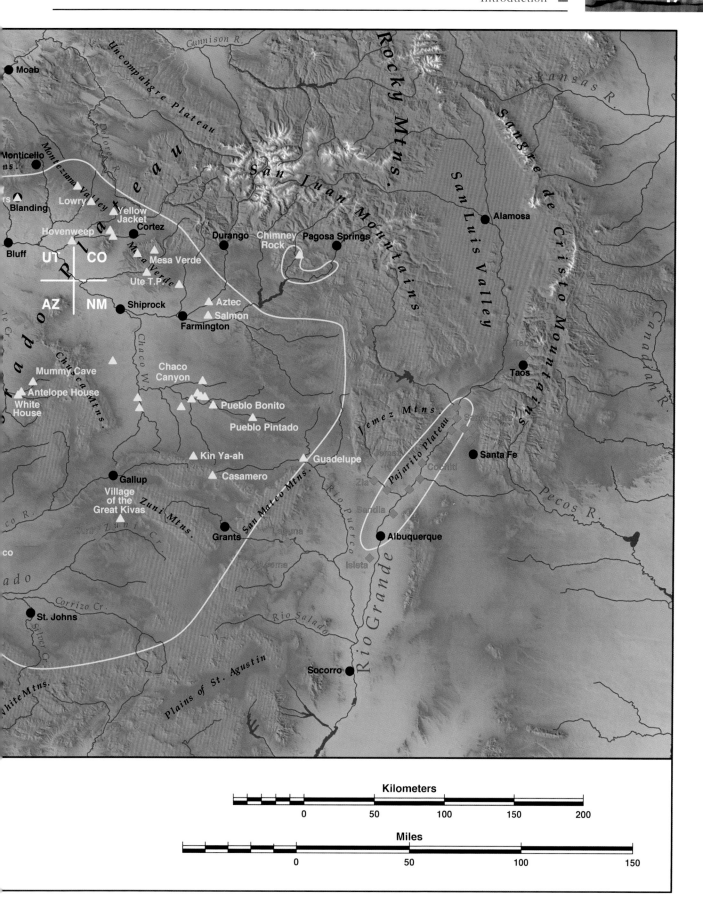

Moab

Monticello
ns.

Blanding

Bluff

Lowry

Yellow
Jacket

Hovenweep

UT | CO

AZ | NM

Mummy Cave

Antelope House

White
House

Durango

Chimney
Rock

Pagosa Springs

Alamosa

Cortez

Mesa Verde

Mesa Verde

Ute T.P.

Shiprock

Aztec

Salmon

Farmington

Chaco Canyon

Chaco
Canyon

Pueblo Bonito

Pueblo Pintado

Kin Ya-ah

Guadelupe

Casamero

Gallup

Village
of the
Great Kivas

Grants

Taos

Santa Fe

Albuquerque

Isleta

St. Johns

Socorro

Rocky Mtns.

Arkansas R.

Gunnison R.

Uncompahgre Plateau

San Juan Mountains

Sangre de Cristo Mountains

San Luis Valley

Colorado Plateau

Chaco W.

Chuska Mtns.

San Mateo Mtns.

Zuni Mtns.

Zuni Cr.

Corrizo Cr.

Silver Cr.

White Mtns.

Plains of St. Agustin

Rio Salado

Rio Grande

Rio Puerco

Jemez Mtns.

Pajarito Plateau

Pecos R.

Canadian R.

Kilometers

0   50   100   150   200

Miles

0   50   100   150

The 1927 Pecos Conference divided the early Pueblo sequence into Pueblo I and II. In 1935 Frank Roberts combined these two stages into his designation "Developmental Pueblo."

The eighth century (700s) saw a dynamic blending of both peoples and cultural patterns (fig. 1-9). Pithouses continued to be built, but now as prototypes for the small kivas that flourished during Pueblo II and III times. Rows of Modified Basket Maker storerooms and *ramadas* (outdoor shades) evolved into wattle-and-daub (*jacal*) blocks of living and storage rooms built on top of the ground. Wattle-and-daub construction involved upright wall posts interlaced with brush and faced with adobe.

Both painted and unpainted pottery evolved as the potters began to take full advantage of the free expression encouraged by this plastic medium of clay. Agriculture became even more dominant for the supply of food, bolstered somewhat by the incipient development of farming terraces. Cotton textiles appeared, although cotton plants were grown only in warmer settings such as Canyon de Chelly.

PUEBLO II (A.D. 900 to 1050–1150). Architecturally, stone masonry began to supplant wattle-and-daub construction for above-ground living and storage room blocks and to provide lining for the once earthen-sided subsurface pithouses that evolved into kivas. Roof and ceiling construction remained essentially the same as it had been in the earliest pithouses, ultimately persisting into twentieth-century pueblos—successive crisscrossing layers first of large space-spanning timbers (*vigas*), topped by smaller poles or split pole shakes, then bark or reeds, and finally a layer of earth.

During this stage, the residence unit took on the modular appearance that would persist into historic times. Pueblo II unit pueblos consisted of jacal and/or masonry–walled room blocks facing an open outdoor work space containing hearths, grinding bins, storage pits, and the entrance to an underground kiva. Such kivas had formalized earlier pithouse features such as the ventilation opening, draft deflector, hearth, and symbolic *sipapu* (representing communication into a spirit world) into a south-north axis. These kivas served both domestic and ritual functions for the extended families occupying the residence units.

Most unit pueblos stood apart from one another and only a single story high. Invariably, they clustered into settlements of steadily increasing size and population. Settlement-wide features such as great kivas, artificial reservoirs supplying domestic water, systems of farming terraces and irrigation, plazas, shrines, and celestial tracking devices all became formalized. Clearly, these features helped to identify and bond together the members of the community of people residing in each settlement.

In the Chaco Region, stone masonry wall construction allowed builders to experiment with partial two-story room blocks. Increasingly, they butted once separate unit pueblos together into larger contiguous buildings that presaged the multistoried, multiroom large "apartment houses" of Pueblo III and following stages.

Ceramic arts continued to flourish with clearly recognizable regional styles of painted black-on-white pottery. Some red wares, painted with black designs, also assumed regional styles. The distinctive exterior corrugated surfaces dominated gray utility (cooking and storage) vessels. Trade expanded significantly in ceramics and jewelry, especially as the Puebloans began to settle west of the Colorado River into the canyons of southern Utah and the Grand Canyon while expanding their occupation into the Virgin River drainage in extreme southwestern Utah and southern Nevada (fig. 1-10).

The rest of Puebloan material culture changed little from previous times, although some tool forms

1-12. Aerial view of Pueblo Bonito in Chaco Culture National Historical Park illustrating the large size and complexity of some of the Pueblo III buildings.

such as stone arrow points, axe heads, and hammerstones took on slightly different appearances. Although turkeys had been domesticated during Basket Maker III, their meat did not become part of the human diet until late in Pueblo II.

PUEBLO III (A.D. 1050–1150 to 1300). During this stage, the once relatively dispersed (suburban-like) unit pueblos agglomerated into contiguous, usually multistoried, massive buildings that many observers have likened to apartment houses. Of course they lacked the communal hallways and staircases and the "master planning" found in real apartment houses, even though they had been assembled by modular residence units. The largest settlements probably claimed two thousand to twenty-five hundred residents in up to forty or more separate buildings. These settlements usually included plazas, shrines, a great kiva and/or tri-wall structure, and some sort of artificial or enhanced domestic water supply (fig. 1-11).

Some of the buildings, such as Pueblo Bonito in Chaco Canyon, stood up to five stories in height (fig. 1-12). In the Northern San Juan Region, the larger settlements clustered around springs and reservoirs, while on the Mesa Verde and in Kayenta's Tsegi Canyon, many people built their homes beneath natural rock overhangs in vertical cliffs. Such architectural feats have inspired many writers to rhapsodize about those as representing the "Classic" or "Great" phase of Puebloan achievement.

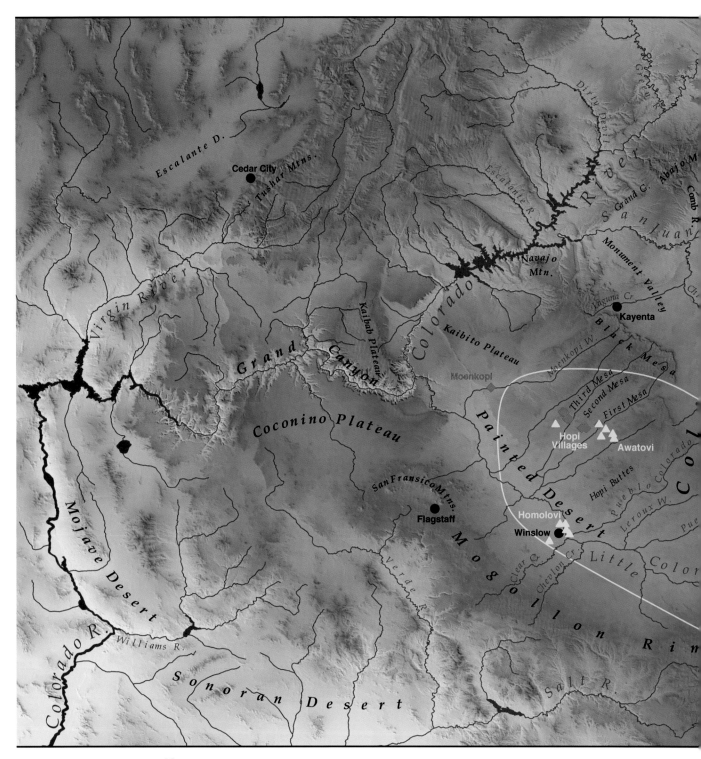

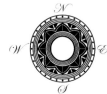

Key

- ● Modern City
- ◆ Modern Pueblo
- ▲ Pueblo IV Site
- ⬡ Regional Limit

1-13. Regions occupied by Pueblo IV people after the Great Migrations of the 1100s and 1200s and up to the arrival of the Spaniards in 1540. Modern pueblos evolved out of these late prehistoric population centers.

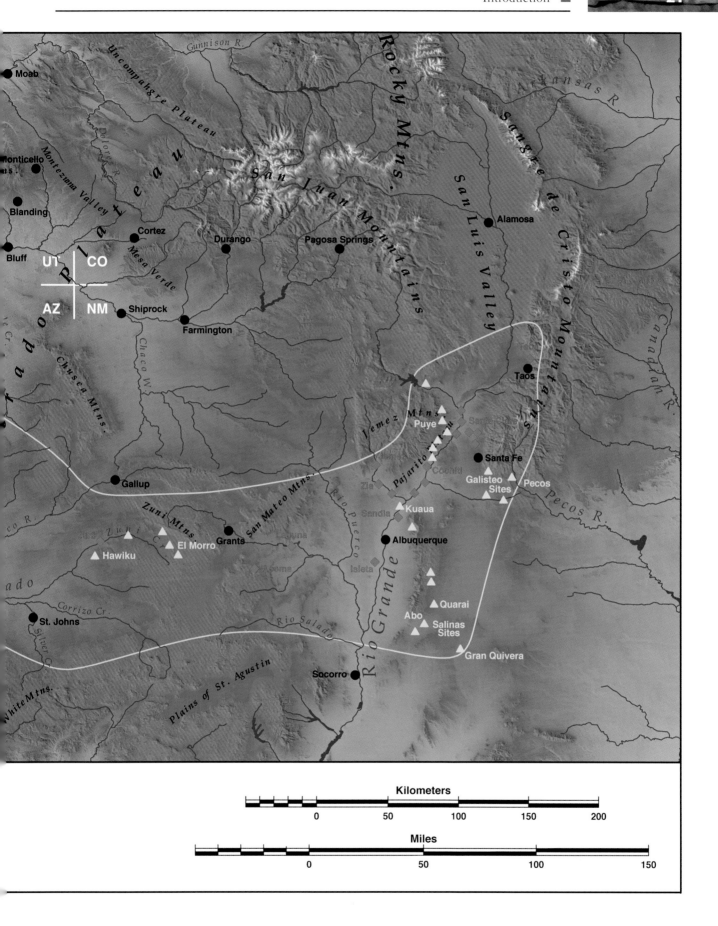

Actually, Pueblo III saw the cementing of cultural qualities into a way of life those people have preferred to experience ever since. Even when whole communities migrated out of the San Juan drainage, totally abandoning their core homeland, they soon reconstituted this basic cultural pattern in the Rio Grande and Little Colorado River regions.

Regional styles became marked in stone masonry, room sizes, kiva features, ceramic decoration and shapes, and even some patterns of trade (see fig. 1–11). While Chaco Canyon dwellers experienced wider trade in shell, turquoise, macaw feathers, and copper bells, people living in the Kayenta and Northern San Juan regions saw considerably less trade than they had seen earlier. This pattern could reflect the return of colonists who had expanded westward across the Colorado River during Pueblo II, but now returned to their Kayenta roots. At the same time, the Chaco and Cibola regions seem to have had more available contacts southward into northern and western Mexico.

Pueblo III culminated in the Great Migrations, during which people moved in family and lineage/clan groups from their old homes to new ones. Rich finds of abandoned pottery and stone utensils in many of the older homes suggest that many of these migrants had planned to return. The migrations began during the mid-1100s, and they had mostly ended by 1300. When they ended, the Northern San Juan, Kayenta, and Chaco regions had been completely vacated, and new settlements had sprung up in the Rio Grande and Little Colorado River regions. Yet, their overall cultural pattern had not changed significantly.

PUEBLO IV (A.D. 1300 to 1540). This stage encompasses the reconstituted settlements and lifestyle of the Puebloan peoples following the Great Migrations until the profound disruptions caused by the arrival of Spanish conquistadors led by Francisco Vásquez

de Coronado. The new settlements ranged from the Chama district west of Taos, through the Pajarito Plateau and Galisteo Basin flanking Santa Fe, past Albuquerque, to the Salinas district east of Socorro, and westward through the Acoma/Laguna district to the Cibola (Zuni) and Tusayán (Hopi) regions of the Little Colorado River drainage (fig. 1–13).

Along the Rio Grande, the Puebloans expanded ditch irrigation farming. In the canyons of the Pajarito Plateau, they often built their homes against vertical cliffs of tuff (volcanic ash), frequently burrowing into the soft tuff to carve out additional living and storage spaces. Some builders of valley floor pueblos began to utilize sun-dried adobe blocks for wall construction. Several historically occupied pueblos such as Acoma and Hopi's Oraibi trace their beginnings to this time frame.

PUEBLO V (1540 to 1860). Spanish conquistadors greatly reorganized Puebloan settlement and life. They occupied some towns like Zuni and San Juan Pueblo. They relocated others from the canyons and mesa tops of the Pajarito and Jemez plateaus into more accessible valley pueblos. They built new towns for themselves at places like Santa Fe and Albuquerque, and they established mission churches at Pecos Pueblo; at the Salinas towns of Gran Quivira, Abó, and Quarai; at Acoma; at Zuni's Hawikuh; and at Hopi's Awatovi.

The Spaniards also appropriated Puebloan lands for themselves; imposed new governance and names on the Indians; required them to trace descent through their fathers (patrilineally) rather than through their mothers (matrilineally) as they had done traditionally (actually making many of them bilateral); impressed many into labor to farm Spanish lands, build missions and Spanish haciendas, and fight alongside Spanish soldiers; and converted them to Catholicism. They introduced horses, cattle, sheep, goats, and donkeys, along with many new crops such as wheat and fruit trees. They introduced metal tools and utensils along with Spanish majolica pottery. And, they provided a market for agricultural products, textiles, buffalo hides, and tallow.

By the late 1600s, the Pueblo Indians had tired of Spanish oppression, and in 1680 they rose in rebellion against the conquerors. This one and only case of concerted effort by all the Pueblos actually drove the Spaniards out together with some southern Rio Grande Puebloan sympathizers. However, success proved to be elusive when the Spanish returned ten years later with a large army to reimpose their domination and rule on the now disparate villages. Only the Hopi, then ensconced in their mesa-top eminences, resisted reconquest.

PUEBLO VI (1860 to the present). When first the Texans and then the fledgling United States militarily defeated Mexico during the middle 1800s, a shift from Spanish/Mexican rule to United States governance took place. Anglo-American exploration and settlement soon entered the Southwest. New settlers traveled westward along the Santa Fe Trail into New Mexico and Arizona. This change in political and social influence marks the beginnings of this stage.

Anglo-American tourism along the railroads and highways has encouraged twentieth-century Puebloan artisans to produce both traditional and contemporary styles of pottery, basketry, some textiles, kachina dolls, drums, rattles, jewelry (especially turquoise and silver), and other items for sale. All these crafts draw heavily on traditional practices and materials, but they have also evolved into quite distinctive art forms.

Even as the Pueblo peoples have adapted to electricity, indoor plumbing, automobiles, farm machinery, schools, and other modern Western conveniences, they have maintained much of their

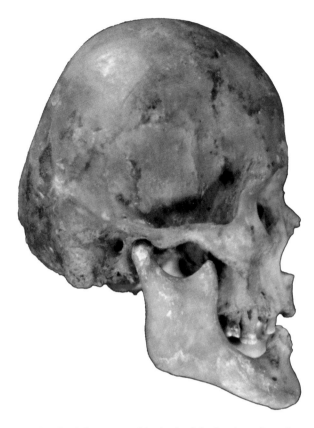

1-14. Artificial flattening of the back of the head resulting from use of hard wooden cradles.

traditional culture. Many of their artistic, social, and spiritual concepts continue to remain strong despite intense outside influences.

Physical Appearance and Disease

Two lines of evidence help us envision what the ancient Puebloan people looked like. Their direct cultural descendants, the modern-day Pueblo Indians, almost certainly have descended genetically from these prehistoric people as well. Hence, the ancient people must have resembled the modern ones. A second body of evidence derives from the many human remains excavated from graves associated with Puebloan sites.

These excavated remains describe a relatively short, stocky build that often tends to be quite barrel-chested.

1-15 Lesions on vertebrae in the spinal column caused by tuberculosis.

Men averaged around five feet four to five feet six inches tall and women around three inches shorter. Of course, some men reached up to five feet eight or nine in height, while the shortest women fell below five feet. The earlier Basket Makers had rugged, long heads, while the later, naturally round-headed Puebloans exhibited artificial flattening caused by wooden cradle boards (fig. 1-14). Many researchers have attributed this artificial head flattening to the replacement of more flexible withe-backed Basket Maker cradles by wooden cradle boards with wooden pillows in Pueblo I.

Puebloan faces tend to be large for their heads with prominent noses, high cheekbones, and shovel-shaped upper incisor teeth. Mummified remains preserved naturally in dry recesses of caves testify to a brownish skin and coarse, straight black head hair along with sparse body hair. All these features, found also among the modern Pueblos, probably reflect their distant ancestors who migrated from Asia across the Bering land bridge into the western hemisphere.

The skeletal remains also reveal signs of relatively heavy usage along the vertebral column in the back suggesting repeated heavy lifting and carrying of heavy loads. Additional stress signs in women's elbows may have stemmed from long hours spent each day grinding corn and other seeds on sandstone metates. This very process also contributed grit to the ground food that seems to have worn Puebloan teeth severely.

Aside from such wear, physical anthropologists have reported caries (cavities), abscesses, and lost teeth in the prehistoric mouths, brought on by heavy reliance on corn in their diet together with the tooth wear. Some of the most severe cases must have caused considerable pain.

Analysts have estimated that just under half the babies born did not live past three to four years of age (a common figure for anywhere in the world prior to the twentieth century). Once past infancy, however, a typical person could expect to live into their late thirties or even forties. Some of the elderly lasted into their sixties.

None of the New World Indians, including the Puebloans, had suffered from the common Old World diseases, such as measles, mumps, smallpox, scarlet fever, whooping cough, diphtheria, and most venereal diseases, until Europeans introduced them during the sixteenth and seventeenth centuries. They did suffer from spinal and joint arthritis caused by heavy use of joints. Skeletal studies show that tuberculosis (fig. 1–15) was apparently endemic in their populations prior to European contact. Many suffered broken bones. Thus, although they led somewhat demanding lives, their general health appeared to have been relatively good.

1-16. The three staples of the Puebloan diet: corn, beans, and squash. These farmed products combined with meat from wild game fed the Puebloans for more than two thousand years.

1-17. Grinding bins in many Puebloan sites during Pueblo III and later could allow two or more women to grind corn at the same time, thus making a daily, tedious chore into a cooperative semisocial event.

Food, Clothing, and Shelter

During their earliest recognized stage, Basket Maker II, the Puebloans had already begun to adapt simple gardening to the hunting and gathering subsistence practiced by their Desert Culture forebears. These earlier peoples had survived by hunting small game animals such as deer, rabbits, wood rats, squirrels, and wild turkeys while gathering a wide variety of seeds, nuts, berries, fruits, and greens.

Without doubt, both the idea for growing crops and the domesticated plants themselves originated in central Mexico at a much earlier date. Although archaeologists have found dried remains of some of these plants in cave deposits in western New Mexico dating as early as 3000–2500 B.C., we have no hard evidence these plants had been cultivated on the Colorado Plateau prior to the beginnings of Basket Maker II. The Basket Makers first planted common squashes and Indian corn or maize. Beans became part of the complex along with the advent of pottery manufacture in Basket Maker III. Interestingly, many other early Mexican domesticates—such as chili peppers, tomatoes, and avocados—failed to accompany the main triad during this northward diffusion. Perhaps the Puebloans had no taste for these foods or did not wish to expend the necessary energy to grow them.

The Basket Makers living in the Animas River valley of southwestern Colorado regularly snared water fowl, but elsewhere neither these birds nor ground birds other than wild turkeys appeared in the diet. When the Basket Maker III people domesticated turkeys, probably also in response to a central Mexican practice, they did not consume turkey meat. Instead, they harvested turkey down feathers for incorporation into feather robes, and they used larger feathers for ornamentation. Only late in Pueblo II did turkey meat show up in the Puebloan diet and turkey bones get made into tools. While elk and bighorn sheep bones occasionally occur in Puebloan refuse middens, their meat did not form an important part of the diet. Perhaps these animals primarily inhabited mountain settings well beyond the boundaries of Pueblo-land.

Of equal significance to what they did eat is what they did not eat. Like their historic Pueblo descendants, the prehistoric Puebloans did not consider fish, reptiles, or amphibians (frogs and turtles) to be food.

Despite the availability of grouse, quail, and other land birds, they, too, did not appear in the diet. The taking of water fowl—ducks and geese—by Basket Makers in the Animas River valley reflects an exception, rather than a common practice. Even those elk and mountain sheep bones found in some middens could have been acquired through trade for the manufacture of bone and antler tools. No predatory animals—coyotes, bobcats, skunks, etc.—nor birds—hawks, eagles, owls—ever seemed to have been taken by the Puebloans for food. Dogs shared domestic status with turkeys, but they served as pets and companions, never as sources of meat, bones, nor hides, although dog hair did very rarely see use in Basket Maker woven sashes.

Thus, by the time Puebloan culture became well established in Pueblo III, the people raised the great bulk of their food—corn, squash, beans (fig. 1-16), and turkeys—but they continued to gather the traditional wild nuts, seeds, berries, cactus fruits, and greens, and to augment their meat supply by hunting primarily rabbits and deer. This pattern remained unchanged until the Spaniards introduced sheep, goats, cattle, wheat, melons, tree-borne fruits, and other crops including chili peppers from Mexico.

Men and women divided economic tasks along fairly fixed lines. Men hunted the animals for meat, frequently relying on hunting charms representing nature's successful predators such as the puma (mountain lion), bear, eagle, and badger. Hunting equipment included the bow and arrow, which had supplanted the older atlatl and dart by A.D. 600. Curved wooden throwing sticks designed for stunning rabbits also doubled as clubs. Traps and net snares caught small animals.

Men also performed most of the farming tasks—working ground and planting with digging sticks, cultivating, watering—although women and children usually assisted with the harvesting. Both sexes braided ears of corn together, cut squash into strips, tied bean

1-18. A Puebloan robe made from turkey down feathers or rabbit fur strips wrapped around cords held together by spaced, twined wefts.

plants into bundles, and dried them all for storage. The women usually gathered wild plant foods, and they had the onerous tasks of preparing and cooking meals. The daily grinding of corn kernels and other seeds into meal and flour constituted a wearing and never ending burden in every woman's life. They would have to kneel behind a tilted sandstone *metate*, often set in a bin (fig. 1-17), and draw the smaller handstone or *mano* back and forth across it for hours at a time. They then added the resulting meal to the ever present stew or baked it into cakes on flat stones.

The stew, kept simmering in a pot over hot coals, and corn cakes provided standard fare at mealtime. A basic stock contained water, chunks of meat, animal grease, sometimes even whole small animals, pieces of vegetables such as squash or beans, flavorings derived from wild fruits and berries, and a host of other items to provide variety. In the days before pottery, the Basket Makers boiled similar ingredients in

1-19. A yucca fiber apron and juniper bark menstrual pad worn by a Puebloan woman during the ninth century A.D. in Pueblo I times in Big Cave, Canyon del Muerto, Canyon de Chelly National Monument. Such a fiber skirt or a breechcloth and sandals constituted standard attire for both men and women. Feather and animal skin robes could be added in winter.

tightly woven baskets sealed with piñon pitch by adding hot stones, since the basket could not be exposed directly to the fire.

In addition to the stew, they often parched whole corn kernels by shaking them against hot coals in baskets; they roasted whole ears of corn in the husks; they roasted cuts of meat directly over the fire; and they probably consumed some wild nuts and berries raw. Detailed examinations of human feces from Mug House at Mesa Verde revealed that they frequently ate prickly pear cactus pads without bothering to remove the short flexible spines, and they consumed small rodents whole—bones, hair, and all.

Like much of their food, the Puebloans derived their basic clothing styles from their Desert Archaic Culture beginnings with modifications through time. The remains found in dry caves offer surprisingly complete evidence for this reconstruction. They employed both animal skins and plant fibers with the latter becoming more prominent through time. The amount of clothes the Puebloans wore depended upon the season. As standard garb, the women wore sandals and aprons and the men sandals and breechcloths. Winter temperatures required additional items, especially at night. The daytime sun provided warmth, even in winter, but high altitude night temperatures— sometimes below zero—could easily overtax the ability of live coals in hearths to heat the indoor spaces.

Basket Maker peoples manufactured warm robes by wrapping strips of rabbit fur around yucca cords and loosely twining them together. Some made deerskin robes and occasionally robes from elk and mountain sheep hides. They stitched hides together with yucca fiber twine, and sometimes even with human or dog hair.

After turkeys had been domesticated, the later Basket Maker III (A.D. 700) and subsequent Puebloan peoples produced light, fluffy, and very

1-20. Twilled yucca leaf sandals, mirroring the shape of the foot, were worn by Puebloan people during Pueblo II and later. Juniper bark padding would offer warmth during cold weather. The wearer would fasten the sandal to his/her foot by lashing cords through loops along the sides. Prior to the introduction of cotton, the Puebloans made their clothes from natural plant fibers, wild animal skins, and feathers.

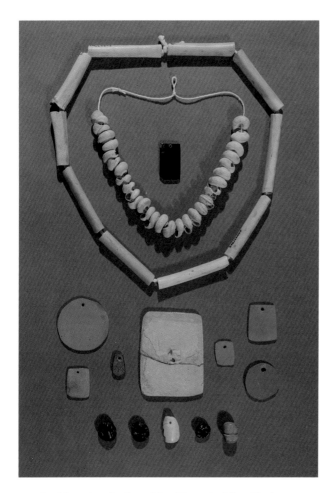

1-21. Puebloan jewelry from Mug House in Mesa Verde National Park. The beads were made from land snail shells and wing bones from golden eagles and Canada geese; pendants were fashioned from red shale and black jet; and the three buttons in the bottom row were also made from jet. The pendant in the center of the bottom row came from a *Conus* shell, a Pacific Ocean shellfish.

warm feathered robes. They wrapped split brown and white turkey down feathers instead of rabbit fur around twisted yucca fiber strings to fashion fluffy cords. They then loosely twined these cords into a blanket or robe (fig. 1-18). They also made lighter garments from deerskin tanned into a soft leather. Cotton became available in Pueblo I (A.D. 750) for belts, sashes, and robes. To protect the feet and legs in cold weather, the Puebloans wore warm calf-length socks made from feather-wrapped cordage or wadded juniper bark tied to the lower legs by the sandal lacings. Men sometimes wore sleeveless leather jackets and short leggings, although generally the people preferred loose-fitting garments.

Robes usually covered the shoulders or wrapped around the waist. Sashes woven from cotton or yucca fibers held them in place. A weaver twined sashes and aprons on a narrow loom attached to the waist. They used upright looms stretching from floor to ceiling to weave larger cotton robes and to twine feathered robes. Some robes with central slits could be worn like ponchos.

Women's aprons consisted of yucca fiber cords hanging down from a string belt tied around the waist (fig. 1-19). These cords passed between the legs to be looped over the belt again in back and hang down over the buttocks. Sometimes juniper bark fibers substituted for yucca. More creative artisans wove designs into the front part of the apron belt where the hanging cords attached. Women generally employed absorbent wads of juniper bark for menstrual pads.

Sandals regularly protected the feet of both men and women. Basket Maker sandals were coarsely twined of thick yucca fiber cords, or even willow withes, ending in square toe ends and rounded heels. A yucca fiber cord passing around the ankle and through both toe and heel loops fastened the sandal to the foot. Basket Maker III peoples fashioned their sandals from finer yucca cords woven by tight twining that produced a concave or "scalloped" toe end. Some wove geometric designs into their sandals, usually beneath the ball of the foot. By Pueblo II, and continuing afterward, the Puebloans wore sandals made of split yucca leaves plaited, usually twilled (over two, under two), into the shape of the foot (fig. 1-20).

Puebloan jewelry varied considerably from region to region and from one individual to another. Some of this variation depended on availability of suitable materials from which to fashion jewelry. Most people wore their jewelry around their necks as bead string necklaces or pendants (fig. 1-21). Some smaller pendants seem suited for wear as earrings. Obvious bracelets, finger rings, buttons, and toggles have also been found.

Local materials from which to manufacture beads and pendants included turkey wing bones, juniper berry seeds, land snail shells, various shales, lignite (jet), hematite, and some other stones. Materials that had to be imported ranged from wing bones of eagles and Canada geese, turquoise, and some forms of hematite to marine shells—*Olivella*, *Oliva*, *Conus*, and abalone from the Pacific coast plus *Glycymeris* from the Sea of Cortés (Gulf of California). Most or all of the imported materials arrived through trade.

Again, what they did not do to decorate themselves bears equal significance to what they did do. Unlike their distant neighbors in central and western

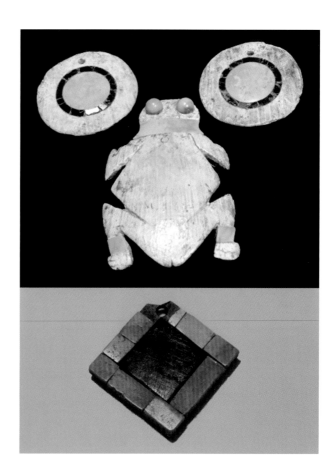

1-22. Four mosaic pendants created by gluing pieces of shell, turquoise, specular hematite, and jet onto a wooden backing. Dominguez Ruin in southwestern Colorado.

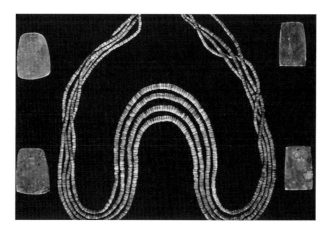

1-23. Turquoise necklace consisting of twenty-five hundred beads and four pendants recovered from Pueblo Bonito in Chaco Canyon. This represents perhaps the most spectacular find of Puebloan jewelry.

Mexico, they did not pierce their lips or nasal septa to insert labrets (lip plugs) or nose plugs, and they did not distend their earlobes for the insertion of large ear spools. Their teeth display no traces of decorative filing or drilling for inlays, and finally, apparently not everyone wore jewelry.

Turquoise appeared late in Basket Maker III (A.D. 700), and with it came the technique of producing mosaics. Pieces of turquoise, jet, and shell were affixed with pitch to a shell or wooden backing (fig. 1-22). Work with turquoise culminated during Pueblo III after the Cerrillos turquoise mines east of Santa Fe had been developed. One necklace made from sky-blue turquoise found at Pueblo Bonito in Chaco Canyon contained twenty-five hundred beads and four pendants (fig. 1-23). All the stones had been shaped and polished by hand using only stone and reed implements.

We really have no idea what form of shelter the pre-Puebloan Desert Culture people occupied. Some of their campsite rubbish has been found in natural rock shelters and caves, but most sites lie in the open. Presumably, they constructed simple huts or lean-tos from brush much like the historic Paiutes used in the Great Basin.

The earliest known Puebloans of Basket Maker II had already begun to erect substantial houses, with floors excavated slightly into the ground's surface. They also built sturdy storage facilities to protect food surpluses for use during times of scarcity. Both kinds of structures elaborated on features employed by the preceding Archaic hunters and gatherers, but as the Puebloans became steadily more sedentary through time in response to more reliable food supplies provided by farming, they rapidly transformed their architecture into a style now famous around the world.

Architecture

Puebloan architecture provided sheltered spaces in which people lived, stored foodstuffs and material items, and conducted sociopolitical and spiritual practices. Their architecture encompassed both indoor and outdoor spaces. Its style evolved rapidly from the early pithouses and storage cists into solid masonry buildings representing a distinctive "Pueblo" style. Some neighboring peoples, such as the Fremont to the north and the Mogollon to the south, even imitated various features of Puebloan architecture.

Pithouses

The early Basket Maker II people had already begun to build relatively small houses, set partially below ground level (hence the label "pithouses") and built up with timber, branches, and earth. They excavated the floor about a foot or so into the ground in a roughly circular shape, retaining the natural earth as the floor surface (fig. 1-24). This surface ultimately became compacted through use. Upright sandstone slabs set against the earthen side walls of this shallow pit prevented any loose earth from leaking in. The builders then erected a superstructure by cribbing horizontal logs on the ground surface at the side walls to form a crude dome-shaped roof. In other cases, they leaned side wall poles against a central vertical roof support post. Smaller sticks, bark, and mud plastered over the logs provided weatherproof shelter. We do not know whether the occupants gained entrance to the pithouse through one side (most likely), through the roof (not really substantial enough), or both.

A group of about ten such houses have been well preserved in Mummy Cave at Canyon de Chelly National Monument (see fig. 3-34). These houses had a rectanguloid shape and measured only nine or ten feet across. Upright sandstone slabs up to three feet tall had been mudded to the sloping bedrock beneath the cliff overhang. Horizontal logs, branches, and reeds held together with mud formed a beehivelike superstructure above the stone slabs. The slanting bedrock

1-24. The excavated remains of a Basket Maker II pithouse from northern Black Mesa in northeastern Arizona.

floors required that benches be leveled by hacking out the bedrock or by building up with logs and mud. Several of these houses contained internal storage bins and shelves, and one had a hearth. These early dwellings probably had holes in their roofs to allow smoke to escape and possibly to allow their occupants a means to enter via a ladder or notched log, unless side entrances existed. A normal-sized person could barely stand up inside, and the very uneven floors suggest that the people carried on most of their daily activities outdoors while using the houses primarily for sleeping and storing their material possessions.

From such rudimentary beginnings, Basket Maker III people developed a quite substantial semi-subterranean earth-covered lodge or pithouse. This lodge tended to be larger than the earlier Basket Maker II pithouses, ranging up to twenty-five feet across. Its clay-paved floor was also dug beneath the ground surface. Upright sandstone slabs occasionally lined the excavated pit, and its shape varied from circular to squarish with rounded corners. A second smaller room, or antechamber, provided both a ground-level entry and additional storage space.

Four upright wooden posts set into the floor well inside the side walls supported both a square roof and sloping side walls. Four horizontal logs laid on top of these posts formed a square on which the roof timbers rested. Sloping poles, footed either on the ground surface or on a very shallow ledge (banquette), leaned against the square central construction and made the side walls. Successive layers of sticks laid at right angles to the timbers and juniper bark or brush were then sealed with earth to complete the pithouse, making it weatherproof and giving it the general appearance from outside of a flat-topped earthen mound (fig. 1-25). A stranger would soon recognize its true nature by observing smoke rise through the hole in the center of the roof or seeing people sitting on the roof grinding corn or performing other household tasks.

The pithouse interiors exhibited several clearly defined features (fig. 1-26). A clay-lined fire pit occupied the center of the floor in the main chamber. A stone slab or set of poles plastered with mud stood between the fire pit and the antechamber passageway to deflect air drafts away from the fire. Low partitions, or wing walls of stone slabs, poles, and mud, linked the two southern roof-support posts to the side walls. Together with the deflector, situated between those same two posts, the wing walls effectively partitioned off the southern fourth of floor space. In this space behind the wing walls, the occupants usually prepared food on metates and stored bulky household items. One could easily step over the wing walls to reach this space. Many occupants also created internal storage bins by tunneling through the lower earthen side walls, by constructing a double set of wing walls, or by walling off spaces next to or on the banquette on which the sloping wall poles rested. Small circular depressions in the smooth clay floor, often filled with sand, provided places to set round-bottomed pots so they would not fall over. One small circular hole in the floor between the fire pit and the north wall in many pithouses represented the earliest expression of the symbolic entry into the spirit world, called "sipapu" by the Hopi.

A classic example of a Basket Maker III pithouse may be seen in Mesa Verde National Park. Site 117, Earth Lodge B, on the Ruins Road (described later), exhibits almost all of the standard features. Tree-ring dates place construction of Earth Lodge B close to A.D. 600. Elsewhere on the Mesa Verde, at Step House Cave, the stabilized remains of four other pithouses of the same age may be visited. These four demonstrate individual variability in this kind of structure, yet all differ from the typical pattern by having short ventilating tunnels in place of antechambers. Entry to these houses must have been through the roof smokehole-

hatchway. One has been partially reconstructed to illustrate construction of the roof and upper walls (see fig. 1-25).

Many basic details of pithouse construction persisted long after pithouses had been replaced by newer building forms. Roof construction especially has continued in all later Puebloan buildings into the twentieth century. The practice of constructing walls, later vertical walls, of poles laced with sticks and mud, often incorporating sandstone slabs in the base, continued for seven hundred years, even after stone masonry walls came into vogue. The use of clay to plaster floors and walls and to line features such as fire pits has continued to the present day. Orientation

1-25. This partially reconstructed pithouse has been based on the remains of a Basket Maker III structure in Step House Cave in Mesa Verde National Park. Its floor was dug partly below ground surface with a superstructure of poles covered by earth above it. A roof hatchway served both for smoke escape and entrance. Through time the Basket Maker III pithouse gradually evolved into the distinctive Puebloan kiva.

of the house features along an axis, running from the sipapu on the north through the fire pit, an ash-holding pit, and the deflector to the antechamber or ventilator tunnel on the south became a rigid pattern for the later Puebloan kivas.

Pithouse architecture evolved rapidly during Basket Maker III. By 700, pithouse builders dug floors more deeply into the ground—up to three to four feet. This necessitated a distinct banquette on which to rest the now shorter sloping side wall poles. Antechambers gave way to longer ventilator tunnels. Occupants had to enter through the roof hatchway. Internal storage bins grew more scarce.

The Deep Pithouses at Site 101 along Mesa Verde's Ruins Road exemplify these changes. This site actually displays two pithouses, a later one built inside the burned remains of an older one. The earlier house, constructed just prior to 700, had an antechamber. After it burned, the later house with a ventilator was built just after 700, possibly even by surviving residents of the earlier house, by enlarging the older antechamber. A stone slab wall held back the loose fill of the older house's main chamber.

By 800, Pueblo I pithouses had become almost totally subterranean with only slightly domed roofs to shed water. The standard shape varied from round to square, but virtually all other features remained the same: four-post roof support, wing walls, sipapu, central fire pit, ash pit, deflector, ventilator tunnel, and north-south orientation. An example of this pithouse style may be seen at Twin Trees on Ruins Road at Mesa Verde (described later).

As Pueblo I architecture evolved into Pueblo II, the people lived less and less in the pithouses and nascent kivas and more in the newly developing above-ground room blocks. They retained the pithouses, however, for places to conduct a growing number of religious rituals. Thus, by 900, these structures became readily recognizable as the specialized

1-26. Archaeological excavation of this Basket Maker III (A.D. 600s) pithouse from the Yellow Jacket district in southwestern Colorado reveals the typical ground plan of antechamber, main room with hearth and storage bins, and the pattern of postholes where wooden posts once supported sidewalls and roof. The burning of this house preserved a full record of the materials used to construct it.

underground ceremonial chambers labeled "kivas" by the Hopi.

Living and Storage Spaces

During Basket Maker II and III (700 B.C. to A.D. 700–750), the Puebloan people lived in semisubterranean pithouses containing some internal storage bins. They constructed additional detached storehouses to the north of the pithouses by lining slightly tapering pits with stone slabs (fig. 1-27) and constructing low domed covers of stone, sticks, and mud, a practice

1-27. The slab-lined cist used to store foodstuffs represents one of the earliest forms of Puebloan construction. Archaeologists believe Basket Maker peoples began building these storage receptacles even before they settled into permanent year-round settlements.

1-28. Jacal (wattle-and-daub) wall construction generally preceded the masonry walls of later Puebloan buildings. A framework of posts and limbs was plastered with mud. This construction continued alongside stone masonry through Pueblo III as this wall of a living room from Keet Seel demonstrates.

carried over from the preceding Archaic peoples. Groups of such stone-lined cists, without pithouses, have also been found in rock shelters near Kayenta and in southern Utah. By the 600s, Basket Maker peoples built additional above-ground granaries of upright poles woven into a latticework with branches and sticks and covered with mud. Archaeologists call this style of construction "jacal" (fig. 1-28). At the same time, the Puebloans began to build simple roofs resting on four posts, with no side walls, to shade themselves from the hot summer sun while working out-of-doors. They arranged these ramadas in rows in front of the storerooms to the north of the pithouses.

Once this pattern became established, it required few modifications to turn these structures into the first typical pueblo-style houses. Jacal walls added to the rows of ramadas created enclosed living spaces. Stone slabs helped reinforce the bases of the wattle-and-daub wall construction (fig. 1-29), and small hearths provided warmth. Smaller jacal storerooms attached to the north (back) side replaced many of the old separate granaries. A portico of ramadas attached to the south (front) side of the rooms provided shaded outdoor work space. Such a combination of buildings typified the Pueblo I transition from living in pithouses to living in above-ground room blocks. Each household would occupy one or two living rooms with attached storerooms and portico space, all constructed using stone slabs, wooden poles, branches, and mud.

The earliest stone masonry appears during the 800s in late Pueblo I. Roughly shaped sandstone blocks or cobblestones were laid in uneven horizontal courses in thick mud mortar. Initially, such elemental masonry appeared in the storeroom walls, but it soon spread to the back and side walls of the living rooms. Front walls, in which doorways had to be framed, continued to be built of jacal. The flat roofs of logs, sticks, bark, and earth rested directly on wall corner posts, sometimes supplemented by additional posts set into the floor inside the room corners. Those roofs had ample strength to hold people working outdoors.

The pace at which stone masonry walls supplanted jacal walls varied greatly from one place to the next. Some Puebloans built their entire housing and storage room blocks out of masonry by the early 900s, while others persisted in using jacal for their houses into the mid-1000s. Single walls of jacal have been found in late Pueblo III cliff dwellings of the Mesa Verde and Kayenta's Tsegi Canyon (see fig. 1-28).

Early stone masonry employed large amounts of mud mortar. Most walls had a thickness of a single stone that then required trimming for both inside and outside faces. Neither such relatively thin masonry nor jacal could support more than a one-story building. However, by the late 1000s in Chaco Canyon, walls of two or more stones in thickness (fig. 1-30) permitted rooms to be stacked atop one another from two to three stories high. Several Chacoan buildings, such as Pueblo Bonito, reached five stories by the early 1100s. To help support such increasing height, the curved back wall of Pueblo Bonito tapered from a basal thickness of more than four feet to about one foot on the fourth story.

Stone masonry construction flourished in the Chaco Canyon during the time of greatest building activity from 1070 to 1130. The masons quarried naturally tabular blocks and small slabs of sandstone, dressed their faces to a smoother surface by pecking away undesired bumps, and laid them in even courses with only small amounts of mud mortar. The close fit of the stone building blocks has kept Chacoan walls standing in the face of ravaging erosion.

Chacoan wall builders expressed considerable artistic individuality in their work. Some used relatively uniform sizes of stones, be they large or small, in a single wall. Others alternated one course of larger stones with several courses of smaller stones to produce a banded effect (fig. 1-31). Individual tastes and skill may even be seen in different banding patterns. Still other masons persisted in using a much

1-29. Stone slab–based jacal walls, adaptations from the earlier pithouse walls, developed during Pueblo I, as seen at the Duckfoot Site in southwestern Colorado.

1-30. Chaco-style stone masonry walls, such as these at Pueblo Pintado, contain tabular stones, two or more stones thick, bound together with mud mortar.

1-31. This wall from Wijiji in Chaco Canyon displays banded masonry—courses of thicker stones interspersed with closely fitted smaller tabular stones. It reflects the most sophisticated form of Puebloan masonry.

1-32. Mesa Verde–style masonry employed sandstone blocks of mostly uniform size in double-coursed walls such as this one from Hovenweep House.

higher proportion of mud mortar to building stones, or they employed masonry veneers on both sides of a core consisting of unshaped stones and earth. Neither of these last two styles produced walls as strong as the solid stone masonry.

Multistory construction appeared somewhat later, after 1100, in the Northern San Juan and Kayenta regions. Mesa Verde–style masonry employed walls from one to three stones thick, with faces pecked or ground smooth. A single wall contained building stones of a relatively uniform size (fig. 1-32). Larger stones usually faced a wall's intended exterior with smaller stones on the interior face. Small sandstone spalls, and occasionally pottery sherds and even corn-cobs, chinked the mortared spaces between building stones. Kayenta builders used larger quantities of mud mortar between thinner stones with wedge-shaped edges, filling the intervals with dense chinking (fig. 1-33). Those same masonry styles also occurred in kivas, but mostly without any chinking.

Despite the individual artistry expressed in masonry wall construction around Pueblo-land, most wall faces had been covered with coats of mud plaster, especially on the inside of rooms. Painted decoration frequently covered interior plastered wall faces, which were painted a reddish basal color on the lower half

1-33. Kayenta-style builders constructed walls a single stone thick using large quan-tities of mud mortar, as in these walls at Big Cave in Canyon del Muerto, Canyon de Chelly National Monument.

1-34. Many Puebloan builders plastered and painted the interior walls of their living rooms in two colors: pinkish red around the lower third and white above. These rooms may be seen in Spruce Tree House at Mesa Verde National Park.

1-35. Flat roofs rested on poles laid across the tops of room walls, and they consisted of successive layers of smaller poles, split twigs, juniper bark, and mud as exemplified by this well-preserved original roof in Keet Seel.

and topped by a white or cream color on the upper half of the wall (fig. 1-34). Both geometric and life figures sometimes appear. The painters commonly placed a horizontal row of red dots just above the red-white junction, or they extended the red zone upward to create a series of triangles, presenting the impression of mountains on the horizon. Mural decorations in living rooms never exceeded two colors, although a tan sometimes substituted for the red or white figures painted against a dark gray background.

Throughout all the changes in wall construction, the roofs continued to be fabricated in the same way—successive layers of smaller and smaller poles, branches, and twigs set at right angles to one another and covered with bark and earth, all resting on one or more main beams built into the tops of the walls (fig. 1-35). The earth covering of one room's roof provided the floor for the room above. Basic construction of these rooms remained the same whether the houses stood in the open or beneath rock shelters as cliff dwellings. Beneath the cliff overhangs, the cliff itself sometimes would form a wall or ceiling for a room.

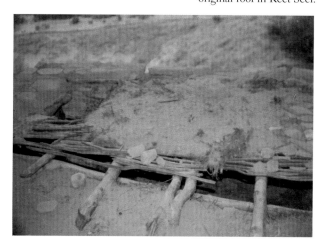

Doorways through masonry walls required positioning a lintel across the top of the opening and a sill across the bottom. Long, thick stone blocks or sets of short poles made strong lintels, and smooth, flat stones served as sills, sometimes projecting slightly from the wall face. Where doors consisted of rectangular stone slabs, wooden doorstops in the form of twigs mudded into the sides and top of the doorway (fig. 1-36), combined with a shallow groove in the doorway sill's top surface, held the door slab in place.

1-36. Room doorways often had stops of twigs and/or clay at the top and sides to support a stone slab door. This doorway appears in a cliff dwelling in Johnson Canyon in the Ute Mountain Tribal Park, southwestern Colorado.

1-37. Doorways could be rectangular or sometimes T-shaped as in these two examples from Pueblo del Arroyo in Chaco Canyon. The small, squarish opening served as a ventilator.

The door could even be locked from the outside by sliding a pole through loops on either side. A woven mat covered some doorways (as in Aztec Ruin).

Most doorways consisted of rectangular openings through walls with raised sills and low lintels, requiring someone passing through to crouch and squeeze. The high sill blocked out cold floor-level drafts, and the small size accommodated smaller, more readily handled stone doors. Chacoan doorways (fig. 1-37) were consistently larger than those in Northern San Juan and Kayenta sites. Some doorways in Chaco and the Northern San Juan have been constricted on both sides above the sill to produce a generalized T shape. Access to many living rooms in Keet Seel near Kayenta involved first passing through jacal front walls at floor level and then over a low wall draft deflector inside the room.

Inside the living rooms, small hearths lined with clay or stones lay in a corner or along one wall; small openings at floor level provided fresh air; and openings in the roof or at roof level carried away smoke. Wooden pegs projecting from the walls and short beams across the corners just below the roof allowed the tenants to hang up their possessions. Twig loops set in some walls served as attachments for string or ropes, and small valued possessions could be placed in wall niches. Smaller rooms without hearths and with poorly faced and unplastered walls functioned as storerooms. Some rooms contained batteries of grinding bins, while others appear to have housed domestic turkeys. People performed many daily activities outdoors on rooftops and in courtyards where hearths and grinding bins customarily occurred. Additional outdoor space was gained by constructing narrow balconies on roof beams extended through the walls (fig. 1-38).

Yet another stylistic difference set Chacoan rooms—at least those in the big pueblos in the Chaco Canyon—apart from those elsewhere in Pueblo-land. Chacoan living rooms covered decidedly more floor space, up to two to three times, and had higher ceilings than those of Kayenta and the Northern San Juan. With the exception of these larger Chacoan rooms, the average Pueblo Indian could rarely stand up straight in the rooms. Once inside, people would sit or lie down on woven mats spread across the earthen floors. We have already seen how indoor spaces provided room primarily for storage and for sleeping, while most other household tasks took place outdoors.

Not even the Great Migrations at the close of the thirteenth century seriously disrupted average domestic architecture. The biggest changes resulted from the different nature of building materials available in the Rio Grande Valley. Hopi and Zuni architecture remained essentially unchanged from that of their Pueblo III ancestors. The evenly bedded sandstones of the Colorado Plateau did not occur in the Rio Grande Valley. There the Pueblo IV Puebloans used lava boulders, rough blocks of volcanic tuff (consolidated ash), and sun-dried adobe bricks to build multistoried pueblos either in the open, as at Kuaua, or against cliffs, as at Bandelier National Monument. The relatively soft tuff cliffs of the Pajarito Plateau west of Santa Fe allowed some Puebloans to carve niches and roof beam sockets into the cliff face, to smooth portions of the cliff face for room walls, and even to carve entire rooms (cavates) entirely inside the cliff (fig. 1-39). Yet even with these changes, the Puebloan housing style continued directly into the historic architecture of such settlements as Pecos Pueblo and Gran Quivira.

1-38. Narrow balconies built upon extensions of interior roof poles often provided access to upper story rooms as did this balcony in Balcony House at Mesa Verde National Park.

1-39. Soft volcanic tuff enabled the Puebloans in Frijoles Canyon at Bandelier National Monument to carve rooms out of the cliff face. Additional masonry-walled rooms stood in front of these cavate rooms.

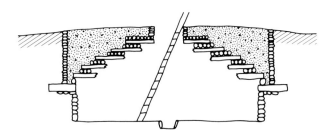

1-40. Kiva roofs consisted of horizontally laid logs built up in crib fashion to form a dome with a central access hatchway. Earth fill then leveled the roof's top and made the kiva entirely below ground. (After National Park Service pamphlet.)

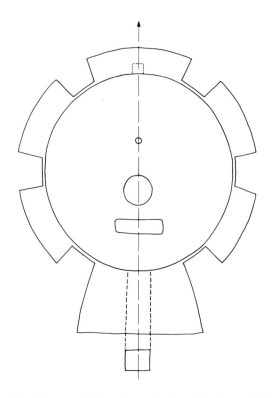

1-41. Mesa Verde–style kivas in the Northern San Juan exhibited very distinctive features, including a banquette level recess on the south side of the circular kiva to produce a keyhole-shaped outline.

Kivas

Kivas evolved directly out of the pithouses of Basket Maker III and Pueblo I. All their salient features originated as pithouse features, even though they changed in form and sometimes function through time. That evolution tells a remarkable story in itself. As kivas evolved, they even took on distinctive regional qualities. Small kivas served kinship groups, while the great kivas served whole communities.

Development of the smaller kin-group kivas has been most completely documented from studies at Mesa Verde. Twin Trees Site and Site 16 along the Ruins Road illustrate how the earlier four roof-support posts first had been set into the front edge of the banquette around A.D. 900, then replaced by four short masonry columns or pilasters footed on the banquette around 1000, and finally increased to six tall masonry pilasters by 1100. The increase from four to six pilasters signaled a shift to a cribbed-log, dome-shaped roof construction not unlike the old Basket Maker II cribbed superstructure for pithouses, leaving the space surrounding the dome to be filled with earth to make a level courtyard surface at ground level (fig. 1-40).

Chaco-style kivas often had eight, sometimes more, low pilasters formed around horizontal log stubs projecting from the upper walls onto the banquettes. Kayenta-style kiva roofs often rested on four upright posts set into the walls at the corners. They also frequently lacked banquettes.

As the kiva roof-support system changed, so did other features. Stone masonry lining began to replace the old clay-plastered earth sides of the pit. At first, this masonry merely shored up weak spots of loose earth on the front of the banquette, but by 1100 it lined the entire structure. The builders then applied coats of clay plaster over the face of the masonry. By the 1200s, painted murals appeared on kiva wall plaster, although the actual beginnings of this practice may date back considerably earlier. By the time of the Spanish conquest in 1540, kiva mural painting had reached a very sophisticated state, as exemplified at Kawaika-a and Awatovi on the Hopi Mesas and at Kuaua in Coronado State Monument near Bernalillo, New Mexico.

The interior alignment of the sipapu, fire pit, deflector, and ventilator on a north-to-south axis remained quite standard in most Puebloan kivas into Pueblo III. Mesa Verde–style kivas added new features to this axis (fig. 1-41). With the advent of stone masonry linings, small storage niches were frequently built into the masonry facing. Quite commonly, one of those niches fell on the axis directly opposite the ventilator opening. When six roof-supporting stone pilasters became common, the builders deepened the space between the two southernmost pilasters and directly over the ventilator tunnel to form a recess at banquette level. From above, the plan of one of these kivas resembled a keyhole shape.

Keyhole-shaped kivas with six masonry pilasters and ventilator tunnels entering at floor level characterize the Pueblo III style at Mesa Verde and in the adjoining Northern San Juan Region. Similar distinctive styles may also be recognized for Pueblo III Chaco and Kayenta kivas. Chacoan kivas tend to be larger than their Mesa Verde–style counterparts: ventilators enter the chamber below floor level, opening adjacent to the fire pit, thereby obviating the need for a separate deflector. They have a very shallow southern recess at floor level—really more an offset in the wall—and they most commonly have eight low pilasters to support the cribbed roof (fig. 1-42). Chaco-style pilasters consist of short logs embedded into the kiva wall with thin masonry veneers on each side. The roof-cribbing logs rested on these pilaster logs. Caches of turquoise have been found in pockets on the top surface of many such log pilasters in Pueblo Bonito kivas.

Chacoan kiva fire pits tend to be stone lined. Many kivas have one or two long vaults set into the

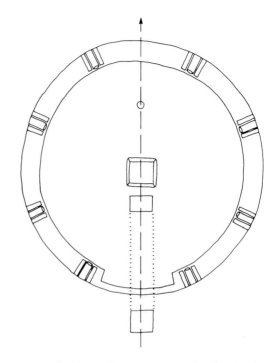

1-42. A typical Chacoan kiva was masonry lined with a banquette around the circular wall upon which eight or more stone and log pilasters supported a cribbed roof. The ventilator tunnel entered from below floor level.

floor flanking the fire pit. The function of these vaults remains obscure, although some have suggested they would make excellent foot drums when covered with wooden planks. The typical Chacoan masonry style of small, closely fitting sandstone blocks sets this kiva style apart from the Mesa Verde style, where larger stones and some upright slabs above banquette level rested in thicker mud mortar.

Kivas in the Kayenta Region tend to be small and somewhat squarish with rounded corners (fig. 1-43). They have four roof-support posts set into the corners, and they lack banquettes and recesses. Some actually have a rectangular shape, foreshadowing the historic Hopi rectangular kivas. A number of kivas in the southern Cibola region exhibit a D shape with a southern recess and floor-level ventilator tunnel on the straight side.

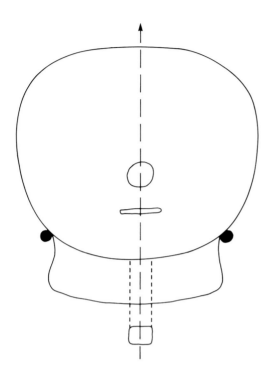

1-43. Kivas in the Kayenta Region display more variability than do Chacoan or Mesa Verde–style kivas. Wooden posts set into the masonry walls often replace pilasters as roof supports. Most have a squarish outline with rounded corners, while others were clearly rectangular.

Of course, not all kivas exactly fit these standards. Within a single settlement, no two exactly duplicate one another. This probably reflects specific needs of the kin-group rituals and the kiva's setting. Bedrock cave floors forced many kivas to be constructed above ground, where the builders surrounded them with rubble and earth held in place by walls to create an underground atmosphere. Kivas built within caves and rockshelters required ventilators to lead toward the cave opening, whatever the direction, although many shrewd architects angled the tunnel toward the traditional orientation once at the mouth of the cave.

Residents of upper-story rooms had access to kivas set among the room blocks of lower stories, hence creating the subsurface impression. A third-story resident could go out his door onto the courtyard and down into his kin-group kiva in the same way that ground-level dwellers could enter a subterranean kiva.

Not all kivas were round. Several kivas on the Mesa Verde and in the Little Colorado River Region actually had a square shape. Numbers of pilasters varied from none (roofs resting directly on walls) to as many as ten. Deflectors consisted of stone slabs, poles and mud, masonry wall stubs, arcs of masonry, and movable stone slabs. Some kivas even lacked a sipapu while others had two or more. Other features found in kivas included loom anchors, wall pegs set in pilaster faces, horizontal pole shelves between pilasters, and stone anvils set into the floor. The loom anchors and stone anvils indicate that the kivas served as men's workshops or craft centers (men wove textiles and chipped stone into tools) as well as gathering places for kin groups. Tunnels occasionally connected to other kivas, to adjacent rooms, or to nearby towers.

The tower kivas in Chacoan sites such as Chetro Ketl and Salmon Ruin stood at second-story levels on top of rubble platforms surrounded by walled-in rubble. Their central position in those sites suggests a specific community-wide function rather than a kin-group one.

Pueblo III marked the epitome of kin-group kiva construction and use by the Puebloans. Probably every kin group had its own kiva for both ceremonial and domestic use. Following the Great Migrations of the 1200s, kin-group kivas became less numerous. More people used fewer kivas, especially in the Rio Grande Valley. Typical kiva features continued to be incorporated into many Pueblo IV kivas, but a new style also developed. The Pueblos of the Pajarito Plateau west of Santa Fe built many of their houses and kivas against the bases of vertical volcanic tuff cliffs. They burrowed many rooms and kivas into the cliffs themselves. Such cave kivas tended to be ovoid with fire pits and side entries (fig. 1-44). These spaces did not need roof supports; sipapus, cut into the rock floors, occurred only occasionally; side entries provided ventilation. Rows of loom anchors commonly occurred. Because of the Spanish attempts to suppress Pueblo Indian religion, kin group–style kivas exist today only in Taos Pueblo and in the Hopi pueblos.

Great Kivas

The so-called great kivas followed a path of development separate from that of the small kin-group kivas. They may be distinguished primarily by their large size—more than forty-five feet across—by the presence of raised masonry fireboxes and floor vaults, and by rooms attached to the exterior of the main chamber. Unlike the small kivas, great kivas seem to have grown out of unusually large pit structures that differed from ordinary pithouses primarily in size and in elements of wall construction.

They mostly had been dug partially below ground surface, and they exhibited a circular shape ranging from thirty to eighty feet in diameter. Most (eleven) of them fell within thirty to forty feet in diameter. Vertical wooden posts stood between upright stone slabs to form both side walls and the front of an encircling low banquette. Four large posts, in two instances six, set well in from the side walls, supported a flat roof. Where preservation permitted, investigators reported central hearths, at least two of them raised, and ventilators, and less commonly deflectors, floor vaults and cists, wall niches, side entries, wing walls, and in two cases several peripheral rooms. Southern and southeastern orientations predominated.

At least fifteen of these nascent great kivas have been identified, all but three of them lying north of the San Juan River. Two of the others occur in the Kayenta Region, with only one in Chaco Canyon. Four of them, Shabik'eshchee Village in Chaco Canyon, Broken Flute Cave and Juniper Cove in Kayenta, and Site 60 on Mesa Verde, date to Basket Maker III times, while all the others fall into the

1-44. On the Pajarito Plateau, including Bandelier National Monument, Pueblo IV people sometimes carved kivas into cliff faces. This cave kiva with rock art decorations belongs to a settlement in Ancho Canyon.

Pueblo I stage. All of these large structures seem to have served entire communities rather than single kin groups, since only two settlements contained more than one, and those may not have been contemporary.

No fully or partially excavated great kivas have been unequivocally dated to the Pueblo II stage, although many of the later Pueblo III structures may well have been built originally during Pueblo II and later remodeled into their Pueblo III versions. The unexcavated Cahone settlement in the Montezuma Valley consists of both Pueblo II and early Pueblo III settlements clustered around an unexcavated great kiva.

1-45. This great kiva at Pueblo Bonito in Chaco Canyon served as a center for the local community. Its roof probably resembled that of the restored great kiva at Aztec Ruin to the north. Internal features include an encircling bench, a raised masonry firebox, two oblong masonry vaults that possibly served as foot drums, and four masonry-lined seating holes for the bases of roof support columns or timbers.

A typical Pueblo III great kiva had a circular shape, forty-five to seventy feet in diameter dug partway into the ground (fig. 1-45). Stone masonry lined the pit and carried the walls above ground level. Chaco-style masonry characterized the great kivas of Chaco Canyon and its obvious outliers, while those north of the San Juan River have Mesa Verde–style masonry. A set of four columns footed on sets of large sandstone disks supported the flat roof. These columns, usually square, consisted of alternating layers of stone masonry and horizontal poles. Large logs linked the columns to one another and to the side walls, forming the bottom layer of a typical Puebloan layered roof of successively smaller wooden elements covered with bark and earth. In the center of the floor stood a raised, rectangular masonry firebox (fig. 1-46). Similarly raised, oblong masonry vaults stretched between roof-support columns on the east and west sides. One, sometimes two low masonry banquettes (resembling benches)—presumably where spectators sat—encircled the floor area.

Entry usually could be gained down staircases from the south and north sides. The north staircase normally led to a ground-level masonry room, attached to the exterior circular kiva wall, in which an altarlike platform stood. The Aztec Ruin great kiva had a set of masonry rooms completely encircling the structure's exterior. Each room could be accessed through an exterior doorway or from inside the kiva by climbing a ladder of short sticks set in the interior wall. Many great kivas lacked this circle of rooms but instead had a circle of niches in the inside circular wall. Others, such as Casa Rinconada in Chaco Canyon, had a tunnel leading from the north altar room beneath the kiva floor to an opening near the center of the floor. Archaeologists speculate that masked performers could emerge from the opening of this tunnel as from out of the earth during a ceremony reenacting the Puebloan origin story. Great kivas shared the same north-south orientation as the small kin-group kivas. This axis ran from a north altar room through the north entry, firebox, and sipapu, to the south entry, with other features arranged symmetrically on either side.

Not all great kivas fit this circular pattern. Possibly because they had been built in limited quarters

1-46. Great kivas occurred at many of the large pueblos in Chaco Canyon and in the Northern San Juan. This great kiva sits in the court-yard at Chetro Ketl. Note the large, round sandstone disks that served as footings for the columns that supported the roof.

beneath cliff overhangs, two such structures on the Mesa Verde exhibited a rectangular floor plan. One, Fire Temple, may be seen from an overlook into Fewkes Canyon on Chapin Mesa (fig. 1-47); the other occupies a central position in Long House on Wetherill Mesa. Despite their rectangular shape, these buildings exhibit typical great kiva features including masonry firebox and floor vaults, low banquettes, a north altar room, and wall niches.

Wherever they may be found, the great kivas appear to have served as places to hold community ceremonies, perhaps both spiritual and sociopolitical. Each Pueblo III town or other central settlement had a great kiva or similarly functioning structure. Following the Great Migrations when the smaller kiva styles grew less common during Pueblo IV, great kivas continued to function as community ceremonial structures, together with open plazas. Except at Taos where kin-group kivas still survive, kivas in the historic Rio Grande pueblos have descended, often in pairs representing the ceremonial moieties, from the prehistoric Puebloan great kivas.

1-47. Fire Temple at Mesa Verde National Park served as a great kiva for the Cliff-Fewkes Canyon community of cliff dwellings. It probably had no roof.

1-48. The triwall structure at Pueblo del Arroyo in Chaco Canyon illustrates the basic plan of a central kiva surrounded by two concentric walls with spaces between the walls subdivided into compartments.

Concentric Wall Structures, Towers, and Shrines

Many Pueblo III settlements contain several features about which we know far too little. A series of walled buildings stand apart from others by having two or three walls trace concentric paths around a central circular space. This central space usually contains the basic elements of a kiva, while cross walls subdivide the surrounding spaces between walls into compartments, many of which have no apparent means of access. Overall ground plans describe either a circle or the generalized shape of a capital D.

These concentric wall structures occur almost exclusively north of the San Juan River. The Hubbard Ruin at Aztec Ruin has three circular walls around an above-ground kiva with a second kiva underground outside the south walls. The Sun Temple on the point between Cliff and Fewkes canyons at Mesa Verde has two concentric walls outlining a D shape around three ground-level kivas. A circular tower stands slightly

apart from the main building. The Hovenweep villages in the Montezuma Valley each contain a D-shaped building with two walls enclosing an above-ground kiva. Those structures have been called horseshoe houses. The only triwall circular structure south of the San Juan River may be visited behind Pueblo del Arroyo in Chaco Canyon (fig. 1-48)—some archaeologists refer to this structure as part of the "McElmo influence." They suggest that Northern San Juan peoples constructed it when they migrated into Chaco Canyon during the 1100s. Since their painted pottery style dominates the canyon's ceramic assemblages, these "McElmo" arrivals apparently lived side by side with the Chacoans.

Because of their positions in the larger towns and villages, concentric wall structures probably supported community ceremonial activities in much the same manner as great kivas. They seem to reflect a characteristic unique to the Northern San Juan and limited to Pueblo III in that region. We know nothing about possible antecedent structures prior to 1100, nor what happened to these features after abandonment of the San Juan drainage around 1300.

Another structure found almost exclusively north of the San Juan River is the round tower. A circular masonry wall stands one to two stories high within a settlement or in an isolated setting, usually on the point of a ridge or finger mesa. When in villages, towers usually stand adjacent to the southern side of kivas with an underground tunnel linking the two. Tower masonry consists of unusually well-dressed stones without any chinking, a style common in kivas, but absent in domestic buildings. For these reasons, archaeologists have interpreted the round towers as ceremonial buildings rather than as watchtowers or granaries. An underground tunnel at the isolated tower at Cedar Tree Tower on Mesa Verde led to both a nearby kiva and a small subterranean room. A sipapu had also been laboriously

1-49. The tower and kiva combination, such as this one at the Far View Settlement in Mesa Verde National Park, exemplifies another ceremonial or religious complex. A tunnel links the two separate structures. The locations of such buildings within the heart of their settlements belie their possible defensive nature.

1-50. Many prehistoric and modern Puebloan shrines consist of a small masonry box, a U-shaped arc, or an alcove such as this one on Chapin Mesa in Mesa Verde National Park. Shrines apparently served as receptacles for ritual offerings or objects.

pecked into its bedrock sandstone floor. Towers generally appear around 1100 and cease to be built after 1300. Towers have also been reported from the Gallina district in extreme northern New Mexico.

The kiva-tower combination set apart in some settlements may have functioned as the community ceremonial building. For example, Far View Tower at Mesa Verde (fig. 1-49), built on the ruins of an ancestor's house, probably served the whole early Pueblo III Far View community. Isolated kiva-towers occupy settings in nature similar to typical locations for shrines—in isolated places on mesas or in canyons, often with striking vistas, that held special significance for the Puebloans.

Another kind of feature has so far defied interpretation. A series of arrangements of loose stones outline at least twenty crude circles (really ovoids) along the canyon rims flanking Chaco Canyon. Most occur on the north side of the canyon walls and on the lower of two rock benches (ledges). They vary in size from about twenty-eight to almost one hundred feet in length by about twenty-two to over sixty feet in width. The loose stones lie directly on exposed

bedrock. Occasionally some dry masonry walls and other crude features accompany them. Both round and rectangular basins had been pecked into the bedrock within these outlines. All have a direct view of a great kiva located on the canyon floor.

Chaco Center archaeologists believe these crude stone outlines relate to the large towns on the valley floor, even though some towns cannot be seen from them. They suspect some role in ceremonial behavior, perhaps as places where ritual performers could prepare for their participation in a public ceremony, out of general public view.

Like their modern Pueblo descendants, the prehistoric people constructed a variety of shrines. None have been clearly dated before 1100, but good examples do occur in Pueblo III and IV contexts. Besides the kiva-towers and some isolated towerlike structures, many shrines take the form of rectangular boxes, U shapes, or alcoves (fig. 1-50). The boxes are formed by stone slabs set in the ground or by low masonry walls without mud mortar resting on the ground surface. Occasionally, an old dressed building stone or piles of small sandstone spalls fill the

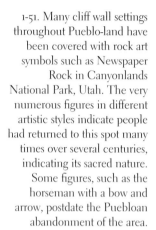

1-51. Many cliff wall settings throughout Pueblo-land have been covered with rock art symbols such as Newspaper Rock in Canyonlands National Park, Utah. The very numerous figures in different artistic styles indicate people had returned to this spot many times over several centuries, indicating its sacred nature. Some figures, such as the horseman with a bow and arrow, postdate the Puebloan abandonment of the area.

interior. U-shaped shrines resemble dry masonry boxes, but with only three sides and rounded corners. These U-shaped shrines often open toward a cardinal direction or a prominent feature on the horizon. Alcove shrines consisted of piles of unmortared stones with a niche or alcove built within.

An unusual stone enclosure shrine stands on a finger mesa of the Pajarito Plateau west of the Bandelier National Monument Visitor Center. Pueblo IV Pajaritans had built it, and modern Pueblo Indians continue to use it today. A crude circle of large stones loosely piled together encloses a space about thirty feet in diameter inside which a pair of crouching mountain lions has been sculpted on two low boulders. These two stone lions occupy the southwest portion of the enclosure, and a large stone-lined passage leads due south from its southeast corner.

Probably much of the rock art in Pueblo-land marks shrine locations. Concentrations of rock art, such as Mesa Verde's Petroglyph Point, the huge panel at the confluence of Butler Wash with the San Juan River, and numerous places labeled "newspaper rock" (fig. 1-51), often exist well apart from settlements. Painted Cave in Capulin Canyon at Bandelier National Monument contains a dazzling array of paintings with prehistoric Puebloan pictographs mingled with more recent ones done by the Cochiti Pueblo Indians.

Modular Residence Units

Any discussion of Puebloan architecture must go beyond a mere description of the Pueblo style. The arrangement of various buildings—for living, storage, group activities, ceremonies, and so forth—relative to one another reflects an organizational design in the minds of the builders. The most consistent concept may be seen in the modular residence units as expressed in the unit pueblo. This concept first appeared with the rows of outdoor storage units and ramadas arranged in a row to the north of Basket Maker III pithouses. This layout steadily evolved through Pueblo I and II into the easily recognized unit pueblo. When these units agglomerated into larger buildings during Pueblo III and later, they formed the primary construction unit.

During Pueblo I, a subdivision within the residence unit first appeared. Two- or three-room sets, or suites, consisting of one large living room containing a hearth, two or more rooms for storage and/or sleeping, plus outdoor work space, shared a single pithouse and trash dump (fig. 1-52). Even as standard residence units became more difficult to trace in Pueblo V, these suites (room sets) persisted into twentieth-century societal organization.

We now believe each suite of rooms housed a household consisting of one adult male, one adult female, any children produced by these two, and possibly one or more other related persons. The two or three households that shared a common pithouse or kiva probably also shared common ancestry. They thus would have comprised a segment of a line of descent, or lineage. Consequently, we may surmise that such lineage segments built and inhabited the various modular residence units. This interpretation of past Puebloan societal organization closely mirrors what modern ethnographers have described for historic and modern Pueblo Indian society.

Village Layout

Yet another significant principle of organization can be seen in the layout of villages or settlements. Throughout Puebloan prehistory, buildings occurred in clusters, and rarely does a single structure constitute a prehistoric community. Basket Maker II and III settlements contained groups of three to a dozen pithouses with associated storage units, ramadas, outdoor hearths, and other features. Single houses have been found, but usually within an hour or less walking distance to a village. The standardized housing units with their southern orientation generally formed east-west rows fronting an open space toward the south or southeast. Along the northern frontier of

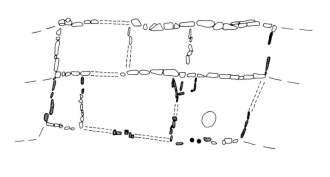

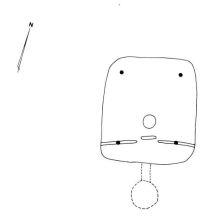

1-52. The central unit from the Duckfoot Site in the Montezuma Valley typifies a Pueblo I (A.D. 750–900) modular residence unit. Each of the two living rooms has its adjacent storage rooms, and both resident households shared the outside courtyard work space and the pithouse in which some ceremonies probably took place. A rubbish dump lies south of the pithouse.

Pueblo-land, wooden post stockades surrounded all or major portions of some Basket Maker III villages. The largest of these villages probably housed around 100 to 150 persons. Proto–great kivas, serving community needs or several villages, generally stood outside the village itself.

With the shift to Pueblo I, village size began to grow dramatically. The standardized housing and storage units still formed east-west rows, quite often directly abutting one another. The southern or southeastern village orientation remained strong. Populations of the largest villages doubled, and smaller outlying settlements sprang up. In the Northern San Juan, at least, great kivas provided for community ceremonialism at many of the larger villages.

1-53. Ground plan of the Lowry town in the Montezuma Valley during Pueblo III (1100–1300). Probably eighteen hundred people inhabited the various buildings while sharing the central water supply and the surrounding farmlands and attending ceremonies held at the great kiva or in the two plazas. Several streets connect various parts of the town and lead away to the neighboring small villages and hamlets.

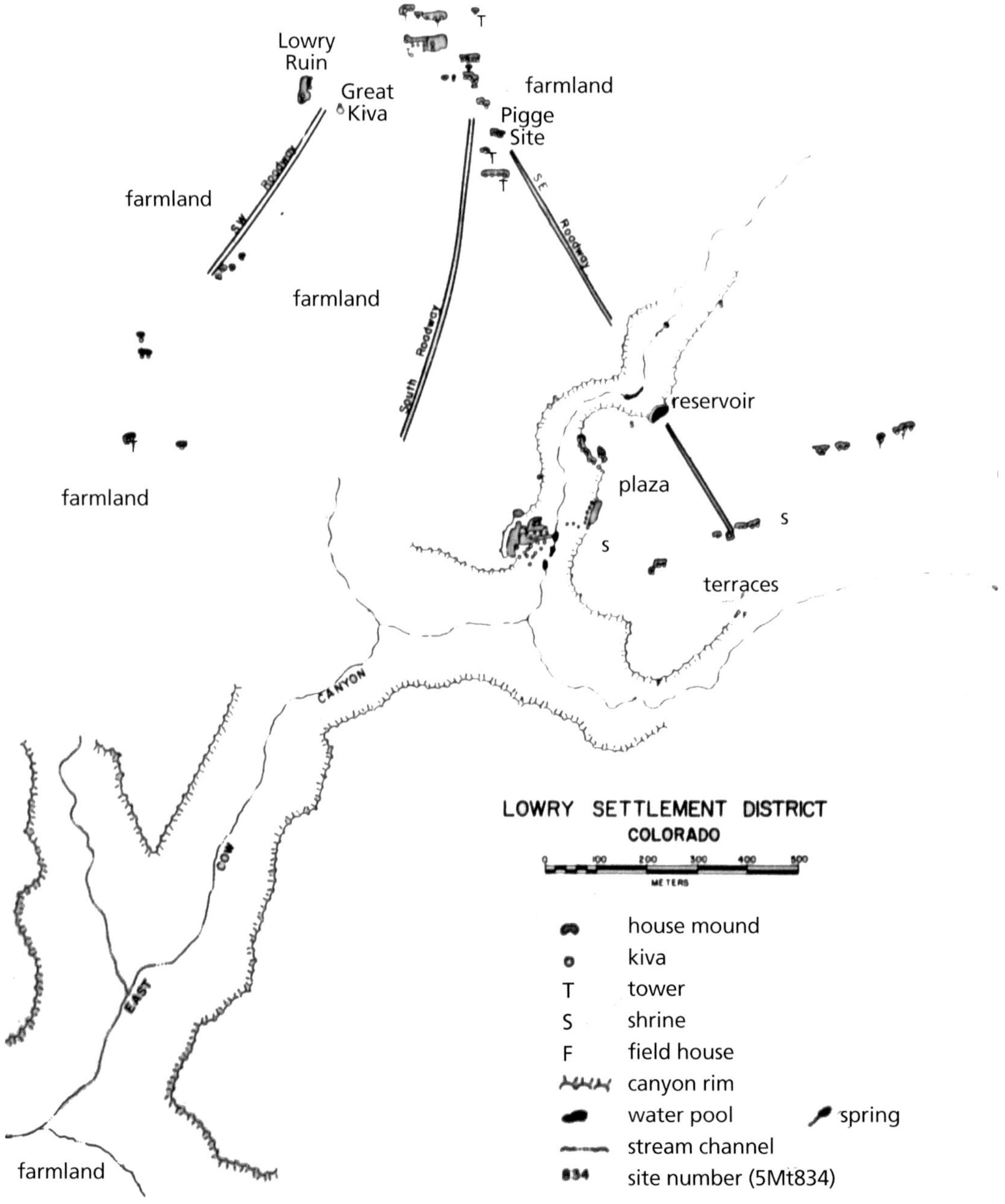

farmland
Lowry
Ruin
Great
Kiva
farmland
Pigge
Site
farmland
S.W. Roadway
SE Roadway
South Roadway
farmland
reservoir
plaza
farmland
terraces
CANYON
COW
EAST
farmland
LOWRY SETTLEMENT DISTRICT
COLORADO
0 100 200 300 400 500
METERS
house mound
kiva
T tower
S shrine
F field house
canyon rim
water pool
spring
stream channel
834 site number (5Mt834)

Complete settlement plans for Pueblo I and Pueblo II have not really been fully investigated except in a few rudimentary cases. About all we can note in Pueblo II villages is the continued growth in population in the largest villages and further differentiation in sizes of outlying smaller settlements. We do have evidence for the construction of reservoirs to supply domestic water for community use (e.g. Mummy Lake at Far View on Mesa Verde).

By Pueblo III, the larger towns of the Montezuma Valley, Mesa Verde, the San Juan River valley, Chaco Canyon, and the Little Colorado River drainage had grown to house up to a thousand or more people each. The standardized residential modules continued to face southward in east-west rows, while streets and plazas focused traffic flow among them. Artificial reservoirs and other devices promoted a steady water supply for the community. Each of the larger settlements contained a great kiva or a similarly functioning concentric wall structure as a kind of ceremonial center not only for the town itself, but also for surrounding smaller villages and hamlets.

Both the large towns, such as Lowry (fig. 1-53), and smaller villages, such as Mug House, reflected a two-part physical division—at Lowry, two clusters of the house blocks shared a common water source; at Mug House an unpenetrated wall divided the cliff site into two sections of unequal size. Settlements of all sizes faced south.

Except for Chaco Canyon, the largest Puebloan towns housed up to around twenty-five hundred people. In Chaco Canyon proper, a relatively closely arranged group of six large pueblos contained a total population of four thousand to six thousand—enough people to qualify as a small city. This view assumes that the six pueblos comprised a single community rather than six separate ones. Five of those six did have one or more great kivas. A network of roadways that connect Chaco Canyon to numerous out-lying settlements in the Chaco Basin has been cited as evidence to support the interpretation of incipient urbanization. Should this view be correct, the urbanization experiment failed. Chaco Canyon's florescence collapsed after about two generations, and the maximum populations of settlements in the rest of Pueblo-land never surpassed twenty-five hundred to three thousand persons.

Modern Pueblos follow the independent pueblo organization. Each pueblo operates autonomously in government and society with maximum populations of twenty-five hundred to three thousand. They arrange housing units along streets or around plazas. Kivas focus ceremonial activities. Many, such as Zuni, have outlying villages whose residents return to the main pueblo on ceremonial occasions. Pueblo organization and size have thus changed little during the seven hundred years since Pueblo III times.

Settlement Locations

The Puebloans located their settlements in a variety of settings—open valley floors, mesa-top ridges, rims of canyons, or in rock shelters beneath cliff overhangs. Basket Maker II and III peoples tended to select rock shelters and mesa-top ridge locations (Los Pinos settlements southeast of Durango, Colorado, lay near mesa edges), while Pueblo I and II peoples opted more frequently for mesa-top ridges and valley floors. Pueblo III saw a preference for canyon rims and rock shelters, although many very large settlements lay in valley floors. During the same stage, many communities settled around the heads of canyons where they could more readily manage their water supply.

After the Great Migrations, Pueblo IV villages chose valley floors and mesa edge locations in both the Rio Grande and Little Colorado River regions. Some Pajarito Plateau inhabitants built against vertical cliffs on the tops of talus slopes. Vertical cliffs had

1-54. Puebloans often built their pueblos around canyon heads where springs occurred or in the cliffs below them. In many places they constructed dams on the mesa tops to prevent rapid runoff and to cause the water to seep down through the sandstone bedrock to enhance the flow of the spring below. (Drawing by Joan Foth.)

1-55. The Puebloans often created garden plots by constructing masonry dams in dry waterways to collect and hold moisture and sediments. These dams fill a ravine near Cedar Tree Tower in Mesa Verde National Park.

always been popular locations where people inscribed rock art.

When the Spaniards arrived, many communities retreated to high mesa locations. However, wherever they could, the Spaniards forced them, except the Hopi, to resettle in open settings on valley floors.

This picture of shifting settlement locations points out several factors that helped select those situations. Those locations on valley floors and mesa-top ridges seemed to focus on available farmland. On the other hand, locations at canyon heads and around springs emphasized water supply. Rock shelter settings may

have provided some protection against weather. Cliff edges, butte tops, and most rock shelters offered defensive situations against potential attack. Clearly the Puebloan peoples adapted through time to changing necessities and desires.

Water Management

The prehistoric Puebloan culture developed in the semiarid American Southwest where the people required reliable access to water. Their ability to manage water for household and crop usage marks one of their major accomplishments. Locations of towns and villages had to take into account appropriate water sources. They occasionally would build along the banks of a permanent stream as did the residents of Aztec or Kuaua, but most often they relied on springs. Because so many streams in their environment ran only seasonally, they learned how to impound runoff rainwater to augment the springs, as the Far View Settlement on Mesa Verde illustrates.

Most springs developed from rainwater percolating downward through porous sandstone to an impervious shale layer along which it then flowed until it came out at the canyon wall, most frequently in the head of a canyon. The Puebloans obviously recognized that if they built a dam across the runoff channels above such locations, like they did above Long House and at the head of Fewkes Canyon on the Mesa Verde, the springs would generate more water flow from the trapped runoff water percolating through the bedrock sandstone (fig. 1-54). Whether or not they understood the mechanics of this relationship, or simply attributed its success to magic, does not matter. They benefited from the end result.

Puebloan water management focused mostly on supplies of water for domestic consumption—drinking, cooking, washing, and pottery making. However, they also developed methods for irrigating their crops, especially in districts with inconsistent natural

1-56. Pueblo IV (1300–1540) peoples on the Pajarito Plateau farmed both on the plateau top and on natural benches in White Rock Canyon cut by the Rio Grande. The sloping ground prompted the farmers to build stone-walled terraces such as these to hold rainwater and in some cases irrigation water.

rainfall. They commonly constructed systems of check dams in shallow ravines (fig. 1-55) or on gentle slopes (fig. 1-56) to slow rainwater runoff and accumulate silt in terraces. In several locations, they diverted runoff rainwater into ditches leading to the agricultural fields. Chacoan irrigation engineering included floodwater irrigation of fields where ravines spilled out from the cliffs, systems of check dams, and large earthen dams designed to catch and store rainwater for diversion into fields. They controlled the direction of water flow through irrigation canals with stone-lined headgates. Other Puebloan regions had less elaborate canal irrigation systems.

Ceramics

The Puebloans manufactured pottery to serve as storage containers and as utensils for cooking and eating. Many scholars believe prehistoric peoples more likely learned the art of making pottery from neighbors rather than inventing the process independently from others. Southwestern archaeologists believe the ideas and techniques for producing pottery spread northward out of central Mexico to the Hohokam and Mogollon south of the Colorado Plateau and finally to the Puebloans.

Basket Maker III peoples had been fabricating a well-made and highly fired pottery by the late 500s, and possibly earlier. Unfortunately, our archaeological record contains very sparse information for the time from A.D. 300 to 600. These early Puebloan potters founded a fourteen-hundred-year tradition of distinctive and outstanding ceramic artistry. Through judicious stacking of fuel, they restricted the flow of oxygen during the firing process to produce gray and white colorings. They decorated many vessels with geometric designs painted in black against either a white (most commonly) or reddish background. The painted wares served much as our dinnerware would—for eating and drinking vessels—while unpainted vessels, some bearing corrugated exterior surfaces, functioned as cooking and storage containers.

Since historic Pueblo women produced the pottery, we assume that women made prehistoric Puebloan pottery also. Making ceramics requires the

1-57. Corrugated jars used for cooking and storage from Pueblo II through Pueblo III and into early Pueblo IV (A.D. 900–1450).

potter first to find a source of suitable clay, collect it, and clean it. Sometimes a soft shale needed to be ground on a metate and winnowed. Then, to prevent the formed pot from cracking while the clay dried and to give it body, a coarse tempering material had to be added, much as we add aggregate to cement to make concrete. This temper might be unprocessed sand or crushed rock. In later times, crushed old potsherds often replaced both as a tempering agent.

The potter built up the vessel's shape by rolling ropes of moist clay and coiling them up the side walls. She then bonded the coils together by smearing and scraping the surfaces. Between 900 and 1350, potters produced distinctive corrugated cooking pots by bonding the coils together only on the interiors of the vessels and finger crimping the exteriors of the coils (fig. 1-57). Vessel surfaces intended for painted decoration were smoothed more thoroughly than others and often polished by the intense rubbing of a smooth pebble over the surface. To achieve white backgrounds for the black designs, the potter coated the surface with a slip of fine white clay. The artisan made paint pigments from powdered iron oxides or from an organic material such as boiled beeweed.

While most painted decorations formed geometric patterns, the intricate combinations of figures, the balance of black versus white, the symmetry, layout, and overall patterning bespeak numerous talented artists. Occasionally, stylized humanoid and animal figures appear as decoration as well as some stylized modeled effigy vessels. Obviously, these decorations went far beyond the mere functions of the pottery vessels. Some figures and whole designs may have been symbols, although we do not understand their significance. We assume that most decoration, however, served as mere artistic expression by individual potters within the bounds of their culture.

Before firing, the potters dried their "green" vessels slowly in the shade to prevent cracking from too rapid shrinkage. Modern Pueblo potters fire their pots in open fires by piling fuel around them. Prehistoric potters may have followed a similar practice, although archaeologists have found and excavated a number of shallow oblong trenches in the Northern San Juan that seem to have been prehistoric kilns. Experimenters have recently conducted firings of similarly made pots to test this interpretation. Wichita State University's ceramics professor Richard St. John has been the most successful at replicating the prehistoric ceramics and their firing temperatures by piling wood around and arched above the pots that had been stacked on top of heated stone slabs.

Undecorated gray and corrugated jars served primarily as cooking pots (soot deposits often covered much of their exteriors), although larger jars also provided storage. These utility jars generally had a globular or ovate shape with wide mouths to allow easy access to their contents. Circular stone lids held in place by clay usually sealed the storage jars. Large globular jars with narrow vertical necks and strong handles held water during both transport and storage. Smaller canteen-size containers held liquids for travelers.

1-58. Mesa Verde–style black-on-white painted pottery vessels from Mug House illustrate several shapes for different uses—clockwise from upper left: a food bowl, a canteen, a large water-carrying and storage jar, a dipper, a small jar for storing valuables, and a drinking mug.

Dippers could be used to scoop water from spring to pot, from pot to pot, and from pot to mouth. Drinking vessels often took the form of handled mugs, some of which resemble pitchers. A very common shape, the hemispherical bowl with rounded bottom and sides, apparently functioned as a food bowl and sometimes as a general container. Bowls ranged in size from small dipper-size bowls to large ones equal to half a basketball. Some smaller jars— seed jars, effigy jars, kiva jars, and oblong ceramic boxes—held valuable items such as feathers, charms, scarce raw materials, and pollen for safekeeping.

All ceramic forms, except the gray and corrugated utilitarian jars, generally bore decorations, on the interiors of bowls and dippers, and on the exteriors of jars and mugs (fig. 1-58). Sometimes decorations appeared on both interior and exterior bowl surfaces. Both decorated ceramics and some small utilitarian pots frequently occurred in graves with the dead, possibly containing food and drink for the afterlife.

Each separate locality, village, and social group had its own style of manufacture, form, and decoration.

1-59. A group of Pueblo I (A.D. 750–900) potsherds from Big Cave in Canyon del Muerto at Canyon de Chelly National Monument. The four painted sherds represent Kana'a Black-on-white; the two dark gray pieces show neck banding typical of Pueblo I cooking jars; and the lower right fragment comes from a sun-dried mud platter showing the impression of a basket.

1-60. Basket Maker III pottery vessels from Step House Cave in Mesa Verde National Park depict the most common plain gray ware and one simply painted pot. Note the shape adapted from the shape of a gourd.

1-61. Pueblo I (800s) gray utility pots from the Duckfoot Site in the Montezuma Valley.

The Puebloans also followed fads and changing styles through time, thus providing a means for recognizing where a particular pot had been produced, when, and by whom. A skilled archaeologist can examine the broken fragments of pottery vessels scattered across a rubbish deposit and read the probable ages of occupation, the regional affiliation of the residents, whether more than a single occupation had occurred, and possible trade connections. The relatively brittle ceramics broke frequently and had to be replaced by new vessels, thus providing archaeologists with a running record of the pottery made and used in any community (fig. 1-59).

Utility wares have chronicled well some of the changes through time across Pueblo-land. The earliest Basket Maker III people produced cooking pots with a plain gray surface, mostly tempered with sand except in the Northern San Juan where they used crushed igneous rock temper. These early vessels did not exceed medium size, and many jars had no necks, resembling the *tecomates* of Mesoamerica (fig. 1-60).

Pueblo I cooking vessels had tall, straight necks, many of which exhibited concentric bands formed by not obliterating the construction coils on the exterior surface (fig. 1-61). True corrugation—finger indenting unobliterated spiral coils—appears by 900 and marks the Pueblo II and III stages. Fine details in the treatment of corrugations, such as alternating bands of crimped and uncrimped coils or incised designs cutting across the coils, in details of vessel shapes, and in tempering materials denote both regional and time differences. By the fourteenth century during Pueblo IV, corrugation steadily died out to be replaced by very large, thick, plain gray cooking pots.

Decorations and shapes of painted wares reflected in even more detail both the passage of time and regional styles. During Pueblo III, densely painted black zones with patches of underlying white slip showing through created a negative pattern

1-62. The distinguishing feature of Kayenta Black-on-white pottery may be seen in the extensive use of black paint causing the underlying white surface to show through in a sort of "negative" design. Food bowls, canteens, dippers, and large jars predominate, and mugs do not occur. Many orange-red polychrome vessels also appear in Kayenta sites, and they were widely traded throughout Pueblo-land (specimens from the collections of the Arizona State Museum).

1-63. Chaco-style painted pottery exhibited broad line figures filled in with close, straight, parallel line "hatching" to create a half-tone effect against a white background. Distinctive shapes include food bowls, tall mugs with expanded bases, and cylindrical vases.

popular in the Kayenta Region, especially in Tsegi Canyon and the Long House Valley (fig. 1-62). Designs carried in figures filled by fine line hatching and bordered by heavier black lines characterized Chacoan pottery (fig. 1-63). Symmetrical and inter-locking band designs on thick-walled bowls and on distinctive mugs marked the Mesa Verde and the Montezuma Valley (see fig. 1-58).

Other features of pottery also contribute to this stylistic story. Kayenta potters almost always painted with organic pigments, while Chacoan and Little Colorado River artisans used mineral pigments. North of the San Juan River, potters used both, with once popular mineral pigments giving way to organic paints between 1050 and 1150.

Red pottery, often painted, first appears in the western Montezuma Valley by 700, then becomes popular in the Kayenta Region shortly afterward while dying out north of the San Juan River by around 950.

Three-colored vessels on this red base produced by Kayenta potters (see fig. 1–4) soon became treasured objects of trade all over Pueblo-land between 1000 and 1300. A separate invention of red pottery took place in the Little Colorado River Region by Pueblo II, and ultimately inspired the protohistoric and historic polychromes, some of which employed glaze paints, in the Rio Grande Valley. Shortly after 1300, ancestral Hopi potters began to fire their pots using coal as a fuel. This method produced a high-temperature firing background of orange or yellow coloring that identifies Hopi-made pottery to this day.

While many more examples of stylistic variation could be cited, Puebloan pottery offers an extremely valuable tool for recording both chronology and point of origin. The obvious trends can be comprehended easily, but it takes a great deal of knowledge and study to read the finer details.

1-64. Small bag woven from cotton yarns during Pueblo III times (1100–1300). The design resulted from interspersing wefts dyed in different colors.

Basketry and Fiber Utensils

Puebloan people made and used baskets throughout their entire history. In fact the fine-quality baskets and bags exhibiting multicolor decorations manufactured by the earliest Puebloans inspired the name "Basket Maker" for them. Unlike pottery, baskets do not break frequently, and hence become far less susceptible to fashion changes. Even when they do wear out, they can be repaired.

The Basket Makers wove supple bags and pouches employing the twining technique where weft fibers are twisted around parallel warp cords. They employed this same twining technique when fashioning fur and feather robes and blankets. They also ornamented most of these bags with two- and three-colored geometric patterns. This practice continued through later Pueblo stages (fig. 1-64). Twining also served to produce bands that could aid in supporting burden baskets, and later pottery vessels, suspended from them across the forehead. Such tump bands often displayed decoration, too.

A very shallow utilitarian bowl basket was made by plaiting (over one, under one) or by twilling (over two, under two) a mat using split yucca leaves, then

1-65. Ring basket made by plaiting two colors of split yucca leaves in an over two, under two twilling technique. Ring baskets first appeared in Basket Maker II times over two thousand years ago and have been continually made by Puebloan peoples into modern times.

1-66. Basket Maker II people produced this coiled basket tray almost two thousand years ago in the Falls Creek locality north of Durango, Colorado. Like the ring baskets, Puebloan artisans have continued to manufacture coiled basketry up to the present.

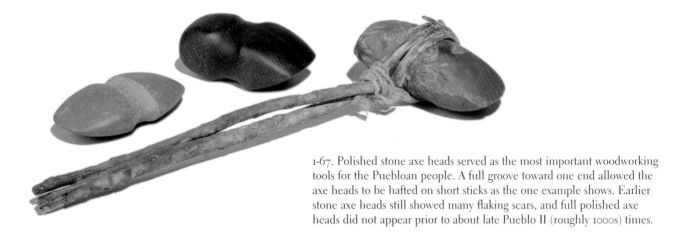

1-67. Polished stone axe heads served as the most important woodworking tools for the Puebloan people. A full groove toward one end allowed the axe heads to be hafted on short sticks as the one example shows. Earlier stone axe heads still showed many flaking scars, and full polished axe heads did not appear prior to about late Pueblo II (roughly 1000s) times.

pushing the mat through a willow ring roughly ten inches in diameter and tying off the overlapping cut ends (fig. 1-65). Such ring baskets became standard household items, never varying in basic style from the earliest Basket Maker times to the present day.

The Puebloans constructed many baskets in a variety of shapes by coiling reed and grass bundles stitched together by closely set loops of rabbitbrush, yucca, and sumac bark that tied each successive coil to the one beneath it. Different-colored stitches allowed the creation of designs encompassing both geometric and natural figures. The various shapes included trays (fig. 1-66), plaques, shallow bowls, globular jars with no necks, and conical burden baskets. As pottery became steadily more popular and versatile during Pueblo I, it replaced basketry vessels except for the trays and shallow bowls. Many of the painted designs on early Basket Maker III pottery actually mimicked the stitched designs on the coiled basketry.

Modern Pueblo Indians, especially the Hopi, still manufacture twilled ring baskets and coiled trays, bowls, and plaques. The Hopi have also added stiff wicker twined baskets of similar shapes. They decorate these coiled and wicker baskets with both geometric patterns and life forms, including some mythical figures, for use on special occasions and during rituals.

Stone and Bone Tools

Each Puebloan family produced its own food, clothing, and shelter. Because no craftsmen specialized in building or tool making, each family also manufactured all of its own tools for farming, hunting, building, garment making, and cooking. Some evidence indicates a division of labor between men and women, and there may have been some exceptional potters, basket weavers, or tool makers. However, on average, each family produced the necessary items to be self-sufficient.

From stone, the Puebloans made grinding tools, hammers, axe heads (fig. 1-67), cutting knives, scrapers, saws, drills, and arrow or dart points. They formed the knives, scrapers, saws, drills, and points by chipping appropriate cherts (flintlike stone) to sharp edges and points; they pecked grinding stones into shape; and they ground the cutting edges of axe heads. In addition, they made scrapers, reamers, awls, weaving tools, and needles from animal and bird bones.

Although the basic functions of these various tools remained the same through time, successive tool makers often adopted new forms and new details of manufacture. Just as pottery styles can be seen as reflections of chronological changes, so too can differing styles of tool making also carry temporal significance.

1-68. This Mesa Verde cliff dwelling called Mug House contained over ninety living and storage rooms, eight kivas, two round towers, and a turkey pen. About one hundred people lived here during the 1200s raising crops on the mesa top above and burying their dead along the steep talus slope below. Trails led out of this small village along the base of the cliff, toward their water supply to the right, and to a trail leading to the mesa top to the left.

Life in the Mug House Cliff Dwelling

Because of its fine state of preservation, little complicated by extensive remodeling, Mug House (fig. 1-68) provides an excellent case for illustrating how the Mesa Verde cliff dwellers lived. The hundred or so inhabitants of Mug House belonged to about twenty households, each occupying a cluster of rooms (apartment or suite) (fig. 1-69). A central living room with hearth and small ventilator was surrounded by smaller rooms for storage and sleeping, and by an outdoor courtyard space where general household work including cooking usually took place.

Several households shared outdoor space in one courtyard, usually atop the roof of one subterranean kiva. Such households seem to have been related through common descent to form a sort of lineage or clan group. Traces of Puebloan duality may also be

1-69. Well-preserved living and storage rooms one and two stories high on the upper ledge of Mug House allowed the plotting of interconnections that defined suites of rooms occupied by separate households. Each suite contains one larger living room, several smaller storerooms, plus outdoor work space.

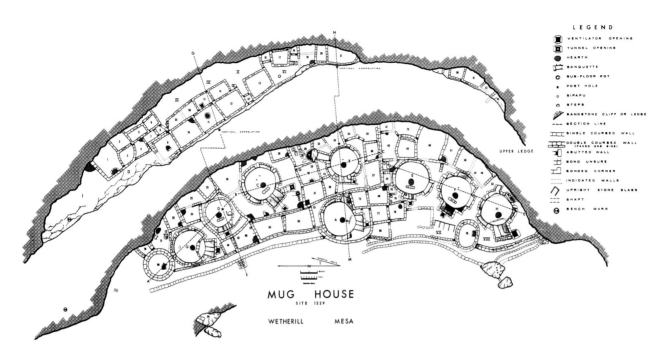

LEGEND

VENTILATOR OPENING
TUNNEL OPENING
HEARTH
BANQUETTE
SUB-FLOOR POT
POST HOLE
SIPAPU
STEPS
SANDSTONE CLIFF OR LEDGE
SECTION LINE
SINGLE COURSED WALL
DOUBLE COURSED WALL (FACED ONE SIDE)
ABUTTED WALL
BOND UNSURE
BONDED CORNER
INDICATED WALLS
UPRIGHT STONE SLABS
SHAFT
BENCH MARK

UPPER LEDGE

MUG HOUSE
SITE 1229

WETHERILL   MESA

1-70. Site plan of Mug House. The upper ledge has been set back from directly above the lower rooms to clarify the horizontal relationship.

seen in the separation of the northern two-thirds of the site from the southern third by a row of six rooms that obstructed access between the two sectors, by a round tower at each end of the site, and by marked differences in kiva construction between the two parts (fig. 1-70).

The inhabitants of Mug House cultivated corn, beans, and squash on the mesa top reached by two trails, one from the north side of the pueblo, the other from the south side. Stone-walled terraces in nearby ravines and on the steep slope below the village augmented the mesa-top farmland. Stone axe heads mounted on short wooden handles helped to clear trees and brush from land for farming, while sharpened hardwood sticks served to loosen the soil for planting (hence the use of hills rather than rows) and to remove weeds.

The inhabitants ground most of their corn into a meal or flour on sandstone manos and metates, usually set in stone-lined bins. They then cooked the

meal in rough-surfaced (corrugated) jars to form a gruel or stew flavored with meats, berries, or wild plant parts such as yucca and cactus fruits. Piñon nuts, greens, and seeds were also gathered. Meat could be obtained by butchering domestic turkeys or by hunting deer, rabbits, rock squirrels, and wood rats. They kept turkeys penned in a large room in the south part of the site or allowed them to roam about while tethered to stone weights. Curiously, these people ate no fish, reptiles, or wild game birds. They did impound runoff rainwater from the mesa top in a small reservoir about fifty yards south of the village and transported it to the households in large painted water jars, filled with the aid of painted ladles.

When someone died, the family buried the body in a shallow, oval grave in the small cave to the north of Mug House or along the steep talus slope below the cliff face. They dressed the corpse in ordinary clothing, wrapped it in a turkey-feather robe or woven mat, and gave offerings to assist in an afterlife. Often a decorated food bowl and drinking mug contained sustenance, while a small corrugated jar might hold useful possessions such as a charmstone, paint pigment, or stone arrowheads. One man took two stone axes and a bone tool kit for weaving into his afterlife.

The people wore only simple clothing consisting of a breechcloth or apron and sandals, but they added woven feather robes and leggings or socks during cold weather. They sat and slept on matting placed directly on the floors. Personal possessions included tools for working sandstone into building blocks and grinding implements, tools for cutting firewood and roofing timbers, and tools for working both wood and fibers into many items such as cradles, bows, weaving sticks, cordage, and textiles. They used other implements made from the bones of turkeys, deer, and other animals to weave baskets and cloth and to serve as general household utensils.

Jewelry consisted of pendants, beads, and buttons fashioned from attractive stone materials, from bone, and even from rare pieces of shell acquired through trade all the way from the Pacific coast. The people of Mug House were frugal. They saved shorter lengths of twine, knotting them together into longer lengths; they repaired pottery vessels, baskets, sandals, and textiles; and they reused broken tools for new functions.

These people were always subject to the caprices of nature. Inadequate rainfall not only threatened their crops, but often caused their nearby reservoir to dry up, necessitating the carrying of water from springs located a mile and a half away. Consequently, religious practices seemed to focus on aspects of nature. Well-preserved murals in one kiva suggest a symbolic horizon line of mountains and other features. Several kivas seem to have been dedicated to animals such as the turkey and cottontail rabbit. A mass of corn tassels suggests the collection of pollen to use in rituals.

1-71. A group of painted mugs found tied together with string through their handles reportedly inspired the name Mug House.

Much religious activity took place in the kivas, out of sight of the rest of the community. At this time in Puebloan history, kiva ritual probably most strongly related to the clan or lineage group living around the courtyard formed in part by the kiva roof. Perhaps some portions of ceremonies were held in the open courtyards, but most likely the residents of Mug House attended (perhaps also participated in) larger rituals with both public and secret events held at Long House with its rectangular great kiva. Long House lies only one mile to the south and most probably functioned as the ritual nucleus for all the cliff dwellers of Wetherill Mesa and neighboring Long and Wildhorse mesas.

Many other activities also took place in the kivas. After all, these buildings were the best-made and most comfortable enclosed spaces in the entire village. Here, the men fashioned their ceremonial costumes, headdresses, prayer plumes, and other sacred objects. Here, too, we find evidence for the weaving of textiles, the knapping of stone tools, and other craft activities generally associated with males. Around the fire in the central hearth, young men and boys undoubtedly learned from their elders all the history and lore of these people. If we can assume that these Pueblo III people had customs similar to those of the modern Pueblo people, the sons of the family likely received instruction in the kiva of their mother's kin group, from her brothers, rather than from the boys' fathers, since kiva society most likely followed the organization of kin groups through the female line. Even though men participated more regularly in activities there, the kivas were not closed to women, and we can picture all members of several families clustered around the kiva fire during inclement weather.

The Puebloans abandoned Mug House sometime near 1300. They left behind a large portion of their material belongings, almost as if they had intended to return (fig. 1-71). From this evidence, we have been able to reconstruct how they lived over seven centuries ago.

Government and Society

Since the prehistoric Puebloans left no written records, archaeologists cannot reconstruct their social organization with certainty. However, the historic Pueblo Indians—from Taos, Acoma, Jemez, San Ildefonso, Zia, Zuni, and the Hopi pueblos among others—trace their descent from the prehistoric Puebloans. In addition, many basic customs and practices have changed little, despite the influence of the Spaniards, who arrived in 1540. Puebloan society had been, and continued to be, essentially egalitarian. The Spaniards even expressed surprise and frustration when they could find no identifiable Puebloan leaders or chiefs.

The modern Pueblo people govern themselves largely through their social customs and ritual practices. Residents of each community (pueblo) choose administrators to serve on a temporary basis. Any member of the pueblo who actively seeks power, influence, or wealth becomes ostracized by the remainder of society. Leadership seems to be vested in those who show reluctance to exercise it—those who do not seek to press their views on others and, oftentimes, those on the lowest economic scale. These chosen ones direct rituals and guide other necessary decisions.

Historic Pueblo social organization expresses itself in four levels of complexity: households, lineage/clan groupings, the entire community, and a dual division within the community.

A husband, wife, their children, and occasionally another relative such as an aunt/uncle or grandparent make up the household unit. They share living spaces and basic subsistence activities such as food preparation, and they provide mutual economic and emotional support. Average household size ranges around five, but no household contains less than one adult male and one adult female.

The clan/lineage group comprises several households that are related to one another, generally through the female line. That is, all members of the kinship unit trace their lineage to a common female ancestor. Males marry into other clan/lineage groups while women remain in the clan/lineage home area. Consequently, sons generally receive instruction from a maternal uncle who belongs to the matrilineal kinship group rather than from the father who belongs to another group. These clan/lineage groups participate together in many ritual activities.

The residents of each Pueblo community recognize a special relationship with each other by virtue of common identity with that community. The pueblo owns land and hunting territories, allocating them to clan/lineage groups who, in turn, allocate them to individual households. The pueblo also forms the primary unit for governing them and for conducting religious ceremonies.

Each Pueblo community recognizes a dual division of its members. Among the Hopi and Zuni, this duality expresses itself almost entirely in following the calendar of religious activities. The Winter People bear responsibility for communal religious activities during the winter half of the year, while the Summer People have the same obligations during their tenure. Among the Rio Grande Pueblo communities, this same duality not only covers ceremonial activities, but also regulates marriage patterns and some other social behaviors.

Ritual activities involve teaching and reemphasizing the traditions, customs, and folklore of the pueblo. Each child learns his/her obligations to society and his/her relationship to the kin group, not only through formal rituals, but also through storytelling. During winter evenings, the elders would tell stories in front of the fire around which the kin group would gather, probably in the kin-group kiva. In this way the children would learn about their expected behavior and about actual and legendary happenings from the past.

One such legend relates the origin of the Puebloan peoples. Their ancestors once lived in a spirit world far below the earth's surface. Over time, these ancestors emerged into successively higher levels of existence until they finally emerged into the present world through one or more "holes" in the ground. This point of emergence is called "sipap" or "sipapu," and the small holes in kiva floors symbolize this connection to the spirit world.

The strongest sanction against antisocial behavior took the form of ostracism by other members of the community. The offender would be ignored, not spoken to, and excluded from group activities. Since Pueblo society relies heavily on communal sharing, an outcast suffers a very severe punishment.

When the Spaniards arrived at the close of Pueblo IV, they encountered this basically egalitarian society. Additionally, evidence from Pueblo III

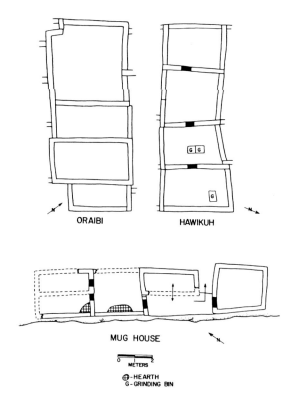

1-72. Plan of a typical suite of living and storage rooms from Mug House compared with similar units from Pueblo IV–V Hawikuh (Zuni) and from historic-modern Oraibi (Hopi). The striking similarities suggest the basic Puebloan social unit of the household has existed for at least seven hundred years with little or no change.

architecture and burials indicates that essentially this same pattern had already existed during that time. No clear evidence for an elite class has yet been found in either housing, personal possessions, or symbolism. Household room clusters may be seen in Pueblo III, Pueblo IV, and historic pueblos (fig. 1-72). The kivas and great kivas indicate that kin groups and communities used them in much the same way as the historic Pueblos. Numerous Pueblo III sites, including Mug House and Pueblo Bonito, reflect an apparent dual division in their layout.

Of course this pattern had evolved from a somewhat less complex society that existed during Basket Maker times. Each pithouse with its attendant storage structures and outdoor ramadas constituted a larger household that probably emerged later as the lineage/clan group. Such pithouse units congregated into relatively small villages of no more than about 150 people. Thus, only two levels of societal structure existed then. During Pueblo I times, the pithouse units seem to have divided into the smaller household units of Pueblo II and III, while the dual division apparently arose as the villages reached much larger sizes during these same two stages.

These same times saw the beginnings of a potential fifth level of sociopolitical organization linking several communities together. In such cases as Chaco Canyon with its outliers; Sun Temple and Fire Temple in the Cliff-Fewkes Canyon Settlement on the Mesa Verde with the other Chapin Mesa settlements; Long House with the Wetherill Mesa settlements; and at Yellow Jacket, Lowry, and the other large towns in the Montezuma Valley, one locality or town functioned as the center for locality-wide activity—a sort of budding ceremonial center concept. It did not survive the Great Migrations, however.

The community organization found during Pueblo III persisted after the migrations to the Rio Grande and the Little Colorado River regions where it has survived into modern times.

Spiritual Concepts and Rituals

Pueblo Indian folklore features a combination of origin and migration legends handed down from generation to generation by the storytellers. Following the emergence of the earliest Puebloan ancestors from the spirit world beneath the earth's present surface, they began searching for the proper sacred place to live. Spirits and kachinas from the spirit world both guided them to their central place and taught them the ways of life. The supernatural kachinas left their masks with the people, who could use them in appropriate dances and rituals to bring rain to nurture their crops and accomplish other good works.

These folktales have doubtlessly been told during the Pueblos' fire-lit ceremonies for centuries.

Representations of migrations appear in Puebloan rock art in many places throughout Pueblo-land, such as in Cow Canyon near Lowry. At Petroglyph Point on the Mesa Verde south of Spruce Tree House, several Hopi have traced a migration story from the figures depicted there (fig. 1-73). The spiral immediately below the large handprint (the storyteller's?) represents the sipapu from whence the ancestral Puebloans emerged from the earth. The two figures to the left mark the Eagle Clan and the Mountain Sheep Clan. Farther to the left may be seen representations of the Parrot Clan. Below the Parrot Clan bird figures and to the left are two figures that may be horned toads or lizards, representing either the Horned Toad Clan or the "lizard spirit." Still farther to the left is an animal figure that may represent an animal spirit or possibly the Mountain Lion Clan. The five humanoid figures to the right and below the mountain sheep may be "whipping kachinas" in the act of influencing and directing the people. Sets of human footprints as well as turkey, bird, and bear tracks probably illustrate this story further.

The Pueblo Indians and their forebears practiced an animistic religion in which animals, plants, and inanimate objects and places in nature possessed souls (anima) that could affect human activities. Humans represent only one of several classes of beings inhabiting the earth and spirit world, none of which had a more important or unique status. Birth and death simply marked changes in the state of being. Hence offerings found with burials—food and water vessels, tools, clothing, and jewelry—show the belief in a spiritual existence after death. Even the position of the body in the grave assisted in this transition. For example, burials at the Pueblo III Village of the Great Kivas near Zuni had been oriented so that their heads pointed toward the horizon

1-73. Puebloan rock art contains many representations of legends recounting ancient migrations. A meandering line usually marks the key element, wandering about among symbols for clans (lineages), for significant geographic features or events, and for supernatural beings. Such symbols may take the form of animals, birds, kachina figures and masks, hand- and footprints, and geometric forms. This legend has been pecked into the face of the Cliffhouse Sandstone at Petroglyph Point about a mile south of Spruce Tree House in Mesa Verde National Park.

1-74. An ogre kachina figure from Puerco Pueblo Ruin in Petrified Forest National Park. To the Pueblos, kachinas carry messages from humans to the supernatural forces that control nature, thereby governing the growth of crops and the availability of wild food resources.

1-75. The Puebloans pecked a kokopelli figure (humpbacked flute player) on the rock face at Sand Island on the San Juan River in southeastern Utah.

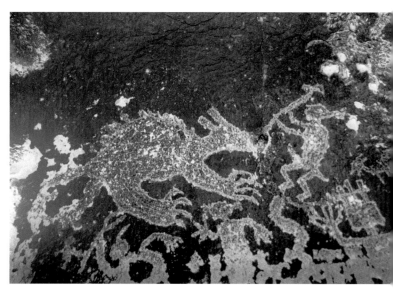

1-76. A Puebloan hunter disguised as a deer shoots a wild fowl, probably a turkey, with a bow and arrow. This rock art appears in a cave kiva in Sandia Canyon near Los Alamos, New Mexico.

1-77. Sandia Canyon (near Bandelier National Monument) cave kiva art pictures a man fighting a bear with a club. The figures have been pecked through heavily smoke-blackened walls and ceiling.

where sunrise would occur either at winter solstice or at summer solstice.

Puebloan rock art apparently contains much information about such beliefs, if only we could understand it. Glimpses reach out when a humanlike figure in the rock art panel (fig. 1-74) can be identified with a kachina in current ritual use. One category of figures that usually represent what has been called the "humpback flute player," or Kokopelli (fig. 1-75), may be found all over the North American Southwest, even far beyond the bounds of Puebloan culture. The meaning of Kokopelli is not understood, partly because the figure has so many different expressions, sometimes quite obviously male and other times unclear. Some have suggested the figure represents traveling merchants, while others have identified him/it with the spiritual "trickster." Tricksters appear in many North American Indian legends as spirits to test human behavior.

Artistic expression may also depict magic and magical practices. The placement of a representation of a corn plant next to a cornfield may have been intended

to induce good crops. Puebloan hunters have regularly invoked the aid of selected predatory animal and bird spirits through charms and rock art depictions to improve their own prowess. One scene found inside a cavate in Sandia Canyon near Bandelier shows a hunter disguised in a deer skin shooting a large bird (turkey?) with a bow and arrow (fig. 1-76). A Pueblo II bowl on display at the Mesa Verde museum shows a humpback hunter with bow and arrow and a kokopelli surrounded by what appear to be ducks. Numerous other bow-wielding figures aiming at deer and other creatures appear on both ceramic and rock art.

Still other depictions probably represent scenes of legendary feats, often performed by a real or legendary culture hero. Perhaps the scene from Sandia Canyon in Bandelier National Monument showing a human with a huge erection fighting off a large bear with a club illustrates such an event (fig. 1-77). Such scenes may have helped the religious practitioners prepare for their ceremonial roles.

Remarkably well-preserved painted murals in the kivas at Kuaua, in Coronado State Park north of

1-78. Beautiful examples of Pueblo IV kiva mural painting cover the walls of kivas at Awatovi and Kawaika-a in Hopiland. This mural from Awatovi depicts two stylized animals facing a central circle that contains an elaborate feather bundle on top of a staff.

Albuquerque, and at the Hopi sites of Awatovi and Kawaika-a, clearly depict Puebloan views of their cosmos. Various kachina figures and spirit forms of birds and animals seem to show the bounty bestowed upon humans by these supernatural beings (fig. 1-78). By reenacting such scenes during ceremonial performances in the pueblo kivas and plazas, the human practitioners could ensure the continuation of such bounty.

Locations of the many shrines found throughout Pueblo-land further attest to their reverence of nature. While some may be found within the pueblo grounds, most occur away from the villages on promontories facing into canyons, near springs, in

rockshelters, or on prominent cliffs. All these locations closely interact with natural phenomena, and what figures have been portrayed represent animals and plants found in nature or spiritual beings with elements of nature as part of them. Some other shrines located on top of the ruins of past house sites may also signify recognition and respect for ancestors who once lived there.

In the modern pueblos, the dual organizations of Summer People and Winter People share responsibilities for conducting religious rituals on behalf of the entire community. While community-wide rituals may have been conducted throughout all of Puebloan history, the duality seems to have first appeared during Pueblo II. Ceremonial practices conducted by the lineage/clan groups (fig. 1-79) probably date back to the earliest Basket Maker times, but they seem to have become less important as ceremonial societies developed during late Pueblo III and the dual ceremonial organization grew in importance.

Celestial Observations

Each of the modern pueblos maintains a system for making solar observations in order to determine solstices and equinoxes and for marking the yearly calendar of ceremonial activities. Movements of the sun

1-79. Depiction of a private ceremony practiced in a small kin-group kiva by the ancient Puebloans. (Drawing by Lisa Ferguson.)

1-80. The pecked rock spirals known as the Sun Dagger are located on a ledge near the top rim of Fajada Butte in Chaco Canyon.

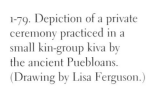

1-81. Diagram showing the position of the sun relative to the Sun Dagger rock spirals. (Courtesy of National Geographic Society.)

from winter to summer and back to winter stand out among people who lack electric lighting.

Puebloan farmers have planted and harvested corn, beans, and squash in the same general way for hundreds of years. These farmers knew when to plant by the length of the days and the warmth of the weather, both of which related to where the sun rose on the horizon. Even though everyone could make these general observations, the ceremonial calendar helped to formalize these essential activities and involve the supernatural world in their success.

Many students of Puebloan culture have made rather exhaustive observations of the sun's reflection through windows, doorways, and portholes in various structures throughout Pueblo-land, hoping to find a deliberate design to mark solstices or equinoxes. They have pored over Pueblo Bonito, Casa Rinconada, Peñasco Blanco, and Wijiji in Chaco Canyon; Hovenweep Castle, Unit-Type House, and Cajon at Hovenweep; and buildings constructed by the Zuni and Hopi. But they could not demonstrate that any of these buildings had actually been built for that primary purpose.

However, the Puebloans did construct observatories demonstrably designed to follow solar movements. The most famous such site has been found on a high ledge near the top of Fajada Butte in Chaco Canyon (fig. 1-80). Here, the noonday sun shines through three parallel slabs of sandstone that lean nearly vertically against the top of a small overhanging ledge to cast daggers of light on the back wall of the overhang. Through the seasons, these daggers move through and around two spiral figures that the Puebloans had pecked there. The precise positions of these daggers mark spring equinox, summer solstice, fall equinox, and winter solstice (fig. 1-81).

Another solar observatory lies near the Holly Ruin at Hovenweep. Two spirals, one set of concentric circles, and several small figures had been pecked into a vertical rock face beneath an overhang on a huge boulder slightly separated from the sandstone cliff (figs. 1-82 and 1-83). At sunrise on the spring equinox, summer solstice, and autumn equinox, a shaft of sunlight cuts across the two spirals and concentric circles in distinctive patterns. The sun does not reach the markers in winter.

The mere placement of upright sticks in the ground to cast shadows would permit the careful observer to also mark the sun's movements through the seasons. By recording the movements of these shadows, the same person could concoct a crude determination of north and south, perhaps accounting for numerous north-south axes on which buildings

1-82. Dr. Arthur H. Rohn examining the solar spirals near Holly Ruin in Hovenweep National Monument. During the summer solstice, a thin horizontal shaft of sunlight splits the spirals and concentric circles just beneath the overhang ceiling.

1-83. Rock art figures at the Holly solar observatory in Hovenweep National Monument where a sliver of sunlight shines through the centers of the two spirals on the left and the concentric circles on the right for several days before and after summer solstice.

had been constructed. Undoubtedly, the people also watched the phases of the moon and possibly bright stars. However, we have no evidence that the Puebloans actually followed the movements of celestial bodies other than the sun.

By comparison, many historic and prehistoric Indians of the Great Plains had observed and recorded not only the movements of the sun and moon but also the visible planets and many bright stars. The Pawnee and their ancestors recognized numerous constellations and bright stars as supernatural beings. They recorded in their artwork, often on skins, the activities of both evening and morning stars (Venus and Jupiter) and the heliacal risings of stars such as Aldebaran, Sirius, and Capella.

Trade and the
Mesoamerican Connection

Many of the basic elements of Puebloan culture originated in Mesoamerica. The three major food crops—maize (corn), squashes, and beans—were first domesticated to the south. Cultivated squashes—three species—have been found in dry caves in the mountains of northeastern Mexico and in the Tehuacán Valley of central Mexico dating to the seventh millennium (7000 to 6000) B.C. Common beans appeared about two thousand years

later in both places, while cultivated maize occurred in levels dating to as early as 4800 B.C. in the Tehuacán Valley. All three plants had begun to find their way into far northwestern Mexico and the southern Southwest by at least 1000 B.C., although beans seem to have been slowest to arrive.

Several other cultural ideas also probably emanated from Mesoamerica including domesticated turkeys, the growing of cotton for textiles, and the idea for manufacturing pottery. Puebloan ancestors then combined these imported ideas and materials with their own preexisting cultural practices to create the unique pattern of Puebloan culture. Subsequent contacts with Mesoamerica appear to have been primarily in the form of a two-way trading relationship, although some scholars see more significant additional transmission of ideas from south to north.

Prehistoric Mesoamerica encompasses most of Mexico except its northernmost tiers of states plus Guatemala, Belize, and the far western portion of Honduras. Within this broad area developed the civilizations of the Olmec, the Maya, Teotihuacán, Oaxaca, Veracruz, and the Toltecs and Aztecs. Following the domestication of many agricultural plants including avocados, chili peppers, tomatoes, amaranth, and the triad of plants that later moved into the Southwest, ancient Mesoamericans settled into year-round villages around 1500 B.C. and began the remarkable cultural growth that culminated in the Mayan and Toltecan/Aztecan civilizations. While some ideas radiated outward from this center of rapid cultural growth, other ideas and peoples moved into the area from both north and south to contribute to this very growth.

During the development of Mesoamerican civilizations, the northern border between Mesoamerica and the Gran Chichimeca to the north—which included the North American Southwest, northeastern Mexico, and the southern Great Plains—shifted considerably. The Toltecs, who themselves had originated in northwestern Mexico, became dominant around 900. From their capitol at Tula, on the northern edge of the central Valley of Mexico, they expanded this northern frontier into the northern state of Durango where they could maintain close trading contacts with the cultural horizons of the southern Southwest and northwestern Mexico.

Some archaeologists see this closer contact with Mesoamerican culture as a time when additional concepts, especially concerning architectural features and possibly some religious ideas, came in. They cite rubble-cored, masonry-veneered walls, terraced "platforms," and stone columns as evidence for a Mesoamerican connection. However, the thickest Puebloan walls contain stones throughout their cores, not just rubble. Furthermore, rubble-filled walls characterize Mayan architecture in the far southeastern portion of Mesoamerica, and they were built quite differently from the cited Puebloan walls.

Both round and square columns appear commonly in Toltec architecture, even as far north as La Quemada in northern Durango. The only "columns" cited in Puebloan architecture consist of a row of square "columns" rising above a low masonry wall at Chetro Ketl with the spaces between them filled in by solid stone masonry. Roofs over some great kivas rested on four square masonry and log columns. Again, these do not really resemble Toltec use of columns. But perhaps the large stone discs upon which the roof supports stood in the great kivas in Chetro Ketl and Pueblo Bonito do come from Toltec inspiration.

The Puebloans have regularly leveled ground on which they planned to build houses, frequently building low terrace retaining walls along the downslope side. Such simple terraces hardly resemble Mesoamerican platforms that rise above the surrounding ground, faced on all sides by stone masonry.

Some other scholars mention circular structures such as round towers, tower kivas, and concentric-wall structures as qualities associated with the Toltec god Quetzalcoatl, the feathered serpent. However, these features do not occur in Mesoamerica. Mention of the T-shaped doorway as a possible Mesoamerican feature faces the same dearth of occurrences there. Finally, if some individual characteristics did travel northward out of Mesoamerica into Pueblo-land, why did not other traits also diffuse? We must evaluate equally those qualities we feel might have diffused and those that obviously did not.

The Puebloans definitely did carry on trading relationships with their immediate neighbors. Some of the goods acquired through trade probably originated even farther away. During late Pueblo III and Pueblo IV, the Rio Grande Pueblos obtained fine lithic materials such as Alibates silicified dolomite from the Texas panhandle, from which to chip arrow points, drills, and knife blades. They also acquired typical Plains beveled knives and sandstone arrow shaft abraders, neither of which have been found elsewhere in Pueblo-land. The presence of bison and pronghorn bones in the rubbish heaps of Pecos Pueblo together with hide-defleshing tools made from bison bones strongly suggests the Pueblos also received both bison and antelope meat and skins from their neighbors on the Great Plains.

Toward the west and south, many marine shell materials found their way into Puebloan possession. Shells of *Glycymeris*, *Olivella*, and *Oliva* found favor as items of jewelry. The beads and bracelets (fig. 1-84) appear to have been made before they were traded to the Puebloans, for we find no debris from shell working in Puebloan sites. The center for marine shell jewelry manufacture fell within the Sonoran Desert reaches of the southern Southwest and northwestern Mexico among the Hohokam, Trincheras, and Casas Grandes cultures.

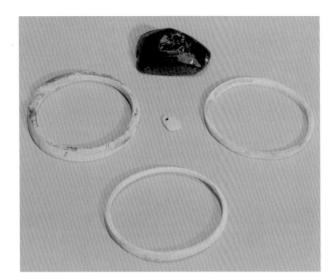

1-84. Three *Glycymeris* shell bracelets from the Pueblo I McPhee Pueblo in the Dolores River valley. *Glycymeris* shellfish live in the Pacific Ocean and the Sea of Cortés, so the occurrence of these bracelets at McPhee reflects ancient trade.

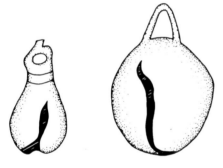

1-85. Cast copper bells, the only metal objects known to the Puebloans, had to be acquired through trade from western Mexico.

1-86. Scarlet macaws from tropical Mesoamerica were prized trade items to the Chacoan people. According to Lyndon L. Hargrave's exhaustive study of these birds, they must have been imported alive, but not bred, by the Puebloans.

Through these same groups, copper bells and macaw feathers and body parts also reached Puebloan villages. The copper bells (fig. 1-85) had been made by the lost wax method in West Mexico, while the macaws were native to the Mexican coast as far north as northern Sinaloa. Evidence from Paquimé (Casas Grandes) in northwestern Chihuahua indicates that macaws, both the military macaw and the scarlet macaw (fig. 1-86), had been bred there in pens. In return, turquoise, salt, and copper ore traveled southward into Mesoamerica. Thus, the Puebloans most likely never experienced direct contact with Mesoamerican peoples. They received ideas and trade goods through the many filters of their immediate neighbors to the south.

Violence, Warfare, and Weapons

The historically known Pueblo peoples have been characterized as being more peaceful than most of their neighbors, such as the Ute, Navajo/Apache, and Comanche, as well as less warlike than the peoples of the Great Plains, the lower Great Lakes, and certainly Mesoamerica. Despite this image, the archaeological and historical records indicate that considerable violence occurred among the Puebloan peoples. However, none of this violence fits a pattern of regular warfare.

As early as Basket Maker times, some evidence points to violent behavior. In 1915 Alfred Kidder and Samuel Guernsey discovered within a Basket Maker slab-lined storage cist in a Marsh Pass cave in northeastern Arizona, beneath the shoulders of a mummy, the full scalp and facial skin of a human being that had been sewn back together to resemble a human head. A suspension cord from the top of the scalp, postmortem hair styling, and painted zones on the skin suggest this specimen served as a trophy, perhaps taken from the body of some deceased enemy, either tribal or personal. Rock art figures of Basket Maker vintage, pecked into a sandstone cliff face along the San Juan River near Bluff in southeastern Utah, depict isolated "heads" without bodies hanging from suspension cords (see fig. 2-128). These quite closely resemble the trophy scalp found by Kidder and Guernsey. While this represents rather sparse evidence, we may suspect the early Basket Makers collected trophies in the form of scalps, and possibly heads, from some enemies.

Other traces of violence may be found throughout Puebloan history. Excavators encountered the sprawled body of a woman with a broken neck on the

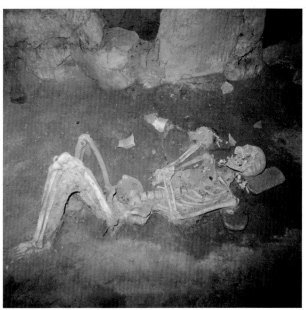

1-87 and 1-88. Evidence of violence may be suggested by the sprawled positions of these human skeletons that represent bodies thrown into a burning pithouse at the Pueblo I Duckfoot Site in the Montezuma Valley.

floor of a Modified Basket Maker pithouse in Yellow Jacket; Crow Canyon archaeologists recorded sprawled and burned skeletons on the floor of a burned pithouse at the Pueblo I Duckfoot Site west of Cortez (figs. 1-87 and 1-88); Joe Ben Wheat found what he suspected might be evidence for cannibalism (bases of skulls bashed in) among jumbled and broken human remains in a Pueblo II context at Yellow Jacket; broken and fragmented human bones were found at the Cowboy Wash Site south of Ute Mountain and at Castle Rock and Sand Canyon pueblos in McElmo Canyon; and Tim White documented other remains from the Mancos Canyon on the south edge of Mesa Verde that he felt also reflected cannibalistic behavior. Finally, Christie Turner has assembled all these potential cases for cannibalism in his synthetic volume *Mancorn*, together with a complete list of characteristics he believes indicate cannibalistic behavior.

Historically, the most dramatic violent event involved the destruction of Awatovi Pueblo and the massacre of its residents by Hopi villagers from neighboring First Mesa during the winter of 1700–1701. The Hopi had united with all the other Puebloan peoples in a revolt in 1680 that threw out all the Spanish priests and soldiers. However, when the Spaniards returned a decade later in greater military strength, the eastern Pueblos and Awatovi received the missionaries back into their villages, allowing them to build new churches, while the rest of the Hopi successfully resisted reconquest. This led to a social and spiritual "sickness" that gained control over Awatovi until the Awatovi leaders themselves requested the destruction of their own pueblo.

In reality, the Awatovi destruction probably best falls into the category of the destruction of witches, who also represent social and spiritual sickness, among the Pueblos. When witches are identified, the remaining population feels it must destroy the witching influ-

ence by killing the witch and the witch's entire family. Furthermore, the bodies must be chopped up, burned, and reduced to broken fragments so the witch power cannot revive. Such a description would also fit the various remains that Turner and his supporters describe as evidence for cannibalism.

Warfare involves conflict between two or more sociopolitical groups, usually to gain land, resources, and/or power. Most warfare among North American Indian groups took the form of raids on enemy traveling groups or villages, where the raiding party swooped in, did what damage they could, and then rapidly retreated. Such practices characterized the traditional enmities among Plains groups and between the Iroquois Confederacy and their Huron enemies.

Without doubt, the Puebloans became targets of raids by surrounding Apachean and Ute peoples who counted such raiding as a means to obtain food and other resources. This probably accounts for the relatively defensive locations for many Puebloan villages, beneath cliff overhangs, on the edges of mesas, and surrounding natural water sources. Such positioning, however, reflects a passive response to the threat of warfare. Taking an active posture by sending out raiding parties or raising combat forces who carry military weapons seems not to have been practiced by the Puebloans.

In many cultures, warriors have been celebrated in art, literature, and folklore. But Puebloan rock art and ceramic decorations totally lack any depictions of warriors or battle scenes. Even the so-called war chiefs of the historic Pueblos help to organize cooperation among their fellows, sometimes for defense, but most often for the accomplishment of communal tasks. Only once during the Pueblo Revolt of 1680 did the Puebloan peoples act in concert to expel the oppressive Spaniards.

They neither made nor used any specific weapons. Coronado during his conquest of the

Pueblos reported that the Zuni of western New Mexico fought with hammers, bows and arrows, and shields. The hammers appear to have been stone mauls or axe heads hafted in short wooden handles, designed for wood working. Bows and arrows were used to hunt deer and other wild animals for food. The shields probably served more of a ritual function than a defensive one. An oval-shaped coiled basketry shield, thirty-six by thirty-one inches across, with a hardwood handle and coated with pitch was found at Aztec Ruin. Spanish explorers reported that Southwestern Indians (presumably including the Pueblos) employed round shields of buffalo or elk hide between twelve and twenty-six inches in diameter. Such shields may have been the only kind of specialized weapon, and that for defensive purposes.

The little evidence we have concerning Puebloan warfare indicates they were not as aggressively warlike as their neighbors. They did defend themselves and their villages, which they would often position in somewhat defensible settings. They did express violent behavior, especially against witches and witchcraft. Any sign of pitched battles such as those fought among the Yuman-speaking peoples of the lower Colorado River and Gila River valleys or among the budding states of Mesoamerica is completely absent.

The Great Migrations

By 1300 the Puebloans had totally abandoned the Kayenta, Northern San Juan, and Chaco regions. This abandonment did not occur all at once, but rather it extended over at least a century and a half. People began moving out of the Chaco Region during the middle 1000s. Populations in the Northern San Juan and Kayenta began consolidating their towns and villages in more defensible locations, as some of them appear to have begun moving away. The appearance of strong "Mesa Verde" influences in architecture and

ceramics in the Chaco Canyon during the mid-1000s and after suggests that some Northern San Juan people had already moved that far.

Meanwhile, other Puebloan peoples continued to occupy the cliff and canyon head sites in both Kayenta and the Northern San Juan almost up to 1300. But by 1300, even these people had all moved away. Unlike virtually all other human migrations in the world where only a portion of the total population actually moved away, no one stayed behind—they ALL left! That bespeaks a cause for migration quite different from most other human migrations.

The migration stories told by Pueblo elders to their children talk of lineage groups traveling together to find new places to live. In the new locations, they might link up with other members of the same clan, or they might establish a new clan. The stories relate the order in which some clan (lineage) groups arrived at a new location.

Why did they move away from their longtime heartland in the San Juan River drainage of the Four Corners? Certainly, the defensive nature of the last occupied settlements hints at possible threats from outsiders moving into the area. However, any outsiders would have been ancestors of the modern-day Ute and Navajo peoples, whose numbers must have been far fewer than those of the settled town dwellers. To be sure, these outsiders would have been more aggressively warlike than the Puebloans, but their attacks would most likely have been no more than short raids by relatively small numbers of attackers who would seize resources and escape. Such raids would have had considerable nuisance value, but it becomes difficult to see them as an explanation for the total abandonment of the Four Corners.

Numerous scholars have invoked environmental causes to explain this drastic population movement. Some mention the "great drought" of the very late 1200s; others suggest the growing season had become

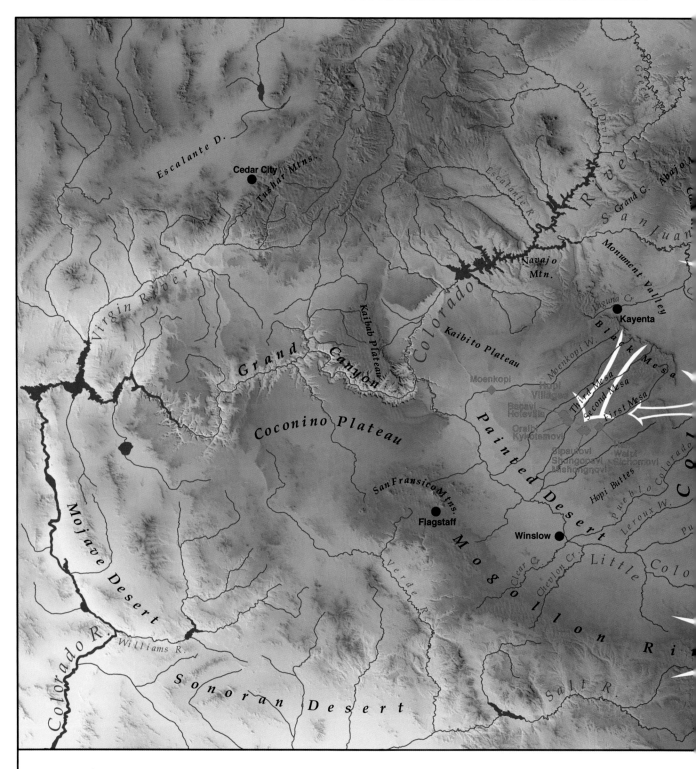

Key

● Modern City

◆ Modern Pueblo

1-89. The Great Migrations of the late 1100s and 1200s emptied the entire drainage of the San Juan River including the Montezuma Valley, Mesa Verde, Kayenta, and the Chaco Basin. Subsequent population centers concentrated in the valleys of the Rio Grande and the Little Colorado River's Cibola and Tusayán subregions.

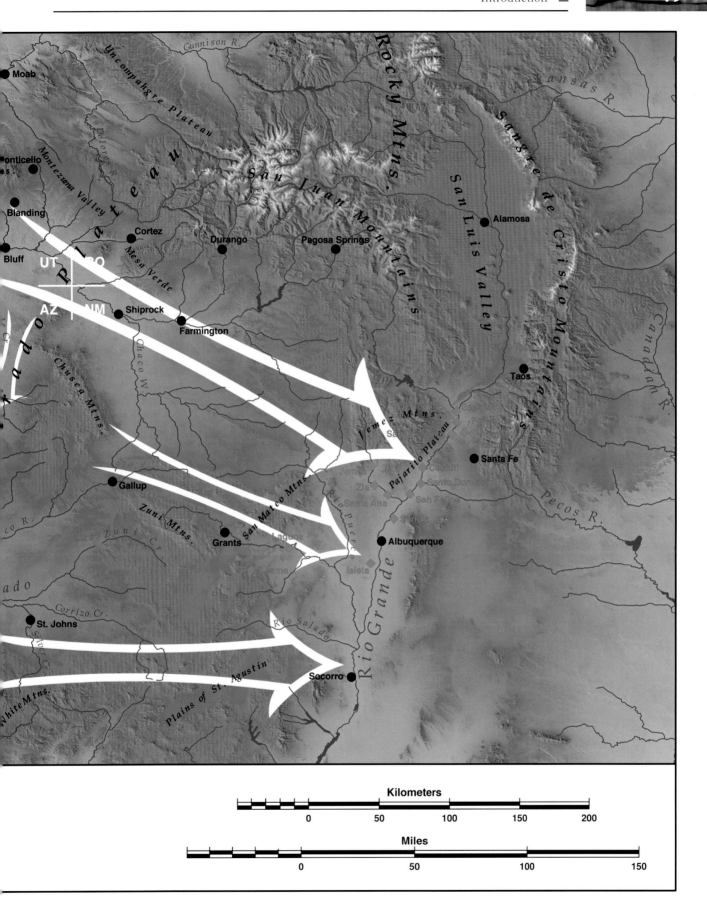

too short to allow dependable crop production; still others cite the possibility that the dense populations had started to exhaust available resources, such as fertile land, wood for construction and fuel, wild food sources, and the like. However, on the Colorado Plateau, all such environmental factors vary with changes in elevation. Hence, we might expect the people to have responded to shortening growing seasons by moving down in elevation, while additional wild resources and moisture could be found at higher elevations. They had already developed water management practices to gain some control over needed water supplies. And, even if some had left because of environmental constraints, why did every last one of them leave?

There have even been attempts to blame the exodus on increasing incidents of disease or on internal competition for resources, citing the violence noted earlier. But once again we must ask why everyone, including the victors, left.

Historic Pueblo Indian folklore tells of long periods of wandering after emergence from the spirit world until the people had located their proscribed "central place" where they were to settle in permanent villages. Each pueblo recognizes its present location as the central place for that pueblo, reached after long wanderings guided by supernatural powers. One potential explanation for the total migration out of the Four Corners could take the form of recognition by the Puebloans there that the San Juan River drainage was not the proper central place as indicated by numerous unpleasant omens, whether of an environmental nature, or one of sickness in the society (remember Awatovi). Such an interpretation would fit into the patterns of Pueblo folklore about their past.

Evidence for major migration is quite obvious. But, where did they go? As the San Juan River drainage of the Four Corners steadily emptied of its once sizeable population, other regions in the Southwest grew significantly in population. The most obvious of these may be seen in both regions of the Rio Grande Valley. A few colonists had begun to arrive during late Pueblo II, more during the late 1100s, and an explosion in numbers of people took place at about the beginning of Pueblo IV in the 1300s. It has also been possible to trace some ceramic styles from Four Corners districts to the Rio Grande, and yet other signs of movement into the Little Colorado River regions. Hence archaeologists feel quite comfortable interpreting major population movements out of the Four Corners regions and into both the Rio Grande and Little Colorado River zones (fig. 1-89).

Once in their new locations, the various Puebloan lineage groups began to reconstitute the settled community lifestyle. The different clan groups sorted themselves into appropriate societies to assume roles in managing the ceremonial calendar. Thus, early in Pueblo IV, large town-size communities reappeared. It was these large settlements that the Spaniards encountered in 1539 and 1540. The Spaniards conquered these Puebloan peoples and founded first a Spanish colony, later to become a possession of Mexico, and ultimately of the United States. During their more than three centuries of domination, the Spaniards attempted to enforce some changes upon the Pueblos—appointed leadership, Christian religion, a more patrilineal form of descent that resulted in bilateralism among the Rio Grande Pueblos, and new crops and technology. Despite this huge influx of new materials, ideas, and governance, the Pueblos have retained many important elements of their traditional lifeways and beliefs to make them the undoubted descendants of the prehistoric people who built the remarkable buildings and settlements described in the following chapters.

CHAPTER TWO

Northern San Juan Region

The Northern San Juan comprises that part of Pueblo-land lying north of the San Juan River and drained by streams flowing into it from the north. The region stretches from the upper San Juan River valley around Pagosa Springs, Colorado; through the lower drainages of the Piedra, Pine, Florida, Animas, La Plata, and Mancos rivers of southwestern Colorado and northwestern New Mexico; and across the Mesa Verde and the Montezuma Valley to the Abajo Mountains and Comb Ridge in southeastern Utah. Its frontiers shifted through time, sometimes to include the Cedar Mesa and Grand Gulch to the west and the Dolores River valley to the north. Following Pueblo I, the Puebloans abandoned the entire eastern portion—essentially east of the La Plata River—except around Chimney Rock.

Introduction to the Mesa Verde

Between Mancos and Cortez, the northern escarpment of the Mesa Verde rises up to fifteen hundred feet above the valley floor with vertical sandstone cliffs capping steep talus slopes. At Point Lookout, the entrance road winds precariously upward to the southward-sloping, flattish mesa top that has been deeply cut by a series of north-south canyons that make east-west travel least difficult along the northern rim. The western and eastern sides of this sloping mesa, or more accurately cuesta, steadily decrease in height as the canyons approach the Mancos River, which forms the southern limit. The national park occupies the northeastern portion of this landform, while the remainder falls within the Ute Mountain Ute Indian Reservation.

Dense piñon and juniper woodland covers most of the mesa with thick brush along many parts of the north rim and isolated stands of Douglas fir on north-facing slopes in some canyons, although recent fires have caused considerable damage to the vegetation. The park can be visited year-round although

Wetherill Mesa stays open only during the summer. Chapin Mesa with stabilized ruins at Far View, near the museum, and along the Ruins Road including Sun Temple, Cliff Palace, and Balcony House can be visited year-round.

Within the park boundaries, some forty-six hundred sites have been identified, including over six hundred cliff dwellings. Additional sites occur in the Ute Mountain Tribal Park to the south and west. At its peak during late Pueblo III, the population of the Mesa Verde probably reached up to twenty-five hundred to three thousand, while two separate researchers have produced estimates of ten times as many Puebloans living in towns and villages in the Montezuma Valley to the northwest of Mesa Verde.

The Puebloan people occupied the mesas and cliffs of the Mesa Verde (fig. 2-1) for over seven hundred years from the late 500s to about 1300, when they abandoned the entire Northern San Juan and migrated mostly southeastward to the Rio Grande Valley. This occupation encompassed the time of rapid cultural development during Modified Basket Maker (about 550 to 750), Pueblo I (750 to 900), Pueblo II (900 to 1100), and Pueblo III (1100 to 1300). They built and inhabited the spectacular cliff dwellings only during the terminal phase of the occupation between 1200 and 1300.

B. K. Wetherill and his sons Richard, Alfred, John, Clayton, and Win settled on a ranch in the Mancos River valley during the 1880s. They befriended the neighboring Ute Indians, who allowed them to pasture cattle in the Mancos River canyon. In December of 1888, Richard and his brother-in-law, Charlie Mason, rode up out of the canyon onto the mesa top in search of strays and stumbled across an overlook where they saw in a great cave opposite them the ruin they soon dubbed "Cliff Palace." Al had actually caught a brief glimpse of the same ruin a year earlier while on foot, but he

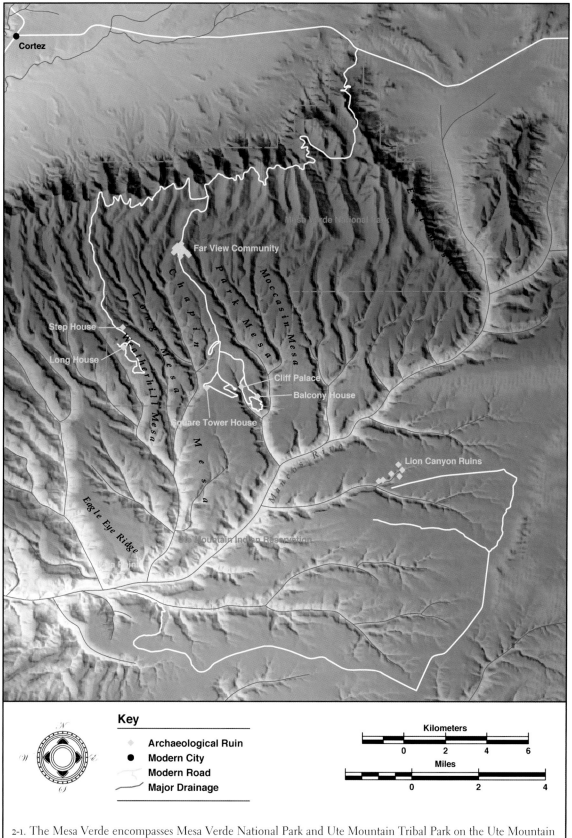

Key

◆ Archaeological Ruin
● Modern City
⌐ Modern Road
〰 Major Drainage

Kilometers

0   2   4   6

Miles

0   2   4

2-1. The Mesa Verde encompasses Mesa Verde National Park and Ute Mountain Tribal Park on the Ute Mountain Ute Indian Reservation. Ruins may be visited on Chapin and Wetherill mesas and in Mancos and Lion canyons.

did not have time to examine it more closely. Richard and Charlie then explored further, encountering Spruce Tree House on that same day. During the following years, the Wetherill brothers explored some 180 buildings, removing and selling artifacts that now rest in private collections and museums throughout the world. In 1891 with the help of the Wetherills, Gustaf Nordenskiöld from Sweden excavated several ruins both in the cliffs and on the mesa top of Wetherill and Chapin mesas. His collection has ended up in the National Museum in Helsinki, Finland, but he published the first scientific study of "The Cliff Dwellers of the Mesa Verde" in 1893.

Mesa Verde became a national park in 1906, and Jesse Walter Fewkes began systematic investigations two years later. His work continued into the 1920s when park superintendent Jesse L. Nusbaum continued the work. In the 1930s, Earl H. Morris made repairs and stabilized Cliff Palace, Spruce Tree House, Balcony House, and Far View Ruin. From 1958 through much of the 1960s, the Wetherill Mesa Archeological Project excavated and stabilized Long House, Mug House, Step House, and several mesatop ruins all on Wetherill Mesa. The National Park Service continues to maintain the ruins to preserve them and to allow public visitation.

Ruins Road

Mesa Verde's Ruins Road displays a series of excavated and stabilized Basket Maker III and early Pueblo pithouses, kivas, and dwellings that enable visitors to see the evolution of Puebloan architecture from 600 to 1200. Nowhere else in Pueblo-land can such a sequence be observed.

Site 117 (**Earth Lodge B**) on Ruins Road represents a typical Modified Basket Maker pithouse (fig. 2-2). Tree-ring dates indicate its construction in 595. The pithouse consists of a large room, twenty feet across, with a centrally located clay-lined fire pit.

Entry was gained through an antechamber to the south, which also provided ventilation and storage space. Stone slabs installed in the passageway between the two rooms and in front of the fire pit deflected air drafts blowing in through the antechamber entrance. Other features include low wing walls setting off the general living area from a southern corn-grinding area, storage cists in the walls and floor, and a sacred sipapu.

Four upright posts supported a squarish solid roof formed by cross members covered with brush and earth, leaving a smoke hole in the center directly above the fire pit. Additional poles set on the ground surface leaning against the square roof formed side walls that were also covered with brush and earth. The builders dug the floor level twelve to fourteen inches below the ground surface. From the outside, the finished product appeared as a flat-topped earthen mound.

Such pithouses usually clustered into small villages of four to eight or nine. Another seven pithouses lay around Earth Lodge B. Each probably housed a small extended family of six to ten including a father, mother, children, and possibly some grandparents, aunts and/or uncles, or even the spouse of a married child. The Puebloans of all stages also lived and worked outside their dwellings, for we have found fire pits, storage cists, and work spaces, some shaded by ramadas, between and around the pithouses. They also utilized the flat roofs of the houses from Basket Maker times on.

Step House Cave on Wetherill Mesa contains the remains of six pithouses, four of which have been excavated with one's superstructure partially restored. The other two lie beneath the late Pueblo III cliff dwelling. At this time, around 600, most Mesa Verde Puebloans lived on the mesa tops, but a few chose the natural rock shelters in the cliffs to build their houses. The Modified Basket Makers of Step House Cave

2-2. Earth Lodge B, constructed around A.D. 600, plus seven other similar partially subterranean dwellings with earth-covered timber and brush walls and roofs made up a Basket Maker III village. This typical pithouse had an antechamber attached by a stepped passageway to its south side, a circular fire pit, four holes where roof support posts once stood, and a storage cist built into the side wall.

2-3. The larger Deep Pithouse at Twin Trees Site 101 (lower right) on Mesa Verde. Tree-ring dates place its construction just before A.D. 700.

2-4. The smaller Deep Pithouse at Twin Trees Site 101 was built just after A.D. 700 inside the burned ruins of the earlier and larger one's antechamber.

employed some variations on construction by digging their floors slightly deeper, resting their side wall poles on distinguishable banquettes just below ground surface, using a ventilator tunnel in place of the antechamber, and entering exclusively down a ladder through the roof's smoke hole (see figs. 2-64 and 2-65).

A hundred years later, around 700, at **Twin Trees Village** on Ruins Road, the Modified Basket Makers constructed two pithouses, one inside the ruins of the other, at Site 101. The earlier pithouse nearly replicated the features of Earth Lodge B, although its floor had been excavated somewhat deeper and a banquette encircled the main chamber (fig. 2-3). The later **Deep Pithouse** utilized the inside of the charred antechamber of the earlier one. Like the pithouses in Step House Cave, the later Deep Pithouse had no antechamber. Its occupants had to enter through the roof. This roof hatch/smoke hole could be totally or partially closed with a stone slab to retain

warmth inside or to keep out rain. The floor stood about twenty-four inches below ground level, and a banquette on which side wall posts rested surrounded the room (fig. 2-4). Otherwise the functional plan of the house closely resembled that of Earth Lodge B. The most significant change that occurred during that hundred years of construction evolution appeared with the tunnel ventilator. This concept for bringing fresh air into the chamber evolved into the

2-5. A deep Pueblo I pithouse at Twin Trees Site 103 showing a squarish shape, ventilator tunnel, wing walls, central hearth, five postholes marking the position of a pole and mud deflector, and four postholes for the roof supporting posts.

ventilator system employed in almost all later Puebloan kivas.

A further development in Mesa Verde pithouse architecture can be seen at nearby Twin Trees Village. Site 103, constructed during Pueblo I, has two excavated, very deep squarish pithouses constructed during the 830s (831 for one and 833–834 for the other). One has been backfilled for preservation. The fire pit, ventilator tunnel, stone slab deflectors, wing walls, sipapu, and roof hatch remained basically unchanged from the earlier Basket Maker III pithouses. But the overall depth of six to seven feet below ground level made these pithouses essentially subterranean so that their roofs stood at the ground surface (fig. 2-5). Thus, the basic elements of kivas had developed.

2-6. Segment of four Pueblo I living rooms at Twin Trees Site 103 built during the 830s. The room floors had been sunk slightly below ground level; wooden posts covered by mud formed walls and roofs; upright sandstone slabs lined the bases of many walls; and several rooms contained hearths. Many adjacent rooms have not been excavated.

2-7. Two rooms constructed of crude stone masonry and a circular kiva mark early Pueblo II Site 102 at Twin Trees on Mesa Verde. This small pueblo, built in the mid-900s on top of the ruins of Pueblo I Site 103, illustrates the beginnings of stone masonry pueblo architecture.

2-8. The circular kiva at Twin Trees Site 102 shows an early stage in the evolution of kivas from earlier pithouses. Construction features that carried over from pithouse antecedents included use of native earth side walls, a circular hearth, sipapu, and ventilator tunnel. The round shape and the four low, stone masonry pilasters resting on the earthen banquette that replaced the former four upright, wooded posts in supporting the roof represent new features. Most likely, a movable sandstone slab served as a deflector.

As part of Pueblo I architectural change, the Puebloans expanded the old above-ground ramadas and storage units into both storage and living quarters. At first they employed jacal construction above upright stone slabs, but later they began to add stone masonry. These units formed a single-story line to the north of the pithouses. During this Pueblo I stage, the Puebloans lived in both the subterranean pithouses and the above-ground living rooms. These surface living rooms were rectangular, often containing hearths and with upright sandstone slabs lining the lower walls (fig. 2-6). Jacal construction formed the vertical side walls and the flat roofs. A row of smaller storerooms backed the row of living rooms, and covered porticos often fronted them.

Thus Twin Trees Village represents three separate occupations. The Deep Pithouses (Site 101) represent late Basket Maker III around 700; the slab-lined rooms and squarish pithouse (Site 103) reflect part of a larger arrangement of Pueblo I during the 830s; and the third, a two-room crude masonry above-ground living unit fronted on the south by a circular kiva (Site 102), belongs to early Pueblo II during the early 900s. The masonry in the rooms consists of little more than random stones stuck into heavy mud mortar (fig. 2-7). The kiva is round with an encircling banquette on which four short masonry pilasters stand to support the roof, a sipapu, a fire pit, a ventilator tunnel, and probably a movable stone slab deflector (fig. 2-8). Its walls retained the natural earth sides of the excavation that had simply been plastered over. Ceramics and architectural style date this kiva to about 950.

Next along the road, **Site 16** also shows the remains of three separate superimposed structures: an early Pueblo II unit pueblo with six rooms and a kiva, a late Pueblo II four-room unit pueblo with its kiva, and a Pueblo III ceremonial platform with three towers and a kiva (fig. 2-9). Remains of yet earlier houses had been noted by the excavators, but they did not stabilize them as part of the exhibit. A most interesting feature may be observed in the stratified

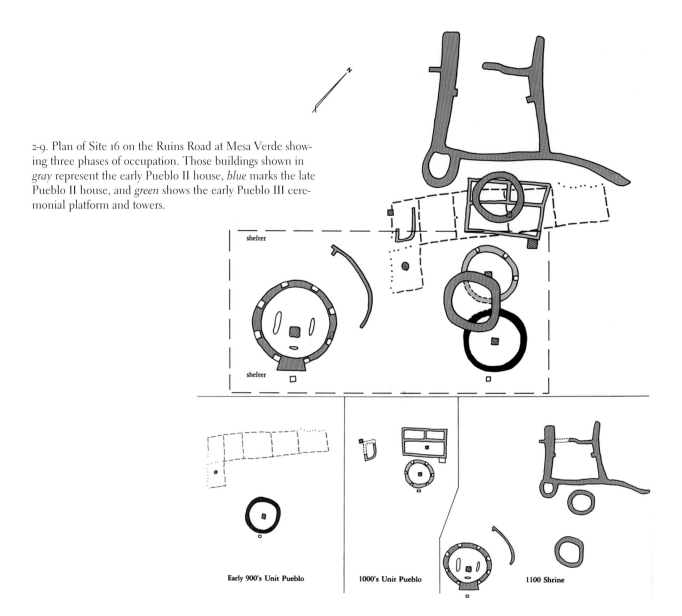

2-9. Plan of Site 16 on the Ruins Road at Mesa Verde show-ing three phases of occupation. Those buildings shown in *gray* represent the early Pueblo II house, *blue* marks the late Pueblo II house, and *green* shows the early Pueblo III cere-monial platform and towers.

shelter

shelter

Early 900's Unit Pueblo   1000's Unit Pueblo   1100 Shrine

fill of the earliest kiva. When the residents of the late Pueblo II house dug the pit for their kiva (the north one), they deposited their back dirt in the older kiva in reverse order (fig. 2-10). Thus, the archaeologists encountered the whitish band of sterile caliche that had come from the bottom of the newer kiva on top of the human rubbish left by Site 16's previous inhabitants.

The latest structures at Site 16 belong to the Pueblo III stage after 1100. They consist of a rectan-gular space outlined by a low masonry wall (fig. 2-11), three round stone masonry towers (fig. 2-12), and the

large kiva beneath the western shelter (fig. 2-13). The low rectangular wall seems to have outlined an earthen platform or stage for religious ceremonies.

Two tree-ring dates of 1074 from the large kiva suggest it had been constructed in that year or slightly later. This masonry-lined kiva had eight stone pilasters to support its roof and a rectangular stone-lined fire pit. Two long rectangular vaults in the floor on either side of the fire pit may have functioned as foot drums or storage space.

2-10. Four wooden posts set into the front edge of an earthen banquette held up the roof of this early Pueblo II kiva at Site 16. The kiva had been filled in by earth layers excavated out of the nearby late Pueblo II kiva, which were redeposited in reverse order. The base of an early Pueblo III round tower overlaps both kivas.

2-11. Site 16 displays stabilized foundations from three phases of Puebloan history. The charred post stubs mark the position of an early Pueblo II (900–1000) wooden post and mud pueblo, the block of rectangular masonry rooms at center represents a late Pueblo II (1000–1100) unit pueblo, while the circular tower and low, thick walls to the right belong to an early Pueblo III (1100–1200) ceremonial platform. In 1984 the National Park Service erected a protective structure over the excavated kivas of all three phases.

2-13. The large kiva at Site 16 associated with the early Pueblo III (1100s) ceremonial platform and towers. Eight masonry pilasters supported the roof, and two elongated floor pits may have been foot drums. Two tree-ring dates argue for construction in A.D. 1074 or later.

2-12. This early Pueblo III tower rests on top of the ruins of the late Pueblo II rooms. The tower belonged to a complex of towers and low platform walls to the north and with the large kiva under the shelter to the west.

2-14. Tower and kiva complex at Sun Point Pueblo, an early Pueblo III (1100s) unit pueblo on Mesa Verde's Ruins Road. A tunnel opening into the kiva leads directly into the circular tower.

This latest group of structures lacked any domestic living quarters or refuse. They more probably represent an early Pueblo III ceremonial unit consisting of the low-walled platform with its radiating walls, three towers, and the larger than usual kiva. It appears to have been built intentionally on top of the ruins of the earlier houses. This site reflects a pattern of the Puebloans to build ceremonial buildings, including shrines, on the remains of ruined former residences. Similar examples may be found at Far View Tower, Site 1 near Twin Trees, and numerous other sites. Such ceremonial structures may have been located over the older residential building ruins to show respect and veneration for their ancestors.

Sun Point Pueblo, the last excavated ruin along Ruins Road, exhibits the remains of a block of roughly twenty surface rooms arranged around a core kiva and tower that had been connected to each other by a tunnel (fig. 2-14). Wall masonry showed the typical Pueblo III pattern of two or more stones in thickness. The kiva reflects a typical Pueblo III masonry-lined subterranean structure with six pilasters. No tree-ring specimens could be found here, but the pottery indicates a brief occupation during the 1100s.

[Overleaf] 2-15. *National Geographic* artist Peter V. Bianchi recreated this scene of the Far View Settlement to approximate its appearance during the 1100s. Inhabitants of the scattered houses, including Far View and Pipe Shrine houses in the upper right, cooperated in constructing a rainwater collection system (seen in upper left), the half-million-gallon reservoir called Mummy Lake (next to canal fork), and an irrigation ditch leading to terraced fields in the lower left. This settlement of about four to five hundred people also shared a common ceremonial center in Far View Tower (upper center). Around 1200 these people moved into the cliff dwellings in Cliff-Fewkes canyons, about five miles farther to the south on Chapin Mesa and one thousand feet lower in elevation. They took their water supply with them by constructing a ditch from Mummy Lake around the Far View buildings and down Chapin Mesa's ridge for some six miles. (Courtesy of National Geographic Society.)

The Puebloan people left this mesa-top site and moved into the cliffs in the canyons to the east. Very little fallen building rubble remains because they apparently dismantled their former houses and took the building stones with them to build new houses. All that now remains for visitors to see are the bottom courses of room walls, the stub of the tower, and the kiva.

Far View Locality

On the northern part of Chapin Mesa, beginning in early Pueblo II times (during the 900s), the Puebloans developed a farming community. A fan of ditches on the hill to the north collected rainfall and channeled it into Mummy Lake (Far View Reservoir), primarily for domestic use. A diversion above Mummy Lake irrigated fields of corn, beans, and squash (fig. 2-15).

Another ditch constructed in late Pueblo III times extended the intake system to carry water several miles south down the mesa. This ditch circled around the Far View Settlement sites and extended southward to the vicinity of the Cliff-Fewkes Canyon group of late Pueblo III cliff dwellings.

The Far View Group consists of a cluster of individual sites within a stone's throw of one another. An early Pueblo II village of thirteen to fourteen unit pueblos accompanied the initial construction of Mummy Lake. Later development, during late Pueblo II times, encompassed about thirty-six unit pueblos, many of which overlay their earlier counterparts. By early Pueblo III, in the 1100s, the number of separate buildings had decreased to around eighteen, but the population had almost doubled because many of the newer buildings contained up to five conjoined modular housing units, each one equivalent to a unit pueblo. A newer masonry style, a changed structural arrangement, and changes in ceramics denote the latest village, many of whose buildings directly overlay or represented remodeled

2-16. Mummy Lake could store up to half a million gallons of water for domestic use by the inhabitants of the Far View Settlement. It was originally built around A.D. 900 and added to at least twice. Water entered the stone-lined reservoir through an intake channel at the southwest corner where a 180-degree turn caused sediment to settle where it could be readily dredged out. A flight of steps in the south wall allowed access for water carriers. The reservoir had no outlet.

2-17. Five excavated ruins toward the upper end of Chapin Mesa at an elevation of about 7,700 feet belong to the Far View Settlement of the 1100s: Site 820 (lower left), Far View House (just right of center), Pipe Shrine House (far right), Far View Tower (just left of center), and Mummy Lake (white patch at far left next to bend in road). Additional unexcavated ruins lie among these and across the road to the west. Mesa Verde's undulating north rim extends across the top of the photograph beyond Soda Canyon. (Photograph taken with the assistance of L. A. Villarreal.)

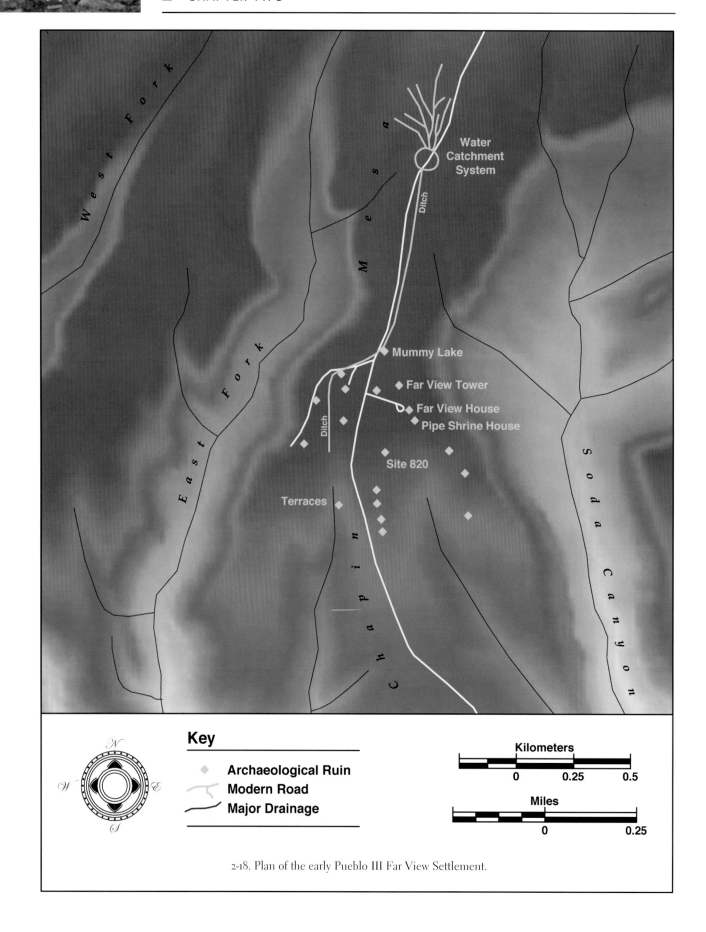

Key

◆ Archaeological Ruin
Y Modern Road
∿ Major Drainage

Kilometers
0   0.25   0.5

Miles
0   0.25

2-18. Plan of the early Pueblo III Far View Settlement.

2-19. Far View House, with about fifty rooms and five kivas, stands on an artificial terrace behind a low retaining wall. Several rooms reached three stories in height, and several walls exhibit core and veneer construction. Rooms surround four kivas, while the fifth lies outside the room block. The large central kiva has eight stone masonry pilasters and oblong floor vaults.

earlier buildings. Far View House, Pipe Shrine House, Site 820 (Coyote Village), Site 875, and Far View Tower represent the remains of the latest construction around Mummy Lake.

Mummy Lake itself could have stored a half million gallons of water within its masonry-lined earthen embankment (fig. 2-16). Its intake at the southwest corner would have forced the incoming water to turn sharply and drop much of its sediment in the intake channel. A set of stone steps in the south wall allowed access to varying water levels, and thus it would have provided domestic water for the inhabitants of the successive villages around it. By early Pueblo III times (1100s), the total community probably housed some four hundred to five hundred people in about 375 rooms with thirty-two kivas arranged in eighteen separate buildings (figs. 2-17 and 2-18).

Far View House contains four kivas incorporated in the room block with a fifth subterranean kiva outside. The roofs of the interior kivas served as courtyards for the second-story rooms located along the north and east sides of the pueblo (fig. 2-19). The larger central kiva stands apart from the other four kin-group kivas by having eight pilasters, oblong vaults in the floor, and a clearly larger size. Presumably it, too, served as a kin-group kiva, albeit with a more specialized role. Another large kiva with similar features accompanied the ceremonial platform and tower complex at Site 16. A low masonry wall supports a built-up terrace along the south side of the pueblo.

Pipe Shrine House, so named by Dr. Jesse Walter Fewkes, who found a cache of tobacco pipes in a small shrine built into the terrace wall to the south when he dug the site in the 1920s, exhibits both late Pueblo II and early Pueblo III stone masonry. It contains twenty-two masonry dwelling and storage rooms, one kiva, and one tower (fig. 2-20). The two rows of nine rooms along the north side had been originally built during late Pueblo II using loaf-shaped stones in walls only one stone thick. The later masonry walls added to the south around the remodeled kiva contain sandstone blocks with flatter edges often dressed by pecking laid in courses two or more stones thick. Thus, this site displays original construction in late Pueblo II masonry

2-20. Construction of the northernmost nine rooms of Pipe Shrine House in the Far View Settlement dates to the 1000s, and the round tower and other rooms were added during the 1100s along with remodeling of the kiva. Stone steps led down through the terrace retaining wall past a small shrine. When excavated, this shrine yielded a number of smoking pipes, inspiring J. W. Fewkes's name for the ruin.

2-21. Site 820, Coyote Village, in the Far View Settlement, comprised five kivas enclosed within their associated blocks of rooms sitting on a low earthen terrace supported by low stone walls visible in front and to the right. Some of the back rooms stood three stories tall. The round tower standing next to three kivas functioned with those kivas in ceremonial activities. It did not serve defensive or lookout purposes.

style with later additions and remodeling in early Pueblo III masonry style.

Site 820 ("Coyote Village") lies southwest of Far View and Pipe Shrine houses relatively near the highway. It contains five kivas and a round tower, all incorporated into the room block (fig. 2-21). One room next to the kiva in the southwest corner of the building contains six stone-slab-lined grinding bins for food preparation. Within each bin a sandstone metate would have been set at an angle. Puebloan women would have kneeled behind the higher end of the metate and leaned forward to grind the corn kernels into meal or flour using stone manos. The meal or flour collected at the lower end of the metate could then be scooped out for use. The six bins in a row indicate the women often treated food grinding as a group activity.

All five kivas are circular and masonry lined with ventilators, built-in stone slab or masonry deflectors, hearths, sipapus, banquettes, southern "keyhole" recesses, wall niches, and usually six masonry pilasters to support a cribbed roof, in typical Mesa Verde fashion. In one kiva near the southeast corner, two wooden poles connected each pair of pilasters about midway up the column. These poles did not support the roof, but rather functioned as storage shelves and/or hangers. Their presence shows that banquettes provided storage space and did not serve as benches for sitting. The kiva occupants sat on mats on the floor.

Far View Tower represents a ceremonial structure superimposed on top of the rubble of older residential rooms and a kiva (a unit pueblo) that formed part of the late Pueblo II village (fig. 2-22). The second kiva was probably built contemporaneously with the tower in early Pueblo III times, while the original late Pueblo II kiva was remodeled to fit the complex. Note the differences in stone masonry between the residential room wall bases and the round tower.

Another ceremonial complex similar to Far View Tower may be seen at **Cedar Tree Tower** (fig. 2-23),

2-22. Far View Tower, a round building with two associated kivas, served a ceremonial function for inhabitants of the early Pueblo III (1100s) Far View Settlement. The tower sits on top of the ruins of an older late Pueblo II (1000s) dwelling, and one of the kivas has been remodeled from an earlier kiva belonging to that older house.

located on Chapin Mesa near the edge of Soda Canyon about three-fourths of a mile north of the entrance to Ruins Road. Here, an ovoid tower, originally probably twice its present visible height, had been built with double-coursed stone masonry walls. Nearly every stone had been dressed by pecking its outer surface to fit the curvature of the walls. Inside, a sipapu has been carved out of the bedrock sandstone on which the tower stands. A natural crack in this sandstone foundation within the tower leads to a tunnel beneath the south wall. This tunnel divides once it reaches beyond the tower wall, one portion leading into a low room walled up beneath the sandstone ledge off to the west, the other portion opening into a subterranean kiva to the south. The tunnel enters the kiva at banquette level adjacent to one of the pilasters. This kiva contained all the standard features of a Pueblo III kiva—ventilator, deflector, pecked-face masonry, banquette, six pilasters, hearth, and wall niches—everything except the sipapu, which could be found in the floor of the tower. A low retaining wall supported a plazalike space over the kiva roof. No precise dates have been determined for

2-23. Cedar Tree Tower, with its associated kiva and underground room, all three connected by a tunnel, played a ceremonial role in the lives of Pueblo III (1100–1300) peoples living on Chapin Mesa on the Mesa Verde. The structure stands near the end of a ridge projecting into the west side of Soda Canyon, the kind of location favored for the many shrines of all sizes by these people.

2-24. Spruce Tree House, across the canyon from the museum at Mesa Verde National Park, contains 114 rooms and eight kivas. This late Pueblo III village, occupied between A.D. 1200 and 1300, is the best preserved of all Mesa Verde's cliff dwellings, with three-story walls extending to the cave roof, many intact roofs and balconies, and painted plaster covering many wall surfaces. Visitors can discern individual workmanship by different stone masons from wall to wall. Spruce Tree House formed the core of a community of fourteen sites holding 150 to 200 residents packed into this canyon head around a strong spring. The other Spruce Tree Canyon sites range in size from one to fifteen rooms each.

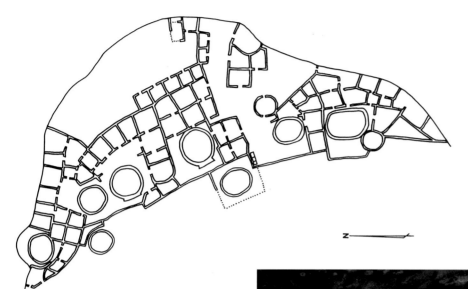

2-25. The ground plan of Spruce Tree House shows the relationships of rooms and kivas to one another. Roofs over the kivas would have formed open courtyards that together with a few streets and passages would have allowed access to all the household suites. Upper stories have not been marked on this plan. Trails entered the site along the base of the cliff from both ends.

2-26. North courtyard at Spruce Tree House formed by the roofs over two underground kivas. These roofs have been restored to create a sense of courtyard life in a Mesa Verde cliff dwelling during the 1200s. Entrance to the second-floor rooms at the rear of the courtyard would have been gained from the roofs of a row of one-story rooms now collapsed, while the third-floor rooms had to be reached via a balcony across the extended second-story roof beam ends. Hearths and stone slab–lined storage bins in the courtyard indicate the people prepared food and cooked in the open spaces in front of their homes.

the Cedar Tree Tower structures, but the architecture fits the Pueblo III style.

While the Puebloans utilized series of check dams in ravines all over Mesa Verde, one restored set of these may be visited along a trail below Cedar Tree Tower. More than sixty dams make up this series. The dams formed small terraces for farming by holding soil behind them and inhibiting rainwater runoff (see fig. 1-55).

Spruce Tree House

Located just across Spruce Tree Canyon from the park headquarters and museum, Spruce Tree House may be one of the most visited pre-Columbian ruins in the Americas (fig. 2-24). It has been seen by many hundreds of thousands of people following its excavation and opening by Dr. Jesse Walter Fewkes in 1908. Its discoverers Richard Wetherill and Charlie Mason mistook the tall Douglas fir trees growing in front of the ruin for spruce

2-27. The so-called Main Street runs from the front of Spruce Tree House to the very back of the cave. The row of two-story rooms on the left have been almost perfectly preserved, with roofs still in place showing how some residents climbed up ladders through hatchways to reach the second floor. Remains of several hearths indicate this passageway also served as outdoor work space for the nearby residents.

2-28. Mesa Verde's cliff dwellers often painted their plastered wall interiors using a reddish color on the lower portions and white above. The inhabitants of this second-floor room in Spruce Tree House added a rectangular geometric design in red on the white upper wall. Smoke blackening in the lefthand corner above a bright red stain marks the location of a fire pit.

trees, hence the name. Between 1907 and 1926, Fewkes excavated and stabilized some sixteen sites, including Spruce Tree House, Cliff Palace, Sun Temple, and several ruins in the Far View locality.

The inhabitants of Spruce Tree House drew water from the strongest known spring on the Mesa Verde at the head of this small canyon. Tucked beneath ledges along the sides of the canyon between the spring and the larger ruin are a number of small masonry buildings that members of the Spruce Tree House community built and used.

This cliff dwelling ranks third in size at Mesa Verde, consisting of 114 rooms and eight kivas (fig. 2-25). Two kivas located in the northern portion of the ruin have been restored with cribbed roofs based on a half-complete kiva roof found at Square Tower House. With their roofs at plaza level, these two kivas illustrate the role of courtyard spaces in all cliff dwellings and mesa-top pueblos. An outdoor courtyard work area would be surrounded on one, two, or three sides by living quarters. The great overhang of the cave roof provided Spruce Tree House residents with maximum sunshine during winter months and maximum shade during summer months.

Two- and three-story rooms face the roofed kivas (fig. 2-26). Some of the doorways are rectangular while others have a T-shape. Second-story roof timbers protrude from one of the buildings behind the north courtyard to provide support for a narrow balcony with access to third-story rooms. A refuse dump area occupied the large space behind all these rooms.

With its many intact roofs and doorways, Spruce Tree House represents one of the best preserved cliff dwellings. Completely preserved rooms line a sort of street that leads from the front of the cave to its back (fig. 2-27). One three-story building with a collapsed front wall stands slightly to the north of center in the ruin. Its interior back wall on the third story retains its original plaster, cream on top and reddish below,

2-29. At the north end of the Spruce Tree House overhang, the builders employed a stone masonry column to support a horizontal log spanning the room below and on top of which they erected a masonry wall for the topmost room. Such a device illustrates how an individual builder solved a difficult problem. It has only been observed in one other Mesa Verde cliff dwelling, Spring House.

with a rectangular abstract design in red visible behind and beneath an intact horizontal roof timber (fig. 2-28). At the far north end of the ruin, a masonry column may be seen supporting an upper-story wall containing a T-shaped doorway (fig. 2-29). This feature has been noted in only one other Mesa Verde cliff dwelling, Spring House.

Two ancient trails entered Spruce Tree House from the mesa top. One of the trails may be seen to the south of the ruin leading to a ledge, on which two white painted stone slabs have been propped, and thence to the mesa top. The other trail goes up the west side of the canyon where a set of hand- and toeholds hewn out of the sandstone cliff face (fig. 2-30) occupy the inside of a horseshoe bend in the visitor trail. The east trail also connects with a mile-long trail along the canyon's east side leading to Petroglyph Point, an apparent ceremonial shrine (see fig. 1-73) that appears to have been associated with Spruce Tree House.

Cliff Palace and the Cliff-Fewkes Canyon Ruins

The magnificent Sun Temple sits on the point where Fewkes Canyon joins Cliff Canyon. It serves as the focal point for a cluster of dwellings located in the cliffs of the two canyons. Fewkes considered it to be a ceremonial structure, apparently correctly, but not dedicated to the sun.

Beginning in early Pueblo III times, probably around 1150, the Puebloan people began to move off the mesa tops and into the cliffs, and by 1200 they had begun the construction of the cliff dwellings. The Cliff-Fewkes Canyon Settlement comprised some thirty-three separate cliff dwellings with a combined total of over five hundred living and storage rooms and sixty kivas. Included in this settlement are Cliff Palace and Sunset House on the east side of Cliff Canyon across from Sun Temple, and Mummy House, Oak Tree House, and New Fire House on the north side of Fewkes Canyon. Another ceremonial structure, Fire Temple, lies near the head of Fewkes Canyon. All of these sites may be seen from overlooks along the Ruins Road (fig. 2-31).

Sun Temple consists of two concentric D-shaped, rubble-cored walls, the space between them divided into compartments. These walls enclosed a pair of kivas built on the ground surface—the entire structure rests on bedrock sandstone. A westward extension of the D-shape surrounds a third kiva, several compartments, and a circular unit that may have been the base of a tower (fig. 2-32). The builders of

2-30. A toehold trail descends the west side of the canyon opposite Spruce Tree House to meet a trail at the cliff base that led past the spring and into the north end of the village. Similar trails connected the cliff dwellers with their mesa-top farming areas.

[Facing page] 2-31. Many of the Puebloan ruins on Chapin Mesa may be reached or viewed from the Ruins Road. Stabilized sites chronicle the history of Puebloan development from about A.D. 600 to 1200. The many cliff dwellings visible from overlooks in Cliff and Fewkes canyons make up most of the Mesa Verde's largest community of some six hundred to eight hundred people residing during the 1200s in thirty-three cliff dwellings including Cliff Palace, Sunset House, and Oak Tree House. The entire Mesa Verde at that time housed approximately twenty-five hundred people.

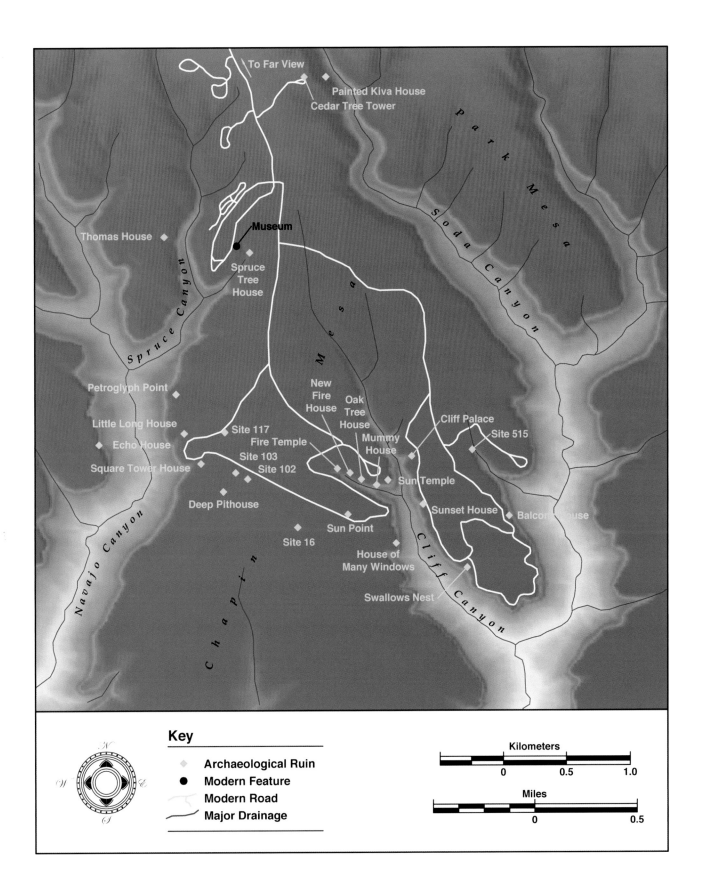

Key

◆ Archaeological Ruin
● Modern Feature
— Modern Road
⌒ Major Drainage

Kilometers
0   0.5   1.0

Miles
0   0.5

2-32. Sun Temple's basic structure consists of two circular above-ground kivas within a D-shaped courtyard surrounded by two concentric walls. The space between these two walls has been segmented into narrow compartments connected to one another by doorways. A later extension on the west end added another kiva and several more compartments, but maintained the overall D-shape. A circular tower stands outside to the east. Sun Temple occupies the prominent point between Cliff Canyon (behind) and Fewkes Canyon (lower right) directly above Mummy House (in shadow, lower right).

2-33. Sunset House occupies two ledges beneath a high arching overhang in the east wall of Cliff Canyon. It is one of thirty-three late Pueblo III (1200s) cliff dwellings that make up the Cliff-Fewkes Canyon Settlement. These people would have obtained their water from one of two springs, one at the head of Fewkes Canyon and the other at the base of the cliff beneath Sun Temple. Their chief access to these springs and to their farmlands on the mesa top would have taken them to the south-end trail out of Cliff Palace.

2-34. Cliff Palace, the largest individual cliff dwelling on the Mesa Verde, contains some 220 rooms and twenty-three kivas.

Sun Temple used sandstone blocks with carefully pecked, even ground surfaces, almost exclusively for the wall facings, both exterior and interior. Roofs probably capped the kivas. Courtyard space surrounded the kivas within the enclosing walls. Another tower stood outside.

Its architecture and positioning indicate that Sun Temple was contemporary with the late Pueblo III cliff dwellings in the Cliff-Fewkes Canyon Settlement. It stood in a prominent position directly above the strongest spring in the complex, essentially surrounded by the residential sites.

Sunset House contains thirty rooms and four kivas arranged on two ledges (fig. 2-33). The lower level comprises three groups of rooms—two rooms and a kiva at the north end, three two-story rooms in front center, and seven rooms with a kiva at the south end. Three dry-wall masonry turkey pens occupy the rear of this same level. An irregular cave floor that remained somewhat damp made this ledge less desirable for living than the very dry upper ledge on which the remainder of the buildings stand. Access to Sunset House depended on trails near Cliff Palace to the north and Swallow's Nest to the south, which led

2-35. The southern portion of Cliff Palace from the round tower (left) to the four-story building (right). The circular tower provided added ceremonial efficacy for two adjacent kivas, and the four-story building has preserved a very fine wall painting.

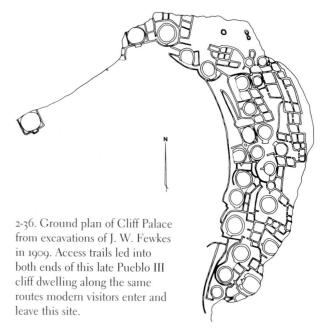

2-36. Ground plan of Cliff Palace from excavations of J. W. Fewkes in 1909. Access trails led into both ends of this late Pueblo III cliff dwelling along the same routes modern visitors enter and leave this site.

to their mesa-top fields. Their water came from the spring beneath Sun Temple.

Cliff Palace is he largest of the Mesa Verde cliff dwellings. It contains about 220 rooms and twenty-three kivas, and during the thirteenth century it housed probably 250 to 350 people (fig. 2-34). A round tower that tapers inward as it rises (fig. 2-35) stands to the south of center. Two- to four-story buildings rise at both ends of the ruin. Retaining walls support the six kivas that range across the front (fig. 2-36). These kivas follow the generalized Mesa Verde kiva style (fig. 2-37), even though considerable variation occurs among them.

The best-preserved rooms in Cliff Palace form what Fewkes called "speaker chief tower," although they probably simply represent multistoried residences (fig. 2-38). The four-story building at the south end displays colorful wall paintings on its interior third-story room (fig. 2-39). A solid red band covered the lower portion of the room walls with white above. Where the two colors meet, several red triangles project upward in groupings as if to represent mountains on the horizon. A row of red dots runs between the sets of triangles. Two figures

2-37. Even though no two of Cliff Palace's twenty-three kivas look exactly alike, most of them follow a generalized pattern: circular in plan, usually dug beneath courtyard level so their roofs would form part of the courtyard, central fire pit, ventilator tunnel in the south side, raised air deflector, and usually six masonry pilasters rising above an encircling banquette to support a cribbed log roof. Variations among kivas probably reflect the different ritual needs and ideas of the different kin groups (lineages) who built and used them.

2-38. The north end of Cliff Palace contains the best-preserved buildings in this large cliff dwelling. Excavator J. W. Fewkes labeled the tallest building the "speaker chief tower" with the suggestion that the village sun watcher announced his findings from there. Most likely, however, these were ordinary residences.

2-39. Painted interior walls on the third floor of a four-story building at the south end of Cliff Palace. The upper portions of the walls have been painted white, the lower portions red, with red triangles projecting upward like mountains on the horizon. Rows of red dots run between the triangles. Both rectangular designs painted in red on the white upper walls resemble textile designs. While most Mesa Verde cliff dwellers decorated the interiors of their living rooms, few have been preserved as well as this one.

painted in red over the white portion of two walls appear to represent textile designs. Originally, floors separated the stories from one another. The occupants would have gained access to the upper rooms through hatchways in these roofs, although a lower building, now collapsed, once fronted this four-story structure. The T-shaped doorway in the top story indicates a balcony once existed below it.

Interior wall plaster and painted surfaces occurred frequently in the Pueblo III cliff dwellings, usually following this same pattern of white above red. However, most have deteriorated over time leaving this room as one of the best preserved examples. The red paint derived from powdered hematite mixed with water and fine clay. The white consists of a nearly pure kaolin clay.

Several other cliff dwellings occupy overhangs along the north side of Fewkes Canyon running northwestward from Sun Temple. Mummy House, Oak Tree House, New Fire House, and Fire Temple all belong to the Cliff-Fewkes Canyon Settlement (fig. 2-40) and community. **Mummy House**, located directly below Sun Temple, consists of twelve rooms and two kivas (fig. 2-41). Fewkes named the ruin after a well-preserved mummy he found in the two-story building located in the small ledge above the main block of rooms. This ledge could have originally been reached by a ladder from the now fallen roofs of the main room block.

Oak Tree House, in the high arching cave to the northwest, contained fifty-two to fifty-five residential and storage rooms and six kivas on two separate ledges

2-40. Fewkes (left) and Cliff (right) canyons on Chapin Mesa contain thirty-three cliff dwellings that made up the late Pueblo III (1200s) Cliff-Fewkes Canyon Settlement. Two communal ceremonial buildings served the entire community—Sun Temple on the point between the two canyons and directly above a spring, and Fire Temple in the north cliff of Fewkes Canyon near its head. The Puebloans had built a dam across the bare rock area above the head of Fewkes Canyon to feed water into the spring below. The wooded mesa top would have been cleared for farmlands, for construction timbers, and for firewood. This large community may have been the nucleus for other smaller Chapin Mesa communities focused around Spruce Tree House, around Balcony House, and around Square Tower and Little Long houses.

2-41. Mummy House, near the mouth of Fewkes Canyon in the Cliff-Fewkes Canyon community. Only the wall stubs of ten rooms and two kivas remain on the lower ledge of this cliff dwelling, but several rooms must once have stood two and three stories high in order to provide access to the perfectly preserved two-story building tucked beneath the upper shallow overhang. A well-preserved mummy found in this building prompted the name. Sun Temple stands on top of the cliff at the upper left.

2-42. Oak Tree House in Fewkes Canyon is the second-largest cliff dwelling in the Cliff-Fewkes Canyon community with six kivas and fifty-two to fifty-four rooms. Ladders from the tops of multistory rooms, now fallen, in the lower cave provided access to the narrow upper ledge crowded with many storerooms and only a few living rooms. Retaining walls had been built to form level terraces for the construction of rooms and kivas. These retaining walls have been restored by the National Park Service to protect the original standing walls from further deterioration.

2-43. New Fire House in Fewkes Canyon contains remnants of twenty rooms and three kivas on two separate ledges. A ladder resting on the wall between the two left kivas led to a set of small steps or toeholds onto the upper ledge between two sets of buildings. The Puebloans employed similar steps or toehold trails to traverse cliffs throughout the Mesa Verde and all of Pueblo-land.

(fig. 2-42). As at Mummy House, the upper-ledge storage rooms would have been easily accessible via ladders from the roofs of the multistoried rooms beneath them. A well-preserved jacal walled structure may be seen at the very back of the cave. One kiva exhibits a D-shape. The people would have discarded their trash down the talus slope in front of the cave, as did the inhabitants of all the cliff dwellings.

Still farther to the northwest and nearer the canyon head stands **New Fire House**. It, too, occupies two levels with most of the twenty domestic rooms on the top ledge and the three kivas and some living rooms on the lower one (fig. 2-43). Both overhangs are very low, providing natural rock roofs for many rooms, but restricting their height to one story.

Between New Fire House and the head of the canyon stands **Fire Temple**. This rectangular structure exhibits many features found only in the round great kivas of Aztec Ruin and Chaco Canyon. Hence it and a similar structure at Long House on Wetherill Mesa most likely represent rectangular versions of the great kiva, perhaps limited in shape by their locations beneath rock overhangs.

An elevated masonry-lined firebox and two masonry-outlined floor vaults occupy the center of the main rectangular space (fig. 2-44). This open space probably had not been roofed. A variety of ritual performances probably took place here, for benches lined the north, east, and south sides. White plaster may be seen on the upper walls. Rooms abut

2-44. Fire Temple was a great kiva built beneath a cliff overhang near the spring at the head of Fewkes Canyon. Its large central rectangular chamber contains an encircling bench, red and white painted walls, a raised circular masonry firebox, and two oblong masonry floor vaults. It may never have been roofed. Rooms have been attached at both right (southeast) and left (northwest), with one of the left group containing a raised altar. Ceremonies held here and at Sun Temple probably attracted residents from the Cliff-Fewkes Canyon community and perhaps people from the other smaller cliff-dwelling villages on Chapin Mesa.

at both ends of the central space with an altar in the rooms to the northwest. The location of Fire Temple nearest the spring in the head of Fewkes Canyon resembles the position of Sun Temple above the other chief spring in this canyon complex. Both appear to reflect communal reverence for sources of water. The Puebloans had constructed a dam in the water course leading to the head of Fewkes Canyon. Water impounded behind this dam would soak into the porous bedrock sandstone until it reached an impervious shale layer that directed the water to the spring at the canyon head. Could this have been attributed to magical ritual practices?

The Fewkes Canyon ruins all occupy rock shelters in the northeast wall of the canyon where no access trail exists. There is a trail on the southwest wall, where no overhangs occur, across from the space between Oak Tree House and New Fire House. A second trail follows the base of the northeast cliff to the spring below Sun Temple and beyond, where a toehold trail leads to the mesa top northeast of Sun Temple. While evidence for a dual division in Pueblo III society might not always be easy to discern, this concept might be represented by the two distinctive ceremonial structures of Sun Temple and Fire Temple, each associated with a good spring.

The Cliff-Fewkes Canyon community with both Sun Temple, a concentric wall structure, and Fire Temple, a rectangular great kiva, probably functioned

2-45. The west cliffs of Chapin Mesa in the vicinity of Twin Trees show the late Pueblo III cliff dwellings Little Long House (extreme left) and Square Tower House (extreme right). Together with five other small cliff ruins, these buildings housed 120 to 150 people in more than 110 rooms and twelve kin-group kivas. They shared water sources in a spring below Square Tower House and a reservoir/seep complex next to Little Long House. They also shared the only two trails to their farmlands and wood supply on the mesa top, now covered by piñon-juniper woodland. During earlier times, the Basket Maker III Earth Lodge B village stood on the mesa top near the center in the photograph, and the subsequent Twin Trees villages at the extreme right. The distant La Plata Mountains loom above the Mesa Verde's north rim in the background.

as the nuclear settlement/community for all the Chapin Mesa cliff dwellings including Balcony House and Site 515, Square Tower House and Little Long House, Spruce Tree House, and a cluster at the head of Pool Canyon on the Ute reservation to the south. Based on room and kiva counts, it housed half of the total population then living on Chapin Mesa.

Square Tower House

Square Tower House, Little Long House, and several small structures—mostly one- and two-room storage buildings—constituted a midsized cliff dwelling settlement (fig. 2-45). Neither of these ruins may be visited by the public, although Square Tower House can be viewed from an overlook reached by a short trail off the Ruins Road.

Water could have been obtained from three sources. A weak spring runs immediately below Square Tower House. A second weak spring in the draw near Little Long House had been augmented by rainwater trapped behind a Puebloan dam built on the bedrock area above it. Finally, a natural, deep depression in the bedrock sandstone near this dam holds water for some time after rains and snowmelt.

Toeholds leading into this depression indicate the nearby people did obtain water from it.

Located in the eastern cliff of Navajo Canyon, Square Tower House represents a relatively large cliff dwelling containing some seventy or more domestic rooms and seven kivas (fig. 2-46). Two of the kivas have portions of their roofs still intact, providing models for the restoration of the kiva roofs at Spruce Tree House. One half-roofed kiva nestles between the "square tower" and the building immediately to the right.

Square Tower House faces south-southwestward. Its name derives from the four-story building of four domestic rooms built one above the other that only appears to be a tower (fig. 2-47). Originally, a three-story building stood in front of the "tower" with a two-story building in front of that creating a stair-step appearance. These latter two buildings have collapsed into the nearby kiva depressions, leaving only the four-story structure standing.

Two trails led into Square Tower House. A still visible toehold trail to the south of the visitor overlook descended the sandstone cliff and then continued along the base of the cliff, going behind a large

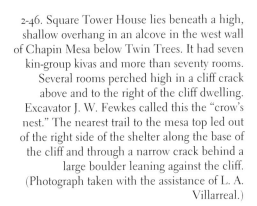

2-46. Square Tower House lies beneath a high, shallow overhang in an alcove in the west wall of Chapin Mesa below Twin Trees. It had seven kin-group kivas and more than seventy rooms. Several rooms perched high in a cliff crack above and to the right of the cliff dwelling. Excavator J. W. Fewkes called this the "crow's nest." The nearest trail to the mesa top led out of the right side of the shelter along the base of the cliff and through a narrow crack behind a large boulder leaning against the cliff. (Photograph taken with the assistance of L. A. Villarreal.)

sandstone block that had slipped from the cliff face and tilted back against it, and thence into the southeast corner of the site. The second trail descended some distance to the northwest, coming down a sandstone projection opposite Little Long House, then around the small tributary canyon, through the lower ledge of Little Long House, around the cliff point, and into Square Tower House from the west. This second trail can still be used with proper permission.

Little Long House, around the cliff point to the northwest of Square Tower House, faces west. It has twenty-four rooms on a narrow upper ledge with four kivas built into the upper talus below. A series of small rock-cut basins at the back of the upper ledge had been designed to capture rainwater runoff streaming down the cliff from above. Little Long House cannot be viewed from any overlook.

Balcony House

From the standpoint of the visitor, Balcony House at Mesa Verde offers one of the most exciting and spectacular adventures among ancient ruins in North America. It sits under an overhang on the west wall of Soda Canyon (fig. 2-48). It can be reached from

2-47. The "square tower" that inspired the Wetherill brothers' name for this cliff dwelling is actually a four-story building that once had a three-story building in front of it and a two-story building in front of that. The upper walls of these front buildings have collapsed. Immediately to the right of this four-story building may be seen a well-preserved section of kiva roof that the National Park Service used as a model for the reconstruction of kiva roofs in Spruce Tree House.

2-48. Balcony House occupies a low overhang halfway up the cliff on the east side of Chapin Mesa overlooking Soda Canyon. Of all the cliff dwellings on the Mesa Verde, this one displays the most defensive setting. Visitors approaching along the base of the cliff from the south would have to climb up a steep toehold trail to a masonry tower and traverse a narrow ledge before entering the cave on hands and knees through two low tunnels behind the leaning boulder at the extreme left. Residents of Balcony House could obtain water from one spring in the back of the overhang behind the two-story building toward the left or from a second spring under the base of the cliff at the extreme right. Turkeys were penned at the base of the cliff just left of the National Park Service ladder. A seemingly disproportionate ratio of forty-five rooms to two kin-group kivas can be balanced by the rooms and kivas in eleven other cliff dwelling sites belonging to the Balcony House village along the adjacent cliffs.

the Cliff Palace–Balcony House road on a guided tour via a lengthy trail and a series of ladders.

Balcony House and several smaller neighboring cliff dwellings formed a small settlement consisting of some twelve separate sites containing a total of eighty-one rooms and six kivas scattered along the west cliffs of Soda Canyon. This community's population has been estimated at over a hundred people. Site 515, with eleven rooms and three kivas, occupies the head of the small tributary canyon just north of

Balcony House. Pueblo III settlements in the Mesa Verde averaged about eleven rooms to one kiva, although many separate cliff dwellings such as Site 515 and Balcony House had far different ratios.

Balcony House presents one disproportion with forty-four rooms and only two kivas. Thus, by combining the numbers from Site 515 and the other nearby sites, the kiva-to-room ratio becomes proportionate to those of other cliff-dwelling settlements. Because of its overrepresentation of kivas, Site 515 may actually have been the most important site in this settlement, probably because it stood next to where the Puebloans had constructed both a dam above the cliff to trap rainwater runoff, allowing it to soak into the bedrock sandstone, and a reservoir below to collect water coming out of the enhanced seep at the base of the cliff. This same water conservation system had also been employed at Spruce Tree House, at Little Long House, and at Long House on Wetherill Mesa.

The trail into Balcony House entered along a narrow ledge from the south behind another huge sandstone slab that had slipped away from the cliff face, leaving a narrow crevice between it and the cliff face. The Balcony House residents further narrowed this passageway by building two stone masonry walls, leaving only a small doorway in each, separated by a crawl space, thus creating an easily defensible entry (fig. 2-49).

Once outside, this trail led south along the narrow ledge until it narrowed to nothing. At that point, the people built a small circular tower directly over a toehold trail that descended to the top of the talus slope at the base of the cliff. From there, the trail led northward beneath Balcony House, and past the dry-wall masonry turkey pens and spring located there, and several hundred yards farther to a point halfway between Balcony House and Site 515 where another toehold trail led to the mesa top. Another very precarious toehold trail led directly down to the entry ledge. These trails made access to Balcony House so difficult that archaeologists surmise the people probably lowered most supplies into the living area by ropes. A strong spring at the back of the main cave provided water for its inhabitants.

Three features in the north courtyard command interest. A very well-preserved balcony stretches along the front of a complete two-story building (fig. 2-50). This balcony rests on the protruding ends of

2-49. One or two persons could adequately defend this entrance to Balcony House by positioning themselves above the two tunnels to strike any intruder trying to crawl in. Burdens for residents, of course, could simply be raised out of the cave or lowered into it by ropes.

the first-story roof beams. A layer of small poles topped by juniper bark and mud, the same as in roof construction, completed the balcony (fig. 2-51). Rectangular doorways opened into all four of these rooms, the top two leading inside from the balcony. Smaller openings in the room walls allowed fresh air into the rooms.

A second feature takes the form of the low parapet wall that runs along the outer edge of the courtyard. Finally, the intact room at the far north end of this north courtyard has both an intact roof and a series of

2-51. The perfectly preserved balcony that gave Balcony House its name was constructed on the ends of roof beams projecting beyond the walls by laying wooden poles, twigs, and/or split juniper shakes at right angles, then adding juniper bark, and finally mud. Inhabitants of the two second-floor rooms could emerge onto the balcony through the rectangular doorways and then climb down ladders to the courtyard below.

2-50. The north courtyard in Balcony House on the east side of Chapin Mesa contains both this remarkably preserved balcony on the two-story building and a low rampart wall across its front. The obvious protection against small children falling over the edge that this rampart affords does not appear in other cliff dwellings. Inside the room at the far end of the rampart wall, a series of horizontal poles halfway up formed a drying rack for preserving foodstuffs.

poles stretching across it halfway up the walls. Such poles would have been ideal for hanging foodstuffs to dry—such as strings of corn ears, or cut strips of squash—or for hanging clothing, utensils, and tools.

A solid wall separated this north courtyard from the southern one, allowing access between the two only at the very back of the cave. Communication between the two courtyards could have taken place through the opening in the wall. An old walled-up doorway suggests that access had been easier in the past. Such a separation possibly reflects two separate

kinship units, although both kivas were in the south courtyard. Their floors, fire pits, and sipapus had to be pecked out of the solid bedrock cave floor. Both their ventilators opened eastward toward the cave mouth, possibly to maximize air flow, although once there they turned toward the preferred south direction. When roofed in the usual manner, supported on the six masonry pilasters in each, the kivas would have lain beneath an open courtyard that would have closely resembled the reconstructed north courtyard in Spruce Tree House. Most activities,

2-52. A view of the south courtyard in Balcony House through an opening or window in the wall that separates the two courtyards reveals a room whose walls have collapsed into adjacent kivas, leaving only the one roof beam projecting from the room next door. Rectangular openings of this size, like the two flanking the T-shaped doorway in the visible wall, functioned more as air vents than as windows. This solid wall across Balcony House from front to back, with only one narrow passageway at the rear of the cave, separated social groupings within the site.

including food preparation, would have been conducted in these courtyards, leaving the rooms for sleeping and storage.

A long pole projecting outward above a T-shaped doorway in a two-story room in the south courtyard remains as the sole evidence for a room that once stood in front of it between the two kivas. This log once helped support the roof of this now missing room (fig. 2-52). Smoke blackening on the cave roof behind the rooms indicates that cooking fires once burned in that space outside the rooms.

Wetherill Mesa

Wetherill Mesa forms another one of the many long, narrow fingers of the Mesa Verde separated by steep-walled canyons. It lies at the west edge of the park between Long and Rock canyons about two miles as the crow flies west of Chapin Mesa. Wetherill Mesa is home to the second-largest grouping of cliff dwellings on the Mesa Verde, including Long House, Mug House, Kodak House, Step House, and

others (fig. 2-53), plus a development of mesa-top sites similar to that displayed on Chapin Mesa. Long House and Step House plus several mesa-top ruins—a Basket Maker III pithouse, a Pueblo I room block, Two Raven House, and Badger House—have been stabilized for visitors.

The steep canyons between these two finger mesas require visitors to drive to Wetherill Mesa, about twelve miles from the Far View Visitor Center along a scenic and winding road that traverses Mesa Verde's north rim to the head of Wetherill Mesa, and thence southward to a parking lot near Step House. From this parking lot, trails lead to two nearby ruins—Step House and the Badger House community—and a minitrain offers transportation to the trailhead into Long House and an overlook for Kodak House with additional stops at mesa-top ruins. Mug House, not yet open to the public, has already been discussed and illustrated in the introduction (see figs. 1-68 to 1-72).

Long House lies beneath a great overhang, facing south, at the head of a small canyon tributary to

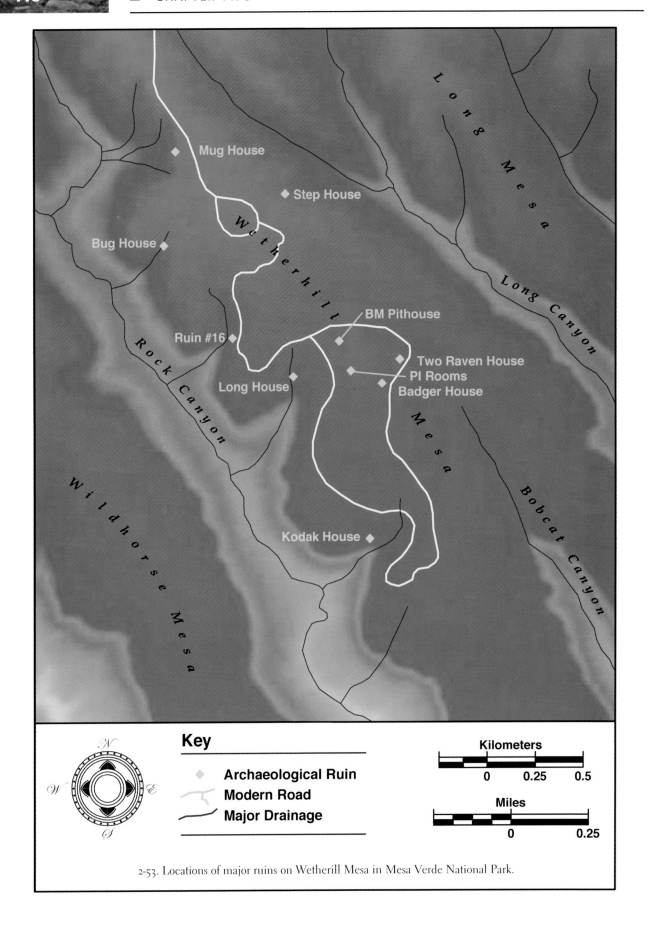

Key

◆ Archaeological Ruin

Modern Road

Major Drainage

Kilometers

0   0.25   0.5

Miles

0   0.25

2-53. Locations of major ruins on Wetherill Mesa in Mesa Verde National Park.

2-54. This aerial view of Wetherill Mesa from above Long House shows how the tableland slopes from about 8,500 feet in elevation on its north rim past 7,000 feet near Long House to about 6,500 feet where the Mancos River cuts through it. Steep canyons, such as Rock Canyon in front of Long House, further subdivide the Mesa Verde into many long and narrow finger mesas such as Chapin and Wetherill mesas. (Photograph taken with the assistance of L. A. Villarreal.)

2-55. Long House on Wetherill Mesa, the second-largest cliff dwelling on the Mesa Verde, housed some 150–200 people in more than 150 rooms and twenty-one kin-group kivas. Its name derives from its long extent around the full arc of this magnificent overhang. In the center front of the ruin, National Park Service excavators uncovered the remains of another rectangular great kiva in the same style as Fire Temple on Chapin Mesa. Upper ledge rooms on the left were probably for storage, and could have been reached by a ladder atop the roof of a room below. A single long, crude wall riddled with peek holes encloses space on the high ledge above the center of the ruin.

Rock Canyon (fig. 2-54). This overhang sheltered an estimated 150 rooms and twenty-one kivas. It can be reached from the minitrain stop via a trail that descends over the bedrock sandstone cliff very close to where an ancient toehold trail had been used by the Puebloans. This trail enters Long House at its west end where terraced buildings cover the slope of the main cave, and a row of low masonry rooms extends along a narrow ledge above them (fig. 2-55).

These upper rooms once had been reached by ladders set on the roofs of now collapsed buildings below them. One can still see vertical grooves worn into the edge of the sandstone by ladder poles just to the left of the well-preserved jacal wall. The three doorways that open toward the front provide additional evidence of the one-time height of the lower level buildings. Some of these buildings had been built on top of a large split boulder fallen from the

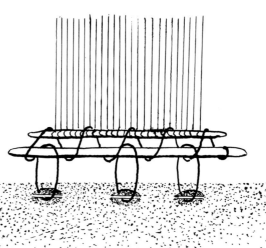

2-56. Puebloan weavers often set up their upright looms in the small kin-group kivas, tying the ends of the looms both to roof beams and to special anchors in the floor. This set of three loom anchors had been carved out of the bedrock sandstone floor of Kiva E on the west side of Long House on Wetherill Mesa. (Drawing by Joan Foth.)

overhang. At some time after these rooms had been built, and probably after their abandonment, the boulder slipped farther, bringing the walls crashing down. To prevent further slippage that might endanger visitors, National Park Service stabilizers constructed the big masonry supporting wall now visible beneath it. The three-story building against the cave wall to the left of this split boulder has a perfectly preserved roof segment visible from below.

Among the buildings on the lower slope is a row of six kivas built quite close to the back wall of the cave. On the plastered wall of one of these kivas, a painted geometric pottery-style design has survived, while a row of three loom anchors had been pecked into its bedrock floor (fig. 2-56) to anchor a vertical loom. The builders of this kiva made the earliest known use of

coal in Pueblo-land when they packed crushed coal between the kiva's lining wall and the cliff base. This coal packing would absorb any moisture seeping from the cliff and keep the kiva interior dry. Four more kivas occupy lower positions in front of this row of six, one at the far western edge of the ruin, two below the central portion supported by a thick retaining wall, and the fourth to the northeast below a two-story room block, also supported by a retaining wall. This last kiva and the upper one of the two in the center both have rectangular shapes (fig. 2-57).

In front of the center of Long House lies a rectangular great kiva (fig. 2-58), strikingly similar to the Fire Temple in Fewkes Canyon. It has a raised masonry firebox in its center, two masonry-lined floor vaults flanking the firebox, a stone-lined sipapu, and

2-57. Square kivas such as this one in Long House occur only occasionally in Puebloan sites. However, since no site contains more than one, or at most two, they apparently reflect a specific quality that many Puebloan communities desired in their ceremonial practices.

2-58. The rectangular great kiva in Long House exhibits typical features such as the raised masonry firebox in the center of the large chamber, flanking masonry-lined floor vaults, low benches along the interior walls, and the altar room extension on its west side. A stone-lined sipapu may be seen between the firebox and the bedrock sandstone back wall where a shale lens (dark band) just above floor level forces moisture out of the bedrock. The main spring used by the Long House residents occupies the east end of the main cave. Ceremonies held in this structure probably attracted people from all of Wetherill Mesa's cliff dwellings.

remnants of benches along both narrow ends. A masonry pilasterlike construction against the north wall in the room at the west end of this structure may or may not have once formed the base for an altar. The doorway near the northeast corner of the building leads into a passageway containing six steps leading from the east bench level to the floor of the adjoining room.

Immediately to the north of this adjoining room stand the lower remnants of walls that once reached up to five stories high, just above the remaining wall remnant still standing. The fifth-story room had extended outward from that wall, allowing a ladder placed on its roof to permit access to another upper ledge upon which a masonry wall had been constructed. The space behind this wall had not been subdivided into rooms, but numerous peep holes through the wall suggest this space may have served as a defensive refuge or as a secure place for ceremonial leaders to retreat.

A single row of one- and two-story rooms and two kivas range along the front edge of the bedrock cave floor behind the great kiva. Because of the hard bedrock, both kivas had to be built above ground. Actually, rectangular walls surrounded each kiva with the space between them and the round interior walls filled with earth to present a pseudo-underground feeling. Half the roof of the easternmost kiva remains intact along with one side of its roof hatchway/smoke hole (fig. 2-59). Unlike most Mesa Verde–style kivas, this roof had not rested on top of masonry pilasters rising from banquette level, but instead its main support timbers had rested directly on the upper side walls. Then, successive layers of split smaller poles running crosswise on top of the main timbers, of cornstalks with leaves and cobs, and of earth completed the roof.

The space behind these central rooms stays damp because of moisture seeping from the spring in the

2-59. A partially preserved roof resting directly on the side walls, rather than on the tops of pilasters, covers this kiva near the center of Long House.

horizontal crease where the bedrock floor and the overhang meet. This spring provided the residents of Long House with their main water supply. They pecked grooves in the bedrock floor to lead water from the spring to a series of pecked depressions in the floor, from which they dipped out the water with ladles into jugs. To further enhance the flow of this spring, they built a dam on the mesa top above the cave to capture runoff and allow the water to soak into the sandstone so it would percolate out at the spring. A second, much weaker seep came out just behind the great kiva.

A dense cluster of kivas and living rooms occupies the eastern end of the overhang. Tunnels connect two of the kivas with an adjacent room to the east. The only round tower found in Long House stands at the edge of this eastern room block. Beneath this eastern room block, and cut into by one of the kivas, archaeologists found the remnants of a Basket Maker III pithouse. Obviously, some Basket Maker III people chose rock shelter locations for their pithouses, such as here and in Step House Cave.

The grouping of living rooms and kivas, ten on the west and eleven on the east, leads one to suspect the

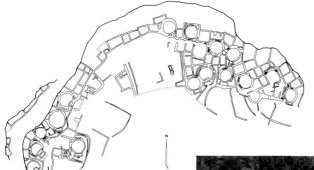

2-60. Ground plan of Long House on Wetherill Mesa at Mesa Verde National Park. The rectangular great kiva lies in the center between two clusters of houses and kin-group kivas that appear to represent a two-part (dual) social division, each with its own trash slope. (Drawing after Cattanach 1980).

2-61. Gustav Nordenskiöld named this cliff dwelling, located in an alcove of Rock Canyon on the west cliffs of Wetherill Mesa, Kodak House because he stored his camera here during his pioneering archaeological investigations on the Mesa Verde in 1891. Sixty to seventy rooms stretch along two separate ledges with seven kivas on the lower ledge. Like the inhabitants of other cliff dwellings on Wetherill Mesa, these people probably attended important ceremonies at the great kiva in Long House, about a mile to the north.

presence of a dual division at Long House, with the great kiva in the center (fig. 2-60). We also suspect the Long House great kiva, situated next to the strong water source, probably served all the cliff-dwelling communities on Wetherill Mesa, from Mug House in the north to Kodak House in the south, in much the same way that Sun Temple and Fire Temple served the Pueblo III inhabitants of Chapin Mesa.

Kodak House was named by Gustav Nordenskiöld in 1891 because he used to store his camera in the ruin when not in use. It contains about sixty to seventy rooms and seven kivas arranged on two levels (fig. 2-61). Only single-story rooms, using the natural cave roof for ceilings, extend along the narrow upper ledge. One of them has a jacal wall.

The lower-level builders had to overcome a steep slope on which to place many of the buildings. Although visitors cannot enter Kodak House, the overlook provides an excellent view of the entire ruin.

Many of the buildings here have been badly damaged by nineteenth-century looters seeking pottery vessels and other artifacts for sale on the antiquities market. Activities such as these continue today both in the Southwest and in many parts of the country, causing loss of information about peoples of the past and the loss of associations between the objects and their context.

Step House Cave lies almost directly north of Long House, but on the west wall of a small canyon off Long Canyon. It faces eastward (fig. 2-62). A small

2-62. Step House Cave in the east cliffs of Wetherill Mesa overlooks Long Canyon. Late Pueblo III cliff dwellers built a small hamlet of thirty living and storage rooms with three kin-group kivas on the pile of boulders at the right (north) side of the overhang. These masonry houses and the rubbish discarded by their inhabitants covered the remains of a village of six Basket Maker III pithouses, four of which have been stabilized in the center of the cave. The Basket Maker III people lived here during the early 600s and buried several of their dead in the back of the shelter. A series of prehistoric stone steps leading down the talus slope into the left (south) end of the cave inspired the name "Step House."

2-63. This view of Step House Cave shows the small late Pueblo III cliff dwelling dating to the 1200s in the foreground and the much earlier Basket Maker III pithouses constructed around A.D. 600 toward the rear.

Pueblo III cliff dwelling of thirty ground-floor rooms and three kivas perches on and around a pile of huge boulders fallen from the overhang in the northern part of the cave. One of the kivas had been squeezed down among several of these blocks of sandstone. Numerous stone axe–sharpening grooves have been worn into the top of one of these boulders. The Puebloan people sharpened both stone axes and bone awls by rubbing the sides of the edges back and forth on exposed sandstone surfaces—natural emery boards. Over time, these grooves assumed the reverse shape of the tools ground in them. Most cliff dwellings have one or more such natural tool-sharpening boulders.

The three kivas manifest some variation in style. The kiva squeezed among the rocks did not need masonry pilasters to support its roof. Another kiva has a relatively large number of niches in its side walls. The northernmost kiva has both a continuous arcing masonry deflector wall and a row of mountain sheep with rectangular bodies painted on its plaster.

A series of grinding bins for food preparation lies just north of the southernmost kiva, where they would once have sat at the edge of the courtyard formed by the kiva roof. A row of masonry-walled rooms extends along a narrow ledge directly above the north end of the ruin. One room yielded a tree-ring construction date of 1226.

The floors and lower walls of four Basket Maker III pithouses have been excavated and stabilized in the flat central portion of Step House Cave (fig. 2-63).

2-64. This close-up of a stabilized Basket Maker III pithouse in Step House Cave shows typical construction features such as the upright sandstone slabs lining the lower wall, an encircling banquette on which the side walls rested, four charred roof support posts (this house had burned), and a circular clay-lined hearth. The house had a ventilation tunnel, but no antechamber.

2-65. Four of the six Basket Maker III pithouses dating from around A.D. 600 found in Step House Cave on Wetherill Mesa. One house has been partially restored by the National Park Service to illustrate what a finished building would have looked like. Remains of two other contemporary pithouses, now covered by the later cliff dwelling, completed this village.

2-66. The ancient inhabitants of Step House reached their farmlands on the mesa top by climbing a set of stone steps along the large talus slope at the south end of the overhang.

Remains of two others were found beneath the walls of the Pueblo III cliff dwelling to the north, bringing the total number of pithouses in this settlement to six. Analyses of tree-rings in timbers from these buildings place their construction in the early 620s. Upright sandstone slabs lined the lower walls of each pithouse below banquette level, but above, the original earthen walls have been stabilized to prevent deterioration. Each pithouse has a circular floor plan with four posts to support its roof and side walls, a fire pit, and a ventilator tunnel rather than an antechamber (fig. 2-64). The partial reconstruction of the superstructure for one pithouse shows how the side wall poles rested on the banquette and against the square roof supported on the four upright wooden posts (fig. 2-65).

The inhabitants of Step House Cave had routes to their mesa-top fields at each end of the cave leading up the talus slopes. During the seventh century, Basket Maker people laid a series of stone steps up the talus slope on the southern trail (fig. 2-66) that the later cliff dwellers used as well. The modern visitor trail into the site parallels these steps that inspired the name "Step House."

On the mesa top, the park service has constructed a trail leading to a series of excavated ruins ranging in age from Basket Maker III to early Pueblo III, reminiscent of the Ruins Road group on Chapin Mesa. **Site 1644,** one of several Basket Maker III pithouses in this immediate area, has been excavated and stabilized for exhibit (fig. 2-67). It possesses the

2-67. One of the Basket Maker III pithouses at Site 1644 on the mesa top near Badger House on Wetherill Mesa has been excavated and stabilized by the National Park Service to illustrate the kinds of houses the Puebloans lived in during the middle 600s. Like Earth Lodge B on Chapin Mesa, this pithouse exhibits common characteristics of a partially subterranean floor with native earth lower side walls, an encircling banquette to support the upper jacal side walls, a four-post roof support system, low stone slab and mud wing walls, a circular clay-lined hearth, a stone slab deflector, and an antechamber attached to the south side.

same internal features found in Earth Lodge B—four-post roof support, antechamber, stone slab deflector, wing walls, central hearth, and sipapu. Side wall poles had been set on an earthen banquette. Tree-ring dates indicate it had been constructed during the middle 600s.

Several slab-based jacal rooms represent part of a Pueblo I complex at **Site 1676**. Typical deep pithouses lie in front of them, although none have been stabilized for exhibit. They had been built during the early 800s to about 860. Archaeologists have identified eight separated surface housing units with an estimated seventeen deep pithouses lying to the south of them. Many living and storage room floors had been dug slightly below ground surface. The larger living rooms each contained a hearth and fronted the plaza to the south beneath which the pithouses lay. Smaller storage rooms, often two per living room, abutted the north sides of those living rooms. Most rooms had been built using jacal construction, although a number contained crude stone masonry with stones set in very thick mud mortar.

The large, circular pit structure at the southeastern end of House 1 looks as though it had functioned as a great kiva. It measures thirty-one feet in diameter at floor level, and it had been dug nearly four feet beneath the original ground surface. Four wooden posts once supported the roof, a one-foot-high banquette or bench encircled the interior, and a stone-lined hearth occupied the center of its floor. Ceramics found on the floor suggest it had been used early in the Pueblo I stage.

The small mesa-top pueblo **Two Raven House** had three separate occupations. The first occurred during early Pueblo II and consisted of an early-style kiva plus three to four jacal-walled rooms. The second occupation comprised about ten masonry-walled pueblo-style rooms fronted by a kiva, the roof of which had been supported on four wooden posts.

Numerous tree-ring dates from this kiva suggest it had been constructed about 1032. A small subterranean feature and a masonry oven above ground completed the third occupation, which apparently took place during early Pueblo III. Excavators encountered part of a wooden post stockade around the northeast corner of the site that once apparently encircled this small unit pueblo.

Superimposed occupations may be clearly seen at **Badger House**. Four Pueblo III stone masonry–walled (two or three stones thick) rooms directly overlie the remnants of nine thinner-walled (single-stone thickness) late Pueblo II rooms. The room block had a six-pilaster kiva to the south. A later Pueblo III kiva with eight pilasters and a floor vault (fig. 2-68) was connected to the thick-walled tower (fig. 2-69) that stood a short distance from the southwest corner of the room block by a long tunnel that bypassed the earlier kiva. Tree-ring dates from the Pueblo III kiva indicate it had been constructed in 1257, unusually late for a mesa-top structure. Of course, this kiva-tower unit probably represents a shrine built by cliff dwellers atop the ruins of ancestral houses.

Alden Hayes, who excavated all these mesa-top sites except Two Raven House, referred to them as part of a "Badger House Community." Taken all together, and including the nearby cliff dwellings, they reflect a continuous occupation by people residing in the same locality that spanned roughly 650 years, or more than twenty-five to thirty generations, longer than European colonists have resided in the New World.

Ute Mountain Tribal Park

The Ute Mountain Ute Indian tribe has set aside 125,000 acres along the Mancos River to preserve both prehistoric Puebloan ruins and Ute tribal historic sites. Before establishment of the park, Earl H. Morris conducted the first professional work here in Lion Canyon in 1913 and 1915. He named Eagle Nest

2-68. The late Pueblo III kiva, constructed in 1257, at the Badger House Settlement on Wetherill Mesa. It has eight stone masonry pilasters resting on a banquette to support its roof, a deep southern recess above the ventilator tunnel, a masonry wall stub air deflector, a circular stone-lined hearth, a sipapu, and one masonry-lined floor vault. A forty-one-foot-long tunnel linked this kiva to a tower at the southwest corner of a Pueblo III room block.

House and Ruin No. 5. During the mid-1970s, David A. Breternitz directed additional excavations here through the University of Colorado Mesa Verde Research Center. The U.S. National Park Service then stabilized the ruins for the Ute tribe.

Ute Mountain Tribal Park encompasses the Mancos River canyon where it cuts through the Mesa Verde, plus the lower canyons that drain southward out of Mesa Verde National Park, and tributary canyons that enter the Mancos River canyon from the south. The cliff dwellings in Johnson and Lion canyons to the south of the Mancos River lie only a few miles southeast of the major ruins in Mesa Verde National Park (see fig. 2-1), and they probably belong to those Pueblo III settlements.

The road into the tribal park passes by several other Puebloan ruins and some interesting rock art at Kiva Point. Mancos River canyon also contains several cabins once occupied by Utes and some scenes they painted on the rock cliffs. Visitors to any of these sites require an approved Ute Mountain Tribal Park guide, arranged through park headquarters at Towaoc, to make this trip.

The Johnson-Lion Canyon complex contains several Pueblo III cliff dwellings: Fortified House, Tree House, Lion House, Morris No. 5, and Eagle

Nest House. Tree-ring studies indicate two phases of construction for the buildings, one from about 1130 until 1160 and again from 1195 until about 1240. Because the second building phase had completely dismantled the earlier buildings and used the materials to build the later buildings, we cannot know whether the earlier buildings had once stood on the mesa top or in the overhangs. The latest tree-ring dates mark construction in 1240 and 1241, almost forty years before the latest construction dates from the Mesa Verde park sites.

The Puebloans who inhabited Johnson and Lion canyons probably belonged to the general Mesa Verde population. Together, these five sites would have constituted only one village of some 200 to 250 people, and like the Balcony House Group, the Square Tower–Little Long House Group, and the Spruce Tree House Group, they may have been an outlying village of the Cliff-Fewkes Canyon Settlement.

Tree House sits in the verdant head of a small canyon off Lion Canyon. It has a towerlike multistory building built like a wasp nest against the canyon wall with both a T-shaped doorway and a rectangular one (fig. 2-70). This room block reaches up to additional rooms on the ledge above.

Lion House lies next along the trail down the canyon. It has one stub wall still standing, showing that originally three-story rooms once stood there (fig. 2-71). At the time of its abandonment, Lion House had seven kivas and more than forty-five rooms (fig. 2-72).

2-69. The stabilized Pueblo III tower at Badger House on Wetherill Mesa on the Mesa Verde has an opening in its floor leading into a tunnel that links it to a late Pueblo III kiva forty-one feet away. This kiva-tower complex seems to represent a ceremonial shrine erected on or next to the ruins of older habitation units in which, perhaps, the ancestors of these structures' builders once lived.

2-70. Tree House, a picturesque late Pueblo III (1200s) cliff dwelling near the head of Lion Canyon in Ute Mountain Tribal Park. The multistory building contains both rectangular and T-shaped doorways.

Morris No. 5, the next cliff dwelling, has only ruins of a few standing walls on two levels (fig. 2-73). An excavated kiva reveals stone pilasters that once supported a cribbed roof, a fire pit, and a floor-level ventilating system with a curved deflector wall. Numerous axe head and bone awl sharpening grooves have been incised into exposed rock surfaces.

These ruins had been discovered by the Wetherill brothers—Richard, John, Al, Clayton, and Win—who did some early collecting shortly after discovery. They left their mark by carving "Wetherill" into one of the large boulders. Here, they found several well-preserved human mummies, one of which had been cut in two across its abdomen and then sewn back together.

Eagle Nest House is the most spectacular ruin in the Ute Mountain Tribal Park. The long masonry building on the upper level remains substantially intact. A series of poles extending outward from the building walls (fig. 2-74) originally supported a balcony similar to the one in Balcony House in Mesa Verde National Park.

Fortified House sits just beneath the cliff top on the south side of Lion Canyon. Its principle interest stems from the water impoundment built into the bedrock sandstone surface to furnish domestic water and to enhance the spring below.

The Montezuma Valley

This broad canyon-incised valley stretches northwestward from the Mesa Verde in southwestern Colorado to the Abajo Mountains and Comb Ridge in southeastern Utah. Now, as during prehistoric times, it represents rich, well-watered, dryland farming country. The valley covers twenty-five hundred square miles drained by intermittent stream systems of the McElmo, Yellow Jacket, Montezuma, Recapture, and Cottonwood washes, all of which enter the San Juan River from the north.

2-72. Lion House belonged to a Puebloan community of cliff dwellings built and occupied during the middle 1200s along the north side of Lion Canyon, an offshoot of Johnson Canyon in the Ute Mountain Tribal Park. In addition to Lion House, the settlement included Tree House, Morris No. 5, and Eagle Nest House, and it housed some 250 people.

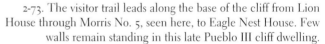

2-73. The visitor trail leads along the base of the cliff from Lion House through Morris No. 5, seen here, to Eagle Nest House. Few walls remain standing in this late Pueblo III cliff dwelling.

2-71. A three-story wall standing in Lion House in Lion Canyon in the Ute Mountain Tribal Park. Construction dates fall between 1195 and 1230 with several reused timbers dating from 1130 to 1160. The upper-story room shows a difference in masonry wall construction from the ones below it.

2-74. The extended beams visible along the front of the buildings in Eagle Nest House once supported a narrow balcony fronting the upper rooms. This late Pueblo III cliff dwelling perches on the edge of a sheer cliff, but no guard rails or protective walls provided safety for small children.

The Montezuma Valley Puebloans have not been well known because few ruins here have been excavated and stabilized for visitors. Yet some thirty thousand people inhabited this broad valley during the 1100s and 1200s. The Mesa Verdeans, scratching a living from the thinner soils on their mesa tops, must have appeared as poor relations by comparison with the Montezuma Valley folk.

A series of eight Classic Pueblo III towns, verging on crossing the threshold into the smallest of urban settlements, marks the Montezuma Valley as an important population center of the Puebloans. Any settlement beyond twenty-five hundred to three thousand residents would need to restructure its society in order to confront the conflicts of the larger community. Here, as elsewhere in Pueblo-land, the people seem to have chosen to hold the population of any one town below three thousand inhabitants.

As viewed from the Mesa Verde's north cliffs, these towns from left to right are: Yucca House at the base of Ute Mountain, Mud Springs in the head of McElmo Canyon, Sand Canyon and Goodman Point ruins on the elevated Goodman Point, and Wilson, Lowry, Lancaster, and Yellow Jacket ruins just to the right of Abajo Mountain. With their associated rural populations and broad cultivated lands, these Pueblo communities, housing close to thirty thousand people, would have made an imposing sight to an onlooker on the Mesa Verde (fig. 2-75). Yucca House forms the center of its own undeveloped national monument; Goodman Point Ruin is an undeveloped, detached unit of Hovenweep National Monument; while both Lowry Ruins and Sand Canyon Pueblo have been incorporated into the newly created Canyons of the Ancients National Monument.

Few traces of pre-Puebloan Archaic and Basket Maker II occupations in the valley have been found. But by the seventh century, Basket Maker III people resided in most of the valley in villages such as the Gilliland and Payne sites enclosed within wooden palisades, and in parts of the Dolores River valley to the east.

Joe Ben Wheat from the Colorado State Museum has excavated a large pithouse near Yellow Jacket, similar to the proto–great kivas from Shabik'eshchee and the Mesa Verde. Pueblo I villages, varying considerably in size, have been excavated across the Montezuma Valley from the Dolores River valley on the northeastern frontier to Alkali Ridge and White Mesa near the western edge. The Dolores Archaeological Project has uncovered great kivas in the Dolores River valley at Grass Mesa and Singing Shelter, while additional unexcavated ones associated with Pueblo I sites are known from Nancy Patterson Village in Montezuma Canyon and from Comb Ridge where the San Juan River cuts across it. The Duckfoot Site west of Cortez represents the typical modular layout found in Pueblo I settlements.

By Pueblo II, in the tenth century, newly developing patterns of social and political organization began to exert themselves in the layout of towns and villages. These patterns can best be seen in the successive Classic Pueblo III settlements, most of which grew out of and overlie their earlier beginnings in Pueblo I and II.

The eight towns along its eastern edge, where the best farming conditions exist today, dominated Pueblo III life in the Montezuma Valley. The largest, Yellow Jacket Ruin, housed as many people as inhabited all of the cliff dwellings of the Mesa Verde. Each town had plazas and either a great kiva, as at Lowry and Yellow Jacket, or a concentric wall structure, as at Sand Canyon and Mud Springs, or sometimes both.

Concentric wall structures were buildings of two or three concentric walls forming either a circular or D-shaped plan surrounding a central above-ground kiva or open space containing kivas. Examples include the excavated triwall structures at Aztec Ruin and Pueblo del Arroyo, the horseshoe houses at

2-75. A Puebloan looking northwestward from Mesa Verde's north rim about eight hundred years ago would see the Montezuma Valley teeming with some thirty thousand inhabitants. About half of them lived in the eight towns marked by plumes of smoke from cooking fires (left to right): Yucca House at the base of Ute Mountain at the left, Mud Springs at the head of McElmo Canyon in the center, Sand Canyon and Goodman Point ruins on the high north side of McElmo Canyon, and Wilson, Lowry, Lancaster, and Yellow Jacket ruins in front of the Abajo Mountains that dominate the horizon in Utah. (Watercolor painting by Joan Foth.)

2-76. Aerial view of the Yellow Jacket Ruin, the largest Pueblo III (1100–1300) town in the Montezuma Valley, home to some twenty-five to twenty-seven hundred persons. The settlement extends for nearly half a mile from the edge of the plowed field at lower left on the north to the junction of the two branches of Yellow Jacket Canyon at upper right on the south. A central avenue passes from the great kiva near the north house to a south plaza, bisecting many east-west rows of houses marked by mounds and kiva depressions. The yellow-green vegetation next to the blue-green sagebrush at center left represents an artificial water reservoir.

Hovenweep, and the D-shaped Sun Temple at Mesa Verde. Such structures probably functioned in ways analogous to the functions of great kivas on behalf of the inhabitants of both the town and its nearby villages and hamlets.

In addition to the rituals, the inhabitants of each town shared a managed water supply, usually including an artificial reservoir, and surrounding farmlands. Internal streets provided communication among segments of the community, and they probably continued as roads beyond the town limits to surrounding villages, resource areas, and shrines. A cluster of pottery-firing kilns has been located on a mesa point at the western end of the hinterland belonging to the Yellow Jacket community.

Yellow Jacket Ruin, the largest town, probably housed around twenty-seven hundred people in some forty-one separate buildings (figs. 2-76 and 2-77). Its layout included at least two and possibly four plazas, a central north-south avenue, crossing streets or lanes, about 165 kin-group kivas, a great kiva, an apparent biwalled tower, six shrines, and an artificial reservoir to impound water above a spring. Natural farmland surrounds the settlement. The surrounding countryside contains some eight villages of 200–250 inhabitants each, numerous small hamlets, dozens of pottery kilns located away from the villages, and several apparently purely religious structures. At least one roadway segment passes between two of the villages.

The **Lowry Ruin** complex, now incorporated into the Canyons of the Ancients National Monument, has some provisions for visitation. The excavated portion of Lowry—a room block and great kiva—lies at the end of a gravel road about nine miles west of Pleasant View, Colorado. The ruin occupies a sort of oasis in the piñon-juniper woods surrounded by presently cultivated fields, telling us that these Puebloans had settled in fertile country good for farming.

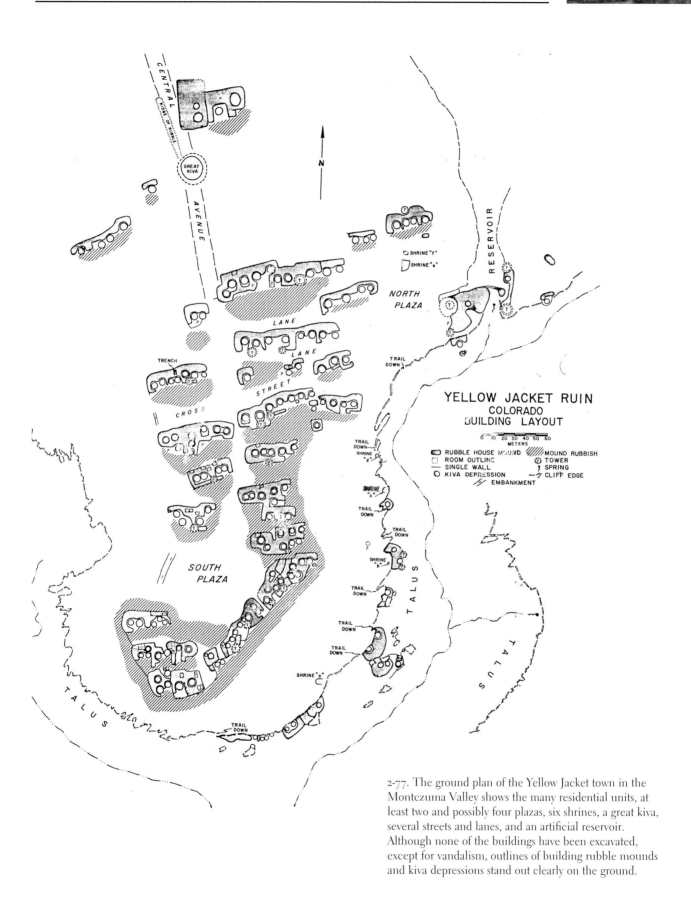

YELLOW JACKET RUIN
COLORADO
BUILDING LAYOUT

```
          0  10  20  30  40  50  60
                METERS
```

▦ RUBBLE HOUSE MOUND	▨ MOUND RUBBISH
▢ ROOM OUTLINE	⊛ TOWER
— SINGLE WALL	⌇ SPRING
○ KIVA DEPRESSION	⌐ CLIFF EDGE
	╱ EMBANKMENT

2-77. The ground plan of the Yellow Jacket town in the Montezuma Valley shows the many residential units, at least two and possibly four plazas, six shrines, a great kiva, several streets and lanes, and an artificial reservoir. Although none of the buildings have been excavated, except for vandalism, outlines of building rubble mounds and kiva depressions stand out clearly on the ground.

2-78. The excavation of Lowry Pueblo and great kiva by Paul S. Martin in the 1930s exposed a building of more than fifty rooms with eight kin-group kivas, only five of which may have been in use at any one time. Construction began here about 1090 and continued well into 1100s. Older rooms display Chacoan architectural characteristics, but all later building typifies Montezuma Valley construction. A kin-group kiva underneath the protective roof retains on its plastered wall portions of a painted mural in a geometric design commonly found on Mesa Verde–style pottery vessels. The excavated pueblo forms the west wing of the northwest housing block that encloses an open plaza where the great kiva stood (see also fig. 1-53). (Photograph taken with the assistance of John Q. Royce.)

2-79. An interior view of the large kin-group kiva in the south end of Lowry Pueblo demonstrates why people did not sit on kiva banquettes. Instead, three sets of wooden poles stretched between each pair of roof supporting pilasters to create extra storage space. A pottery-style geometric design painted in white on the gray plaster lining the lower kiva walls may be seen below the banquette.

Dr. Paul S. Martin, from the Field Museum of Natural History in Chicago, excavated this pueblo unit and the great kiva from 1930 through 1934 (fig. 2-78). He recognized at least thirty-seven ground-floor rooms but estimated as many as fifty may once have been present. Probably second- and third-story rooms would bring the total to between sixty-five and eighty rooms plus eight kivas, although only five can be seen now. However, various episodes of remodeling indicate not all rooms and kivas had been in use at any one time.

Tree-ring dates reveal that the earliest rooms and a then-detached kiva had been built in 1089–1090. The large size of several rooms and some aspects of masonry style resemble construction details found in Chaco Canyon sites, but the kivas contained typical local architectural features. The most extensive building spurt occurred between 1103 and 1120, all in the local Montezuma Valley style. Three small, subsequent additions brought the building to its final form. The excavated rooms and kivas have been repeatedly stabilized in modern times to protect them against weather and visitor wear.

The contrast between Chaco-style and local-style rooms may be seen in the former's much larger size—two to three times larger—and in the use of tabular pieces of sandstone fitted very closely together in the wall masonry. The local Mesa Verde–style rooms are smaller, the building blocks tend to be thicker and less evenly laid, and the thicker mud mortar spaces have usually been chinked with small sandstone spalls. The large kiva built within the room block near the south end retained a remarkably well-preserved mural painted on the plaster of its lower wall. The design resembles a typical pottery decoration. The triple sets of horizontal poles between pilasters reflect a local design feature probably to provide more storage space (fig. 2-79). Stabilizers have reroofed this kiva with a skylight, and they have opened a passage into the kiva's southern end to allow visitor access.

2-80. Lowry's great kiva measures forty-five feet in diameter below bench level and exhibits features typical of other great kivas: an encircling bench, four square stone masonry boxes for seating roof support columns, masonry floor vaults between the roof supports on east and west sides, an altar room attached to the north side, and an entry staircase. This building and the two plazas in the Lowry town probably saw religious ceremonies attended not only by inhabitants of the town itself but also by residents of surrounding villages and hamlets up to several miles away.

The Lowry great kiva became the first such structure to be excavated in Colorado. It is a circular, masonry-lined, partially subterranean building apparently designed for communal ritual activities (fig. 2-80). It measures forty-five feet in inside diameter, and it exhibits features typical of other great kivas from Chaco Canyon and the Northern San Juan regions: a central masonry firebox, two raised masonry floor vaults, four square seatings for roof-supporting columns, an encircling bench, north and south stairways, and a north altar room. A single tree-ring date suggests construction after 1106.

Lowry Pueblo itself represents only about 5 percent of the total domestic buildings that make up the second-largest Pueblo III town in the Montezuma Valley. This town of forty separate structures sprawled over nearly one square mile. Its twenty-four residential sites contained some 108 standardized modular pueblo units, each marked by a small kin-group kiva, totaling close to twelve hundred rooms and housing perhaps fifteen hundred to eighteen hundred persons. The housing blocks clustered into two distinct sectors on opposite sides of their common water supply in a manner similar to Taos and Zuni pueblos (see fig. 1-53).

Several features served the entire Lowry community. A spring in the canyon between the two housing sectors maintained a continual flow of water, supplemented by an artificial reservoir built on the canyon rim above it. A short distance downstream, three naturally formed permanent pools supplied additional water. Land suitable for farming surrounded the town on its west, north, and east sides. A shallow draw running south from Lowry Pueblo contains fertile soil within the confines of the town, and many stone-walled terraces allowed farming in the canyons to the south. Each of the two residential sectors had a plaza in which public portions of ceremonies could be performed. The Lowry great kiva occupied part of the northern plaza, and two of five known shrines stood in the southern plaza.

A series of at least three roadways connected various parts of the Lowry Settlement and led outside to surrounding villages, hamlets, and farmland. One of these roadway segments appears as a thirty-foot-wide shallow ditch leading southwestward from the north plaza between Lowry Pueblo and the great kiva. Even though it disappears in the adjacent cultivated field, it heads directly toward a distant rock art panel and attendant kivas.

While most of the visible features of the Lowry Settlement belong to the Pueblo III stage (1100–1300), some traces of earlier Pueblo I (750–900) and Pueblo II (900–1100) construction may be observed beneath them. Thus this town bears

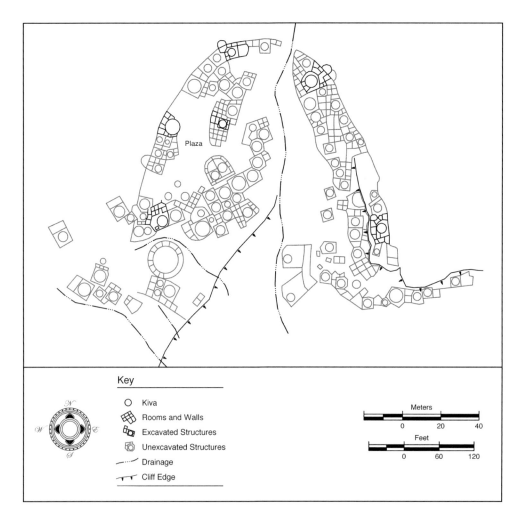

2-81. The ground plan of Sand Canyon Ruin in the recently designated Canyons of the Ancients National Monument in southwestern Colorado, and one of the eight Pueblo III towns in the Montezuma Valley, reveals its horseshoelike layout along the canyon rim surrounding a spring, and suggesting a dual sociopolitical organization. The western sector contains both a great kiva and D-shaped biwall structure, and a site-enclosing wall arcs around the curved uphill boundaries of the town. (Drawing after Bradley 1992).

evidence for roughly four hundred or more years of occupancy.

Sand Canyon Pueblo

As one of the many Puebloan ruins now included within the Canyons of the Ancients National Monument in southwestern Colorado, the public may now visit Sand Canyon Pueblo, roughly twenty miles west of Cortez, Colorado. The rubble mounds here conceal an estimated minimum of 420 rooms,

approximately ninety kivas, fourteen towers, a D-shaped concentric wall structure enclosing two kivas, a great kiva, and an enclosed plaza. Many room blocks stood two or even three stories high.

Sand Canyon Pueblo occupies the north canyon rim, facing toward the south. Its layout resembles a huge capital D with the curved sides standing on the canyon rim and many of the buildings extending down the talus slopes below the rim (fig. 2-81). A stone masonry wall bounds the curved east, north, and west sides of the pueblo on the mesa top. A rapidly deepening canyon divides the pueblo into two parts of unequal size with a spring in the center of the settlement. This probably reflects a dual division in both social and political organization.

Between 1983 and 1993, archaeologists from the Crow Canyon Archaeological Center under the general direction of Bruce Bradley excavated six blocks of rooms and kivas, a portion of the great kiva, and part of one kiva in the D-shaped concentric wall structure. These excavated units have been filled back in to preserve the architecture from further deterioration.

Escalante and Dominguez Ruins

On the south bank of the Dolores River, north of Cortez, stand two small Pueblo III ruins thought to be the pueblos mentioned in the journals of the Franciscan priests Francisco Atanasio Domínguez and Silvestre Vélez de Escalante, who rode across the Montezuma Valley in 1776 in search of a passage from New Mexico to California. Escalante Ruin stands on top of the hill, while Dominguez Ruin lies at the foot of the hill next to the parking lot.

Their setting on the south rim of the Dolores River valley looking downstream to the north over what is now the McPhee Reservoir fits the journal description. Fray Escalante wrote: "On the 13th we made camp, both to allow the Padre to improve, and to take a bearing on the polar elevation of this site and meadow of El Rio de los Dolores where we found ourselves. . . . Upon an elevation of the river's south side, there was in ancient times a small settlement of the same type as those of the Indians of New Mexico."

Escalante is the larger of the two ruins. It essentially consists of a unit pueblo of rooms arranged around one kiva. Double rows of rooms lie on the west, north, and east sides, with a single row on the south (fig. 2-82). Seven of an estimated twenty to

2-82. Escalante Ruin sits atop a hill overlooking the Dolores River valley, now beneath the waters of McPhee Reservoir. Two Franciscan priests, Francisco Domínguez and Silvestre Vélez de Escalante, passed this way in 1776 and mentioned two ruins in such a setting. This Pueblo III site features double rows of rooms built around one kiva that exhibit some Chacoan features such as a few large rooms and the kiva's floor-level recess and subfloor ventilator. The site may be visited by an easy trail from the Anasazi Heritage Center near Dolores, Colorado.

twenty-five rooms have been excavated and stabilized. Several of these display the larger Chacoan size. The kiva displays several Chacoan features: a low banquette with floor-level shallow southern recess, eight low masonry pilasters, a subfloor ventilator, and one crude floor vault (fig. 2-83). The masonry of both the rooms and the kiva plus the pottery fit the Northern San Juan styles rather than those of Chaco.

The Dominguez Ruin, at the foot of the hill, represents one of several small sites around the hill's base. It consisted of only four rooms and a kiva (fig. 2-84). A burial found in one of the rooms contained the remains of a woman interred with two local pottery vessels and various items of jewelry including a shell frog with turquoise inlay and a pair of round shell ear pendants with turquoise and jet inlay (see fig. 1-22), a rectangular pendant with turquoise and shell inlay

2-83. The kiva at Escalante Ruin displays some Chacoan features including eight low, masonry pilasters (but without log stubs), a floor-level recess, and a subfloor ventilator tunnel. However, the masonry and general construction more closely fit the Mesa Verde style.

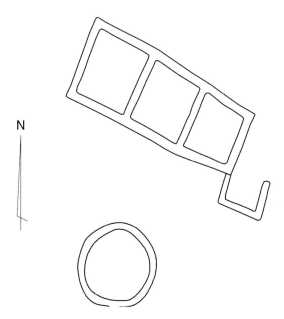

N

(see fig. 1-22), and a string of turquoise and shale beads. Pueblo III burials in the Montezuma Valley rarely contain so much fine jewelry. Both ruins can be visited through the Anasazi Heritage Center adjacent to the Dominguez Ruin. This center/museum houses many of the objects excavated from these and other nearby sites including those salvaged from the McPhee Reservoir.

Additional villages and other small settlements east and north of Cortez, Colorado, either represent rural villages associated with the larger towns, or they may form a separate cluster in themselves. Undoubtedly, more will be identified as investigations progress throughout the valley.

Duckfoot Site

The Crow Canyon Archaeological Center of Cortez, Colorado, conducted excavations during 1983–1984 at Duckfoot, located about five miles west of Cortez. It comprised a block of seventeen rooms, three pithouses, and a refuse pile belonging to the Pueblo I stage in the late 800s (fig. 2-85).

The rooms formed a double row arcing roughly east-west, with nine storage rooms along the north row and six larger living rooms making up the south row. Two additional storerooms had been squeezed between two of the living spaces in the south row. Three pithouses occupied the space to the south about fifteen feet away (fig. 2-86).

The Duckfoot inhabitants employed both jacal construction and very rough stone masonry in building

2-84. Plan of the Dominguez Ruin, at the foot of the hill below Escalante Ruin, represents but one of several small sites around the base of the hill that probably belonged to the same settlement with the Pueblo III Escalante Ruin. A woman interred here in a vacant room had an unusually large amount of jewelry with her. Some archaeologists have cited this case as evidence for an elite class, but quantities of personal jewelry or even pottery vessels in graves, by themselves, do not evoke the symbolism associated with elite class burials elsewhere in the ancient world.

2-85. The Pueblo I Duckfoot Site in the Montezuma Valley, occupied during the late 800s, while being excavated by the Crow Canyon Archaeological Center near Cortez in 1984.

2-86. Duckfoot Site rooms formed an east-west row with storage rooms on the north side of the six living rooms, and with three pithouses, the forerunners of kivas, in the plaza area to the south. Each living room contained a hearth and combined with associated storage rooms and outdoor work space to make up a household suite. An adjacent pair of suites shared a pithouse to form one of the three modular residence units at this Pueblo I site.

their houses. Most room walls had been built by plastering mud over a framework of branches woven horizontally among upright wooden posts with large upright sandstone slabs lining the wall bases. On the other hand, inhabitants of the central third of the rooms laid up sandstone blocks in profuse mud mortar as crude masonry walls. Some walls exhibited a combination of these two techniques. Most likely, such variation reflected the preferences of individual builders.

The central block of two living rooms and five smaller storerooms belonged to the central pithouse, while the eastern and western blocks, each including two living rooms and three storerooms, were associated with the eastern and western pithouses, respectively. Presumably, the people occupying each such unit shared kinship and made up a small lineage or clan segment. Each of the six living rooms contained

a hearth and traces of food preparation activities, such as corn grinding stones, and most likely each housed a distinct household. Thus, Duckfoot would have housed six households organized into three lineage or clan segments of two households each.

Besides this clear picture of Pueblo I society, the excavations of Duckfoot uncovered traces of a prehistoric drama. Many of the rooms, including the western pithouse, had burned. In this pithouse, a large quantity of household equipment including over twenty pottery vessels (fig. 2-87) and a complete corn grinding outfit—a metate propped up on river cobbles and a mano with two pottery platters to catch the meal—had been buried by the collapsing roof. Clearly this structure had been inhabited up to the moment fire consumed it, for the collapsed burned roof also smothered two human skeletons, one

2-87. Plain gray and neck-banded utilitarian pottery vessels, probably used for cooking and for storage of food and water, rested along the wall of this burned Pueblo I pithouse at the Duckfoot Site in the Montezuma Valley.

sprawled across the hearth (see fig. 1-88) and the other along the north wall (see fig. 1-87). Neither had been accorded a proper Puebloan burial, and both had died violently. The burning roof material had charred very small portions of their bones, indicating they still retained flesh when the burning occurred. Both bodies lay atop some charred poles with the knee of one elevated by the debris below.

How did these two people die? Had they been trapped inside the pithouse when it burned, unable to escape? Had they been killed outside and thrown into the burning pit? Could this have been a prehistoric murder or the devastation of an enemy raiding party? The answers will probably never be known, but we do know that these bodies provide evidence of violence that occurred twelve hundred years ago.

Hovenweep

Introduction

Although the large-sized towns do not occur in the central and western portions of the Montezuma Valley, the villages found there tend to cluster into larger settlements. The Hovenweep sites offer a good example, all within easy walking distance of one another and the central Square Tower Group. Great kivas do not occur here, but smaller D-shaped concentric wall structures, called horseshoe houses, probably served similar functions.

Hovenweep includes clusters of masonry-walled buildings concentrated around heads of shallow, arid canyons along the Colorado-Utah border about forty-five miles west of Cortez, Colorado (fig. 2-88). They fit into the Northern San Juan, Montezuma Valley Pueblo III settlement pattern between 1100 and 1300. Prior to 1100, the Indians of the Hovenweep district lived in clusters of unit pueblos on the mesa tops. Then for whatever reason, they moved to the heads of the canyons during Pueblo III. This same phenomenon took place at about the same time at Mesa Verde, Kayenta, and Canyon de Chelly.

During the 1920s, Jesse Walter Fewkes partially excavated several of the Hovenweep sites. However, he confined his work to the larger, more visible structures such as Hovenweep Castle and Hovenweep House, and he did not excavate or stabilize smaller habitation sites. He assigned names such as "Hovenweep Castle," "Stronghold House," and "Square Tower" by what each ruined building resembled in his mind, not for how they had been used. Hovenweep Castle belonged to a residential pueblo, and was not a castle. Around the visible buildings on the canyon edges are sagebrush-covered rubble piles that outline the pueblos that once flourished during Pueblo III times.

The ruins in Square Tower and Ruin canyons near the Hovenweep National Monument ranger station form the center of the Hovenweep villages. Cutthroat Castle, Hackberry, Horseshoe, and Holly ruins lie to the northeast, with the Cajon ruins to the southwest. All occupy canyon heads along the north side of Hovenweep Canyon that cut into the south side of Cajon Mesa, and all may be visited. Additional similar ruins at Cannonball and Pedro Point lie to the

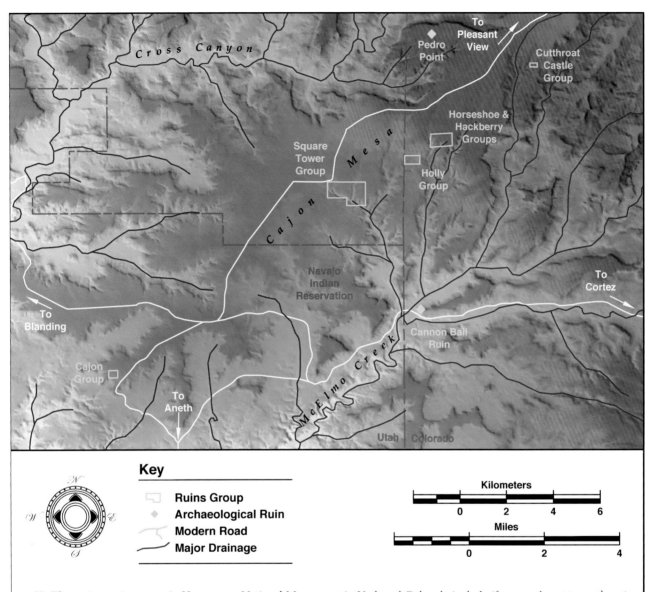

Key

◻ Ruins Group
◆ Archaeological Ruin
⌇ Modern Road
— Major Drainage

Kilometers
0   2   4   6

Miles
0   2   4

2-88. The various ruin groups in Hovenweep National Monument in Utah and Colorado include (from southwest to northeast) Cajon, Square Tower/Ruin Canyon (monument headquarters), Holly, Horseshoe, Hackberry, and Cutthroat. A seventh group on Goodman Point lies far to the east.

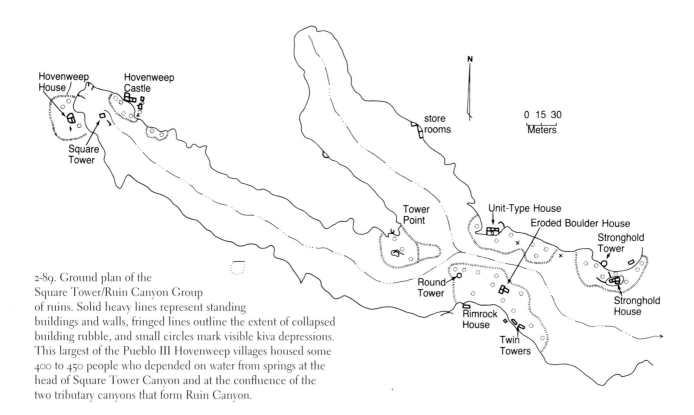

2-89. Ground plan of the
Square Tower/Ruin Canyon Group
of ruins. Solid heavy lines represent standing
buildings and walls, fringed lines outline the extent of collapsed
building rubble, and small circles mark visible kiva depressions.
This largest of the Pueblo III Hovenweep villages housed some
400 to 450 people who depended on water from springs at the
head of Square Tower Canyon and at the confluence of the
two tributary canyons that form Ruin Canyon.

south and north respectively. Because of the limited excavations and difficulties in counting kivas, it is difficult to estimate population accurately, but from the sizes of the pueblos and the number of ceremonial buildings, the Hovenweep group of sites probably once housed twenty-five hundred or more people.

Each village centered around a spring located in a canyon head. They all utilized similar village layouts and construction techniques, and all were located within relatively easy walking distance of one another. None had a great kiva, but each one did have a ceremonial tower or a horseshoe building—a D-shaped structure of two concentric walls around a central kiva in the same style as the Sun Temple on the Mesa Verde.

The population and ceremonial center for the Hovenweep villages probably lay in the Ruin Canyon complex comprising the Square Tower, Tower Point, Twin Towers, and Stronghold House ruin groups.

These buildings perched on both canyon rims and the talus slopes below. Mesa Verde–style architecture and masonry and the predominance of Mesa Verde–style pottery at all the villages indicate that these people participated in the Northern San Juan–Mesa Verde cultural pattern. They had descended from earlier Puebloan peoples who had inhabited the Montezuma Valley from at least Basket Maker times. Then, like the other Puebloans of the San Juan River drainage, these people abandoned their homes, villages, and farms during the very late 1200s and moved southeastward and southward, apparently to the Rio Grande and Little Colorado River regions.

Ruin Canyon Group

This group of ruins concentrates where two smaller canyons join to form the main canyon (fig. 2-89). Here, several lush trees betray the potential existence of subsurface water (fig 2-90). The **Square Tower**

2-90. Within the upper Ruin Canyon complex at Hovenweep National Monument, the greatest cluster of ruined buildings occupies the lower left quadrant of the photograph from Tower Point (between the two canyon forks) past Rimrock House, Eroded Boulder House, and Twin Towers on the left and past Unit-Type and Stronghold houses on the right. Nearly thirty kin-group kivas lie scattered along the slopes on both sides of this canyon among the ruins of many additional stone masonry housing units. At the head of the longer lefthand fork stand the Square Tower (for which the group is named), Hovenweep House, and Hovenweep Castle along with another eleven kivas. A number of granaries tucked beneath ledges in the cliffs and rainwater check dams lie scattered about among the main residences.

ruin subgroup surrounds a very strong spring in the head of the longer tributary canyon to the west. Square Tower itself, more or less the center of this subgroup, sits on a large sandstone boulder in the bottom of the canyon. It originally stood three stories high (fig. 2-91). Its masonry of well-dressed sandstone blocks fits the Mesa Verde–Montezuma Valley style, and a keyhole doorway faces down canyon. Some of the smaller openings in the walls once held ceiling beams, while others between floor levels seem to have been lookout holes.

Towers, both round and square, appear almost exclusively in the Northern San Juan Region. Few occupy positions where they could effectively serve as lookouts or defensive structures. Most have been built into room blocks, and they often associate with adjacent kivas, to which many were linked by tunnels. Several, including Square Tower, stand in canyon bottoms where they would be virtually useless for defensive observation. Hence, archaeologists believe these towers served a more ceremonial function, some related to their nearby kivas, others related to other features. Square Tower at Hovenweep stands in proximity to the strong spring that must have supplied water to the residents of the nearby pueblos.

Remnants of a dam that would have captured rainwater runoff can still be seen on the canyon rim above

2-91. The Square Tower, constructed of sandstone block masonry, rises two stories high from its foundation on a sandstone boulder in the floor of the canyon near the headquarters of Hovenweep National Monument. Such a location would not serve a protective purpose, but it does lie just below the canyon's most productive spring.

2-92. At Hovenweep Castle, next to the head of Square Tower Canyon, the standing walls on the cliff edge represent only the best-preserved portion of the main living quarters for this ruin group.

2-93. Square Tower Canyon with Square Tower in the foreground and the ruins of Hovenweep Castle standing on the cliff rim. Traces of six kin-group kivas and additional residential rooms appear on the talus slope immediately below the standing ruin.

2-94. Artist's reconstruction of the pueblo of which Hovenweep Castle formed only a part. Most of the buildings actually stood on the talus slope below the sandstone cliff and have collapsed into rubble. (Drawing by Lisa Ferguson after an original by Don Ripley.)

this spring. Once prevented from running off, the water would soak into the sandstone bedrock to reappear at the spring immediately below it. Two to three small rooms had been built on the narrow ledge above this spring. The Puebloans commonly employed such a device in canyon settings. Two other dams had been built in this Ruin Canyon settlement, one next to Rimrock House and the other on the south canyon rim halfway between Square Tower and Rimrock House.

Two residential pueblos flanked the Square Tower on opposite rims of the canyon. **Hovenweep Castle** perches on the north canyon rim with two- and three-story walls still standing (fig. 2-92). The standing walls have survived the ravages of time because solid bedrock provided their foundation. Many other one- and two-story rooms built next to them on the boulders and talus slope below have since collapsed into rubble (fig. 2-93). The largest and most complete building contains a D-shaped room and a doorway and several other openings through which some observers believe both solstices and equinoxes could have been observed. However, any opening toward the east would have the same capabilities.

One kiva depression among the ruined walls on top of the rimrock and six more in the rubble from the pueblo on the talus slope have been recognized by archaeologists. This combination of ruins and rubble inspired Don Ripley, a longtime ranger stationed at the nearby Hovenweep National Monument headquarters, to produce a drawing that reconstructed in his mind's eye what this building complex might have looked like during the thirteenth century (fig. 2-94). Together with the other structures around Square Tower, these buildings probably housed well over one hundred people.

Hovenweep House occupies the northwest rim of the canyon opposite Hovenweep Castle. The ruined walls rising out of the center of a rubble mound represent a typical horseshoe house (fig. 2-95), the

2-95. Hovenweep House, a slightly distorted horseshoe house, stands at the head of Square Tower Canyon. The scattered stones on either side of the standing building indicate fallen walls from once standing adjacent structures.

D-shaped ceremonial structure so common to the Hovenweep sites. The round, green spot with a tree in its center marks the reservoir formed by the dam above the spring in the canyon head.

Tower Point is the narrow canyon rim where the two smaller canyons join to form Ruin Canyon. The tower sitting on the junction point does suggest a function as a watchtower. It commands a view up the canyon toward the Square Tower Group and down the canyon toward the southeast past the Twin Towers ruins toward Ute Mountain in the distance. It stands alone on the canyon rim, but adjacent rubble indicates that now fallen buildings once ran right up to it as at Hovenweep Castle. We must remember that most of the canyon interior below the tower once had residential buildings, so this tower probably served a ceremonial function similar to that of Square Tower.

From Tower Point, the visitor can visualize how the canyon looked during the 1200s. Within the

2-97. The Twin Towers in the Ruin Canyon Group of Hovenweep National Monument. A separation of the two sandstone boulders upon which they stand dictated the separation of these two-story buildings, and their curved walls conform to the shapes of the foundation rocks. Such a solid footing has helped their walls survive centuries of weathering.

2-96. Rimrock House (on the canyon rim) and Eroded Boulder House (beneath the boulder overhang) stand among the rubble from many fallen buildings as testimony to the sizeable masonry village that existed at the canyon junction below Tower Point about eight hundred years ago. The rubble atop Eroded Boulder House derives from other buildings farther up the slope.

canyon on the south talus slope stands **Round Tower**. It is surrounded by rubble, including at least three kiva depressions, demonstrating its association with residential rooms, even though the tower itself probably had a ceremonial function. Beyond Round Tower in the middle of the slope lies **Eroded Boulder House**, near which the villagers had inscribed some rock art figures—a spiral and several geometric forms. The probably residential **Rimrock House**, on the south rim of the canyon, would have overlooked the buildings below (fig. 2-96).

Beyond that on boulders split off the canyon rim stand the **Twin Towers**. Each of the two-story, ovoid-shaped buildings had been constructed on a separate boulder (fig. 2-97). Together they contained sixteen rooms. The sagebrush-covered rubble surrounding all these buildings extends from the canyon rim down almost to the canyon bottom, indicating the extent of the Puebloan houses. The eleven or more kiva depressions among this rubble indicate a sizeable residential area.

Across the canyon from Twin Towers, another pueblo unit labeled **Unit-Type House** sits on the canyon rim. This excavated and stabilized building followed the typical unit pueblo design of the Mesa Verde and Montezuma Valley—a block of rooms

2-98. Unit-Type House, near the junction of the two heads of Ruin Canyon, consists of eight to twelve rooms surrounding a kin-group kiva on three sides. Because of the solid bedrock, the kiva had to be constructed on top of the rock surface, at the same level as the residential rooms around it, instead of below ground level. This building exemplifies the typical modular residence unit concept employed by the Puebloans in the arrangement of their living rooms, storerooms, and small kivas.

around a kiva at the south with trash dumped to the south down the slope (fig. 2-98). The kiva had a banquette and stone pilaster configuration with a floor ventilating system. On the talus slope below, six kiva depressions lie among the rubble formed by many other collapsed buildings indicating the one-time presence of a medium-size pueblo.

Still farther to the east of Unit-Type House on the north canyon rim, **Stronghold House** occupies the center of yet another pueblo. Although its walls seem to be isolated on top of a boulder away from the rim (fig. 2-99), they merely formed the top story of the rooms built up from the slope below where seven kiva depressions have been identified. On the rim nearby stands **Stronghold Tower**. Only a portion of this tower remains because the canyon side of the tower had been constructed on top of a log that bridged a crevice through which persons could descend into the canyon. When the log rotted away, more than half the tower fell into the canyon.

When combined, the residential pueblos from Tower Point to Stronghold House, with at least twenty-seven discernable kiva depressions, apparently accommodated up to four hundred to five hundred inhabitants. Add to that number the occupants of the Square Tower subgroup, and the total Ruin Canyon population would have been about five hundred to six hundred people, almost as many as in the Cliff-Fewkes Canyon Settlement on the Mesa Verde.

Holly Ruin Group

The Holly Group of Hovenweep ruins sits in the head of Keeley Canyon (fig. 2-100) about two miles northeast of the Ruin Canyon Group. The site encompasses five named buildings: Tilted Tower, Holly Tower, Curved Wall House, Great House, and Isolated Boulder House (fig. 2-101). **Tilted Tower** originally was a multiroom structure on the canyon rim, where part of the building may still be seen. Sometime after abandonment, the cliff edge on

2-99. Stronghold House stands at the southeastern-most limit of the Ruin Canyon Group. Construction of this building on the separated portion of bedrock sandstone ledge accounts for the remarkable preservation of its walls. Whether the builders intended this setting to be defensive cannot be known. They would have reached it via ladders from the tops of buildings built on the slopes adjacent to it.

2-100. Holly Group at Hovenweep National Monument with Holly House at the left, Holly Tower in the center, and Tilted Tower to the right. Additional ruins, including at least twelve kiva depressions, cover the talus slopes between the standing buildings. A stone and earth dam at the edge of the cliff behind Holly Tower fed the spring in the canyon head.

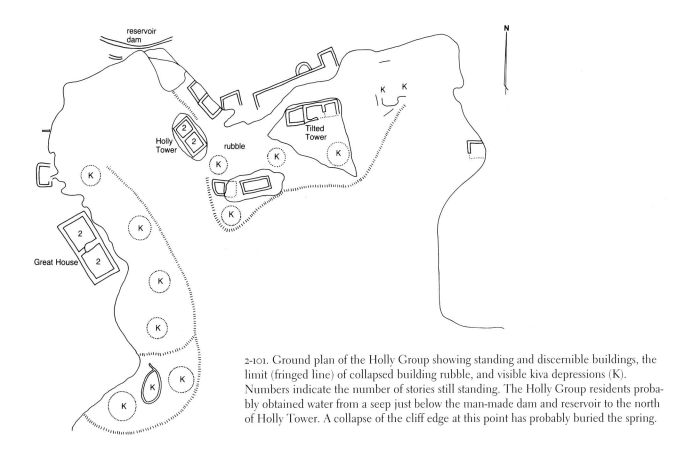

2-101. Ground plan of the Holly Group showing standing and discernible buildings, the limit (fringed line) of collapsed building rubble, and visible kiva depressions (K). Numbers indicate the number of stories still standing. The Holly Group residents probably obtained water from a seep just below the man-made dam and reservoir to the north of Holly Tower. A collapse of the cliff edge at this point has probably buried the spring.

which it had been constructed split off from the cliff, tilting the building so that much of its masonry fell into the canyon.

Isolated Boulder House perches alone on a turtleback boulder to the south of Tilted Tower. Its isolated position well above the collapsed buildings around it suggests a nonresidential function. The nearby room blocks on the canyon rim together with the rubble-covered talus slope around these buildings indicate the presence of a ruined pueblo building that had at least four kivas.

Similar room blocks, now marked by rubble with seven discernable kiva depressions, occupied the opposing talus slope below Curved Wall House and Great House. At the very head of the canyon, now fractured by blocks of the original cliff face, the inhabitants had built a dam to catch runoff rainwater to enhance

the flow of the spring directly below it. **Holly Tower** sits on a boulder just downstream from this spring and to the east side. This building with two ground-floor rooms still stands two full stories tall (fig. 2-102). An entrance doorway on its north side could be reached by a few toeholds cut into the boulder surface.

Great House and **Curved Wall House**, both two stories tall, stand on the west canyon rim. All the visible walls in this group had been laid two to three stones thick using sandstone blocks with carefully pecked faces in typical Mesa Verde style. The stones in the outer wall face of Curved Wall House had been faced to fit the curve of the exterior wall that encircled its rectangular interior, creating an exterior towerlike appearance. A tunnel led out of the bottom through a crack in the rimrock to the buildings on the slopes below. All together, the buildings of the

2-102. The two-story rectangular tower at the Holly Group was erected on top of a sandstone boulder in the center of the small canyon head where it could be reached by climbing a set of toeholds cut into the rock itself. The building fits very closely the limits fixed by its foundation, and it rises gracefully amid the structures of the group around it. As such, it represents one of the finest examples of Montezuma Valley architecture.

2-103. The Horseshoe House in the Horseshoe Group at Hovenweep National Monument consists of a central kiva surrounded on three sides by compartments formed by partitioning the space between the circular kiva wall and a partially enclosing curved concentric outer wall. These compartments could not be entered at floor level either from the kiva or from outside. A low stone dam runs along the cliff edge from in front of the building to the lower left of the picture. A kin-group kiva and several rooms occupy the overhang below Horseshoe House.

Holly Group once housed 120 to 150 people, slightly more than the Spruce Tree House community on the Mesa Verde.

The residents of the Holly Ruin Group had developed a device, located a short distance down canyon to the west of Great House, to record the sun's position at summer solstice and at the two equinoxes (see fig. 1-82), somewhat similar to the Sun Dagger site on Fajada Butte in Chaco Canyon. To accomplish this, they had pecked into the vertical surface of a large detached boulder beneath an overhang a complete three-ring concentric circle with a central dot on the northwest, a spiral on the southeast, and another spiral in the center (see fig. 1-83). At summer solstice, and for several days before and after, a horizontal shaft of early morning sunlight splits all three of these figures. No lighting effect happens at winter solstice.

Horseshoe Ruin Group

Horseshoe Ruin lies about one mile northeast of Holly. It comprised a small village housing only fifty to sixty people contemporaneous with and similar in style to Holly. Horseshoe House itself, a D-shaped structure with a kiva at its center and a curved exterior wall, stands as the most significant building (fig. 2-103). The space between the two curved walls had been divided into three compartments, but none had outside entries unless roof hatchways had been used. Seven loopholes in the outer wall permitted observations of the outside area to the north.

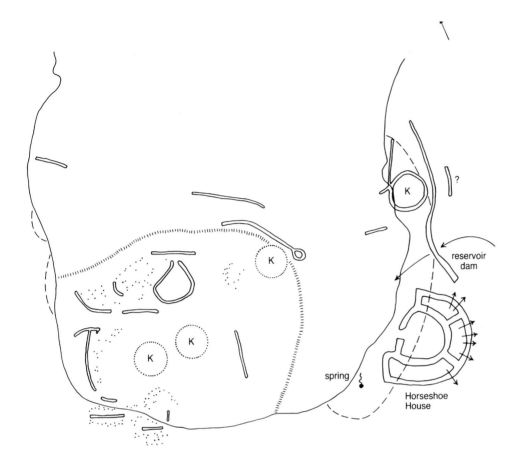

2-104. Ground plan of the Horseshoe Group showing the standing Horseshoe House, a kiva beneath the west end of the overhang, numerous terrace walls, and a small rubble mound containing three visible kiva depressions (K) outlined by the fringed line. The Horseshoe House stands directly above a good spring whose flow had been enhanced by the man-made dam and reservoir immediately west of the building. Arrows in Horseshoe House indicate "peep" holes through its outer wall.

A dam next to this horseshoe building created a reservoir near the canyon rim that fed rainwater into the strong spring beneath the wide overhang on top of which the Horseshoe House sat (fig. 2-104). Several painted handprints may be seen on the overhang's ceiling, and several rooms and a kiva occupy the far west end. The talus slope to the south opposite this overhang reveals traces of wall outlines and fallen building rubble plus three or four kiva depressions.

A well-preserved round tower (fig. 2-105) stands on the point between two short canyons about five hundred feet to the southwest of Horseshoe House. Even though its position would allow good oversight of the canyons below, this position also represents one of several kinds of places with spiritual significance to the

Puebloans. Cedar Tree Tower on the Mesa Verde also illustrates this significance.

Hackberry Ruin Group

Hackberry represents a medium-sized Pueblo III village supporting between 250 and 350 inhabitants, probably as large as Cliff Palace on the Mesa Verde. Two main pueblos faced each other on opposite sides of the head of the east branch of Hackberry Canyon, where two springs flowed (fig. 2-106). A third, smaller building, marked by a rubble mound with wall outlines showing, stood on the canyon rim above the springs. Stone walls attached to this third building formed a reservoir for rainwater runoff to feed into the springs beneath a large overhang in the canyon

2-105. This isolated tower stands on the bedrock sandstone point to the west of Horseshoe House, where it commands an excellent view of the canyons to the south. Despite this overlook, the two-story tower probably served a primarily ceremonial function rather than a defensive one.

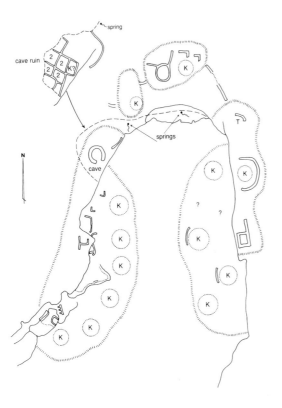

head. Prehistoric handprints also appear on the ceiling of this overhang.

Buildings had been built both on the canyon rim and on the talus slopes below them. The western pueblo's rubble mound reveals numerous wall outlines with at least six kiva depressions. The base of a tower stands on the canyon rim at its north end directly above the west end of the large overhang. Underneath the overhang at this point are the well-preserved walls of a possible kiva and about a dozen rooms, four of which occupy a second story (fig. 2-107). The eastern pueblo's rubble mound covers from five to seven kiva depressions plus the visible walls of one building on the canyon rim and the base of a tower at its north end.

The relative proximity of Hackberry and Horseshoe—less than three-tenths of a mile separates them—raises the question of whether the two formed part of a single settlement, each representing one part of a duality. On the other hand, one can sense a sort of duality in the opposing pueblos similar to that at the Ruin Canyon ruin complex. Might Horseshoe House then have functioned as an external subgroup similar to the role of the Square Tower subgroup at Ruin Canyon?

Cutthroat Ruin Group

One of the most interesting and spectacular of the outlying Hovenweep ruins may be **Cutthroat Castle** ruin. It lies on an offshoot of the Hovenweep Canyon about eight miles by road (seven miles in a straight line) northeast of the Hovenweep ranger station. This Pueblo III village straddles the canyon bottom where it

2-106. Ground plan of the Hackberry Group at Hovenweep National Monument indicating standing buildings and walls by solid double lines, the limits of collapsed building rubble by fringed lines, and visible kiva depressions by Ks. Several two-story rooms stood beneath the overhang west of the springs with numbers designating their discernible height.

bends sharply, with most of the buildings on the west side (fig. 2-108). A dam across the stream between the two main buildings would have backed up a small reservoir to supply water for the village inhabitants. Even today, subsurface water probably exists here since cottonwood trees grow along the streambed (fig. 2-109).

Cutthroat Castle sits on the west side of the stream on the very canyon rim. This three-story building includes a lower level on the talus slope with two stories roughly resembling a horseshoe building rising above it (fig. 2-110). A wall partially surrounded the central kiva. A passageway led from the upper part of the building through a split in the ledge to the small room block on the talus below. Two oval towers rise above the rubble mound to the west and south of the main building. Their sandstone building blocks have been faced by pecking to fit the rounded exterior surface (fig. 2-111).

Both here and on the east side opposite, sage-brush-covered rubble masks the once sizeable pueblos in which the people had lived. Wall outlines can be seen in both. Between nine and eleven kiva depressions show in the west pueblo and five in the

2-107. The overhang and one spring beneath the canyon head at the Hackberry Group. About twelve rooms and a possible kiva once stood at the far end of this shelter. The spring at the extreme right is one of two that provided water for the residents of the Hackberry Group.

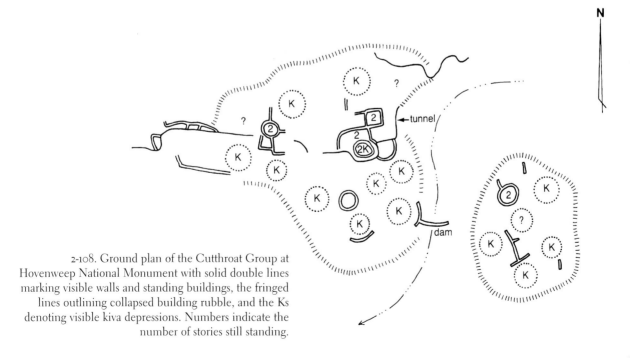

2-108. Ground plan of the Cutthroat Group at Hovenweep National Monument with solid double lines marking visible walls and standing buildings, the fringed lines outlining collapsed building rubble, and the Ks denoting visible kiva depressions. Numbers indicate the number of stories still standing.

2-109. In this aerial view of the Cutthroat Group, building rubble from collapsed houses and kin-group kivas covers virtually all of the ground in the photograph. The standing walls represent only a fraction of the structures that once stood here. The green trees in the center of the group mark the probable location of a spring that would have supplied water to the residents of this community.

2-110. The main preserved building at Cutthroat consists of a horseshoe house with several attached rooms on the right. A tunnel leads through a crevice in the bedrock floor of the kiva inside the horseshoe house to a two-story rounded room below the ledge.

2-111. One of the well-preserved round towers in the Cutthroat Group exhibits walls constructed with carefully pecked sandstone building blocks laid in mud mortar without small chinking stones between them.

2-112. This general view of the Cajon Group at Hovenweep National Monument shows a strong spring flowing out of the back of a cave in the head of the canyon with buildings flanking it on both sides. In addition to the standing structures and walls, piles of building rubble marking the remains of at least seven kin-group kivas and associated houses cover both talus slopes and the rim of the canyon. An earthen dam about one hundred yards upstream behind the cave trapped rainwater runoff that percolated through the bedrock sandstone to feed the spring. (Photograph taken with the assistance of John Q. Royce.)

east one. Another tower graces the eastern pueblo. Combined, these pueblos provided living quarters for some 150 to 200 inhabitants. Despite their uneven size, the two opposing pueblos could reflect a duality in the village's social organization.

Cajon Ruin Group

At Cajon, about eight and one-half miles southwest of the Ruin Canyon Group, the Puebloan people followed the same arrangement of buildings found at the other Hovenweep villages. A set of springs beneath the large overhang in the canyon head provided domestic water (fig. 2-112), while a dam upstream caught runoff rainwater to enhance the springs' flow. Flow from these springs continues strong today, and the local Navajo Indians water their horses in the outflow.

Here, too, a pair of sizeable Puebloan buildings, now largely reduced to piles of rubble, faced each other across the canyon (fig. 2-113). Two readily visible buildings stand on the northwestern canyon rim above the rubble-covered talus slope (fig. 2-114). In addition to the usual wall outlines and at least three visible kiva depressions, a round tower had been fitted onto parts of three fallen sandstone boulders (fig. 2-115).

The eastern pueblo also rested on the canyon rim and the talus below it. Many room outlines can be seen, some having stood two stories high. At least three kiva depressions appear on the talus slope behind a long retaining wall. Several rooms had been built under a narrow ledge beneath the rim. Here, the inhabitants had painted several pictographs: one a typical Mesa Verde pottery-style design with interlocking key-shaped frets connected to a rectangular scroll, and the other a four-legged creature with a birdlike body and a zigzag line. Probably eighty to one hundred people once lived here.

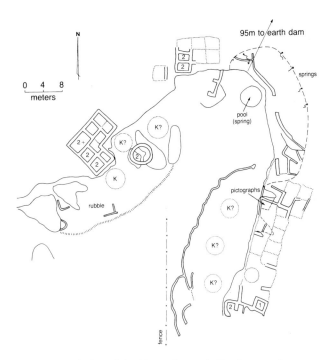

2-113. Ground plan of the Cajon Group indicating standing buildings and recognizable walls, including terrace walls, by solid double lines and dotted lines, seven visible kiva depressions by dotted circles and Ks, and limits of rubble mounds on both sides of the canyon by terrace walls or fringed lines. Numbers show how many stories still stand. The deep cave in the canyon head contains a very strong spring still used by the Navajo Indians to water stock.

Western Montezuma Valley Ruins

The San Juan County Economic Development Board in southeastern Utah has sponsored a map and guide to the many points of interest to visitors to be found in the county. This "Trail of the Ancients" not only features scenic and historic locations, but it also emphasizes many prehistoric Puebloan ruins (fig. 2-116), some of which have been partially excavated and stabilized while others have not. For the most part, visitors are permitted to visit these sites unattended.

An unpaved road leads southward from the Monticello-Blanding highway down most of the length of Montezuma Canyon past several rock art panels, Montezuma Village and Coal Bed Ruin, a very clearly defined hand- and toehold trail leading up the sandstone cliff (fig. 2-117), Three Kiva Pueblo, and the Nancy Patterson Village to Hatch Trading Post. Neither Montezuma Village nor Coal Bed Ruin have been excavated. However, the experienced visitor will recognize the distinctive piles of building rubble that indicate once standing buildings.

2-114. The northwestern cluster of buildings in the Cajon Group, all three of which reached at least two stories in height. Additional buildings, including three kin-group kivas, once stood among these visible structures but have since fallen into rubble.

During the 1980s, archaeologists from Brigham Young University mapped and conducted test excavations in the **Nancy Patterson Village**. They recognized a sizeable Pueblo III D-shaped pueblo with at least six visible kiva depressions and rubble heights that indicated some rooms had stood at least two and perhaps three stories high. Beneath this pueblo, test excavations revealed traces of Pueblo II occupation. Remains of a Pueblo I village with a dozen or more pithouse depressions covered most of the bluff top. Here, too, they identified a circular depression measuring fourteen meters (over forty-five feet) across that they believe represents a Pueblo I great kiva or similar community ceremonial structure. A few traces of both Pueblo II and III occupation also occur near one edge of the bluff top.

Three Kiva Pueblo sits in a broad floodplain area formed by the confluence of Montezuma Creek with a tributary canyon entering from the east. Its occupation ranges from A.D. 1000 to 1300. Masonry-walled rooms surround a round kiva, the roof of which archaeologists from Brigham Young University have restored (fig. 2-118). This ruin contains some fourteen rooms and a turkey pen with traces of two additional kivas. A set of three grinding bins are also visible.

Edge of the Cedars Ruin lies on the northwestern outskirts of Blanding, Utah. It has indications of six residence units with kivas dating to the Pueblo III stage with evidence of earlier Pueblo I and II buildings beneath. Several rooms and one kiva have been excavated and stabilized for visitors (fig. 2-119). An adjacent fine, small museum houses many objects that have been found in southeastern Utah over many past years, as well as exhibits on the historic Navajo and Ute Indians and Euro-American settlers.

The curious traveler may view several small cliff dwellings off the highways leading west and south out of Blanding. The **Little Westwater** or **Five Kiva Ruin** occupies a rock overhang in Little Westwater

2-115. Cajon Group builders constructed this circular tower on and around several large sandstone boulders on the slope of the northwestern side of the canyon. They carefully fitted their masonry blocks to the boulders to produce the desired round structure on a remarkably uneven surface. The space between the large boulders served as a lower-story room with one or more stories on top of that.

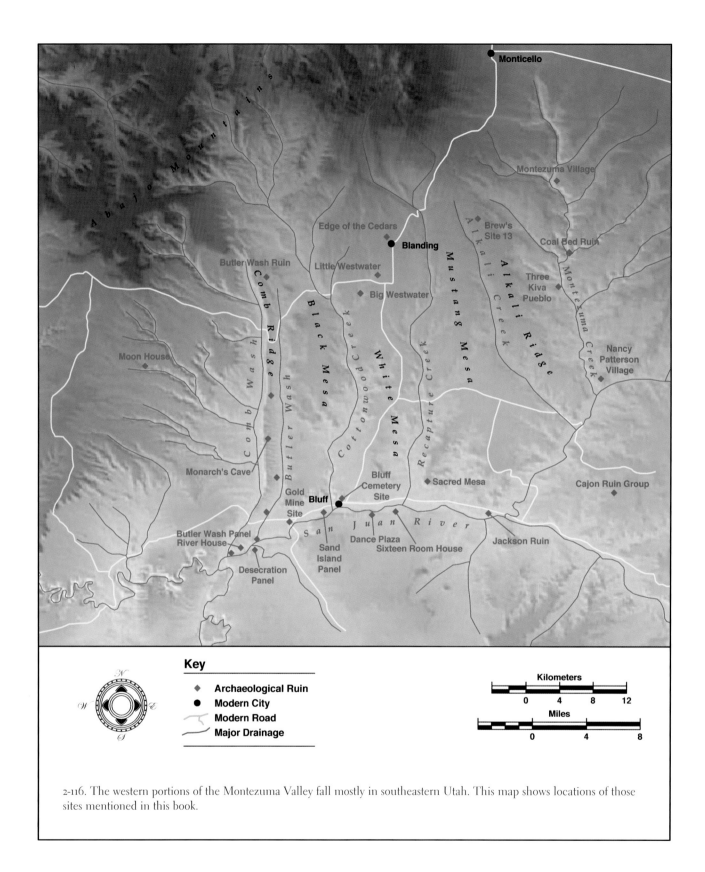

Key

◆ Archaeological Ruin
● Modern City
〰 Modern Road
〰 Major Drainage

Kilometers
0   4   8   12

Miles
0   4   8

2-116. The western portions of the Montezuma Valley fall mostly in southeastern Utah. This map shows locations of those sites mentioned in this book.

2-117. The Puebloans used toehold trails such as this one in the canyon of Montezuma Creek to travel up and down steep cliffs. The individual depressions carved out of the cliff face could barely accommodate the toes or hands of the traveler, who had to be confident of his/her balance.

2-118. Three Kiva Pueblo sits in the broad floodplain of Montezuma Creek where a tributary joins the main stream. It contains roughly fourteen rooms surrounding a circular kin-group kiva plus a turkey pen and evidence for two additional kivas, all dating from 1000 to 1300. Archaeologists from Brigham Young University have restored the central kiva's roof.

2-119. The Edge of the Cedars Ruin near Blanding, Utah, was a Pueblo III village that may have housed approximately 250 people. Puebloan villages such as this one in the western Montezuma Valley tended to be much smaller than the towns found along the valley's eastern side, but their inhabitants participated in the same cultural pattern. Only a portion of Edge of the Cedars village has been excavated and stabilized.

Canyon southwest of Blanding. Here once stood a multiroom pueblo reaching two stories high in some parts with five kivas, numerous storage structures, and open work spaces (fig. 2-120). The kivas had been built above the solid bedrock floor of the overhang in front of the domestic buildings. Puebloan people occupied this site from roughly 1150 to about 1275. Unfortunately, vandals and souvenir seekers have so badly damaged this ruin that we can no longer assess its full extent.

The **Big Westwater Ruin** occupies a south-facing overhang in Big Westwater Canyon farther downstream. It contained at least nineteen to twenty-one rooms, at least five of them on a second story (fig. 2-121). One kiva can be clearly distinguished toward the west end of the room block, while a second may be buried in the eastern end. A narrow upper ledge holds three or more small granaries. A high wall attached to the east end of the main two-story room block encloses an open court with a closable doorway to limit access from the east. Many loopholes open

2-120. The cliff dwelling called Little Westwater Ruin sits beneath a low cliff overhang in Little Westwater Canyon southwest of Blanding, Utah. The Pueblo III rooms here stood up to two stories in height with five kin-group kivas that rest on top of the bedrock cave floor in front of the residential rooms. They had been constructed roughly from 1150 to about 1275. Because relic hunters have so heavily vandalized this site, archaeologists have little evidence left with which to interpret the site's occupation.

2-121. The Big Westwater Ruin in Big Westwater Canyon contained at least nineteen to twenty-one rooms, five of them on a second story. While one kiva occurs at the west end of the ruin, there may be a second kiva buried beneath rubble in the east end. The residents of this Pueblo III cliff dwelling had both a nearby water supply and a clear view down the canyon to the south.

through this wall to provide visibility to the east and downward into the canyon, suggesting a defensive posture for this small pueblo.

Butler Wash Cliff Dwelling lies still farther west of Blanding in the upper end of Butler Wash where it begins its long southward course along the eastern side of Comb Ridge to the San Juan River. Buildings occupy all three alcoves, with the main structures in the northern one (fig. 2-122). Here, four kivas built upward from the bedrock alcove floor fronted rows of living and storage rooms. The northernmost kiva has a rectangular plan. Buildings in the southern alcove appear to have been used for storage, while the dry masonry wall in the central alcove resembles construction often found in turkey pens. This cliff dwelling dates from late Pueblo III times.

Many other rock shelters and alcoves may be found all along the east side of Comb Ridge and the west side of Butler Wash. Many of the overhangs reveal past occupations by Puebloans ranging in time from Basket Maker II through Pueblo III.

2-122. The Butler Wash Cliff Dwelling occupies three adjacent but separate overhangs on the west cliff of Butler Wash, west of Blanding, Utah. The northern shelter contains four kivas built on top of the bedrock sandstone cave floor in front of living and storage rooms, the southern rock shelter contains storerooms, while the central one has dry-wall masonry structures reminiscent of turkey pens in other sites. All date to Pueblo III.

Unfortunately, most of them have been severely damaged by pot hunters and other private collectors.

Among these sites, **Monarch's Cave**, one of the largest cliff dwellings, retains many standing walls (fig. 2-123). The main alcove contains two separated room blocks, both with evidence for two-story structures, representing nine to a dozen rooms. One of these with a rounded front wall may have been a kiva. The masonry fits the Mesa Verde style of the mid-1200s. Dry-wall masonry atop several walls appears to have been a later addition. Entrance to the main alcove from a second ledge requires the traversal of about twenty feet of steep, slippery rock using the ancient hand- and toeholds pecked there. Another cave directly below the cliff dwelling maintains a pool of water, suggesting the presence of a spring.

Comb Wash drains the western side of Comb Ridge, running parallel to Butler Wash on the eastern side, until it empties into the San Juan River. Several sites, such as the Arch Canyon Ruin, cluster in its upper reaches. Leading southward from them,

the remains of an ancient Puebloan roadway has been tracked in several sections of the valley. Recognizable stretches of this roadway run in straight-line segments along the valley bottom (fig. 2-124). Additional roadway segments have also been identified in the bottoms of Butler Wash and Cottonwood Wash between Blanding and Bluff.

Moon House lies considerably farther to the west of Comb Ridge in a canyon on Cedar Mesa. The most visible feature of Moon House is a long continuous wall built across the mouth of most of the long narrow overhang (fig. 2-125). The rooms behind it could be reached through a rectangular doorway in the wall. Several other well-preserved rooms stand to the east of the walled sector. Because of the many peepholes through the wall, it takes on the appearance of a defensive construction. A pictograph of the moon painted on one of the room walls inspired the name for this Pueblo III Mesa Verde–style cliff dwelling.

The broad triangular area bounded by the Colorado and San Juan rivers with Comb Ridge on

2-123. The Pueblo III cliff dwelling known as Monarch's Cave occupies a sandstone rock shelter on the east side of Comb Ridge overlooking Butler Wash. Two separate blocks of nine to twelve rooms each, some two stories high, exhibit typical Mesa Verde–style masonry. One room block may have included a kiva. A lower cave below the ruin contains a pool of water, probably once used by the site's ancient inhabitants.

2-124. This roadway segment, visible as a straight line running from upper left to lower right in the photograph, forms just a part of a prehistoric road that has been traced down the bottom of Comb Wash for at least nineteen miles. It demonstrates clearly that not all Puebloan roadways led directly to or from Chaco Canyon.

the east has been inhabited at various times by Kayenta Puebloans, largely during Pueblo I and early Pueblo II, and by Mesa Verde peoples, during later Pueblo II and Pueblo III times. To the east, the San Juan River valley seems to have served as a sort of boundary between the two regions, and the sites along the river reflect influences from both regional styles.

Many ancient ruins extend along both sides of the San Juan River from Montezuma Creek to Comb Ridge. Some of them can be visited while traveling with one of the river rafting companies that operate on this stretch of river. These include the Jackson Ruin on the north side, with evidence of both Pueblo II and III occupation; the Desert Creek Rock Art Panel, with a procession of Kokopellis and other multicolored figures, Citadel Ruin, Sixteen Room Pueblo, and the Dance Plaza site, all on the south side; the so-called Sacred Mesa site, the Gold Mine site, with associated rock art panel, "Moki" Steps Ruin, and the Butler Wash Rock Art Panel on the north side; Desecration Rock Art Panel on the south side; and River House and the Great Kiva ruin, at the cut through Comb Ridge.

Jackson Ruin appears as massive piles of fallen masonry rubble representing a Pueblo III structure with eight kivas and rooms that once stood three stories high. A smaller two-kiva pueblo on its west side dates to Pueblo II. Three small rooms perch on a ledge below the main ruin. Masonry fits the Mesa Verde style, both for Pueblo III and II. **Citadel Ruin** sits on a high bluff above the floodplain with two- and three-story rooms lining the north and east sides enclosing an interior space that may have held three kivas. Its sparse rubbish of both Mesa Verde and Kayenta pottery suggests a nonhabitation use—possibly for ceremonial purposes.

Sixteen Room House occupies a long, shallow shelter in the cliff on the south side of the San Juan River, facing northward toward the river. The eastern part of the ruin consists of three two-story large room sets with a seventh room that may once have stood two stories high (fig. 2-126). The upper-floor rooms were interconnected by doorways. The western portion contains a single row of nine one-story rooms, all with wall pegs and most with peepholes. Only the easternmost

2-126. Because it sits on a ledge in a high arching rock overhang on the south side of the San Juan River east of Bluff, Utah, Sixteen Room House is one of the very rare Pueblo III cliff dwellings that face toward the north. A block of three, possibly four, two-story rooms at the east (left) end of the ledge counterbalances a row of nine single-story rooms toward the west (right) that would have had to be entered through their roofs.

2-125. Moon House stretches along beneath a long narrow ledge in one of the canyons on Cedar Mesa to the west of the Comb Ridge in southeastern Utah. A continuous wall extends along the front of the ledge with a number of well-preserved rooms behind it. The many "peep" holes through this wall lend the impression of some defensive intent. The name for this Pueblo III cliff dwelling comes from the painted image of the moon on the wall of one room.

room had a doorway opening to the east. Thus all these rooms had to have been entered through their roofs. Only the central two-story room contained a central hearth. Two rows of negative handprints adorned the cliff face at the second-story level.

Sacred Mesa, so named by early Mormon settlers, refers to an erosional butte that rises on the northeast corner of the confluence of Recapture Creek with the San Juan River. Three masonry unit pueblos, each with four to six rooms and a kiva depression surrounded by Mesa Verde–style Pueblo III pottery, stand on the flat top of the butte along

2-127. The Sand Island Rock Art Panel just west of Bluff, Utah, displays petroglyphs of many different ages from pre-Puebloan Archaic times, shown in this photograph, through Basket Maker II and up through Pueblo III. Obviously, this location must have possessed a special spiritual significance for many peoples over a very long time.

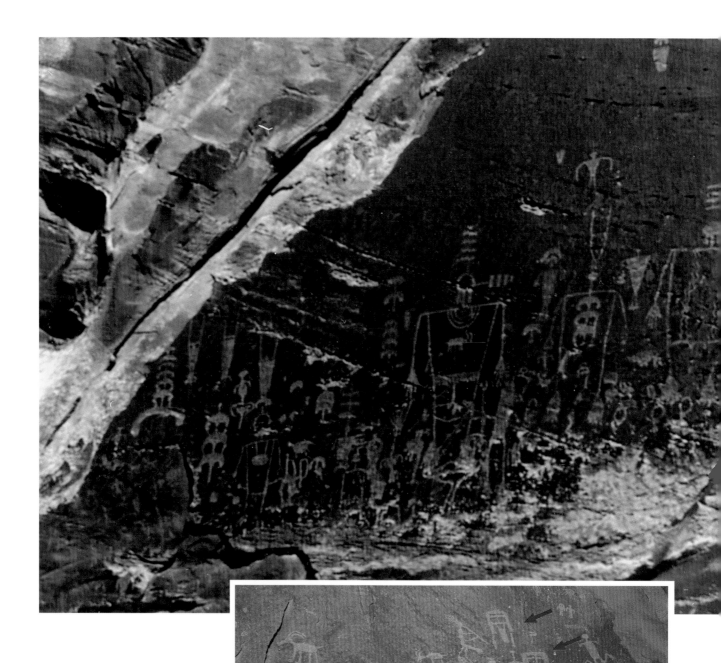

2-128. The two pecked "floating" heads just above and right of center in this photograph from the Sand Island Rock Art Panel along the north side of the San Juan River appear to represent human heads taken as trophies by Basket Maker II people. They bear a striking resemblance to a mummified trophy head found in a Basket Maker II deposit in a cave in northeastern Arizona.

2-129. The Butler Wash Rock Art Panel extends for more than one hundred meters along vertical cliff faces on both sides of the mouth of Butler Wash where it spills into the north side of the San Juan River as it cuts through Comb Ridge. Here, too, the figures pecked into the weathered face of the cliffs range in age from Archaic through Pueblo III. The wide-shouldered humanlike figures shown here represent what Sally Cole labeled the San Juan Anthropomorphic Style, which predates A.D. 500.

2-130. River House sits inside an arched rock shelter in the lower sandstone cliffs of Comb Ridge on the north side of the San Juan River floodplain. This seventeen- to eighteen-room pueblo has two kin-group kivas. The masonry in room walls reflects both Mesa Verde and Kayenta styles, but the two kivas display only Mesa Verde features and masonry style. The ruin derives its name from a painted serpentine figure that seems to depict the river high on the cave's back wall.

with three additional masonry rooms on a slightly lower level where the entrance trail reaches the crest. Scattered among these later buildings are thirteen to fourteen visible depressions that probably represent Pueblo I pithouses, judging from the plethora of typical Mesa Verde–style Pueblo I potsherds found all over the surface. This site bears a striking resemblance to the Nancy Patterson Village.

The **Dance Plaza** site boasts what appears to be a rectangular great kiva measuring twenty-eight meters (ninety feet) long and eleven meters (thirty-five feet) wide on the bluff edge above the river. A series of petroglyphs on two upright sandstone boulders to the south reinforce the probable ceremonial nature of this structure. Both are surrounded by Pueblo III Mesa Verde–style ceramics. A multioccupation residence unit of slab-based room outlines overlain by a rectangular masonry room block lie about fifty-seven meters to the east on the same terrace. Both Kayenta-style masonry and ceramics characterize this part of the site.

Sand Island Rock Art Panel occupies a low cliff face near a heavily used river rafting put-in and take-out location west of Bluff, Utah. This panel contains petroglyphs ranging from pre-Puebloan Archaic times through Basket Maker II up to Pueblo III. Several humanoid figures whose outlines have been filled in by crisscross lines follow the Archaic style (fig. 2-127), while several broad-shouldered humanoid figures depict the Basket Maker style. Two Basket Maker figures have great interest for they appear to show trophy human heads (fig. 2-128) remarkably similar to an actual trophy head found in a Basket Maker II cave in northeastern Arizona during the 1910s.

The **Gold Mine Site** consists of the rubble remains of Pueblo II cobble masonry residence units at the base of the cliff plus two small cliff granaries with pecked toeholds leading up to them. An extensive petroglyph panel extends along the cliff at the top of a steep talus slope to the west, depicting rows of bighorn sheep with a person behind them. The

Moki Steps Ruin, another local settler name, reveals evidence for collapsed residential buildings mostly of Pueblo I vintage with slab-based room outlines visible. Roof beam socket cutouts in the cliff face indicate the onetime presence of one two-story building and one one-story room built against the cliff. The presence of late Pueblo II pottery suggests a date for this structure in the late 1000s. Some Kayenta-style pottery also occurs here.

Butler Wash Rock Art Panel represents perhaps the most spectacular rock art panel in the American Southwest. The figures here reflect styles ranging in age from Archaic through Basket Maker II to Pueblo III (fig. 2-129). The giant broad-shouldered figures toward the western end of the panel represent the San Juan Anthropomorphic style of Basket Maker II art that Sally Cole dates before A.D. 500. The panel stretches for more than one hundred meters on both sides of the mouth of Butler Wash. Traces of three Pueblo II room blocks overlie Pueblo I slab-based rooms about one hundred meters to the west of the panel, and a small rubble pile indicates the former presence of a small masonry room block at the top of the talus slope in about the middle of the panel. This location certainly marked a very important, perhaps spiritual place to the ancient Puebloans and their forebears.

The **Desecration Rock Art Panel** on the cliff on the river's south side exhibits many petroglyphs ranging in age from Basket Maker II through Pueblo III. Many of these figures have been rubbed out or severely damaged. Scholars suspect the damage was effected by Navajo Indians who blamed the spirits on this panel for a very severe epidemic of tuberculosis that occurred in this particular part of the Navajo Reservation during the 1950s. One long zigzag serpent, partially buried, extends nineteen meters along the base of the cliff in this panel.

River House is a seventeen- to eighteen-room Pueblo III masonry pueblo standing up to two stories high with two kivas built in an arched overhang in the cliffs on the north side of the river's floodplain (fig. 2-130). Four granaries perch on the ledge about forty meters to the west. The builders used both Mesa Verde– and Kayenta-style stone masonry, with the kivas exhibiting Mesa Verde–style masonry and features. The ruin's name derives from the bright red and white wavy line painted on the back cliff of the overhang above the buildings, representing either a serpent or the river itself.

The remains of at least three and probably four Pueblo I slab-based jacal residence units stand on the flat a short distance to the west of River House at the toe of Comb Ridge where the San Juan River cuts through it. One unit has six to eight visible storerooms. Pithouse depressions occur in front of them. There is also one masonry house unit belonging to Pueblo II or III. A large circular depression measuring fifteen meters (about forty-eight feet) in inside diameter could be a great kiva or some closely related structure of unknown age. Its encircling wall measures about one meter thick.

The **Bluff Cemetery Site** cannot be reached during a river trip. It consists of a tall rubble mound, four to five meters (thirteen to sixteen feet) high, with at least four and possibly five kiva depressions visible in it. The height of the rubble indicates that some parts of the pueblo must have stood up to three stories tall. It rests on a high terrace at the base of the river's north cliff above the town of Bluff. A great kiva depression, sixteen meters (fifty-two feet) across, occupies the southwest edge of the terrace. Both masonry and layout reflect Pueblo III Mesa Verde–style architecture. This site is a good candidate to have been the center of a somewhat dispersed settlement along the north side of the San Juan River. University of Colorado field schools have conducted beginning excavations here since 2002, revealing several quite large rooms.

2-131. The excavated and stabilized Aztec West Ruin on the fertile west floodplain of the Animas River in Aztec, New Mexico. The restored great kiva occupies the center of the plaza in this pueblo of about 405 rooms and twenty-eight kivas. The Hubbard Site, a concentric triwall structure, lies behind the pueblo next to the road. (Photograph taken with the assistance of John Q. Royce.)

Aztec Ruins

The Aztec Ruins lie on the north bank of the Animas River near the town of Aztec, New Mexico. The name stems from a popular belief during the late 1800s that the many ruins scattered across the Southwest had been built by the Aztecs or Toltecs of central Mexico. However, archaeological investigations have found no such connection between these Puebloan ruins and the pre-Columbian Meso-americans.

The excavated and partially stabilized pueblo known as Aztec West Ruin contained an estimated 405 rooms and twenty-eight kivas, including both Chacoan and Northern San Juan–style structures in addition to the restored great kiva (fig. 2-131). Portions of this pueblo stood three stories high. Some of the rooms were spacious with high ceilings like many Chacoan rooms. Later, these rooms had been reduced in size, older doorways were blocked up, and new floors lay upon debris that partially filled some of the rooms. Newer inhabitants built Mesa Verde–style kin-group kivas and remodeled the great kiva.

Some archaeologists have suggested that Chacoan peoples constructed the West Ruin at Aztec like the Salmon Ruin, located twelve miles to the south on the San Juan River. They argue that the overall site plan, masonry, core and veneer walls, large room sizes, kiva style, and the great kiva closely resemble similar buildings at Salmon and in Chaco Canyon sites. They also suggest that both sites had been constructed around 1100 and abandoned by 1150, after which Northern San Juan peoples reoccupied the site during the 1200s. Other archaeologists feel the West Ruin more closely fits the Northern San Juan style than the Chacoan style. The large rooms and one Chaco-style kiva more

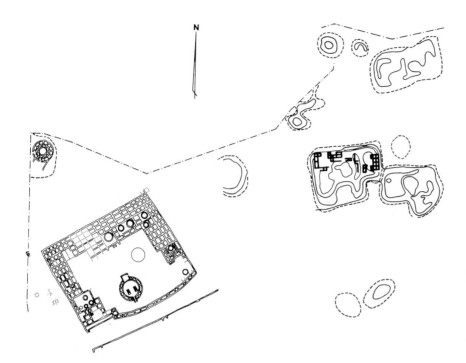

2-132. Plan of the Aztec settlement with the Aztec West Ruin and the Hubbard Site (after Morris 1928) in the lower left and the largely unexcavated eastern portions to the right (after Vivian 1959).

probably indicate a Chacoan colony that once lived at Aztec during the early 1100s.

Aztec West Ruin is but the largest of twelve structures on the twenty-seven-acre Aztec Ruins National Monument. The Hubbard triwall structure to the north of the West Ruin has also been excavated. The unexcavated portions of the tract include the large East Ruin, several smaller house mounds, and a second triwall structure (fig. 2-132). Farming Puebloans occupied the fertile Animas River valley from very early times. Traces of early kivas and some above-ground dwellings have been located beneath the excavated portions of the Aztec Ruins. A substantial population may have lived in scattered settlements along the river, but modern farming has destroyed most of the evidence.

During the 1880s, residents of the town of Aztec broke through the walls on the first floor of the West Ruin to explore and collect relics. Seven of these rooms have intact ceilings. The National Park Service has repaired these breaks in the walls to create a passageway for visitors through this series of rooms.

To one side of the passageway, visitors may observe a mat used to cover a doorway. The original doorways were often aligned in this pueblo to allow communication among rooms (fig. 2-133).

Mesa Verde–style stone masonry dominates the building at Aztec West Ruin, except in the larger Chaco-style rooms. The masons took considerable care to erect a well-built, attractive building. Along the Mesa Verde–style west exterior wall, they incorporated two horizontal bands of masonry using green sandstone blocks that had to be imported to the site (fig. 2-134).

While excavating the Aztec West Ruin, Earl Morris rebuilt its great kiva. No other Puebloan building has been so completely restored (fig. 2-135). It offers the visitor a rare opportunity to sense what the people of ancient times must have felt during activities conducted in this structure, especially when recorded Indian music is played. The inner circular floor of the great kiva measures about forty-two feet in diameter. It had been dug eight feet below

2-133. Aligned doorways through rooms on the east side of the Aztec West Ruin showing Mesa Verde–style stone masonry.

2-134. For this banded west exterior wall of the Aztec West Ruin, the green sandstone blocks in the two bands had to be imported from elsewhere. The fine tablet band suggests a Chacoan quality, but the remainder of the stonework and the green banding itself more closely characterize Montezuma Valley construction.

ground level with stairs leading into it from an altar room on the north side (fig. 2-136). A second stairway once graced the south side, but it was later removed. The National Park Service has replaced it with a wooden staircase. A bench encircles the room at floor level. In the center of the floor stood a square masonry firebox flanked by two elongated masonry floor vaults (fig. 2-137). Four massive columns, erected with alternating courses of stone masonry and horizontal wooden poles, supported the roof, each column resting on top of three massive sandstone disks.

Fourteen arc-shaped chambers surround the great kiva at ground level. At one time each of these rooms had a doorway that opened onto the plaza (see fig. 2-135) and another opening into the kiva. Later the outside doorways were sealed, and access could only be gained via narrow ladders reaching upward from bench level and built into the kiva's interior wall.

The Hubbard Site triwall structure lies to the northwest of the West Ruin. Three concentric walls enclose a central kiva with the spaces between them partitioned into twenty-two small rooms. The entire structure measures sixty-four feet across. Both the central kiva and most of the rooms could only have been accessed through hatchways in their roofs. Earlier kivas lay beneath the building. Triwall structures represent a Northern San Juan architectural feature similar in style and function to the Sun Temple on Mesa Verde and the horseshoe houses at Hovenweep. Pueblo del Arroyo in Chaco Canyon has a similar triwall structure.

The Puebloan people living in Aztec Ruins seem to have had everything needed for a comfortable survival, even during relatively dry times—fertile soil and plenty of water. Traces of an old ditch that carried water from the river to the flatlands around the pueblo indicate they irrigated their fields. Earl Morris suspected the pueblo suffered harassment by outsiders because the great kiva and the entire east

2-135. The exterior of the great kiva, restored by Earl H. Morris in 1934, at Aztec West Ruin.

2-136. A view from the north altar room in the restored great kiva at Aztec West Ruin looking southward into the main chamber toward the stepped southern entry. A white circle had been painted on the top of the raised altar in the north room.

2-137. The interior of the restored great kiva at Aztec West Ruin looking across the main chamber toward the north altar room, past the square, raised masonry firebox flanked by two masonry floor vaults that may have been foot drums, and between two of the four stone masonry and horizontal pole columns that supported the roof.

wing had been destroyed by fire. He also noted the south row of rooms built of cobblestone masonry by the latest occupants enclosed the pueblo's plaza except for a narrow entrance to a hallway at the southwest corner of the pueblo. This seems to have made the pueblo more readily defendable.

For whatever reasons, the Puebloan people abandoned Aztec during the late 1200s. Most likely they participated in the Great Migrations toward the Rio Grande Valley that emptied the Northern San Juan Region by 1300.

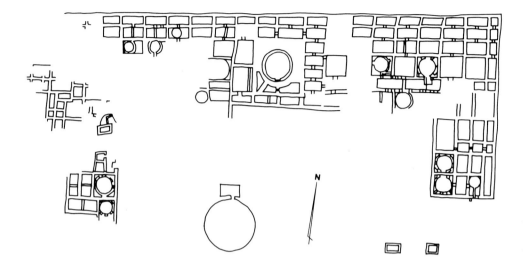

2-138. Ground plan of the Salmon Ruin. (Drawing after Irwin-Williams 1976).

Salmon Ruin

The Salmon Ruin was constructed by Chacoan peoples on the north bank of the San Juan River, some thirty miles north of the Chaco Canyon and about twelve miles south of Aztec Ruins. The site and an accompanying museum lie just south of the highway between Bloomfield and Farmington, New Mexico. Excellent farmland surrounds the site, and the San Juan River provided a dependable water supply.

Tree-ring dates indicate construction of the pueblo took place within a span of only seven years between 1088 and 1095. Its plan resembled a giant capital E with a Chaco-style tower kiva in the center arm and 250 large rooms distributed along the 450-foot-long main northern stem and the two flanking arms (figs. 2-138 and 2-139). The inhabitants constructed the walls of thin, carefully matched sandstone slabs, importing some of them and some roof timbers from up to thirty miles away. A great kiva occupied the plaza in front of the central arm.

The great kiva resembled the restored great kiva at Aztec West Ruin. It measured forty-six feet in diameter, and it was entered by way of an antechamber room on its north side. Four stone and wood columns supported the roof. A central firebox and two rectangular

floor vaults, possible foot drums, lay in the center of the floor. The tower kiva reminds us of the one at Chetro Ketl in Chaco Canyon. It had been constructed inside a room block using special footings to support its extra-thick walls, and it probably extended somewhat above the roofs of the adjoining buildings.

The Chacoans abandoned Salmon about the middle of the twelfth century after only about sixty years of occupation. However, roughly fifty years later, Mesa Verdean peoples reoccupied the pueblo and remodeled it. They subdivided the larger Chacoan rooms, added several kivas around the perimeter of the plaza, and reworked the great kiva. The blockier masonry work of these later peoples can readily be distinguished from the tabular stone masonry employed by the Chacoan builders.

A fire broke out at the pueblo in 1250, during the Mesa Verdean occupation, and some fifty children and one woman were killed when the kiva roof on which they had sought refuge collapsed, tumbling them all into the burning kiva. Another fire in 1270 destroyed the great kiva and much of the pueblo. Archaeologists cannot judge the ultimate causes for these fires, but the latest one could either have instigated final abandonment of the site, or it could have

2-139. Salmon Ruin lies on the north side of the San Juan River between Farmington and Bloomfield, New Mexico. This northeast view shows the E-shaped layout of the pueblo with a tower-kiva in the center and a great kiva across the plaza toward the river. Tree-ring dates indicate most construction took place between 1088 and 1095. Chacoan peoples seem to have occupied the pueblo until about 1150, and Northern San Juan peoples then reoccupied it around 1200. These later inhabitants subdivided some of the large Chacoan rooms, built kivas around the plaza, and reworked the great kiva. (Photograph taken with the assistance of John Q. Royce.)

been set by the last inhabitants as they left. These latest occupants then joined the migration southward and eastward to the Rio Grande Valley.

Chimney Rock Sites

The unique formation called Chimney Rock stands out prominently among the mountains, mesas, and hills among which it stands. The Indians of modern Taos Pueblo, whose legends indicate they came from the Chimney Rock area, consider the twin spires to represent the twin war gods of Taos mythology. Apparently the ancients felt some sort of spiritual connection for this place as well, for they constructed both residences and specialized, probably ceremonial, buildings around the feature and on high mesa remnants near the top (fig. 2-140).

An access road winds northwestward up the mountain to a parking lot on the Chimney Rock high mesa. Here, five ruin clusters have been excavated and stabilized: the Parking Lot Site, Great Kiva

2-140. Several of the ruins around Chimney Rock sit on a ridge high above the Piedra River valley west of Pagosa Springs, Colorado. They include the great kiva in the lower left, the Parking Lot Site nearby, and Chimney Rock Pueblo on the triangular level space in front of the twin Chimney Rocks. The Continental Divide in the San Juan Mountains runs across the horizon.

2-141. Chimney Rock Pueblo sits on a high mesa one thousand feet above the valley floor. It consists of thirty-six ground-floor rooms and two Chaco-style kivas, suggesting that Chacoan peoples constructed it. This pueblo belonged to a much larger settlement, clearly not Chacoan, encompassing as many as two thousand people, which Frank W. Eddy, who excavated the site, calls the Chimney Rock Tribe. The entire district had been abandoned by 1125. (Photograph taken with the assistance of L. A. Villarreal.)

Site, Building 16, the Access Road Site, and the "Guard House," in addition to Chimney Rock Pueblo. Visitation arrangements can be made at the Pagosa Springs Ranger Station.

The most prominent ruin here is **Chimney Rock Pueblo**, built on a triangular remnant of the high mesa at an elevation of 7,600 feet and with sheer drop-offs on two sides (fig. 2-141). Frank W. Eddy suggests that a group of migrants from Chaco Canyon constructed the pueblo about 1076. They built an L-shaped complex comprising two Chaco-style kivas and thirty-six ground-floor rooms (fig. 2-142). The combination of precisely laid wide and narrow courses of tablet-shaped stones marks Chaco-style masonry, and many of the rooms are large, like Chacoan rooms. Eddy believes the builders were

men because they brought all the building skills—men's work—but no pottery—women's craft.

About four hundred yards northeast of the parking lot stands the **Guard House** on a narrow ledge referred to as the Causeway leading to Chimney Rock Pueblo. This structure is a circular masonry room enclosed by a rectangular retaining wall. Its position between Chimney Rock Pueblo and the local community seems to have been intended to keep the two separated. Hence if the Chacoan builders of Chimney Rock Pueblo actually lived in the building, they seem not to have integrated into the community. And then, perhaps the absence of pottery indicates the Chaco-style building had not actually been lived in, but it may have functioned primarily as a ritual place to which only a select few would be admitted.

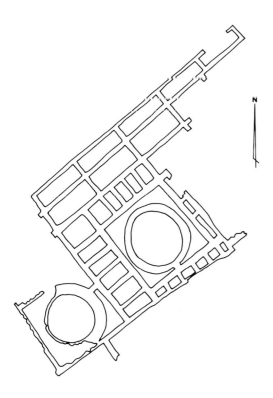

2-142. Ground plan of Chimney Rock Pueblo. (Drawing after Eddy 1977).

2-143. The obviously named Parking Lot Site lies about four hundred yards west of Chimney Rock Pueblo. Although the three circular, thick-walled rooms almost look like kivas, people actually resided in them as above-ground pithouses between about 950 and 1125. A neighboring site, named the Access Road Site, located next to where the access road branches, consists of circular living quarters similar to those at the Parking Lot Site. (Photograph taken with the assistance of L. A. Villarreal.)

The incoming Chacoans encountered a resident population around Chimney Rock and on its high mesa remnants. Frank Eddy estimates that some twelve hundred to two thousand people lived in about a dozen villages here during the 1000s. He refers to these people as the Chimney Rock Tribe. He also suggests there must have been a religious impetus to inspire building on the high mesa where the nearest good farmland and abundant water lay in the valley a thousand feet below. Earlier Pueblo I sites are abundant on Piedra and Stollsteimer mesas nearby.

The **Parking Lot Site** consists of three circular, thick-walled, above-ground rooms linked together with two rectangular rooms attached to them (figs. 2-143 and 2-144). Eddy concluded these circular structures served as domestic living quarters because they lacked any of the features typical of either Northern San Juan– or Chaco-style kivas. Perhaps the shallow soil atop this rocky ridge made it impossible to excavate the floors into the ground as in pithouses. One of the rectangular rooms had been used for food grinding and perhaps preparation while the other provided storage space. The circular houses had to be entered through roof hatchways, but the rectangular rooms had doorways. Five nearby crater-shaped mounds probably mark additional as yet unexcavated houses.

The ruins of the **Great Kiva** lie about two hundred yards to the southwest of the parking lot. This structure probably served as the ceremonial center for the Chimney Rock Tribe. It was a circular stone masonry building with an inside diameter of about forty feet. Fourteen subfloor rectangular

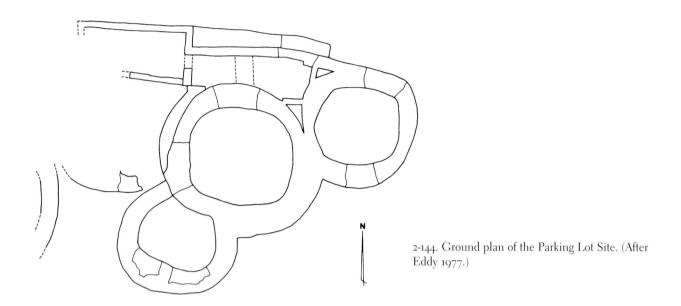

2-144. Ground plan of the Parking Lot Site. (After Eddy 1977.)

cists, probably used to store ritual paraphernalia, ringed the interior space. An altar flanked by subfloor vaults occupied the center of this large room. The building had been roofed, but the nature of that roof could not be determined.

Building 16 stands next to the north side of the Great Kiva. It consists of one stabilized above-ground circular house with a fire pit and ventilator and two masonry rooms, one for storage and the other containing five mealing bins holding metates for grinding corn. It belonged to a Pueblo II village with sixteen unexcavated mounds.

An early dirt road partially destroyed much of the **Access Road Site**. The surviving portion of the ruin closely resembles the Parking Lot Site and Building 16 with circular masonry living rooms and attached work and storage rooms. It, too, belonged to a cluster of some thirteen crater-shaped mounds marking other houses.

Occupation at the Parking Lot Site has been placed from about 950 to about 1125. Together with the other Pueblo II sites here, the community comprised close to forty houses and the great kiva.

Presumably Chacoan peoples built the Chimney Rock Pueblo, or the local people simply copied Chaco-style masonry and construction techniques for a building dedicated to ceremonial purposes. In any event, the entire Chimney Rock district had been abandoned by 1125. Interestingly, the later communities of Taos Indians seem to have preceded other Puebloan peoples into the Rio Grande Valley, perhaps by 150 or more years.

CHAPTER THREE

Kayenta Region

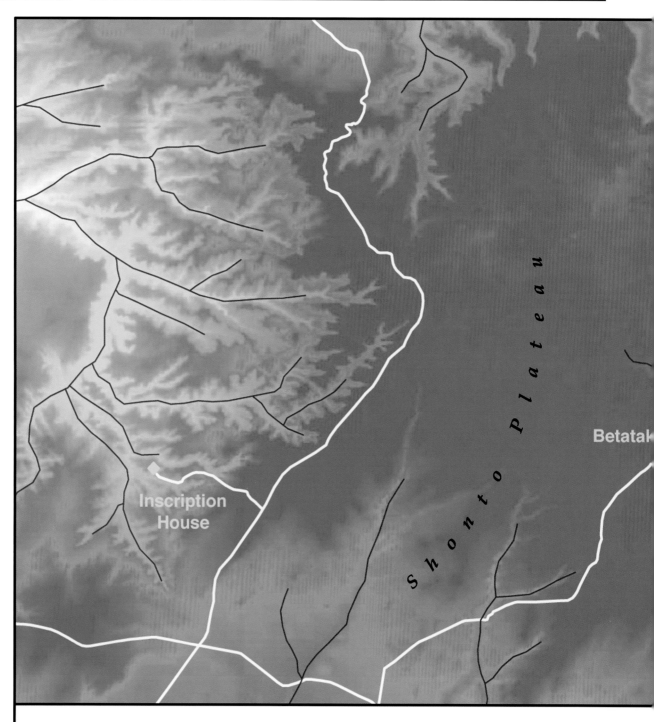

Betatak

Shonto Plateau

Inscription
House

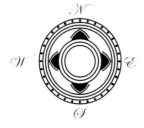

Key

◆ **Archaeological Ruin**

Modern Road

Major Drainage

3-1. The core of the Kayenta Region in Pueblo-land showing the locations of Inscription House, Betatakin, Keet Seel, and Black Mesa.

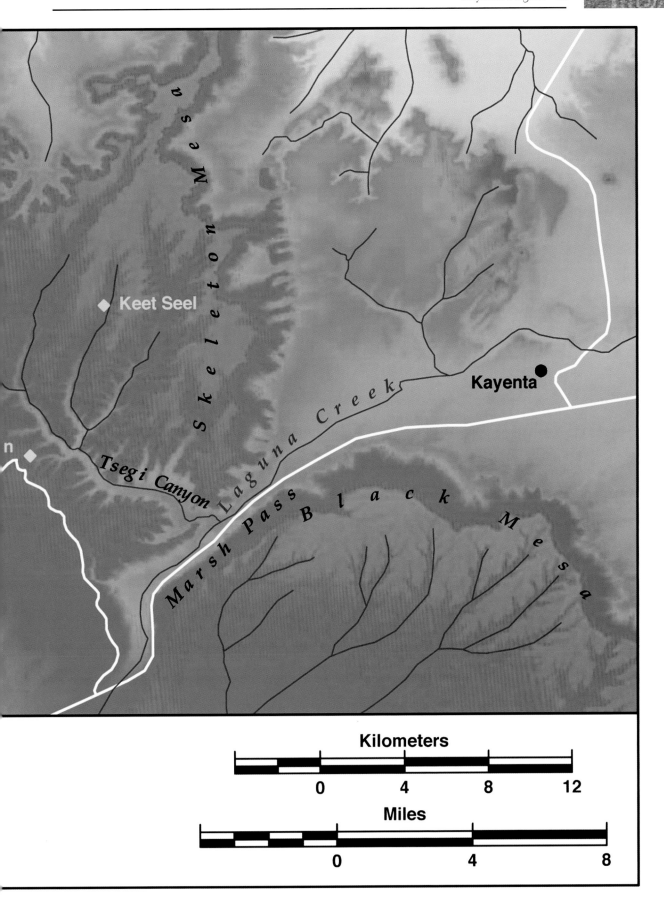

Kilometers

0   4   8   12

Miles

0   4   8

Introduction

From Basket Maker times through Pueblo III, the Kayenta people made up the northwestern branch of the Puebloan tree, the other three branches occurring in the Northern San Juan (Mesa Verde and the Montezuma Valley), in the Chaco Basin, and in the Little Colorado River regions. The Kayenta cultural pattern developed and flourished along the southern side of the Colorado and San Juan rivers from west of Navajo Mountain to Monument Valley, all along the Chinle Wash including Canyon de Chelly, in the Tsegi Canyon–Marsh Pass district, in the Klethla and Longhouse valleys, and on the northern end of Black Mesa. The Grand Canyon and Virgin River districts mark western offshoots of Kayenta culture.

Kayenta Puebloan remains have been found beginning in early Basket Maker II (radiocarbon dates from the northern end of Black Mesa place houses in small hamlets as early as 750 B.C.) to the end of Pueblo III about A.D. 1300, representing a span of more than two thousand years of continuous occupation and cultural development. This region provided the source for population movements during Pueblo II both to the northwest across the Colorado River and to the west as far as the Grand Canyon and the Virgin River drainage of southern Nevada and southwestern Utah. Across the Colorado River, they reached well up the course of the Escalante River to Escalante and Boulder, Utah. Small populations, probably involving only a few hundred people, began to move into those areas between 900 and 950, peaking between 1050 and 1150.

By about 1150, most of the Puebloans left these western and trans–Colorado River zones and returned to the Kayenta heartland. During the last half of the 1200s, perhaps half the populations in and around Tsegi Canyon moved from the broad valleys upstream into canyons and to higher eminences in the valleys. Some built cliff dwellings such as Betatakin, Keet Seel, and Inscription House, marking the Tsegi Phase of Kayenta prehistory. Jeffrey Dean suggests these moves had been caused by arroyo cutting that lowered the water table in previously farmed localities.

By 1270 the Kayenta people had concentrated into relatively larger villages around Navajo Mountain, in Tsegi Canyon (Betatakin and Keet Seel), in Longhouse Valley (e.g., Long House), on the north end of Black Mesa, and in Canyon de Chelly (e.g., White House and Antelope House). Only a few of these later ruins can be visited, and most of those cannot be entered by the general public because of their fragile condition. All Puebloan occupation in the Kayenta Region ended around 1300 as the people moved away, possibly because their farmlands continued to degrade. Most resettled to the south in the drainage of the Little Colorado River as the ancestral Hopi.

The Tsegi Canyon cliff dwellings of Betatakin and Keet Seel lie within the boundaries of Navajo National Monument, along with Inscription House, situated in a steep canyon about fifteen miles to the west (fig. 3-1). In this area, wide, steep-sided canyons have entrenched themselves deeply through high (at nearly 8,000 feet) forest-covered mesas. Both Betatakin and Keet Seel may be visited on guided walking tours leaving from the visitor center, and Betatakin may be viewed from an overlook anytime during regular park hours. Keet Seel can only receive a limited number of visitors each year. Such a visit requires a nine-mile hike or horseback ride each way and permission from park headquarters.

Kayenta-style architecture employed a mixture of stone masonry and jacal (vertical poles twined together with small branches and coated with mud). The stone masonry walls generally had a thickness of only one stone. The building stones would usually be trimmed on both sides by crude flaking to give them a kind of loaf shape with the spaces between stones filled with copious amounts of mud mortar and chinking spalls. Builders often employed such stone masonry for a room's rear and side walls, while using jacal for the front wall through which a door would pass.

The room clusters of the Tsegi Phase Kayenta cliff dwellings resembled those of the Mesa Verde Pueblo III cliff houses, as outlined for Mug House. The Tsegi Canyon people built their suites, or household units, in groups opening onto courtyards, but the bedrock sandstone floors of the rock shelters prevented the excavation of kin-group kivas below ground level. Hence very few such kivas appear in the caves themselves. It is possible, although not yet confirmed, that kin-group kivas may have been built in alluvial deposits found in lower caves on the valley floor or in nearby caves such as Turkey Ruin near Keet Seel. Great kivas have not been found in the Kayenta Region with the possible exception of a related structure in Mummy Cave in Canyon del Muerto.

Each room cluster housed a household, or small extended family, which constituted the basic unit of the village. Several households, probably related to one another, shared a courtyard space and the outdoor activities that took place there. People entered their rooms either through a doorway or through a roof hatch. The floors were leveled and the inside walls plastered. Slab-lined fire pits, located beneath a hatchway or smoke hole, heated the rooms, while deflectors or more complex entry boxes in the doorways controlled drafts.

Other forms of construction included granaries, storerooms, grinding rooms, and kivas. Smoothed plaster covered the exteriors of granaries, but the interior walls generally remained unfinished, since these buildings were designed only to protect foodstuffs from insects and rodents. The storerooms often had jacal walls, since they often housed items other than food. Each grinding or mealing room contained a series of

3-2. A group of pottery sherds from Keet Seel in Navajo National Monument in northeastern Arizona representing several styles of ceramics made and used by the Kayenta Puebloans. The top center of the photograph shows a rim fragment of a gray corrugated cooking vessel surrounded by several polychrome painted pieces decorated in red, black, and white paints on an orange background. Five black-on-white potsherds in the two bottom rows reflect slightly different ages—the two in the lower right corner characterize the 1000s and 1100s, while the other three date from the late 1200s. The three-color polychrome pottery became a popular trade item to eastern Puebloan regions.

stone slab–lined bins that surrounded metates for grinding corn kernels and other seeds with stone manos. Sometimes sets of grinding bins occupied a corner of a courtyard where the onerous daily task of grinding corn and other seeds could have been shared among several individuals, presumably women.

The Kayenta people farmed in the valley bottoms in Tsegi Canyon, Monument Valley, the Longhouse and Klethla valleys, and in Canyon de Chelly and Canyon del Muerto, but they also planted on mesa tops on Black Mesa and in the Navajo Mountain districts. Conditions in the Canyon de Chelly district allowed them to grow cotton in addition to the usual food crops of maize, squash, and beans. Like the other Puebloans, they produced both utility pottery for cooking and storage and decorated vessels for other uses

3-3. Inscription House Ruin, the third largest Pueblo III cliff dwelling in Navajo National Monument, perches in an arched rock overhang high in the cliff of a steep canyon west of the Shonto Plateau and Tsegi Canyon. Like the similar Kayenta sites of Keet Seel and Betatakin, it represents one of the latest Puebloan villages to be built prior to abandonment of the San Juan River drainage.

(see fig. 1-4). The Tsegi Phase black-on-white vessels exhibited such heavy amounts of black paint over the background white slip so as to create a negative painted effect (fig. 3-2, lower left). In addition, they developed an orange ware, often covered with a red slip, painted in black and white designs in both bichrome and polychrome color schemes. By applying the red slip in limited zones, together with black and white decorative lines, they could produce a four-colored result (fig. 3-2, upper right).

Jeffrey Dean has postulated that the Tsegi Phase Kayentans chose to abandon the Kayenta Region because the larger villages could no longer be supported in a deteriorating environment. They had a choice of subdividing into smaller self-sustaining groups or of moving away, and they chose the latter. Most of them moved southward into the Little Colorado River drainage and ultimately back to the southern mesa ends of Black Mesa as the modern-day Hopi. A few intrepid souls continued farther southward through the mountains along the Mogollon Rim in east central Arizona, finally ending up in the Tucson Basin, where they amalgamated with the local Hohokam peoples.

Inscription House Ruin

The smallest of the three fine cliff dwellings encompassed by Navajo National Monument, Inscription House contains approximately seventy-five rooms (fig. 3-3). It derives its name from an inscription

3-4. Puebloan people began building cliff dwellings in Tsegi Canyon, shown here looking south-ward, and its tributaries in the late 1200s. Betatakin lies to the right with Keet Seel about eight miles to the north. Approximately seven hundred people lived in these canyons around 1280, but all of them had left by 1300.

3-5. Betatakin cliff dwelling occupies a high arching overhang in the north canyon wall of an offshoot from Tsegi Canyon in Navajo National Monument.

3-6. Tree-ring dates from Betatakin tell us that its construction began about 1267 and that its population peaked in the mid-1280s with roughly 125 persons who farmed on the canyon floor. Portions of the cliff dwelling have collapsed, but in its heyday more than one hundred rooms, some multistoried, filled the cave. The only identifiable kiva seems to be the rectangular room just to the right of the stone steps.

incised into the plastered wall of one of the rooms. Some think this badly weathered inscription had a Spanish origin during the 1660s, but the point cannot be verified. The one- and two-story buildings have been constructed of stone masonry, adobe, and jacal, employing T-shaped doorways extensively. Two kivas have been identified, one circular, but the other has an irregular shape because of its position next to the natural cave wall.

Only two tree-ring samples from Inscription House have been securely dated, with the only cutting date of 1271 falling within the span of the Tsegi Phase. Harold Gladwin collected five samples during the mid-twentieth century from the site that he dated between 1057 and 1102, but these could not be verified by the later work. Because of its difficult route of access and the fragile nature of the preserved buildings, visitors should not try to enter this ruin.

Betatakin

The Betatakin Cave nestles in a high, arching overhang on the north cliff of a short side canyon off of the main Tsegi Canyon stem. From this location, the residents had an impressive view to the south down Tsegi Canyon toward their farmlands (fig. 3-4). Aspens grow in the canyon bottom with box elder, Douglas fir, and piñon on the talus slopes. Junipers and piñon dominate the surrounding mesa tops. The extensive projection of the rock overhang provided shade during hot summer months when temperatures could approach one hundred degrees, while the southern exposure allowed the lower winter sun to shine into the cave and warm the buildings (fig. 3-5).

Jeffrey Dean's analysis of tree-cutting and construction dates for Betatakin enabled him to reconstruct the forty-year life history of this Tsegi Phase village. The rock shelter had served as a seasonal camp for a few years around 1260. Then in 1267 and

1268, four households, totaling about twenty people, founded the village. These founders seem to have made up an advance party assigned to prepare the site for a move by the remaining residents of the main earlier village. They cleaned the cave floor and then cut trees into standard lengths and stockpiled them for later construction. Later in 1272, they cut, sized, and stockpiled yet more beams. Perhaps conditions had improved at the home village, delaying the main move to Betatakin until the years 1275 to 1277.

By the mid-1280s, the population had peaked at about 125 people (figs. 3-6 and 3-7), among a postulated total of seven hundred residents in Tsegi Canyon at this time. Dean suggests that continued arroyo cutting in the broader valleys downstream had destroyed farmlands there and forced cultivation to shift upstream into the canyons. Sometime after 1286, the Betatakin people began to leave the cave, and by 1300 the entire Kayenta Region had been abandoned, probably because the arroyo cutting continued to move upstream and destroyed the canyon fields and irrigation systems in the same manner as the fields in the wider valleys had been destroyed at an earlier time.

The planning and preparation of the new site and the deliberate and unhurried movement of people from the earlier village to Betatakin indicate a community decision-making process. Yet Dean saw no evidence for the existence of an elite class. The architecture of the village conforms to the Tsegi Phase general plan of construction involving room clusters, or suites, composed of a living room, storage rooms, and outdoor courtyard space. Some of the buildings stood two stories high with courtyard space located on the roofs of adjoining lower structures (fig. 3-8). However, no room suites stood apart from others in their larger size or better construction. Hence, no class separation could be observed, even though some form of community decision-making process must have existed.

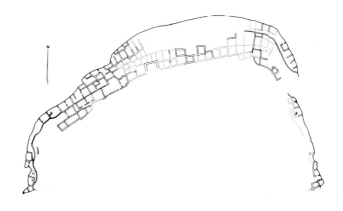

3-7. Jeffrey S. Dean's ground plan of Betatakin shows the foundations of the rooms that filled the entire arc of the cave. The south-facing overhang made the cliff dwelling cooler in summer and warmer in winter.

3-8. Rooms in Betatakin that have retained their original roofs.

3-9. This masonry-walled living room in Betatakin had a fire pit at its center and a deflector between the fire pit and the entrance. One roof timber remains in place, and the blackened walls attest to the amount of smoke with which the occupants had to contend.

3-10. Keet Seel Canyon, a tributary to Tsegi Canyon, winds through Skeleton Mesa, cutting a deep arroyo in front of the Keet Seel Ruin that destroyed portions of the farmlands once cultivated by Puebloan farmers.

The Betatakins built five kinds of buildings: living rooms (fig. 3-9), storerooms, granaries, grinding rooms, and kivas, all arranged around the outdoor courtyard spaces. Dean found only one probable kiva—a large, rectangular room with rubble-cored walls, a bench along the north wall, a triangular bench at the northwest corner, and four loom anchor holes in the floor. Men did the weaving, mostly in kivas all over Pueblo-land. They fastened their vertical looms by looping ropes around the upper loom frame poles to the roof and around lower frame poles to anchors formed by cross sticks mudded into holes in the floor. A pair of such loom anchors would normally mark each loom. Since the room's front wall is missing, any evidence for a recess, ventilator, or fire pit has been lost. Dean based his assessment of this room as a kiva on its large size, the extra height of its ceiling, and its lack of any association with any room cluster. Another, fully subterranean, rectangular kiva occupies a small cave just to the west of Betatakin.

A low masonry wall extends along the edge of a ledge about thirty feet above the rooms in the center of the cave. It could have been reached by a ladder resting on the roof of the tallest room below it, and it would have provided rodent-free storage.

Today, visitors may look into Betatakin from an overlook to the south, but the ruin may only be entered on guided tours because of its increasingly delicate state of preservation. Many of the buildings perch on very steeply sloping bedrock sandstone surfaces, and the shelter overhang has become somewhat unstable with rock falls possible. One such fall of a portion of the overhang destroyed a sizable section of the ruin sometime after its abandonment. Despite these dangers, the remaining portions display well-preserved rooms and buildings that still look much as they did seven hundred years ago.

Keet Seel

It requires a hike or horseback ride of about nine miles from National Park Service headquarters down through the canyon bottom to reach Keet Seel (fig. 3-10). Increasing wear and tear from visitors has led to a limit having been placed on the number of visitors allowed into the ruin itself at any one time. Both advance registration and a guide are required. Once there, though, the visitor gets a great treat with a view of the largest, and perhaps the best-preserved, cliff dwelling in Arizona.

The Pueblo people began constructing the presently visible village of Keet Seel (or "Kiet Siel") in a cliff overhang on the west side of Keet Seel Canyon some five miles upstream from where it joins Tsegi Canyon. Like Betatakin, this large rock shelter had also been occupied in earlier times by the Puebloans and then abandoned before the Tsegi Phase people arrived.

Tree-ring dates indicate a surge of timber cutting and construction activity between 1272 and 1275, which then tapered off and ceased entirely by 1286. By examining the room clusters and dating their construction, Jeffrey Dean estimates the 1272 population of Keet Seel at about 60 people, but by 1286, the total population may have reached between 125 and 150. The complete absence of tree-ring dates after 1286 shows that construction had ceased then. Within twenty-five years, Keet Seel was abandoned.

During the later years of occupation, some people must have moved in and out of the village, for some room blocks had been vacated and then rebuilt. Some unoccupied rooms were converted into granaries, and beams from vacant rooms saw reuse in the building of new ones.

As the best preserved of the larger ruins in the Southwest, Keet Seel retains the feel of a recently discovered ruin (fig. 3-11) with corncobs and pottery sherds scattered about. A large log some twenty feet long laid across the pueblo entrance may have been placed there by its occupants, some archaeologists suggest, to symbolically bar entrance to the cliff dwelling. The extremely dry climate in this part of Arizona, coupled with protection by the cliff overhang, have allowed the preservation of both the buildings and a number of otherwise perishable objects such as baskets and various parts of corn plants. Signs of National Park Service stabilization are minimal, except for the visitors' ladder to replace the original hand- and toehold trail.

Although we assume that individual families constructed their living and storage quarters, the occupants of Keet Seel mounted a community effort, perhaps as early as 1272, to build a 180-foot-long retaining wall extending across the front of the eastern 60 percent of the cliff dwelling. They then filled in the area behind this wall—over ten feet high in some places—by carrying tons of dirt and rubble, probably in baskets supported on tump lines, to create a terraced foundation for this part of the village. They also cooperated in the overall layout of the village by providing for three streets to allow easy access to all the room clusters (fig. 3-12).

At about the center of the village on the lower level facing "Rampart Street," the people built a rubble-core walled, keyhole-shaped kiva with a fire pit, a ventilator, and a rectangular floor vault for storage or perhaps for a foot drum (fig. 3-13). They had plastered the walls and painted two four-inch-wide white bands on them. Next to this kiva, they also constructed a D-shaped ceremonial annex with a jacal front wall. This clearly was not a residence or storeroom, yet it lacks typical kiva features.

Although jacal walls had largely disappeared elsewhere in the Four Corners area, the inhabitants of Keet Seel continued to utilize this method of construction. The builders set small wooden posts along the wall line, filled the spaces between them with

3-11. Keet Seel is the best-preserved large cliff dwelling in the American Southwest. Built mostly during the second half of the 1200s, it may have housed as many as 150 people. The long masonry retaining wall stretching about 180 feet along the front of the cliff dwelling holds back a rubble-filled foundation for buildings behind it and illustrates the engineering skill and cooperative effort of the builders. Its inhabitants, along with the occupants of the other villages in the Tsegi Canyon system, had abandoned this village by 1300.

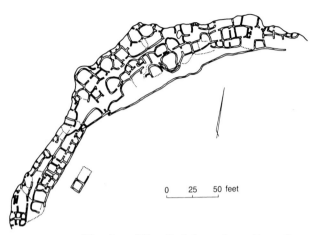

3-12. The plan of Keet Seel shows the outlines of about 150 rooms. The remains of several additional rooms and a round tower lie at the base of the cliff.

3-13. So-called Rampart Street runs along the top of the fill behind the long retaining wall past the keyhole-shaped kiva in the right foreground and the vertical wooden poles of unknown function that had been set in place by the village residents. A barrier log at the end of the street sets off the western section of the village.

twigs and/or reeds, also set vertically, tied everything together with split yucca leaves, and plastered the entire lot with mud.

More than 150 rooms and four kivas had been built beneath the overhang. Those in the western part of the cave rested directly on its bedrock sandstone floor with a couple of rooms perched like wasp nests on the steep sandstone slope below them. Erosion has destroyed most of the buildings at the base of the cliff where a fairly large group of Tsegi Phase structures, including additional kivas, once stood. Visible remains include several rooms and a two-story round tower. The nearby Turkey Cave Ruin contains two, possibly three, additional kivas.

Within the cave itself, Dean has identified twenty-five room clusters or household suites, each consisting of one living room and one to four storage rooms arranged around a courtyard (fig. 3-14). These room clusters at Keet Seel correspond to the suites first identified in Mug House and other Pueblo III cliff dwellings on the Mesa Verde.

Keet Seel's rock art includes several figures painted on the cliff face: a human figure with one arm flailing downward and the other upward, a flute player, and two anthropomorphic figures with large semicircular heads, each with a hooded extension coming off one corner. These could represent masked figures, for there are historic references to kachina masks in that general shape. A bird figure with a white body probably represents a turkey. Some pecked geometric figures may be seen at the east end of the cave. Nearby Turkey Cave also displays numerous painted positive and negative handprints and a row of birds—turkeys or ducks.

Lower Chinle Wash

Kayenta-style ruins occur all along the Chinle Wash from where it empties into the San Juan River at Comb Ridge up into its Canyon de Chelly headwaters.

3-14. For the most part, the Puebloans worked and cooked over fire pits out of doors in small courtyards, surrounded by living and storage rooms, such as this courtyard in Keet Seel. The smoke blackening on the ceiling of the cave indicates the intensity of the cooking and heating activities. The stub remains of a burned jacal-walled room may be seen near the center of the photograph.

3-15. Baseball Man House extends along a narrow ledge on the west side of the lower Chinle Wash in southeastern Utah. It has eight to twelve masonry-walled rooms with the unexcavated ruins of additional rooms and perhaps one or two kivas at the base of the cliff. The upper wall of one second-story room on the ledge appears to have been constructed of jacal.

Several of those in the lower part of the wash are accessible to visitors who boat along the San Juan River. Upstream from the boat landings, hikers will pass by Baseball Man House, the Duckhead Rock Art Panel, several valley bottom sites of Pueblo I and II vintage, and two ruins in high cliff alcoves.

Baseball Man House consists of eight to twelve masonry-walled rooms tucked along a narrow ledge on the west side of the canyon (fig. 3-15). One second-story room appears to have been built of jacal. Unexcavated ruins of additional rooms, probably including one or two kivas, stand in front of the lower cliff. The ruin exhibits a mixture of Kayenta- and Mesa Verde–style masonry. It derives its name from a double pictograph of a red and white circle with baseball-like seams superimposed over an earlier, white, painted human figure (fig. 3-16).

The **Duckhead Rock Art Panel** appears on a vertical cliff face on the east side of the canyon. Among

3-16. The pictograph for which Baseball Man House was named actually consists of two separate paintings of far different ages. Basket Maker II people first painted the white humanlike figure with broad shoulders, big hands and feet, and dangling earrings. Much later Pueblo III people painted a probable shield of red zones outlined in white on top of the earlier figure. The resulting painting fosters the image of a "living" baseball.

3-17. On the east cliff of the lower Chinle Wash, the Duckhead Rock Art Panel presents a number of unusual figures pecked through the dark desert varnish to expose the lighter rock beneath. A series of humanoid figures sporting duck-shaped heads lends this panel its name.

the many figures pecked into the desert varnish one may see a group of humanoid figures sporting ducks where their heads should be (fig. 3-17). Other figures include a broad-shouldered humanoid with gigantic hands raised above its head, a wiggly line emanating from its right foot to a spiral, a large bird (turkey?), and two flute players, one of whom reclines on his back (fig. 3-18).

The towering **Alcove Ruins** occupy two high, arching rock alcoves situated one above the other on the east canyon wall (fig. 3–19). The upper alcove contains several masonry-walled rooms, while the lower cave has ruins of five rooms, including two granaries, along its north side and four rooms along its south side with a square-cornered kiva in the center. Several stone axe–sharpening grooves survive in the southwestern portion of the ledge. Prehistoric hand- and toe-holds lead up the steep cliff on the south side of the alcoves providing access to the upper cave. Rainwater spilling down through the alcoves accumulates in the lower one where evidence of prehistoric attempts to enhance this natural catchment can be seen. Both

3-18. Another portion of Duckhead Rock Art Panel in the lower Chinle Wash depicts a humanoid figure with very broad shoulders and very large hands upraised. A wavy line emanates from this figure's foot and ends in a spiral, beyond which marches a row of turkeylike birds. Toward the right in the photograph, a long-bodied Kokopelli, or hunchbacked flute player, seems to be reclining on his back.

[Facing page] 3-19. Both of these two towering rock alcoves, stacked in the east cliff face of the lower Chinle Wash, contain small Pueblo III masonry buildings— several rooms in the upper alcove and nine rooms, including two granaries, plus a square-cornered kiva in the lower alcove. A natural hole in the bedrock sandstone that captures and holds rainwater below the alcoves would have been an attractive water source for the people living here.

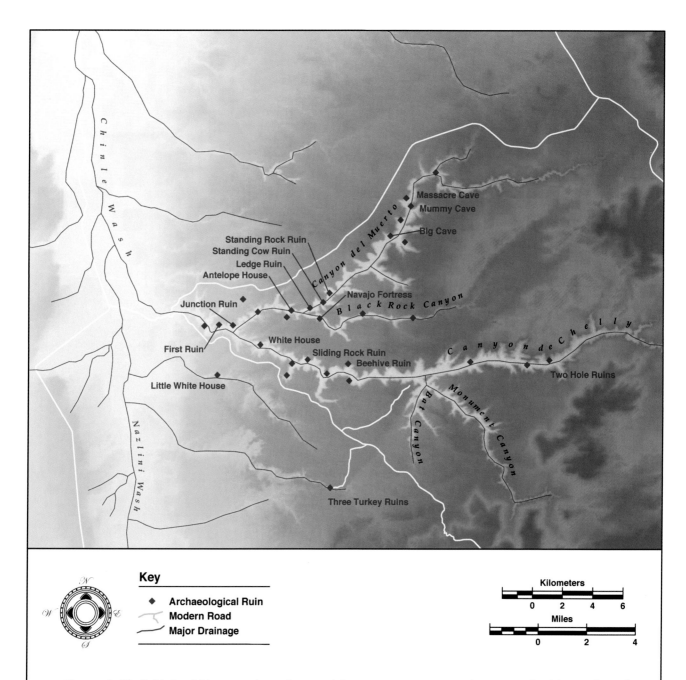

Key

◆ Archaeological Ruin

⌁ Modern Road

⌁ Major Drainage

Kilometers
0 2 4 6

Miles
0 2 4

3-20. Canyon de Chelly National Monument in northeastern Arizona encompasses two major canyons that join together a short distance east of Chinle. Canyon de Chelly gave its name to the monument and contains White House and a number of smaller Puebloan ruins, while Canyon del Muerto extends to the northeast and contains most of the prehistoric ruins including Antelope House, Standing Cow Ruin, Big Cave, and Mummy Cave.

[Facing page] 3-21. The Puebloans and their progenitors inhabited both Canyon de Chelly (to the right) and Canyon del Muerto (to the left) from as early as 1000 B.C. They farmed both on the canyon floors and on the mesa tops. The population of Pueblo III occupants peaked in the canyons about A.D. 1150, when there may have been as many as eight hundred people there, and it declined thereafter until abandonment by 1300. Navajo Indians have occupied the canyons for the past four centuries.

3-22. Navajo farms in the bottom of Canyon del Muerto utilize the same fields farmed by the Puebloans for hundreds of years prior to 1300. The Navajo arrived during the 1600s.

the masonry style and the few pottery sherds reflect Kayenta patterns.

The stream terrace below the alcoves reveals remains of Pueblo I slab-based houses and Pueblo II–III Kayenta-style masonry pueblos littered by fragments of both Kayenta- and Mesa Verde–style pottery. This northern frontier of Kayenta occupation seems to have had close contacts with their Mesa Verdean neighbors to the north.

Canyon de Chelly

Introduction

Canyon de Chelly National Monument's unique natural setting makes it an exceptional and exciting place to visit. Two huge, narrow canyons, de Chelly and del Muerto, with vertical, bare sandstone walls towering up to one thousand feet in height, come together a short distance east of the monument headquarters at Chinle, Arizona. Unless you bring your own four-wheel-drive vehicle and arrange for a Navajo guide, the only way to see and visit ruins in the canyons is by way of arranged tours in old multiwheel-drive, open-top military personnel carriers. The one exception, White House Ruin in Canyon de Chelly, may be visited by way of a hiking trail from the south canyon rim.

Two reasons have made these precautions necessary. Deep, dry sand, running washes, and quicksand fill the canyon bottoms, especially toward their mouths, making travel virtually impossible for standard cars. Secondly, several Navajo families still reside and farm in the canyons, so unauthorized travel would impinge upon their privacy. However, in addition to the canyon tours, self-guided motor trips along both the north rim of Canyon del Muerto and the south rim of Canyon de Chelly afford excellent views of the canyon ruins, of Navajo hogans, and of their cultivated fields.

Canyon de Chelly (pronounced "d'Shay") flows from east to west with the Canyon del Muerto (a Spanish word meaning "death") joining it out of the northeast (fig. 3-20). The headwaters for both come out of the Chuska Mountains, feeding the streams that have cut deeply through the de Chelly Sandstone to carve these very deep, vertical-walled, flat-floored, and well-watered canyons (fig. 3-21) that have provided an almost unique environment for Puebloan residents for over thirteen hundred years and for their Archaic predecessors as far back in time as 1000 B.C.

The Kayenta Puebloans who lived here grew their corn, squash, and beans in the canyon bottomlands, where water regularly flowed beneath but close to the ground surface, in much the same way as the Navajo do today (fig. 3-22). In addition, they hunted wild game and foraged for wild fruits, seeds, and nuts. By Pueblo II, they had begun including domestic turkeys in their diet. Tests at Antelope House have shown that cotton seeds, beeweed, prickly pear cactus, and mule deer formed a regular part of the diet. These unusual conditions allowed the people here to raise cotton, the northernmost place on the Colorado Plateau where this could be done. Remains found at Antelope House include cotton plants, bolls, seeds, and carded fibers. The inhabitants wove these latter into textiles, apparently trading both textiles and fibers to their Puebloan neighbors to the north.

From 700 to 1150, people also lived on the mesa tops surrounding the canyons. Population increased in the entire district up to about 1150, when most people moved into the cliff overhangs in the canyons themselves. From then on, the population declined during the 150 years prior to total abandonment. At no time, even at the peak of population, did more than six hundred people live in this canyon system. During Pueblo IV, some Hopi visited the canyons, either to hunt or for ceremonial purposes, leaving traces of their visits in the form of broken sherds of typical Hopi coal-fired yellow ceramics. When

3-23. Approximately one hundred people lived in the White House Ruin both on the canyon floor and in the cliff over-hang above for about 250 years beginning around A.D. 1060. Floods coming down the Canyon de Chelly have destroyed many of the canyon floor rooms, several of which exhibit Chaco-style features.

Cave, however, a rectangular roofless structure may have functioned as a great kiva in much the same way as did both the Fire Temple and the rectangular great kiva in Long House on the Mesa Verde. Yet, because a small number of Northern San Juan peoples had migrated into Canyon del Muerto during the 1200s, building the central towerlike structure in Mummy Cave and producing Mesa Verde–style ceramics, they could also have influenced the construction of this structure.

Similarly, several large rooms built with Chaco-style masonry at White House suggest influences from the Chaco Basin across the Chuska Mountains to the east. Perhaps both these cases for external contacts reflect a growing restlessness among the Puebloan people in all regions prior to the final abandonment of the San Juan River drainage in the Four Corners.

Westerners first encountered them, the Navajo had settled into the canyons, probably having arrived there during the 1600s.

Most of the best-preserved ruins date to the Pueblo III occupation, and most of them may be found in Canyon del Muerto—Antelope House, Standing Cow Ruin, Big Cave, and Mummy Cave. The other large ruin, White House, rests against the north canyon wall of Canyon de Chelly. Because of their delicate condition, however, visitors may not enter them, although close-up views offer a thrilling experience. Except for the ravages of time and the elements, these ruins still retain the general form and feel they must have exhibited when the Kayenta Puebloans abandoned them during the late 1200s.

Apparently, these Canyon de Chelly occupants did not build as many kin-group kivas as did other Puebloan peoples in the Northern San Juan Region, and no great kivas have been found. At Mummy

White House Ruin

From the White House Overlook on the south rim of Canyon de Chelly, an easy hiking trail (about 1 1/4 miles long) drops some five hundred feet to the canyon bottom and traverses the ankle-deep wash to the White House Ruin (fig. 3-23). Visitors may walk to the edge of the lower ruin, but they may not enter the cliff dwelling portion.

Datable tree-ring specimens taken from the beams used to construct the lower level of this Pueblo III group of buildings indicate that most construction began in the early 1070s and continued to as late as 1275. The big rooms with distinctive close-set, evenly coursed masonry suggest possible Chacoan influence in construction. The lower ruin contained forty-five to sixty rooms with four kivas. The upper ruin in the low cave standing some thirty-five feet above the canyon floor had about twenty rooms (fig. 3-24). White plaster with a decorative band of yellow coats the exterior walls of two of the rooms toward the rear of this cave, giving the ruin its name.

3-24. The white plastered walls in the center of the cliff dwelling at White House give the pueblo its name. Its occupants reached their houses and storage chambers via a ladder resting on top of a three-story-tall building, now mostly collapsed, which led through the gap in the walls to the left in the upper ruin.

3-25. First Ruin, so named for its first location upstream from the mouth of Canyon de Chelly and on its north cliff face, contains sixteen or more Pueblo III rooms and two kivas all on the same level, forming two modular residence units.

Originally, four- and five-story buildings on the lower level allowed access to the upper level by means of ladders resting atop the roofs of the lower buildings. While the walls of all lower-story rooms had been constructed of thick stone masonry, many jacal and adobe walls extended outward and upward from them. At least one T-shaped doorway has been observed. Both pecked and painted figures still survive on the cliff face around and above the rooms. Unfortunately, many of the lower-level rooms have been damaged or destroyed by floodwaters in the wash, which removed about one-third to one-half of the west portion of this lower ruin during the late 1920s and early 1930s. One can even see the remaining half of one kiva where the other half has been washed away. At its peak, White House probably housed up to one hundred people.

First Ruin
First Ruin takes its name from Cosmos Mindeleff as the first ruin he examined during his explorations of

the canyons in 1892. It may be seen both from the canyon floor and from the South Rim Drive at Junction Overlook. It occupies a low ledge on the north side of Canyon de Chelly a short distance west of the junction of the two main canyons. This Pueblo III cliff dwelling contains sixteen or more rooms and two kivas all on one level (fig. 3-25). It probably housed two residence units, each consisting of two or three households of four to six persons each, thus bringing the total population to around fifteen to twenty.

Junction Ruin
Located a few hundred yards to the east and directly overlooking the junction of the two main canyons, the Junction Ruin seems to be a smaller companion to the First Ruin. Nine or more rooms and one kiva occupy the center of this narrow ledge (fig. 3-26). Roughly half the number of people living in First Ruin lived in this Pueblo III structure. Both probably belonged to the larger community focused upon White House and/or Antelope House.

3-26. Junction Ruin, where Canyon de Chelly and Canyon del Muerto join, has nine or more rooms and one kiva, representing a companion residence unit to First Ruin, only a few hundred yards to the west. Both probably belonged to a larger community with White House at its center.

3-27. Antelope House, on the floor of Canyon del Muerto. The visible ruins date to Pueblo III although the remains of earlier structures built during Basket Maker III, Pueblo I, and Pueblo II have been found beneath them. A central plaza, in which a circular low-walled space has been demarcated, separates two distinct room blocks that probably reflect a dual social division. Judging by the large quantities of cotton textiles and all parts of cotton plants recovered from this site, its inhabitants seem to have developed a local specialty in producing both cotton for weaving and the resultant textiles.

Antelope House

Antelope House stands on the canyon floor on the northwest side of Canyon del Muerto (fig. 3-27) about four miles upstream from the junction with the main canyon. Above it the cliff leans outward to provide shelter from most of the elements. Occupation of this site began in Basket Maker III times about A.D. 700 with a pithouse village of unknown extent. A sizeable Pueblo I village occupied an area larger than that of the visible Pueblo III village during the first half of the ninth century. Following a short gap in occupation, a small group of no more than fifteen people built a Pueblo II unit in the southwest end of the site no later than 1050. Between 1100 and 1140, a second group added another small unit pueblo toward the northeast end.

Subsequent Pueblo III construction in the downstream room block took the form of large plastered and decorated rooms, some of which reached two to four stories in height (fig. 3-28). Kayenta-style masonry predominates, with the wall faces plastered both inside and out. White painted geometric designs ornament several room interiors (fig. 3-29). Less-refined room blocks of smaller rooms were added later to the north as needed. After 1200 the residents constructed a low circular wall in the plaza between the two main room blocks, emphasizing the function of this space for community purposes. By 1270 everyone had moved out.

Because so much of the ruin has been eroded away or damaged by the canyon's floodwaters, it is difficult to assess its full size or to estimate the number of people who once lived there. Don Morris, who oversaw a major excavation and analysis of the site during the early 1970s, lists over thirty living rooms alone that housed, conservatively, at least fifty people. Altogether, there once must have been about ninety rooms of all uses here, which would suggest a population at maximum perhaps of eighty to one

3-28. Some standing walls at Antelope House currently reach as high as three stories in buildings that once stood up to two to four stories tall. Kayenta-style stone masonry predominates here with both interior and exterior wall faces heavily plastered.

3-29. Painted plaster on the interior wall of one room in Antelope House illustrates how many residents decorated their living quarters.

3-30. Pueblo III Antelope House contained at least ninety rooms with four or more kivas both in the plaza and in room blocks. Since much of the site has been eroded by canyon floods, we cannot know its full extent. Perhaps similar flooding caused its relatively early abandonment before 1270.

3-31. At the Standing Cow Ruin in Canyon del Muerto, the historic Navajo Indians painted in black and white their view of the arrival of a Spanish missionary on horseback accompanied by mounted soldiers.

hundred. In addition, evidence for four kivas may be seen. Intriguingly, the separation into two blocks of rooms (fig. 3-30) separated by the plaza with its circular low-walled space probably represents a twofold social division.

Morris also oversaw detailed analyses of materials found during the excavations. These studies demonstrated that the people exploited primarily local resources for food and for raw materials for tool making and building. For example, many construction items came from cottonwoods, willows, and reeds that grew at hand in the canyon bottom. They cultivated corn, squash, and cotton (seeds) for food, while gathering products of wild canyon plants and hunting deer and antelope on the nearby mesa tops. While this pattern applies uniquely to Antelope House, it also reflects the generalized Puebloan pattern of exploiting nearby resources and relying only slightly on more distant sources and trade.

3-32. Mummy Cave faces southward in an east-west trending cliff face on the east side of Canyon del Muerto. Seventy to eighty Pueblo III Kayenta-style rooms and four kivas filled the two alcoves of the cave with what appears to be a rectangular great kiva among the rooms in the east (right) alcove. Immigrants from the Northern San Juan Region constructed the prominent buildings, including three kivas and nine rooms, on the ledge between the two caves using Mesa Verde–style construction around 1284.

The long-standing Navajo presence in the canyon complex may be observed in the source of the ruin's name. The local Navajo say a well-known artist named Dibe Yazhi (Little Sheep) painted during the 1830s the series of multicolored antelope that appear to be running along a ledge to the southwest of the tallest prehistoric buildings. Other figures along the same ledge, usually shown in a single color, date to Puebloan times.

Standing Cow Ruin

Canyon bottom tours frequently stop at Standing Cow Ruin, about two miles farther upstream from Antelope House. It cannot be viewed from the North Rim Drive. Here a Pueblo III ruin of eighty-five to ninety rooms and three kivas occupies a long, low cave on the north side wall of the canyon. Here, too, historic Navajo have painted two more realistic scenes on the cliff walls. A large, white cow may be seen toward the

east end of the ruin close to the remnants of an old Navajo hogan (house). The second scene, above a ledge at the west end of the cave, depicts the artist's view of a seventeenth-century Spanish priest on horseback accompanied by several mounted soldiers carrying guns (fig. 3-31). This panel provides an insight into the way the Native Americans saw the arrival of Spanish missionaries and explorers.

Mummy Cave

Mummy Cave lies under a great overhang in the northern portion of Canyon del Muerto about twelve miles above its junction with Canyon de Chelly. Although visitors may not enter this site, excellent views can be had from both the canyon floor and from the overlook on the North Rim Drive (fig. 3-32).

The most spectacular section of this ruin was constructed during late Pueblo III times by immigrants from the Northern San Juan on the ledge between the

3-33. This well-preserved three-story building on the central ledge in Mummy Cave, along with attached two-story rooms and three kivas, was the handiwork of Northern San Juan immigrant builders to Canyon del Muerto. The projecting timbers are original and provided samples to date the building's construction about 1284.

two alcoves that make up this large cave. Tree-ring dates indicate that construction of these three kivas and four ground-floor rooms, including the three-story tower and three two-story rooms, took place about 1284. The tower, with its two levels of roof beams protruding from the walls (fig. 3-33), stands at the south end of this room block. Evenly coursed masonry of dressed sandstone blocks with trim corners characterize these rooms as Mesa Verdean in style when compared with the seemingly cruder Kayenta-style masonry found elsewhere in the ruin.

Before the time of abandonment, probably by 1300, Pueblo III people lived in the visible buildings in the alcoves on either side of the central ledge. The west alcove contained about twenty-five rooms, and it could only be reached from the central ledge. The eastern alcove contains the remnants of fifty-one rooms, four kivas, and an enclosed space that bears a resemblance to the rectangular great kivas at Fire Temple and Long House on the Mesa Verde. In total then, the site had some eighty to ninety ground-floor rooms including storerooms housing about one hundred inhabitants.

The great kiva–like structure permits some interesting speculation. Identified by Roland Reichard during stabilization work on the ruin (hence not excavated), this sub-triangular space measures roughly thirty by twenty feet on its interior. The lower four feet of walls exhibit a reddish brown plaster topped by a band of white where upper wall sections still stand. Interior features include two opposing short benches, two wall niches, and three separate paved areas supported by masonry. Access had to be gained through the now collapsed curving front wall or through a doorway in the northwest end leading out of a neighboring room. All of these features have their closest analogues with the Mesa Verde great kivas; none of them fit the characteristics of ordinary small kivas, living rooms, or storerooms.

3-34. In the lower east end of Mummy Cave, Basket Maker II people constructed a small village of ten small houses and numerous storage cists by mudding upright sandstone slabs to the sloping bedrock cave floor and covering them with logs, branches, and mud. Tree-ring dates place this early occupation between A.D. 300 and 400. The more visible structures belong to the later Pueblo III Kayenta occupation.

Mummy Cave had been occupied prior to the construction and use of the extensive Pueblo III buildings. Remains of some twenty-two Basket Maker II structures, including at least ten houses and many granaries, have been identified at the top of the long talus and rubbish slope at the extreme southeastern end of the overhang (fig. 3-34), while others may have been covered or destroyed by the later buildings. Upright stone slabs and horizontal wooden logs, affixed to the sloping bedrock cave floor with copious amounts of straw-tempered mud, formed the walls probably capped by domed or cribbed roofs. Only one of the houses had an interior hearth; additional hearths had been placed outside. Some houses had simple benches pecked into the bedrock and smoothed, while other benches had been constructed with sandstone slabs, horizontal timbers, and/or adobe. Tree-ring dates place this early occupation between A.D. 300 and 400.

Between these two significant occupations of Mummy Cave, the Puebloans built no structures under the overhang, although scattered pottery sherds throughout the rubbish indicate they had visited the site periodically, perhaps having camped beneath the protection of the shelter. Remains of a small Pueblo I building do appear on the talus slope next to the southeast cliff of the cave, suggesting a small Pueblo I group lived adjacent to the overhang, but not in it. Even the Pueblo IV Hopi had apparently visited this cave site, leaving behind broken pieces of their distinctive yellow coal-fired pottery.

Other Viewable Ruins

Ledge Ruin may be seen from an overlook along the North Rim Drive of Canyon del Muerto between the junction of the two canyons and Antelope House. Like virtually all of the Pueblo III sites on these canyons, it sits in a narrow ledge about one hundred feet above the canyon floor on the north cliff face. It contains approximately thirty or more rooms and apparently more than two kivas. It has not been excavated.

Sliding Rock Ruin occupies a sloping ledge about one hundred feet above the canyon bottom about four miles southeast from White House. It can be viewed from an overlook along the South Rim Drive of Canyon de Chelly. The sloping floor of this ledge on which about fifty rooms and four kivas sit is unstable, giving the Pueblo III ruin its name. Many

3-35. Harold Gladwin excavated the Tusayán Ruin on the south rim of the Grand Canyon in 1930. This small pueblo reflects a westward expansion by Kayenta Puebloans around 1050. It and similar sites lasted for roughly one hundred years, when the Kayenta peoples moved back to their heartland by about 1150.

structures have probably already slid off this ledge. The west and central portions of the site display many rock art figures: a stick flute player, negative and positive handprints, quadrupeds, birds, a frog, running zigzag lines, triangles, circles, and so forth.

Grand Canyon

The modern Hopi Indians claim the Grand Canyon as the place where their ancestors emerged (called "sipap") from the underworld a very long time ago. The Kayenta ancestors of the Hopi first expanded westward into the Grand Canyon during the 900s when a few people camped there while hunting away from home. By 1050 several hundred Puebloans had moved onto the canyon rims and into the canyon itself, where they constructed many small sites over a broad territory. Whatever attracted them to the Grand Canyon, they all left shortly after 1150, returning eastward to their Kayenta heartland. The total Grand Canyon Puebloan population could not have exceeded five hundred persons at any one time.

3-36. An artist's reconstruction of Tusayán Ruin shows a central room block of four two-story living rooms flanked at right angles by two rows of single-story storage rooms. A kiva lies at the southeast corner of the pueblo. (Painting by Gene Foster.)

Besides this short span of occupation, the Puebloan people regularly traveled to the Grand Canyon to hunt and to celebrate their origin tale. Traces of such expeditions date from Basket Maker II to historic times. Evidence of considerable occupation of the Grand Canyon by pre-Puebloan Desert Archaic people lends support to the Hopi origin legend.

Three of the small houses built by the pioneering Puebloans of nine hundred years ago may be visited. The **Tusayán Ruin** (fig. 3-35) lies a short distance from the south canyon rim about three miles west of Desert View at the east end of the south rim road. Harold Gladwin excavated this site in 1930. It consists of a central room block of four two-story masonry living rooms, flanked by two wings of one-story storerooms creating three sides of a square opening to the southeast (figs. 3-36 and 3-37). The smaller one-story rooms in the wings on both east and west sides lacked sufficient space to serve as adequate living quarters. A kiva with a ventilator and its roof supported by four wooden posts occupies the northwest corner of the plaza. A second similar kiva (fig. 3-38), built in the ancient refuse pile south of the east wing, replaced the original one after it burned in the early 1070s.

During the late 1960s, the School of American Research, under the leadership of Douglas Schwartz and in cooperation with the National Park Service, conducted a number of archaeological investigations on Puebloan sites in Grand Canyon National Park. This project recorded sites on the Unkar Delta in the canyon bottom and on the Walhalla Plateau on the north rim. It also excavated several sites in both areas as well as the Bright Angel site near the Phantom Ranch.

Bright Angel Pueblo was built in the bottom of Grand Canyon just to the east of where Bright Angel Creek enters the Colorado River. The pueblo consists of five masonry rooms built above ground forming an L-shaped plan around a masonry-lined subterranean

3-37. The masonry foundations of the ground-floor living rooms at Tusayán Ruin.

3-38. This squarish, mostly aboveground kiva at the southeast corner of Tusayán Ruin had a central, round fire pit, an encircling banquette, a southern ventilator, and a roof supported by four wooden corner posts. People would have entered it through the smoke hole in the roof.

3-39. Artist's reconstruction of Bright Angel Pueblo in the bottom of the Grand Canyon. (Drawing by Joan Foth.)

3-40. Bright Angel Pueblo sits on an alluvial fan next to where Bright Angel Creek enters the north side of the Colorado River in the bottom of the Grand Canyon. The site consists of five masonry-walled rooms and a kin-group kiva with two small granaries tucked under ledges nearby. The Kayenta Puebloans who lived here during the early 1100s farmed on the alluvial fan and had easy access out of the canyon to both the north and the south.

3-41. Unkar Delta, formed by alluvial sediments where Unkar Creek enters the Colorado River from the north in the bottom of the Grand Canyon, offered the Kayenta Puebloans a favorable place to farm and easy access to the north canyon rim up Unkar Creek. The people occupied numerous small sites here between 1050 and 1150, although only three had squarish Kayenta-style kivas.

3-42. The Walhalla Glades Ruin on the Walhalla Plateau on Grand Canyon's north rim represents one of more than one hundred small field houses occupied only seasonally by Kayenta Puebloans while they hunted, gathered wild plant products, and farmed at this 8,000-foot elevation. This building had nine rooms in two separate blocks built and used between 1050 and 1150.

kiva (figs. 3-39 and 3-40) probably dating to the early 1100s. Two small granaries built into the nearby cliffs also probably served the inhabitants of this site. A small pithouse on the same location had been occupied about fifty years earlier.

Bright Angel Pueblo represents only one of several residential sites built on alluvial fans where trails provide access to the canyon rims from the canyon bottom. The largest concentration of such sites spreads across the **Unkar Delta** (fig. 3-41), where Unkar Creek has deposited sediments that bulge out into the Colorado River. None of these Unkar Delta sites was

very large, and only three had squarish Kayenta-style kivas with eastward-running ventilators. A series of small one- and two-room structures, granaries, and use areas ranging along the creek from the delta to the north rim illustrate how people probably traversed the very rugged terrain found within the canyon.

Most of the Puebloan ruins on the north rim of the Grand Canyon consist of small, isolated granaries or seasonal camps. The **Walhalla Glades Ruin** on the Walhalla Plateau exemplifies such camps. Its nine masonry rooms in two separate blocks, with no kiva (fig. 3-42), date between 1050 and 1150. Nearby **Sky**

3-43. Artist's reconstruction drawing of one of the two main room blocks at the Coombs Site near the upper end of the Escalante River in southern Utah at an elevation of 6,700 feet. When the Kayenta Puebloans expanded, they also moved northwestward across the Colorado River to build a sizeable pueblo at the Coombs Site, where tree-ring dates place major construction between about 1129 and 1169. The two distinct room blocks, each with kivas and pithouses, suggest a dual sociopolitical organization.

Island, a seemingly detached portion of the canyon rim, has eighteen masonry-walled rooms in four separate room blocks arranged in a row, but no kiva. Both these sites had a clear view of the Unkar Delta in the canyon bottom as well as a clear line of sight to the Tusayán Pueblo across the canyon on the south rim.

Coombs Site

Yet another example of the Kayenta expansion to the west and across the Colorado River can be seen at the Coombs Site ruins and museum in Anasazi State Park on the northern edge of Boulder, Utah. After crossing the Colorado River, the colonists proceeded up the Escalante River valley to an elevation of 6,700 feet, where they constructed their village on a low promontory with a stream to the east. Such a location offered suitable farming conditions combined with proximity to plentiful wild game and plant food sources.

University of Utah archaeologists under the direction of Robert Lister undertook major excavations in about half of the Coombs Site. They unearthed the remains of ninety-seven rooms, ten pit structures including kivas and contemporary pithouses, and hundreds of thousands of artifacts. The various structures were arranged into two distinct room blocks (fig. 3-43), which suggest a dual social and political organization.

3-44. This living room at the Coombs Site shows the use of basalt block masonry for exterior walls, jacal for inner partition walls, and sloping basalt stones lining a circular hearth. The site also contained many stone slab–lined storage bins inside and outside the rooms.

Many storerooms exhibited typical Kayenta-style masonry, while the larger living rooms combined basalt boulder masonry and jacal partition walls. Circular hearths in the living rooms had sloping basalt stones as linings (fig. 3-44). Slab-lined storage bins could be found both inside the living rooms and outside. Tree-ring dates place the major times of construction between about 1129 and 1169, with abandonment occurring by around 1175.

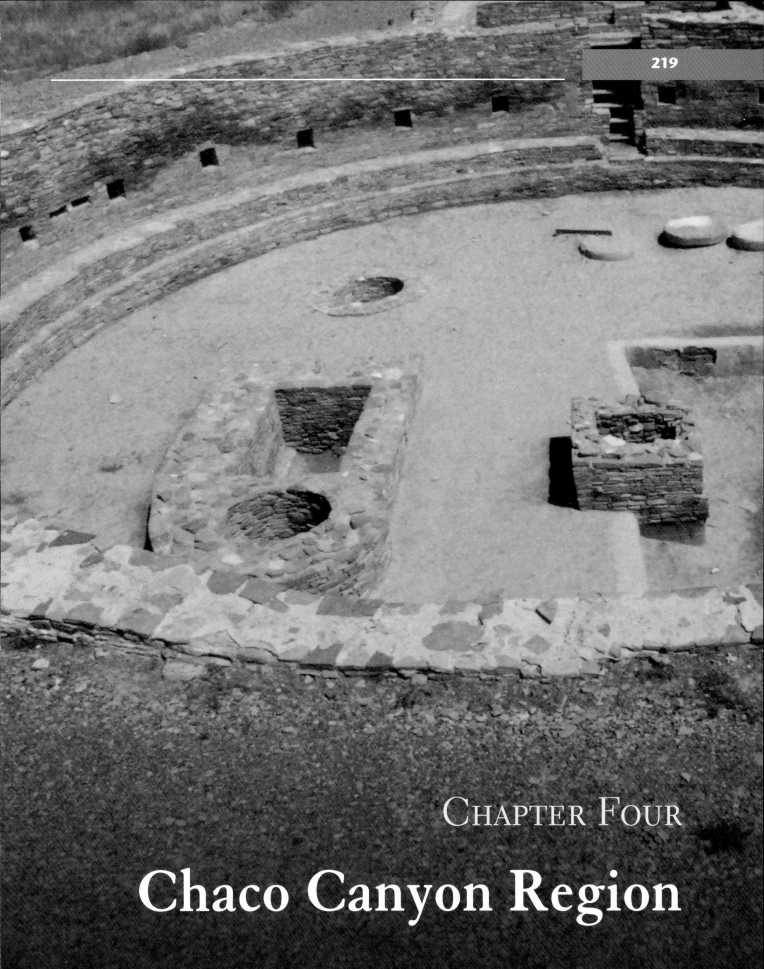

CHAPTER FOUR

Chaco Canyon Region

Introduction to Chacoan Culture

Chaco Canyon, now a part of the Chaco Culture National Historical Park and situated nearly at the center of the high (6,000 to 7,000 feet), seemingly treeless, arid Chaco Basin of northwestern New Mexico, formed the hub of Chacoan Pueblo culture. The park encompasses the magnificent, world-famous ruins of Pueblo Bonito, Casa Rinconada, Chetro Ketl, and others, as well as Fajada Butte, near the top of which perches the well-publicized Sun Dagger site.

Today, during the height of summer, hot and dry conditions in the canyon seem to justify its inclusion in the high desert of the Colorado Plateau. Recent studies suggest that today's climate closely resembles climatic conditions during the times when the prehistoric Puebloan people lived there, except that prior to the middle 1100s somewhat more rain fell during the summer months. The present arroyo that now runs down the middle of the canyon would argue against the use of floodwater irrigation by the Chacoans if it had been there in ancient times. However, some climatologists believe the canyon appeared more verdant in the tenth and eleventh centuries than it does now, and that cutting of the arroyo began with intensive farming of the canyon bottom as ancient populations grew and located their fields and gardens there.

From the hub of Chaco Canyon ancient roadways radiated outward toward contemporary settlements many archaeologists call "outliers." These include Pueblo Pintado to the east, Salmon Ruin to the north, and Kin Ya'a and Casamero to the south. The exact locations of most of these sites have not been revealed to protect them from looters. Chaco culture specialists refer to the burgeoning of the Chaco culture with its outliers as the "Chaco Phenomenon," but unfortunately this flash of cultural expression seems to have been short-lived.

4-1.

CHACO CANYON CHRONOLOGY

Phases	Dates	Site
BONITO		
Early Bonito	920–1020	Pueblo Bonito
		Chetro Ketl
		Una Vida
		Peñasco Blanco
		Hungo Pavi
		Kin Bineola
Early Classic Bonito	1020–1055	Pueblo Alto
		Tsin Kletzin
		Kin Ya'a
Florescent Bonito	1055–1083	Pueblo del Arroyo
		Wijiji
		Pueblo Pintado
Late Classic Bonito	1083–1120	All Bonito Phase sites remodeled and enlarged
Late Bonito	1120–1220	No new construction
HOSTA BUTTE	1040–1154	Casa Rinconada Group and other small sites
McELMO	1050–1154	Kin Kletso
		Casa Chiquita
		New Alto
		Tsin Kletso
		Triwall unit
REOCCUPATION	1250–1300	Some remodeling in older sites
ABANDONMENT	By 1300	

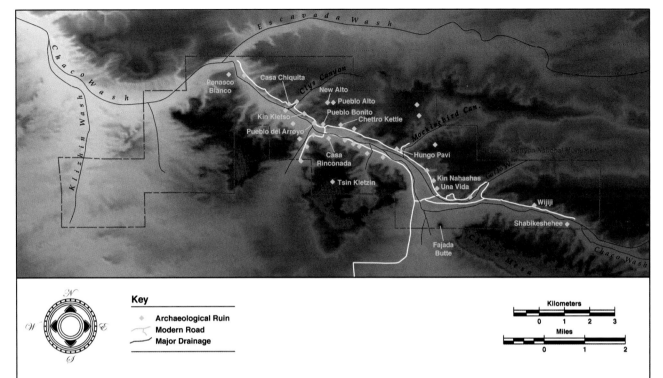

4-2. At the Chaco Canyon in northwestern New Mexico, the Puebloans underwent a remarkable development in architecture and communications by the end of the 1000s. This development left behind for future generations the remnants of some of the most spectacular pre-Columbian buildings in the United States.

The Bonito Phase of Chacoan culture covers the period during which the Chaco Phenomenon begins, flourishes, and starts to wane, roughly between 920 and 1120 (fig. 4-1). According to the interpretations of R. Gwinn Vivian, the Chacoans drew on ideas and practices from both the north and the south to inspire their own distinctive brand of Puebloan culture, especially in architectural expression. The Bonito Phase encompassed both Pueblo II and Pueblo III characteristics. It reached the Pueblo III stage at least fifty years earlier than did other Puebloans. But in turn, after its florescence, Pueblo III Chacoan culture waned more than a century earlier than did its counterparts in the Northern San Juan and Kayenta regions.

During the century prior to 1020, the Chacoans began construction and occupation of the sites that ultimately became the towns of Una Vida, Peñasco Blanco, Pueblo Bonito, Chetro Ketl, and Hungo Pavi. Both Pueblo Bonito and Chetro Ketl underwent additional major construction in the early 1000s. All these pueblos occupied a seven-mile-long stretch of Chaco Canyon from Una Vida, near Fajada Butte at the east end, to Peñasco Blanco, on West Mesa to the west (fig. 4-2).

The earliest buildings were built of unfaced stone slab–type masonry—sandstone slabs laid in a double row and sealed with mud mortar. They began as small arcing Pueblo I– and Pueblo II–style structures with storerooms behind (to the north of) living rooms and open plazas to the south. Through subsequent regular additions to these basic buildings, the occupants created the larger structures.

These early people also learned to control rainwater runoff from the cliffs to irrigate fields in the canyon bottom as a supplement to Chaco Wash

4-3. Wijiji, just over two miles east of the Chaco Canyon visitor center, represents a Classic Bonito Phase pueblo with ninety-two first-floor rooms and two kivas. (Photograph taken with the assistance of John Q. Royce.)

floodwaters. They built dams, ditches, and canals, some with complex headgates, to divert water to the various fields and gardens.

By 1020 the Chacoans had begun to develop a well-ordered cultural pattern reflected in architecture, ceramics, jewelry making, astronomical observations, roadway building, communication systems, and agriculture. Bonito Phase practices essentially became the precursors of the Classic Pueblo III culture of the Puebloan Southwest.

Exact dates cannot be determined, but several additional pueblos began during Early Classic Bonito times after 1020. Pueblo Alto became the terminus for the roadways leading northward. Kin Ya'a, along a roadway to the south, has an impressive tower kiva. Tsin Kletzin lies southwest of the canyon. Pueblo Pintado lies along another roadway seventeen miles east-southeast of Pueblo Bonito. Within the canyon itself, Pueblo del Arroyo became one of the major later pueblos, while **Wijiji** (fig. 4-3) lay about five miles upstream to the east.

Dense clusters of tree-ring dates during the florescent portion of the Classic Bonito Phase between 1055 and 1083 indicate a period of intense building activity. During this active period, most of the larger pueblos approached their final form. At the same time, especially along the south side of the canyon, many smaller sites without any of the finest wall masonry sprang up. Archaeologists have labeled these sites as belonging to the Hosta Butte Phase.

The Hosta Butte Phase (1040–1110) defines a settlement pattern of Chacoans that contrasts with that of the Bonito Phase sites along the canyon's north side. Most Hosta Butte buildings were relatively small with few reaching above a single story. They consisted of blocks of rooms that appear to have grown irregularly. Walls contained only roughly finished stone masonry with liberal amounts of mud mortar. Subterranean kivas lay scattered among the rooms, but rarely conformed to the customary north-south orientation. These smaller structures usually clustered together as we see in the group associated

4-4. Casa Chiquita, located next to where the modern road enters Chaco Canyon from the north, is a small, unexcavated McElmo Phase village of about fifty rooms, originally standing two or three stories high, and at least two kivas. (Photograph taken with the assistance of John Q. Royce.)

with Casa Rinconada, the large isolated great kiva situated opposite Pueblo Bonito on the south side of the canyon. Possibly half of the canyon's inhabitants lived in these smaller buildings, even though they shared most of the rest of Chacoan culture.

The McElmo Phase overlaps somewhat the later parts of both Bonito and Hosta Butte phases. It describes sites constructed by apparent immigrants into the canyon from the Northern San Juan Region to the north. These sites, often located along the north side of the canyon, exhibit smaller room sizes with Mesa Verde–style masonry. Chaco archaeologists consider such sites as Kin Kletso, Casa Chiquita, New Alto, Tsin Kletzin, and probably the triwall structure attached to the west side of Pueblo del Arroyo to reflect this influx of people.

Casa Chiquita contains twenty to thirty ground-floor rooms surrounding a central kiva with a second probable kiva at its northeast corner (fig. 4-4). Many of the rooms in the west and south wings appear to have been two or even three stories tall. The central

kiva rests on a low clay knob that gives it the appearance of elevation even though it had been built below the ground of the knob. Despite three tree-ring dates ranging between 1058 and 1064, the McElmo masonry style and ceramics suggest a more likely construction date between 1100 and 1130.

Interpretations of the Chaco Phenomenon vary greatly and have inspired considerable controversy. W. James Judge suggests that the growing population in the 900s could not be supported by the canyon's agriculture, so the Chacoans developed an industry fashioning turquoise into ritual and other objects to be exchanged with outlying Chaco Basin villages for food and other goods. Judge argues that Chaco Canyon in the 1000s became a ritual center (similar to the Maya cities during the 700s and 800s). By 1050, he suggests, Chaco Canyon served as the center of a social, ritual, and economic system. He sees the large pueblos not as year-round residences but rather as accommodations for pilgrims traveling along the roadways. He would estimate the canyon's permanent population at two thousand rather than the six thousand indicated by the number of rooms in the canyon.

David Stuart also envisions the Chaco Phenomenon as a regional system centered on the canyon with economic activities ebbing and flowing between highland zones and lowland zones as minor fluctuations occurred in rainfall and temperature. Both economic and religious ties to the center held the system together. Both he and Judge infer the concentration of power to be in the Chaco Canyon itself with the surrounding outlying populations following the proscriptions of the powerful.

On the other hand, R. Gwinn Vivian sees the Chaco Phenomenon arising out of a coalescence of influences from both the north and the south that led to construction of the large pueblos. Citing many examples from living and historic cultures around the world, Vivian believes that the entire system could have functioned nicely with a strong basis in an organization of social and political duality, not unlike that of the modern Pueblos. The contrast between the large Bonito Phase buildings along the north side of the canyon and the contemporary, smaller Hosta Butte Phase sites on the south side reflect this duality. Such contemporaneity and their participation in the same social/political community leads one to question the advisability of defining two separate phases. It would not have been necessary to invoke a power-wielding elite class to account for the cultural complexity, which in fact closely resembles that from other Puebloan regions. He envisions the collapse of the Chaco Phenomenon coming from overexploitation of resources in a fragile environment. In this volume, we favor Vivian's interpretations because they better fit the available data.

Architecture

The partially excavated Pueblo Bonito and Chetro Ketl offer good examples of four- and five-story living and storage complexes of room-enclosed courtyards, kin-group or lineage kivas, and great kivas all built according to accepted templates. Pueblo Bonito may have housed as many as one thousand people, with fewer persons in the other pueblos.

During Florescent Bonito times, the older towns of Una Vida, Peñasco Blanco, Pueblo Bonito, and Chetro Ketl underwent extensive remodeling. Several new pueblos also sprang up. Pueblo Pintado, an outlier to the east, contained wood specimens suggesting a mostly single construction phase around 1060–1061. Pueblo del Arroyo, located near Pueblo Bonito in the center of the canyon, and Wijiji, some five miles to the southeast, seem to be among the latest sites to be built. These major building projects occurred between 1055 and 1083, unless some timbers were not incorporated in buildings the same year they were cut.

Coursed masonry of sandstone slabs and blocks characterize the Chacoan construction style. Several individual masonry styles may be recognized. The builders used two main types of stone: the hard, brown tabular sandstone from the bench above the canyon cliffs, and the bedded sandstone from the cliffs themselves. Crude unshaped slabs set in large amounts of mud mortar characterize the earlier walls of Pueblo Bonito. Thicker, rarely shaped blocks of sandstone make up the walls of the smaller Hosta Butte Phase sites on the canyon's south side.

In the larger buildings walls were usually constructed two or three stones in thickness, with some consisting of a stone-packed core faced on both sides with veneers. The wall faces exhibited a variety of different patterns of stone block and slab placement, some of them showing forms of banding (see figs. 1-30 and 1-31). These various styles of wall construction seem to have been more a matter of each individual mason's style rather than improved efficiency. In general, however, the thicker walls were designed to support multiple stories of rooms.

Some archaeologists have suggested that skilled laborers shaped and set the stones while other workers did the carrying and mortar mixing, and that construction of the large pueblos followed master plans conceived in the minds of the builders prior to construction. They argue that in addition to laying up the walls, they needed to plan in advance the necessary thickness for the proposed height of the building. They suggest further that the builders needed to determine locations of rooms, kivas, and plazas in order to allow for doorways, air vents, and interior wall supports. Thus they invoke a division of labor and a system of management that other archaeologists do not accept.

These other archaeologists point out that Chacoan construction actually resembles quite closely, except for the banded masonry, that found at other Puebloan sites in the Northern San Juan, Kayenta, and Little Colorado River regions where specialized managed labor was not needed. Any preplanning would have had to survive the several generations it took to construct them. Impressive as they may be, the large Chaco buildings can also be seen as assemblies of the same kind of modular residential units found throughout Pueblo-land from Basket Maker times onward. Even when abutted together, such modular units provide for doorway access, smoke and air vents, plus kiva and plaza arrangement. For comparison, loosely directed community efforts in rural America have constructed many a barn, farmhouse, and Grange hall according to "plans" held jointly in the minds of the contributing laborers.

Ceremonial Structures

Like their Puebloan relatives, the Chacoans built smaller kin-group kivas, larger great kivas for community use, and a variety of shrines. The one triwall structure at Pueblo del Arroyo appears to have been a McElmo Phase addition. Tower kivas seem to represent an exclusively Chacoan feature.

Typical Chaco-style kivas had eight low log end pilasters—short sections of horizontal logs fitted into the kiva wall, cut end inward, which supported the roof of cribbed logs (see fig. 1-40). Ventilator tunnels regularly entered beneath floor level, doing away with any need for a draft deflector. Many also had a floor vault (see fig. 1-42).

Every large Chacoan pueblo had one or even two great kivas. Three may be seen at Pueblo Bonito, although we cannot tell if all had been in use at the same times. Great kivas generally had semisubterranean floors with flat roofs raised several feet above ground level. Entrance could be obtained through an antechamber on the north side, which also contained a raised altar. Interior features include a circular bench, possibly to accommodate ceremonial viewers, a raised masonry firebox, a pair of rectangular masonry floor vaults, some form of sipapu, and sockets for roof support pillars (see figs. 1-45 and 1-46).

Tower-kivas have been found only in Chaco Canyon at Chetro Ketl, Una Vida, and Kin Kletso and at some Chacoan outliers such as Kin Ya'a and Salmon Ruin. They probably served ceremonial functions, although some investigators have noted they usually stand at the highest point in the pueblo where the best view of neighboring pueblos and probably signal stations could be had.

Ceramics

Chacoan pottery bears a number of distinctive qualities. The utility corrugated jars often display a variety of decorations wrought by modifying the exterior unobliterated coils into patterns or by incising and pinching over the coils. Potters decorated food bowls, drinking mugs, water jars, and vases by painting with mineral pigments a variety of geometric figures in solid black or in a kind of halftone created by hatching (close parallel lines), often bounded by markedly heavier lines. A characteristic Chacoan mug can be

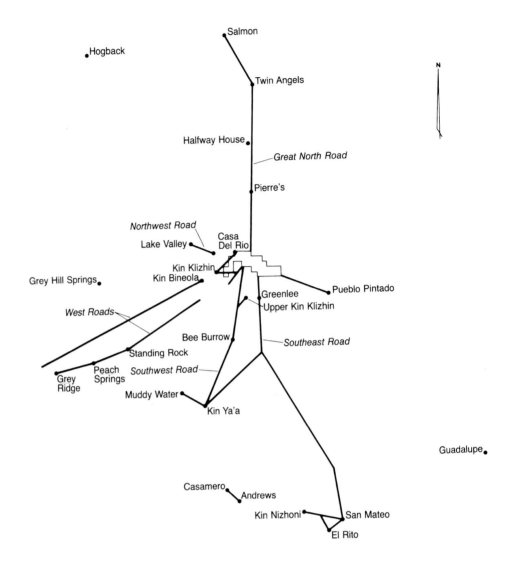

4-5. The Chaco system of roadways linked Puebloan communities throughout the Chaco Basin, focusing on the Chaco Canyon. The map shows many known segments of roadways, totaling more than four hundred miles, recognized through a combination of aerial photography and ground survey. Obviously, many more miles of roadways existed in the past, but they have either been destroyed by modern farming or have yet to be discovered.

identified by its tall cylindrical body with vertical strap handle sitting atop a globular base. Tall cylindrical vases (see fig. 1-63) are unique to Chaco Canyon.

As part of the arrival of northern influences that mark the McElmo Phase in architecture, pottery painted in organic (carbon) pigments using Northern San Juan–style designs appears in the canyon. Both mineral- and organic-pigmented ceramics coexisted during the later Bonito and Hosta Butte phases after about 1050, but the mineral pigments disappear after about 1130–1150. Some vessels have black painted designs of geometric solids or hatching on a red-slipped background.

Population

By 1100 the number of rooms available suggests that up to six thousand people could have been living in some four hundred sites in the Chaco Canyon and its immediate surroundings. This would be about double the population during the Early Bonito Phase, indicating that many people moved into the canyon during the height of construction activity. Perhaps as many, or more, lived in the many so-called outliers scattered throughout the Chaco Basin. Many sites in the Northern San Juan often labeled as Chacoan outliers actually belong to large local settlements, some of which may have contributed to the movement of

4-6. Seven Chacoan road-ways converge on Pueblo Alto, seen here from the northeast. The Great North Road has been traced from here as far north as Kutz Canyon, south of Bloomfield.

peoples into Chaco Canyon during the eleventh and twelfth centuries.

Communication System

The most technically advanced aspect of the Chaco culture involved their systems of roadways and line-of-sight communications. Even though traces of similar systems in both the Northern San Juan and Kayenta regions have been recognized, the evidence from the Chaco Basin has been more completely preserved and studied. The line-of-sight signaling network in use among the Chacoans could have linked communities throughout the Chaco Basin by using fires at night. They often combined shrines with signal stations. A Pueblo III shrine–signal station uncovered near Peñasco Blanco contained a cache of turquoise beads. This shrine (Site 29SJ423) had a clear view of the distant eastern and western horizons. Line-of-sight contact

had also been established between Pueblo III settlements located on high eminences in the Long House Valley of the Kayenta Region.

Survey archaeologists have recorded a number of circles of loose stones situated on exposed rock surfaces near the cliff edge with two or three holes pecked into the bedrock at their perimeters. These holes usually align to another cliff edge location where a similar stone circle occurs, or they may point toward one of the large canyon pueblos. Members of the Chaco Center research staff tested the line-of-sight connections among these features by building fires or shining automobile headlights at a preset time at night. Every station could observe the lights at one or more of the other stations.

Roadways leading to outliers ran north, south, southeast, and southwest from Chaco Canyon. The Great North Road headed toward Salmon and Aztec ruins, but disappeared in the heavily eroded Kutz

4-7. A prehistoric stairway, one of several leading into and out of Chaco Canyon, ascends to the north mesa rim from behind Hungo Pavi in the canyon bottom.

Canyon near a major shrine at Twin Angels Peak. The southeast roadway reached Pueblo Pintado and Guadalupe, the south roadway ran to San Mateo and Kin Nizhoni, the southwest roadway extended to Kin Ya'a next to Crownpoint, and another roadway led to Standing Rock and Peach Springs (fig. 4-5). Additional road segments headed westward toward Skunk Springs.

All told, some nine hundred miles of roadways have so far been recorded, mostly within the Chaco Basin where the land surfaces have been less modified than in other regions, with new traces being found constantly. Not all roadways lead to Chaco Canyon. Segments have been recorded running north-south along the eastern side of the Chuska Mountains, between large settlements in the Montezuma Valley as at Lowry (see fig. 1-53), and along Comb Wash in Utah (see fig. 2-124).

Roadways were formed by pushing aside loose surface stones and sometimes by cleaning surface debris down to hardpan clay or to bedrock and banking this debris along both sides. Where they traversed exposed bedrock surfaces, lines of spaced stones often marked the path. Pueblo Alto on the north rim of Chaco Canyon formed a sort of terminus for several roadways from the north and northeast (fig. 4-6). Where some roadways descended into the canyon, they followed stairways cut by hand into the bedrock cliffs (fig. 4-7). Outside the canyon, these roadways formed virtually perfect straight lines despite occasional obstacles. When a roadway turned, it turned on an angle to another straight line segment.

Roadway widths averaged around twenty feet on the major stems, with a maximum at about forty feet, while spurs ran only about twelve feet wide. Such widths far exceeded any needs for standard foot traffic. Some archaeologists have speculated that such wide avenues supported the transportation of goods for exchange, building materials, people, even armies, in and out of Chaco Canyon. Yet strangely, these roadways exhibit virtually no signs of wear and tear from heavy traffic. For this reason, Michael Marshall has suggested the roadways had not really been intended for human use but for the use of spiritual beings en route to and from the pueblos to ensure that they could find their way.

Astronomical Observations

All ancient peoples, none of whom had the benefit of electric lighting, could not help but notice changes in the night skies from one season to the next. Even in tropical zones, the sun and moon rose and set in different positions on the horizons throughout the year. Anyone spending time outdoors would be aware of the movements of the sun, the moon, and many stars. Modern Pueblo Indians have ritual calendars that mesh with the basic movements of the solar system, and evidence indicates that the prehistoric Puebloans, including the Chacoans, observed such solar phenomena.

No one knows the full extent of Chacoan, or Puebloan, astronomical sophistication. They obviously were aware of the seasonal movements of the sun, and they could determine the equinoxes and solstices by observing sunrises at various points on the horizon. They could also make accurate directional alignments by following shadows cast by the sun as it moved throughout the day. However, they lacked the much more detailed observations of sun, moon, and stars by the Pawnee of the North American grasslands, nor could they devise as accurate a calendar as did the Maya of Central America.

Although several alignments of openings in some buildings such as Pueblo Bonito and Casa Rinconada point toward solstice sunrise points on the horizon, the epitome of solar observation occurs high atop Fajada Butte. At this site daggers of light mark both summer and winter solstice and the equinoxes (see fig. 1-81). Anna Sofaer, who first recognized this

observatory, also suspects it contains a device for recognizing the phases of the moon.

One rock art site located near the foot trail leading to Peñasco Blanco also seems to record an astronomical occurrence. Here a crescent moon, a bright star, and a human hand have been painted in red on the underside of a flat sandstone overhang. Slightly below and to the left, three red concentric circles on a yellow background, painted on the vertical back wall of the shelter, probably represent the sun just below the horizon (probably marked by the crack between back wall and roof of this overhang) (fig. 4-8). Some archaeologists like to consider this group as a representation of a supernova that would have been seen worldwide, including in Chaco Canyon, in A.D. 1064. Since a crescent moon did not necessarily accompany the supernova, however, this scene seems more likely to have represented the concurrence of the very last crescent of the waning moon with Venus, or morning star, just prior to sunrise. Or, the new moon often may be seen close to Venus as evening star as the sun sets in the west. Such events occur several times each year. The astronomer Michael Zeilik points out that the crescent moon would actually face toward the sun rather than away from it, but most likely it was the concept in the mind of the painter that mattered.

Water Management

The management of rainwater runoff to conserve scarce water resources marks another major achievement of the Chacoans. A series of water diversion and distribution devices along the entire canyon from Una Vida to Peñasco Blanco employed dams in many side canyons to impound the runoff and direct the water through canals to larger side canyons where it would feed headgates, from whence it could be directed into a grid irrigation network to water the fields. Key parts of the headgates had stone masonry lining to impede

4-8. Beneath a shallow rock overhang near the trail to Peñasco Blanco, the Puebloans painted a star, a crescent moon, a human hand, and below the crack to the left, the sun. These figures portray the eastern sky just before sunrise showing Venus as the morning star rising near the new moon. The handprint probably belonged to the artist.

erosion and to allow various channels to be blocked off by stone slabs. Stone-lined field borders helped identify what fields belonged to whom. Despite its complexity, R. Gwinn Vivian does not feel any central oversight or control beyond the strong dual organization of the population would have been needed to construct and operate such a system.

End of the Chaco Phenomenon

Bonito Phase people accomplished little new construction, and presumably little remodeling after 1120.

Of course we cannot know if new building efforts employed reused older timbers, since the tree-ring dates record only the year when the tree died or had been cut down. Reuse of both stone building materials and timbers has been recorded at numerous sites throughout Pueblo-land, and since good timbers were scarce in the Chaco Canyon by Pueblo III, it would only make sense to salvage any useable old timbers. No new cutting dates occur after the mid-1100s.

By this time the Chaco Phenomenon had faded, probably reflecting the inability of the sociopolitical

4-9. Pueblo Bonito in Chaco Canyon, the largest and one of the most spectacular single buildings constructed by the Puebloans, stood up to five stories high along its curved back wall. It grew by accretion from the early 900s into the middle 1100s during at least four major and many minor construction episodes. At its peak in the late 1000s, it housed roughly one thousand people in some eight hundred rooms and thirty-seven kivas, including two great kivas.

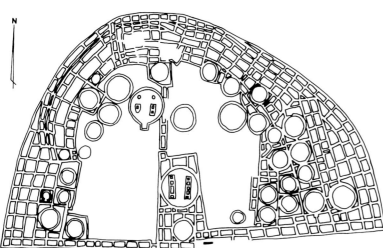

4-10. The ground plan of Pueblo Bonito shows its D-shaped layout and its two-part division.

4-11. The living rooms at Pueblo Bonito were quite large by Puebloan standards and constructed of unusually fine sandstone block masonry. Several different styles of banded and unbanded masonry in this photograph display the workmanship of different individual stone masons. The horizontal grooves in the walls held the ends of roofing beams separating floor levels, at least three of which can be seen here.

duality to overcome worsening environmental and economic conditions. The incoming McElmo Phase people did continue to do some building during the 1100s. But apparently the Chacoan population had begun to move away during the latter part of the twelfth century. If any stayed behind, they became amalgamated into a population of immigrants from the Northern San Juan who remodeled many larger rooms and kivas into smaller versions and who produced McElmo/Mesa Verde–style pottery. By 1300 all the Puebloans, even the latest immigrants, had left the Chaco Basin. From about 1300 until sometime in the 1700s, when the Navajo arrived, Chaco Canyon's buildings simply formed a ghost town.

Where they went and why has been addressed in the introduction to this volume. Yet we might continue to speculate about the nature of the social and political organization of the Chaco Phenomenon. Despite some claims, archaeologists have found no convincing evidence for nobles, kings, or hereditary chiefs. Chaco Canyon ruins have revealed no solid evidence for an elite class, a priestly class, or a theocracy. Hence, the only supportable explanation of the authority that could oversee the building and maintaining of the irrigation works, roadways, and line-of-sight signaling system would be R. Gwinn Vivian's vision of the strong, seasonal dual leadership that also cemented the social fabric of the whole society together. That system continues among the historic Puebloan peoples, especially in the Rio Grande Valley.

Pueblo Bonito

Between 1050 and 1100, Pueblo Bonito could have housed up to one thousand people in some six hundred rooms. It was the largest single Puebloan building and one of the most thoroughly excavated. Lieutenant James H. Simpson of the U.S. Army first described the ruin in 1849, while Richard Wetherill, a trader and rancher, conducted the first excavations there. Wetherill was later shot and killed by a local Navajo. The Hyde Exploring Expedition began in 1896. By its conclusion four years later, it had cleared 190 rooms and kivas and shipped some ten thousand pieces of pottery and a huge number of turquoise beads and pendants to New York. Neil M. Judd and the National Geographic Society worked at the site for seven years beginning in 1921. Judd also began to stabilize the ruin during the 1930s. Research continued at this and other sites in the Chaco Canyon during the 1970s by the National Park Service and the University of New Mexico under the direction of Robert H. Lister and, later, W. James Judge.

The great building we now know as Pueblo Bonito began about 828 as a typical Pueblo I village with pithouses and storage units. During Pueblo II between about 919 and 936, its occupants added an arc of rudely constructed one-story living rooms, with storage rooms in the rear, built of wall-width stone slabs embedded in mud mortar. This marked the first of four major construction phases, during which the pueblo grew both in size and grandeur. The second building phase, during the early 1000s, added several kivas and the great curved rear wall that still stands. This second-phase outer wall has covered the older curved wall, but it did not destroy it.

The vast bulk of construction took place during the Early Classic and Florescent Bonito Phases between 1030 and 1079, based on the tree-ring dates recovered from construction timbers. It included the two great kivas and rooms and kivas located in the front of the site on the east and west sides. The last phase, lasting into the early 1100s, added several kivas and rooms to the southeast corner, bringing the pueblo to its final appearance (figs. 4-9 and 4-10). In all, the process of building and remodeling Pueblo Bonito covered a span of just over two hundred years, roughly ten generations of its inhabitants. Many burials found in some of the earlier rooms demonstrate that not all of the final building had been occupied at the same time.

Four principal styles of stone masonry have been identified at Pueblo Bonito (fig. 4-11). The oldest style employed rough sandstone slabs, double rowed, held together with abundant mud mortar. The second style used dressed and faced sandstone blocks requiring much less mortar, and chinked between courses with thin laminate sandstone tablets. The third kind of masonry wall had a packed rock interior veneered on the outside with banded masonry made up of dressed sandstone blocks alternating with zones of inch-thick tablets of sandstone. The latest walls also had rock-packed interiors faced on both sides with sandstone tablets of relatively uniform thickness.

Many archaeologists do not understand the significance of these different masonry styles. At Pueblo

4-12. The cooperative effort required to construct this high curving back (north) wall for Pueblo Bonito has led to speculations that the builders followed a grand design in laying out and building the large Chacoan pueblos. The wall's distinct taper from the bottom toward the top suggests it had been intended to carry a heavy architectural load of multistory rooms, and its cross section reveals the packed-rock core and veneer technique for construction.

Bonito they fit into a sequence of construction, but only at Pueblo Bonito. At other pueblos the styles as well as the sequence of construction differ. It had nothing to do with strength or durability, since all but the first style possessed equally effective capabilities. The differing styles hardly seem to have been ornamental since most of the masonry walls had been plastered over. Still, it seems most likely these masonry variations reflected style preferences among individual stone masons. Overall the elegant close-fitting masonry, made possible by the availability of tabular sandstone outcrops, stands as a hallmark of Chacoan style.

4-13. Chaco-style kin-group kivas in Pueblo Bonito and other Chaco Canyon ruins display a circular shape with a floor level recess on the south side, an encircling banquette, an average of eight low masonry and stub log pilasters on the banquette to support the cribbed log roof, a ventilator tunnel that enters from the south below floor level and thus required no separate deflector, and a centrally positioned hearth.

The huge curved rock-packed wall forming the back side of the pueblo tapered from bottom to top, presumably to support the massive weight of five stories of rooms (fig. 4-12). Throughout the pueblo, rooms were arranged in terraces to allow access without an interior system of stairways. With its high back wall, its enclosed plazas, and its inward focus of living rooms and kivas, the later stages of Pueblo Bonito almost resembled a fort. The single entrance, located in the south wall in the southeast corner of the west plaza, originally opened only seven feet ten inches in width. Later, a single cross wall with a doorway in its middle narrowed this entrance to only thirty-two inches in width. In addition all external doorways in the previously constructed outer walls were sealed. We will probably never know whether these measures provided defenses against marauding tribes or against their neighbors.

Because many of the upper walls have collapsed since the pueblo's abandonment, we can never know the exact number of rooms in the building or how many may have been occupied at any given time.

Many of the older rooms had been filled with rubbish to provide footings for upper levels that reached five stories high along some parts of the rear wall. Archaeologists estimate the building may have contained as many as eight hundred rooms, although probably no more than six hundred had been in use at one time. The pueblo also contains thirty-seven kivas, but not all were used at the same time.

Pueblo Bonito represents a spectacular architectural achievement for a people living a Neolithic lifestyle who possessed no metal tools, no wheel, no form of writing, and no beast of burden. Archaeologists disagree over whether this great masonry structure required some form of master plan or whether the builders, over roughly ten generations, simply followed a generalized cultural concept by putting together smaller pueblo modular units using techniques known to the Puebloan people since Pueblo I times. Some of the long outer walls and the great kivas may have needed cooperative efforts, but most interior rooms and smaller kivas could easily have been family/lineage undertakings.

Community efforts and cooperation can be seen throughout Pueblo-land, not just in the Chaco Canyon sites. The residents of Keet Seel pooled their labor to construct the large rampart wall supporting the entire eastern end of the site. Puebloan farmers throughout the Four Corners country combined their energies to build extensive systems of farming terraces and water collection works such as Mummy Lake on the Mesa Verde. Town dwellers contributed to the building of the communally used great kivas and concentric-wall structures.

Pueblo Bonito stands near the north cliff of the Chaco Canyon about midway between Escavada Wash and Fajada Butte. As the pueblo grew, its occupants recognized that a great balanced rock that had separated from the cliff face posed a threat to the building if it should ever fall. We can realize their concerns because

4-14. The great plaza in Pueblo Bonito with a north-south wall dividing it into east and west sides and a great kiva on each side indicate a duality of social and political organization among the Chacoan Puebloans that resembles the dichotomy of Winter People and Summer People among the modern Pueblos.

the Bonitians placed a series of support timbers combined with tons of earth and masonry beneath this rock, apparently to forestall its collapse. As insurance, they also placed some prayer sticks and perhaps other offerings behind the rock. These features inspired the historic Navajo to call the ruin Sa-bah-ohn-nee, "the house where the rocks are propped up." Apparently these measures taken by the prehistoric Bonitians worked, for the great monolith of Threatening Rock did not fall until January of 1941, when it produced an avalanche of rubble that tore through the back wall of the ruin.

The ruins of Pueblo Bonito exhibit the characteristic arrangement found in Puebloan residential buildings throughout the Southwest. Masonry rooms, often two or more stories high, were placed to the rear, generally on the north side, of the pueblo. Living rooms faced the plaza with storage rooms behind them. The small kin-group kivas lay in the plazas, sometimes partially or wholly surrounded by rooms. They usually have a subfloor ventilator, a central hearth, and a low encircling banquette on which sit four to ten horizontal log pilasters to support the

cribbed roof (fig. 4-13). Each level kiva roof became part of the plaza or of a courtyard among the rooms. A trash dump lay beyond the open end of the plaza. At Pueblo Bonito a row of rooms built across the front of the plaza separated it from the trash dump. The presence of great kivas reflects the size and possible importance of the pueblo, for they served as community-wide ceremonial centers of the complex, and they may have served smaller surrounding villages and hamlets as well. Pueblo Bonito has no tower-kiva.

Two great kivas, forty and fifty feet in diameter, respectively, lie on either side of a north-south row of rooms that divides the main plaza into two (fig. 4-14). A possible third great kiva may once have existed. The rooms in the dividing row contained many manos and metates. The metates were arranged in a line of bins where several women could work together grinding corn for the daily meals. This dividing row of rooms implies that a dual organization existed within Pueblo Bonito's social and political life to handle community affairs, much as R. Gwinn Vivian has suggested.

Very little rock art has been found at Pueblo Bonito. Yet at the base of the cliff directly behind the curved back wall may be seen a pair of large footprints pointing upward. Strangely each footprint clearly has six toes! Archaeologists had long dismissed this depiction of six-toed feet as mere artistic license, until physical anthropologist Ethne Barnes discovered an actual case of six toes on the skeletal remains of a person found buried in one of the pueblo's rooms. Thus, the ancient artists had actually been anatomically accurate.

Pueblo Bonito functioned more or less as a self-sufficient social and political entity. As a farming community, it encompassed gardens, resource areas, housing, work areas, clan or lineage group kivas, and great kivas. It was not an ancient equivalent of a modern apartment complex. It operated as one of several independent, but associated, towns and villages strung out along the Chaco Canyon. However, its residents must also have participated in community endeavors such as irrigation works, roadways, and communication systems that incorporated them into a much larger social entity.

Chetro Ketl

The Chetro Ketl (also spelled "Chettro Kettle") ruin displays four particularly noteworthy qualities: its great kiva, its tower-kivas, a supposed courtyard colonnade, and the nearby Talus Unit No. 1 (fig. 4-15). We do not know the meaning of its name, but it probably stems from Lieutenant James Simpson's transcription of a Navajo word to English spelling after his expedition in 1850. This second largest of the Chaco Canyon pueblos lies about one-half mile east of Pueblo Bonito.

The pueblo contained five hundred or more rooms, more than a dozen kin-group kivas, two tower-kivas, and two great kivas. Investigators believe the buildings reached four stories in height along the north wall. The many tree-ring dates obtained from excavated specimens have produced the best dated building sequence for any of the Chaco Canyon pueblos. Stephen Lekson has identified fifteen separate construction stages, with a number of substages, ranging from about 1010 to 1105 with abandonment coming at some unknown time after the latest variable noncutting date of 1117. The heaviest construction took place during the Pueblo III Early Classic and Florescent Bonito phases between 1020 and 1080.

Slightly less than half of Chetro Ketl has been excavated over the century and a half since its initial recognition by explorers and archaeologists. The east-west rock-packed back wall runs nearly five hundred feet long and helped support the four-story room blocks next to it. The core of this wall consisted of unshaped stones laid in adobe mortar, while both its faces were veneered with coursed tablets of sandstone, forming a typical Chacoan banded pattern. The wall tapered inward as it rose in height.

Wings of rooms formed the east and west sides of the pueblo, and an arcing row of small one-story rooms enclosed the plaza on its south side (fig. 4-16). Two parallel walls, set about two feet apart and standing about seven feet tall, and attached to the south exterior of these rooms, inspired the label of the "moat" from excavators. The overall pueblo layout has suggested to some analysts that its builders followed a predetermined plan throughout its many construction and remodeling phases. This would be a remarkable feat for a people with no written records since the work encompassed nearly a century and probably five generations.

The front wall of the central building, facing the main plaza, was constructed sometime around 1087 as a row of square columns rising up from a low masonry wall and supporting horizontal timbers in the roof of a gallery. Later, builders filled in the open spaces between these columns to create a series of

4-15. Chetro Ketl and Talus Unit No. 1 (against the cliff to the left) have yielded construction dates from 1010 to 1117. Chetro Ketl contained over five hundred rooms and twelve kivas including a tower-kiva and a great kiva. Although only a small portion of the ruin has been excavated, the photograph clearly shows the outline of the pueblo and its front (south) wall enclosing its plaza.

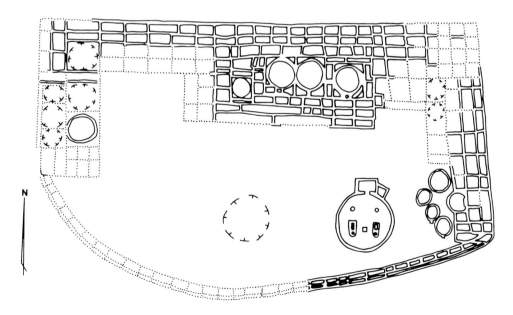

4-16. Chetro Ketl's ground plan.

4-17. The front wall of Chetro Ketl's central room block shows it had originally been built as a low wall with square masonry columns set at intervals along its top to form a kind of colonnade. The spaces between these columns were later filled in with stone masonry to create a solid wall. Some archaeologists have suggested this construction offers evidence for Mesoamerican influence.

rooms (fig. 4-17). A few archaeologists have suggested that this pillar-fronted gallery resembles Mesoamerican architecture of pre-Columbian Mexico and consider it to be evidence of contact between Chaco Canyon and Mexico. However, columns springing from a low wall do not occur in Mesoamerican architecture, making it doubtful that this feature represents solid evidence for a Mexican connection. Better evidence for such a connection has been found in Chaco Canyon's pueblos in the form of copper bells and macaw skeletons that probably came as trade items.

The round tower-kiva on the east side of the central room block originally stood three stories high with the kiva on the top story (fig. 4-18). The room block completely enclosed it, with the spaces between the circular tower and its square enclosing structure completely filled with rubble. No floor features could be observed because of the ravages caused by exposure to the elements. What part the kiva roof may have played in the complex of rooms is not known. The tower-kivas in Chaco Canyon may have been part of the signal

network connecting several of the pueblos with other high points on the canyon rim. We suppose a person standing on top of the tower could see a fire at night burning at another station.

The excavated great kiva at Chetro Ketl is a circular subterranean room with a diameter of more than sixty feet, an encircling bench, niches in the vertical walls, a raised masonry firebox, two masonry-lined floor vaults, and a plaza-level antechamber containing a masonry altar on its north side through which people could enter the kiva down a series of steps (fig. 4-19). Its floor and walls had been constructed over the floor and walls of an earlier great kiva that measured only fifty-four to fifty-five feet in diameter but with a depth below the present plaza level of fourteen feet. Construction of the new outer wall and encircling bench that lies above the original bench completely remodeled the original building. While excavating these two superimposed buildings, archaeologists found ten carefully sealed niches in the older wall just above bench level. Each niche measured about one foot square and contained a

4-18. The tower-kiva, a circular kin-group kiva constructed within a second- or third-story block of rooms, at Chetro Ketl stands on top of a platform of filled-in lower rooms. It represents a distinctively Chacoan feature seen at some, but not all Chacoan sites throughout the Chaco Basin from Salmon Ruin in the north to Kin Ya'a in the south.

4-19. The great kiva at Chetro Ketl had an inside diameter of sixty feet and a depth of fourteen feet. Its roof extended well above the surrounding ground level, supported on four large pine posts that had been seated on top of large wheel-like stones. Its other features included an altar room attached to the north side, a stepped entryway, an encircling interior bench with niches in the walls above it, and raised masonry hearth and paired floor vaults. The excavation in the lower right revealed an earlier version of this great kiva.

necklace of black and white shell and stone beads with both worked and unworked pieces of turquoise. The ten strands had from 983 to 2,265 beads each and measured from seven to seventeen feet long.

The roof for this large structure stood on four large pine posts that stood in masonry-lined holes in the floor and supported a square frame of heavy timbers on which the roofing material rested. One of these timbers measured twenty-six inches across at its base. Smaller beams spanned the space between this frame and the side walls. The addition of smaller poles, brush, and earth produced a flat-surfaced roof. Within each of the four upright support timber footing holes,

the builders had set four huge sandstone discs, each weighing between one thousand and fifteen hundred pounds and measuring over three feet in diameter, to serve as footings for the bearers of tons of roofing materials. Such measures must have worked, for the excavating archaeologists found no evidence of settling or shifting in the building's superstructure.

A second great kiva, toward the western portion of the great plaza, had been created by remodeling an ordinary kin-group kiva through the addition of great kiva features. We can only speculate whether this pair of great kivas indicates a dual division within Chetro Ketl society.

4-20. Talus Unit No. 1, at the base of the cliff behind Chetro Ketl, can be seen to consist of two typical unit pueblos side by side when viewed from directly above.

4-21. The low platform in Talus Unit No. 1, with three low steps leading onto it, may have been an open shrine.

While excavations progressed at Chetro Ketl, the archaeologists decided to explore one of several small ruins tucked against the base of the cliff behind the big ruin. **Talus Unit No. 1** contains some thirty rooms and five kivas (fig. 4-20). Some of its rooms stood at least two stories high. Ladders placed on these high roofs could have enabled the people to reach a roadway at the top of the cliff that led to Pueblo Alto. Its tree-ring dates indicate it had been built and occupied at the same time as the large pueblo.

Talus Unit No. 1 stands on a low terrace platform with three steps near its center leading to an unroofed space (fig. 4-21) that one archaeologist believes shows Mesoamerican influence. However, similar terraced platforms have been found at many Mesa Verde sites such as Pipe Shrine House, Far View House, and most sites built against cliff bases. Rather than showing Mexican influence, such terracing apparently represents a common method used by the Puebloan builders to level ground surfaces on which to build their houses.

Pueblo del Arroyo

In the eleventh century between 1025 and 1075, the population of Chaco Canyon doubled, mostly from immigration. Pueblo del Arroyo's tree-ring dates show it had been built from 1052 to 1103 during this population explosion. This Florescent and Late Classic Bonito Phase pueblo had an estimated 284 rooms and fourteen kivas. It derives its name from its position next to the Chaco Wash arroyo and away from the cliff, where it faces toward the east-southeast rather than to the south. Because it dated to the same time as the later occupations of nearby Pueblo Bonito and its masonry fit into the better, later styles found there, its excavator Neil Judd speculated that a splinter group from Pueblo Bonito (located only four hundred feet to the northeast) may have built Pueblo del Arroyo.

4-22. Neil Judd, who excavated Pueblo del Arroyo, speculated that a splinter group from Pueblo Bonito built this pueblo during the period from 1052 to 1103 when Chaco Canyon's population expanded dramatically. Then, during the McElmo Phase, immigrants to the canyon constructed the concentric triwall structure behind its long back wall (lower left in photograph) while remodeling both rooms and kivas in the main building into a Northern San Juan style.

The masonry in Pueblo del Arroyo equals the finest found in Chaco Canyon. Veneers on walls generally consist of very closely fitted, light-colored sandstone tablets quarried from the main canyon cliff. Perhaps by the time this pueblo was being constructed, the builders had exhausted the most readily available quarries on the north cliff, from which had come the dark brown sandstone used to build many walls in Pueblo Bonito and Chetro Ketl. The tabletlike stones fitted into the walls required a minimum of mortar, enabling these walls to stand for a thousand years.

The central room block reached heights of three and four stories, while the rest of the rooms stepped down in terraces to two stories and one on the ends (fig. 4-22). An arcing row of one-story rooms enclosed the east side of the plaza. The pattern of doorways connecting adjacent groups of rooms indicates the presence of household suites much like those seen in sites on the Mesa Verde and in Tsegi Canyon. Ground-level rooms tended to be used for storage, while people lived on the upper floors.

One long room next to a kiva facing the plaza yielded the skeletons of three adult macaws. These parrots do not live naturally in the American Southwest, but they do exist along the west Mexican coast as far north as Sinaloa. Consequently, they must have been traded northward into Chaco Canyon, perhaps through the large center of Paquimé in Chihuahua, Mexico, where evidence of macaw breeding has been found. The ancient Puebloans and their historic Pueblo descendants have prized the colorful feathers of these birds for use in their ceremonial paraphernalia.

Two nearby kivas present a contrast in roof construction. In the smaller of the two, long timbers extended across the room from wall to wall to provide the base for a flat roof of poles, brush, and earth through which a hatchway over the central fire pit allowed entry. The other larger kiva fits the typical Chacoan style with a low bench supporting horizontal log pilasters on top of which ever-narrowing circular tiers of logs formed a dome-shaped cribbed roof superstructure. Soil and rubble then filled the spaces between this dome and the surrounding walls to make a flat roof with a hatchway entrance to the kiva below. The subfloor ventilating system eliminated the need

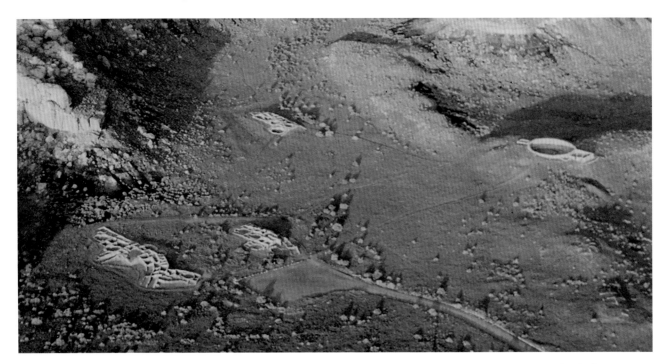

4-23. The Casa Rinconada great kiva along with the surrounding small, Hosta Butte Phase pueblos on the south side of Chaco Canyon existed at the same time as the large pueblos on the north side. Sites to the left of Casa Rinconada, Bc 59, Bc 51, and Tseh So (Bc 50) have been excavated, but many others such as the two mounds just below the great kiva have not. (Photograph taken with the assistance of L. A. Villarreal.)

for a deflector to protect the fire from draft, which was found in most kivas north of the San Juan River.

These two kivas also illustrate the continued remodeling performed by the Chacoans. Several two-story rooms had to be removed to make space for the kivas. And the rooms torn out had been built on top of still earlier kivas that had been filled with trash to make a foundation for the room blocks. This constant rebuilding and remodeling indicates the Chacoans may not have had a master plan for each pueblo, but instead they followed general overall concepts for arranging sections—modules—during the building's growth over several generations of builders and residents.

Toward the end of its span of Chacoan occupation, probably during the McElmo Phase, a unique structure for Chaco Canyon was added next to the back west wall of the pueblo. This building consisted of three concentric circular masonry walls with cross walls between them creating a series of long arcing rooms (see fig. 1-48). An open space in the center possibly once held a kiva. Several masonry rooms and additional kivas abut the south and east sides of the circular walls. The building does not appear to have been finished, and many of the building materials appear to have been robbed for use somewhere else.

This triwall structure resembles very closely similar structures commonly found in the Northern San Juan, such as the Hubbard Ruin at Aztec. Hence we can only suspect that immigrants from the Northern San Juan either built this structure or they strongly influenced its construction. However we interpret it, it probably served a community-wide ceremonial function in the same manner as the great kivas.

4-24. Hosta Butte Phase Sites Bc 51 and Bc 50 (Tseh So), which belong to the Casa Rinconada Group on the south side of Chaco Canyon across from Pueblo Bonito, stood one and two stories high. Such small sites lay scattered about, suburban style, instead of being all incorporated into one large building, urban style, perhaps because their builders employed poorer masonry than did the builders of the large pueblos.

The Casa Rinconada Group

The great kiva known as Casa Rinconada does not occupy a place in one of the large canyon pueblos. Instead it lies among a grouping of small Hosta Butte Phase residential sites including Bc 59, Bc 51, Tseh So (Bc 50), Bc 58, and Bc 57 (these latter two unexcavated) arrayed counterclockwise from the upper left in fig. 4-23. Crews from the University of New Mexico excavated several of these during the 1930s. Although archaeologists once thought these smaller sites predated the large pueblos across the canyon, we now know from many tree-ring dates that both the larger Bonito Phase pueblos and these smaller Hosta Butte Phase sites were contemporary.

The smaller sites range in size from ten to fifty rooms each, plus kivas, and they stand generally only one or two stories high. Their walls exhibit relatively poor masonry of blocky, minimally shaped stones. In the immediate vicinity of Casa Rinconada, the total number of rooms probably exceeded three hundred, all of them belonging to the Casa Rinconada complex. This total surpasses the number of rooms in any of the large pueblos except Pueblo Bonito and Chetro Ketl. Except for the poorer masonry and the presence of fewer luxury items such as turquoise, excavations revealed the Hosta Butte people essentially shared the same lifestyle as the Bonito Phase people across the wash.

The small ruin located next to the parking area for the Casa Rinconada trail is **Tseh So** (Bc 50). This building contained twenty-six ground-floor rooms and four kivas. There may have been some second-story rooms as well. Its companion site to the east, **Bc 51**, included forty-five rooms and six kivas. Both sites show signs of occasional remodeling, just like the larger pueblos, while arrangements of rooms show the presence of household suites (fig. 4-24).

Apparently the largest of the excavated great kivas, **Casa Rinconada** occupies the top of a low hill overlooking the small house sites around it. It had a circular, partially subterranean chamber with a flat roof projecting several feet above ground level and supported by four huge interior pillars. Its interior measures about sixty-three feet in diameter. It had a one-room public entrance at ground level on its south end and a multiroom antechamber with other

4-25. Casa Rinconada, the largest of Chaco Canyon's great kivas, perches on a low hill amidst a clustering of small Hosta Butte Phase pueblos. Constructed and used during the latter half of the 1000s, it exhibits features typically found in such buildings such as a circular shape, partial subterraneity, and probably a roof fashioned in the same manner as the restored great kiva at Aztec Ruin. The subfloor passage probably allowed a figure to appear suddenly in the middle of the kiva during ceremonies. (Photograph taken with the assistance of John Q. Royce.)

4-26. The plan of Casa Rinconada shows an encircling interior bench, the subfloor passage, the raised masonry firebox, a fire screen, two opposing masonry floor vaults (possibly foot drums), seating pits for the four roof support columns, and the north antechamber rooms. (Drawing after Vivian and Reiter 1960).

4-27. Kin Kletso, a McElmo Phase pueblo located just northwest of Pueblo Bonito and Pueblo del Arroyo, was constructed and occupied between 1076 and 1174. It may have been built by the same people who erected the concentric triwall structure at Pueblo del Arroyo, although the two central kivas fit the Chaco style while the smaller kivas on the east fit the Mesa Verde style.

attached rooms on the north. One of the north rooms contained a masonry block altar. Inside the chamber, a bench that could seat one hundred people encircled the inner wall. Interior features included four sockets for the roof support columns, a raised masonry firebox, east and west masonry-lined floor vaults, a fire screen, cists, wall niches, windows, and a subfloor passageway that connected the main chamber with the north altar room (figs. 4-25 and 4-26).

The Chacoans built and used Casa Rinconada during the last half of the eleventh century. Then they reconstructed it and laid a second floor about four inches above the first. At the same time they altered the firebox, changed the floor vaults and bench, and filled in the subfloor passage. The subfloor passage is an unusual feature. It ran about three feet deep, three feet wide, and it had been roofed over. Apparently it had been intended to permit a costumed or masked figure to crawl from the connecting altar room and appear suddenly next to one of the roof support columns near the center of the kiva.

Kin Kletso

This excavated ruin stands alongside the park road between it and the north cliff of the canyon. McElmo Phase people who immigrated from the Northern San Juan Region—Mesa Verde and the Montezuma Valley—constructed it. They brought their own style of masonry, built smaller rooms than those found in other large Chacoan pueblos, and built two Mesa Verde–style kivas into the room blocks (fig. 4-27). In two central kivas, they did adopt the Chacoan style with eight horizontal log pilasters and subfloor ventilator shafts. At the far west end of the building, they raised a tower-kiva fifteen feet tall on top of a huge boulder incorporated into the building. They did not build a great kiva, but they probably contributed to the construction of the triwall structure at nearby Pueblo del Arroyo.

Even though three construction phases have been recognized by investigators, Kin Kletso appears to have had only a single occupation. Tree-ring dates cover about a fifty-year span from 1076 to 1124. Some

4-28. Peñasco Blanco, a large ovoid pueblo located on the mesa top at the west end of Chaco Canyon, had roughly 160 ground-floor rooms, some of which reached four stories in height, seven kin-group kivas within the room blocks, two great kiva depressions in the plaza, and two more outside the village but next to it.

analysts feel this span represents construction that would make it contemporary with the intense growth period of Pueblo Bonito and the other large Bonito Phase pueblos. Stephen Lekson, on the other hand, believes the earlier dates represent reused beams and that the major construction took place between 1125 and 1130, after the end of building in the other Chaco Canyon pueblos. The first building phase encompassed the western half of Kin Kletso surrounding one central kiva, and the second the eastern half surrounding a second central kiva. The two small kivas at the eastern end were added during the final phase.

These varied interpretations raise some interesting questions. Why did the builders employ Mesa Verde–style masonry and build smaller living rooms while adopting the Chacoan style for their main kivas in the two separate building components and for the tower-kiva at the west end? Were they really immigrants from the north, or did they merely accept some northern architectural ideas? Did these builders actually represent the early arrivals of the much larger

Northern San Juan migration into Chaco Canyon, which can be seen in remodeling at most of the large pueblos? A full understanding of the human activities in this fascinating place still eludes us.

Two very late tree-ring dates of 1171 and 1178 derived from the fill of one of Kin Kletso's rooms. They might suggest some activity roughly fifty years after construction was supposed to have ceased. However, their recovery from fill deposits in the room, clearly after its abandonment, cannot be related to construction of this pueblo.

Peñasco Blanco

Peñasco Blanco sits on West Mesa on the south side of Chaco Wash with views toward the east of Chaco Canyon, toward the north of Escavada Wash, and toward the west of the Chaco River. The ruin has a broad oval layout consisting of some 160 ground-floor rooms, some of which reached four stories in height (fig. 4-28). The large depression to the northwest marks an unexcavated great kiva. Another great kiva

4-29. Rock art along the trail to Peñasco Blanco.

4-30. Pecked rock art figures along the trail to Peñasco Blanco.

depression lies outside the main building to the south with two more inside the plaza. Seven kin-group kiva depressions occur among the rooms in the main block. The pueblo underwent several stages of construction with masonry development ranging from the cruder rough slab walls through banded masonry to the rock-packed core with veneer walls evidenced at both Pueblo Bonito and Chetro Ketl.

Construction began at Peñasco Blanco in the early 900s at the same time as at Pueblo Bonito and Una Vida. Its first appearance resembled Pueblo II modular residential units, but during the 1000s, the pueblo grew considerably through the addition of more rooms, upper stories, and kivas, mostly following the curved northern and western portions of the building. The arc of one-story rooms that finally enclosed the ovoid plaza on the east and south were completed after 1090, and the latest dated construction can be placed between 1120 and 1125. How much longer people continued to live here we cannot know. A McElmo Phase building of six to eight rooms, arranged in an L with one kiva, stands on a massive artificial terrace to the northeast of the main building.

Along the trail to Peñasco Blanco, about three-quarters of a mile west of Casa Chiquita, where the trail begins, Puebloan artists pecked into the cliff face two series of petroglyphs. The upper panel located high on the north wall of the canyon depicts a bighorn sheep, a humanoid figure, and a geometric rectangle containing two spirals (fig. 4-29). The second panel occurs farther west at canyon-floor level where a concentration of various humanoid figures, footprints, spirals, wavy lines, and, unfortunately, some recent graffiti may be seen (fig. 4-30).

Una Vida and Kin Nahasbas

Surfaced trails lead from the parking lot at park head-quarters to nearby Una Vida, a largely unexcavated Chacoan pueblo (fig. 4-31). The National Park Service began stabilizing exposed walls from 1956 to 1960, recovering tree-ring specimens as the work pro-ceeded. Although the resulting dates present only a sketchy history of construction at the site, William Gillespie distinguished seven growth stages based on wall abutments and twenty-nine tree-ring dates.

Stage one began with the building of a curved Pueblo I–style masonry unit pueblo of six ground-floor rooms and one kiva around 860 to 865. Extensive remodeling of these early rooms makes it impossible to tell whether they stood more than one

4-31. Una Vida, an unexcavated Bonito Phase ruin on the north side of Chaco Canyon, had roughly a hundred first-floor rooms and four to eight kin-group kivas.

story high. Successive building stages during the mid-900s, and the mid- and late 1000s saw the construction of multistory rooms along the northwestern and northeastern wings of this L-shaped pueblo (fig. 4-32). The arc of low walled rooms that enclosed the plaza was added sometime after 1095.

Poor preservation of the ruin's walls makes it difficult to estimate the size of Una Vida. Gillespie suggests the northwest and northeast wings contained about one hundred ground-floor rooms, with perhaps half of them standing two stories high. Evidence for three stories appears in one limited corner of the main room block. Another forty to forty-five rooms may have made up the plaza enclosure arc. The number of kivas is even more speculative. Anywhere from four to eight kin-group kiva depressions may exist, the northwest wing contains a tower-kiva, and the large unexcavated depression in the south plaza could denote a great kiva.

Another isolated great kiva, Kin Nahasbas, nestles into bedrock and talus on a projection from the north canyon wall a few hundred feet west of Una

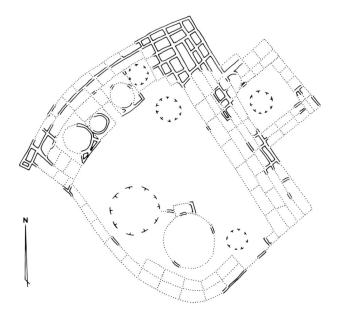

4-32. Ground plan of Una Vida.

4-33. East Ruin (foreground), Pueblo Alto (center), and New Alto on the mesa north of Chaco Canyon looking west toward the junction of Escavada and Chaco washes.

Vida. A team from the University of New Mexico investigated this ruin in 1935. The structure bears no apparent association with the nearby town.

Although smaller in size, Kin Nahasbas resembles Casa Rinconada in many ways. Its floor was dug partially into the ground, and its roof projected above the surrounding sloping surface. It exhibited most of the interior features typical of great kivas, although it had no underground entrance and no southern antechamber. It has yielded no tree-ring dates, but masonry and pottery styles suggest a relatively late date for this site in the very late 1000s and into the 1100s.

The relationships of this isolated great kiva to nearby Una Vida or to several small sites along the north side of canyon remain unclear. However, its situation atop a promontory jutting out from the north canyon wall would have allowed persons stationed there to have lines of sight to several of the canyon floor pueblos, especially the tower-kiva at Una Vida, and to points on the cliff edges marked by stone circles. In this latter scenario, Kin Nahasbas probably did relate to Una Vida.

Pueblo Alto

On the flat open mesa top about two-thirds of a mile from the canyon rim north of Pueblo Bonito stands Pueblo Alto and three smaller ruins (fig. 4-33). This location commands a view across the Chaco Basin to the Chuska Mountains in the west, the San Juan Mountains in the north, to Mount Taylor and Hosta Butte to the south, and to the Jemez Mountains in the east. Archaeologists from the Chaco Center led by W. James Judge conducted investigations at these sites from 1976 through 1978.

Pueblo Alto itself contains 100 to 110 rooms, all of them a single story in height, and eleven kivas, but no great kiva nor tower-kiva. Its ground plan resembles a broad open C with square corners and with a curving row of rooms enclosing its south-facing plaza (fig. 4-34). Chaco Center archaeologists dug ten rooms and examined several kivas. They outlined the tops of all walls by trenching, and they conducted numerous tests into the trash mound and other sections of the ruin. Many of the rooms had quite high ceilings, and Judge feels they appeared to have been intended

4-34. Pueblo Alto contains 100 to 110 one-story rooms and eleven kivas, but no tower-kiva nor great kiva. W. James Judge, who excavated a portion of the site in 1976, has suggested the pueblo might have served as a hostelry for accommodating pilgrims and merchants to the large pueblos in nearby Chaco Canyon.

4-35. New Alto, located just west of Pueblo Alto, is a McElmo Phase site with twenty-eight rooms and a single kiva in the room block.

primarily for storage. He also speculated that this building served as a sort of hostelry for visiting pilgrims and merchants, assuming, of course, that Chaco Canyon had been a major trading and religious center. Had this been the case, the culture should readily have survived the minor environmental problems he attributes as the cause for its collapse by simply importing necessary foodstuffs.

Tree-ring dates from Pueblo Alto cluster from 1010 to 1045. Only one at 1021 came from a construction timber, and the vast majority were recovered from the trash mound, where they clearly had been discarded after having been burned. Despite such inconclusiveness, Thomas Windes postulates five main construction stages on top of remains of still earlier buildings. His Stage I, from 1020 to 1040, consisted of a double row of rooms along the north side with two kivas in front of them to the south in the manner of a typical Pueblo II layout. Successive stages saw the addition of rooms in front and to the east followed by construction of both west and east wings up to 1060 and finally the enclosing of the plaza between 1100 and 1140. His interpretations draw logically on dated masonry styles found at other sites.

All three of the smaller sites near Pueblo Alto appear to represent McElmo Phase construction and occupation. They have never been excavated so no tree-ring dates have been recovered from them. **New Alto** lies four hundred feet west of Pueblo Alto and is connected to the big pueblo by a low masonry wall.

4-36. Pueblo Pintado lies seventeen miles east of the Chaco Canyon visitor center. The photograph reveals the extent of the ruin with about sixty ground-floor rooms with seven kin-group kivas and at least one great kiva. Some rooms stood three stories high. When Lieutenant James H. Simpson first saw Pueblo Pintado, he remarked: "Indeed, so beautifully diminutive and true are the details of the structures as to cause it, at a little distance, to have all the appearance of a magnificent piece of mosaic work" (quoted in Lister 1981:10).

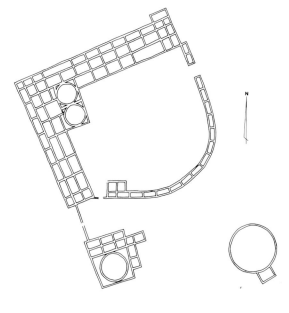

4-37. Pueblo Pintado ground plan.

New Alto contains about twenty-eight rooms, many of them two stories tall, surrounding a single kiva (fig. 4-35). Its masonry clearly reflects the Mesa Verde style. To the east and also connected by a masonry wall to Pueblo Alto lies **East Ruin**, with twelve rooms and one kiva. **Rabbit Ruin** denotes a rubble mound eight hundred feet to the north where limited trenching revealed a plan identical to that of New Alto.

The Pueblo Alto complex in its high mesa location formed a sort of terminus for roadways leading northward. The Great North Road, reaching as far as Kutz Canyon south of Bloomfield, entered the plaza between Pueblo Alto and East Ruin through an opening in the east-west wall that connected the two sites. Fig. 4-6 shows segments of seven of these roadways. Robert Powers of the Southwest Cultural Resources Center believes the building of most of these roads took place between 1075 and 1140. The roadways lead to other large communities, to small settlements, to quarries, and to water sources.

Outliers

Chaco Canyon lies near the center of the Chaco Basin, a relatively flat, semiarid region, bounded on the north by the San Juan River valley, on the west by the Chuska Mountains, on the south by the drainage divide between the headwaters of the Chaco River tributaries and the Puerco River of the west, on the southeast by the Continental Divide, and on the northeast by the divide between the Chaco River and Canyon Largo. This region roughly equates with the area of northwestern New Mexico between Shiprock, Bloomfield, Gallup, and Grants.

Several decades ago archaeologists compared such things as the presence of "great houses," the construction and facings of masonry walls, the size of rooms, the design of kivas, and the existence of great kivas with the buildings at Chaco Canyon and concluded that some seventy Chacoan outliers ranged from Lowry Pueblo

in the Montezuma Valley of Colorado to Guadalupe Ruin near Albuquerque. To Chacoanists the term "Chacoan outlier" still refers to sites that exhibit certain Chacoan architectural features.

The term "outlier" implies a close connection with Chaco Canyon sites. What kind of connection, whether economic, religious, or political, has only been speculated. Such speculations raise questions about whether these outliers were actual outlying colonies, whether they contained enclaves or small migrant settlements of Chaco Canyon people, or whether they merely reflected influence of some Chacoan architectural ideas. The concept of a "great house" has yet to be defined, other than by a generic inference that the large Chaco Canyon pueblos are "great houses."

The system of roadways provides the most persuasive argument for recognizing Chacoan outliers. At least thirty sites located within the Chaco Basin have been connected to Chaco Canyon by ancient roadways (see fig. 4-5). They range in size from sites as large as Pueblo Pintado and Kin Bineola to rather small settlements such as Newcomb and Kin Ya'a. Yet other roadway segments that do not connect or even point toward Chaco Canyon have been identified in other parts of Pueblo-land well beyond the Chaco Basin.

While many of the so-called outliers rather closely resemble the large Chaco Canyon pueblos in architecture and layout, numerous others do not. **Pueblo Pintado**, about seventeen miles to the southeast, comprised some sixty ground-floor rooms with seven kivas and at least one great kiva (fig. 4-36). Some rooms stood three stories tall. Its L-shaped layout with enclosed plaza (fig. 4-37) reminds one of Una Vida. Six tree-ring dates cluster at 1060–1061.

To the southwest about ten miles from Pueblo Bonito, **Kin Bineola** rests on the valley floor of a tributary to the Chaco River. Its ground plan forms a large capital E opening toward the south (fig. 4-38). The

4-38. The layout of Kin Bineola resembles a giant capital E approximately 350 feet long by 150 feet wide with 105 ground-floor rooms, 58 second-story rooms, 34 third-floor rooms, ten kin-group kivas, and one great kiva. Tree-ring dates place construction from the A.D. 940s (Early Bonito Phase) to the 1120s (Late Classic Bonito Phase). Kin Bineola represents one of the principal Chacoan outliers located along one of the major roadways to the southwest of Chaco Canyon.

4-39. Ground plan of Kin Bineola.

building ranges from one to four stories in height with 105 ground-floor rooms, 58 second-story rooms, 34 third-story rooms, ten kin-group kivas, and one great kiva (fig. 4-39). It measures approximately 350 feet long by 150 feet wide. Clusters of tree-ring dates place beginning construction in the 940s or later and the last significant construction from 1119 to 1124.

Some of the other outliers require some squeezing to fit the pattern. **Tsin Kletzin** stands on the South Mesa about one and a half miles south of Casa Rinconada. It occupies a favorable spot for line-of-sight observations. Its forty-five ground-floor rooms and four kivas exemplify the McElmo Phase with Mesa Verde–style masonry (fig. 4-40). Parts of the main room block stood two stories tall with the remainder at one story. The three tree-ring dates fall at 1111 to 1113. Stephen Lekson believes the entire building had been constructed in the twelfth century.

4-40. Tsin Kletzin, seen from the east, lies on the South Mesa of Chaco Canyon about a mile and a half by foot from Casa Rinconada. This small, compact McElmo Phase building, tree-ring dated to 1111–1113, contains at least forty-five ground-floor rooms exhibiting Mesa Verde–style masonry and four kin-group kivas. Some rooms had second stories. Its position puts it in place for line-of-sight observations.

4-41. The Chaco Canyon outlier of Kin Ya'a lies about twenty-four miles south of the canyon on one of the Chacoan roadways. Here around 1106 in the Late Classic Bonito Phase, the Puebloans constructed a four-story tower-kiva, possibly for use in the signaling system, plus two kin-group kivas, and about twenty-two ground-floor rooms with some possible second-story rooms.

4-42. Grey Hill Springs is another Chacoan outlier to the west of Chaco Canyon, constructed during Pueblo II and early Pueblo III. Its most unusual feature consists of a circular wall, probably not roofed, placed on top of a twenty-foot-high natural rock pillar.

4-43. The stone circle at Grey Hill Springs.

4-44. Casamero Ruin sits in the west side of a broad valley about fifty miles south of Chaco Canyon and around four miles north of Prewitt, New Mexico. This probable Chacoan outlier only had about thirty rooms and one kin-group kiva laid out in a backward L. A very large depression seventy feet in diameter indicates a great kiva just south of the pueblo that probably provided a community center for the inhabitants of at least fourteen known nearby small residences.

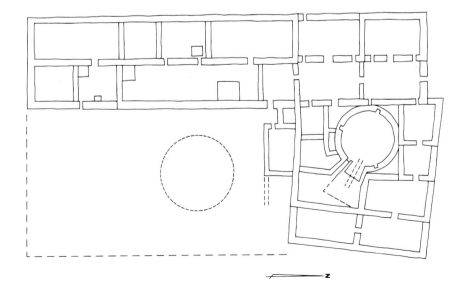

4-45. Ground plan of Casamero Ruin.

Kin Ya'a sits in an open plain twenty-six miles south of Pueblo Bonito on one of the roadways. It contains about twenty-two one-story rooms, perhaps some second-story rooms, two kin-group kivas, and one tower-kiva. The four-story tower-kiva dominates the ruin (fig. 4-41). The few available tree-ring dates cluster around 1106.

The **Grey Hill Springs** outlier is not a real residential pueblo. It consists of two adjacent circular rooms (kivas?), each enclosed in a square masonry block, and a circular masonry wall perched atop a twenty-foot-high natural sandstone butte (figs. 4-42 and 4-43). An isolated masonry room sits on a nearby jutting point. It lies quite far to the west of Chaco Canyon.

Chaco specialists have suggested that additional outliers occur outside the Chaco Basin. They cite Salmon Ruin on the north bank of the San Juan River, Chimney Rock Ruin to the northeast in Colorado, and Casamero across the divide to the south. Other sites such as Aztec probably housed only an enclave of Chacoans. We now know that the presence of a great kiva or of rock-cored masonry walls occurs at numerous Puebloan sites not connected to Chaco Canyon, and hence these architectural features do not necessarily provide evidence for Chacoan influence.

Casamero sits on an east-facing slope in a broad canyon roughly fifty miles south of Chaco Canyon. It is a rather small pueblo with about thirty rooms and one kin-group kiva arranged as a backward L (figs. 4-44 and 4-45). A very large depression seventy feet in diameter marks a great kiva just south of the ruin. Its span of occupation has been estimated at between 1050 and 1220.

Guadalupe Ruin sits atop an isolated narrow mesa remnant overlooking the junction of two canyons east of the Continental Divide. Its estimated twenty-five rooms and three kivas stretch out roughly east-west along the narrow mesa with stubby wings at each end (figs. 4-46 and 4-47). A retaining wall along the south side supports a narrow plaza.

How did this outlier system operate? A number of Chacoanists have suggested that the network of outliers had been designed to bring goods into Chaco Canyon from more favorable surrounding environments. Such items as timbers for construction, food, and pottery would then have been exchanged for turquoise jewelry and mosaics. In addition, they see Chaco Canyon as a redistribution center for food. When one area came up short, others could support it. Some feel that Chaco Canyon functioned as a sort of religious mecca. Had such a system worked as hypothesized, Chacoan culture should easily have outlasted any minor environmental vicissitudes rather than collapsing during the twelfth century.

However, the paucity of evidence of quantities of turquoise jewelry and mosaics anywhere outside Chaco Canyon's large pueblos challenges the marketing hypothesis. Within the canyon itself, only the fine masonry and large size of buildings can offer any sense of a controlling group. Finally, none of the ceremonial (religious?) buildings within the canyon outshine similar structures found throughout Pueblo-land. Thus we come back to the scenario suggested by R. Gwinn Vivian of a well-organized sociopolitical duality that allowed the residents of Chaco Canyon to approach the threshold of an urban society until minor environmental changes or internal factional squabbling caused the society to break up and move away.

The Cibola (Zuni) Connection

Some archaeologists have suggested that the beginnings of Chaco culture occurred during late Pueblo II and early Pueblo III times in the northern Cibola region at sites such as the Village of the Great Kivas, northeast of Zuni Pueblo, or its forerunners. They further suggest that the organization central to the

4-46. Guadalupe Ruin perches high on a ridge overlooking Salado and Tapia canyons, surrounded by visibly ancient cultivated fields, to the northeast of Mount Taylor. Its excavator, Cynthia Irwin-Williams, considers this pueblo to have been part of the Chacoan regional system that failed, causing abandonment of the entire region by 1140.

Chaco culture shifted northward into Chaco Canyon during the late eleventh century to coincide with the Chaco building spurt.

Another view argues that a close connection existed between Chaco Canyon and Cibola and that the towns and villages of the Cibola Subregion fully participated with Chaco Canyon during the Florescent Bonito Phase, making them Chacoan outliers. Inclusion of the Cibola sites would increase the number of Chaco Canyon outliers and make more viable the concept of supportive outlying communities, since the Cibola Subregion is a far more productive region than the Chaco Basin.

The Chaco Canyon–Cibola connection hypothesis adds to the dimensions of the Chaco Phenomenon. If we accept in full the outlier concept, Chaco Canyon residents in their halcyon days would have controlled, influenced, or traded with Puebloan towns and villages spread in a great arc from present-day St. Johns, Arizona, to north of Cortez, Colorado. It appears unlikely, however, that

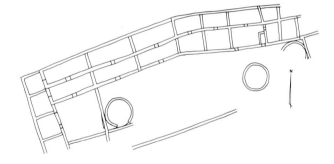

4-47. Ground plan of Guadalupe Ruin.

smaller numbers of Chacoans residing in the starkest Puebloan region could actually control much larger populations living in the more favorable environments of both the Cibola and Northern San Juan regions. Obviously, archaeologists still have much to learn to increase their understanding of the kind and extent of the many relationships of Puebloan peoples in their various habitats.

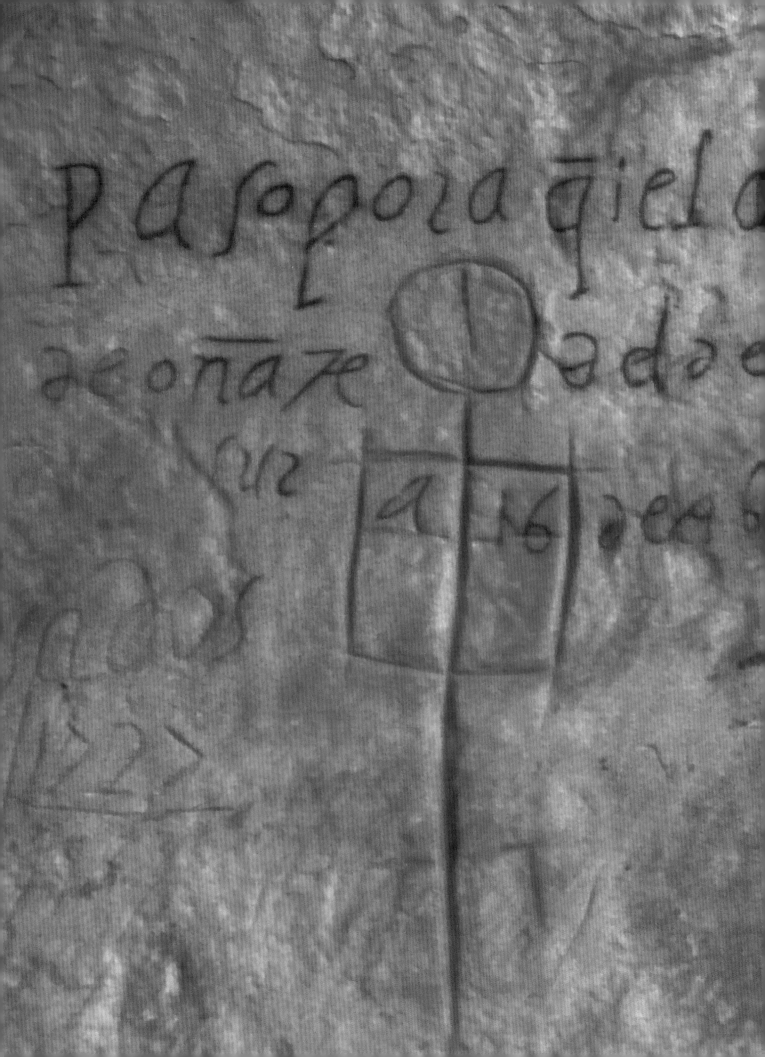

CHAPTER FIVE

Little Colorado River Region

Zuni and Hopi

260

5-1. Modern Zuni Pueblo grew out of Halona, one of six Pueblo IV villages located along a twenty-five-mile stretch of the Zuni River that Zuni people inhabited when the first Spanish arrived in 1539–1540.

Francisco Vásquez de Coronado arrived in the vicinity of Zuni in July 1540, looking for the fabled Seven Cities of Cibola (Zuni villages numbered only six at the time). Coronado never found the expected cities built of gold, but the name "Cibola" remains attached to the region nevertheless.

The Cibola Subregion essentially surrounds Zuni Pueblo in west central New Mexico extending from Petrified Forest National Park on the west to the Continental Divide on the east and from just north of the Mogollon Rim on the south to around Window Rock and Gallup on the north. This region encompasses the upper drainages of the Little Colorado River, the Zuni River, and the Puerco River of the west, all broad valleys covered by grass,

brush, and piñon and juniper woodlands.

Cultural development has been continuous in the Cibola Subregion from Basket Maker times to the present. A sizeable Basket Maker III site has been excavated by William Bullard at Cerro Colorado north of Quemado, New Mexico, and contemporaneous pottery sherds occur at Allentown and White Mound in Arizona. Pueblo I villages have been excavated at White Mound and Kiatuthlanna along the Puerco River in Arizona. Many subsequent sites of Pueblo II, Pueblo III, and Pueblo IV vintage show that people living in this region clearly participated in the general growth of Puebloan culture.

To the west in the lower drainages of the Little Colorado River, ancestral Hopi occupied a broad swath of territory from Petrified Forest National Park westward past Winslow, Arizona, to the Painted Desert on the west, the southern half of Black Mesa on the north, and to the Mogollon Rim on the south. This Tusayán Subregion again exhibits a parallel development of Puebloan culture dating well back into Archaic times.

Cibola (Zuni) Subregion

The fable of the Seven Golden Cities of Cibola seems to have originated in a report by Alvar Nuñez Cabeza de Vaca. After being shipwrecked in 1528 on the Gulf of Mexico coast, he had heard about the golden cities during his wanderings through Texas and New Mexico prior to his rescue. Following a reported actual sighting of such cities in 1539 by Fray Marcos de Niza, Vásquez de Coronado mounted an expedition in 1540 to find them. Instead, he only found the six Zuni pueblos, one of them the pueblo of Hawikuh, all built of yellow (gold) colored sandstone, and grouped around Halona, which later grew into modern Zuni Pueblo (fig. 5-1).

Village of the Great Kivas

The Village of the Great Kivas, located northeast of Zuni, represents but one of numerous eleventh- to twelfth-century villages situated in small valleys off tributaries to the Zuni River. Archaeologist Frank H. H. Roberts excavated this site in 1930 and named it for its two great kivas. He identified three masonry room blocks with associated features. The largest contained sixty ground-floor rooms and seven small

5-2. Village of the Great Kivas on the Zuni Reservation derives its name from the two great kivas that occupy space in the pueblo's large plaza. Some Chaco specialists consider this site to have been one of the outliers to Chaco Canyon because it dates from the late 1000s into the 1200s.

5-3. El Morro designates a massive cliff (*morro* means "cliff") that juts out into the broad Zuni River valley from the south along an ancient trail between Zuni and Acoma Pueblos. A permanent pool of water sits at the base of the cliff, making El Morro an ideal resting place for travelers, both prehistoric and historic, many of whom left inscriptions and/or their names on the cliff face; hence the title of Inscription Rock, now part of El Morro National Monument. The ruins of Atsinna, a Pueblo IV village of an estimated one thousand rooms, lies on the high mesa in the open area at the upper left.

kin-group kivas, three of them set into the room block and four in the courtyard to the southeast (fig. 5-2). Five additional masonry rooms adjoined the cliff next to the block's northeast corner. The smaller of the two great kivas, about fifty-five feet in diameter, abutted the south side of this large room block and exhibited the customary features of a bench encircling the interior, four sockets in the floor where roof support columns or timbers had been set, a raised masonry firebox, two masonry floor vaults, and an antechamber on its north side set into the room block.

A second block of twenty ground-floor rooms stood on the west side of a large plaza in which lay the larger of the two great kivas, with a diameter of more than seventy-five feet. Roberts outlined its walls, but he did not excavate its interior. A third block of only six rooms lay south of this second great kiva.

Most of the village's deceased inhabitants had been buried in three of the site's four refuse mounds where the soil was soft and easy to dig with simple wooden digging sticks. The burials had been laid on their sides with knees drawn up and with their heads pointing either southeastward or northeastward toward

points on the horizon where the sun would have risen at the winter and summer solstices. This seems to reflect affiliations with the Winter and Summer People, who carry responsibilities for ceremonialism and leadership among the present-day Pueblos.

Several of the cliffs nearby display petroglyphs pecked into the rock surface by the prehistoric inhabitants of the area. On some of the cliffs, the modern Zuni Indians maintain painted figures of some of their kachinas and other spirits. The Zunis consider these images to be sacred, and all observers should respect them.

Atsinna (El Morro)

By the 1200s villages in the Cibola Subregion had increased in size, and some of them occupied mesa-top locations. One such settlement was the multistoried pueblo of Atsinna built on top of El Morro, also known as Inscription Rock (fig. 5-3). Although only a small portion of the site has been excavated and stabilized for visitors to see (fig. 5-4), the pueblo contained an estimated one thousand rooms arranged around a square plaza (fig. 5-5). A heavy masonry

5-4. The small excavated portion of Atsinna Pueblo includes the large kiva on the north side of the plaza. The pueblo's location on the high mesa and the absence of external openings into rooms imply a defensive posture. Pueblo IV people lived in this village into the late 1300s.

5-5. Atsinna Pueblo, on top of El Morro, has a rectangular layout around an open plaza where one or more kivas had been built. Only a small group of rooms and one kiva in the northeast corner of the pueblo have been excavated and stabilized to show visitors.

wall, against which the interior room suites abutted, surrounded this plaza. Archaeologists suspect the south side of this enclosing wall may have had a gate or opening. The plaza has both a round kiva and a rectangular one, perhaps indicating influence from the Mogollon regions to the south. Across the box canyon to the north, the visitor trail passes next to a second smaller but unexcavated ruin. The close proximity of these two contemporary pueblos strongly suggests their inhabitants practiced a dual sociopolitical system similar to that found in modern pueblos.

El Morro lay along the trail from Zuni to Acoma and ultimately to the Rio Grande Valley. At the base of El Morro rock could be found El Estanque del Penol, meaning "The Pool by the Great Rock," which Diego Pérez de Luján mentioned in his journal in 1583. This pool provided one of the few sources of drinkable water on the entire route. The Indians had apparently used this trail for centuries, leaving a variety of pecked rock art figures along the base of the rock (fig. 5-6). Later both Spanish and Anglo

5-6. Long before Spanish and Anglo travelers inscribed their messages on Inscription Rock, the prehistoric Puebloans had pecked and incised figures of animals such as these four mountain sheep, handprints, and geometric figures onto the rock face. They, too, had used the great pool of water at the base of the rock and built pueblos both on its top and in the nearby valley.

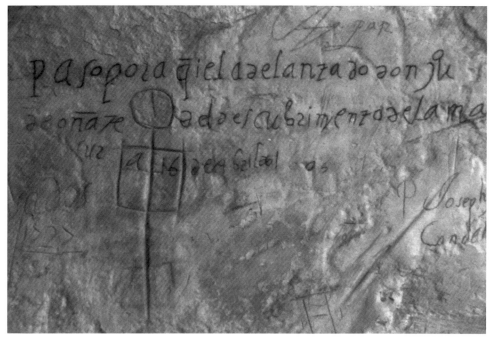

5-7. The oldest Spanish inscription on Inscription Rock in El Morro National Monument reads: "Passed by here the Adelantado Don Juan de Oñate, from the discovery of the Sea of the South, the 16th of April of 1605."

5-8. Puerco Pueblo Ruin, on the south bluff of the Puerco River, is a single-story rectangular pueblo of approximately one hundred rooms laid out around a plaza containing several rectangular kivas. Individual household suites of two or three rooms forming rows from plaza to back wall could be readily identified.

passersby added their own inscriptions at this place. Juan de Oñate carved in Spanish the following inscription: "Passed by here the Adelantado Don Juan de Oñate, from the discovery of the Sea of the South, the 16th of April of 1605" (fig. 5-7). Following the reconquest of the Pueblos after the Pueblo Revolt of 1680, don Diego de Vargas inscribed in Spanish the following on the rock surface: "Here was the General Don Diego de Vargas who conquered for our Holy Faith, and for the Royal Crown, all of New Mexico at his own expense, year of 1692."

Other Puebloan settlements occupied defensive settings to the south of Zuni during Pueblo IV times. By the late 1300s, people had abandoned Atsinna and other eastern sites to move westward into the district of Zuni where they built and inhabited the six pueblos, including Halona, which the first Spaniards observed in 1539.

Puerco Pueblo Ruin and Agate House

In the Petrified Forest National Park, the ruins of a Pueblo III site called Puerco Pueblo Ruin sit on the

5-9. Excavated rooms at the southwest corner of the Puerco Pueblo Ruin on the south side of the Puerco River in the northern portion of Petrified Forest National Park.

south bank of the Puerco River where the Petrified Forest Road crosses it. Prior to 1100 the Indians in this part of the Little Colorado River valley had lived in relatively small settlements, but during the 1100s and 1200s many of them congregated along the banks of the Puerco River into larger pueblos such as this one and nearby Stone Axe Pueblo, about twice the size of Puerco Pueblo. The river valley contains a permanent stream with a marshy floodplain easily adaptable for farming and with ample brush and trees to provide habitat for wild fowl and game.

The Puerco Pueblo Ruin consists of about one hundred single-story sandstone masonry–walled rooms laid out around a rectangular plaza (fig. 5-8). The entire complex measures roughly seventy meters (about 220 feet) north-south by fifty meters (about 160 feet) east-west. Rooms were arranged two to three deep in household suites with living rooms in front

toward the plaza and storage rooms at the rear. The absence of doorways through many walls indicates that some inhabitants gained entry to their rooms through hatchways in the roofs, where they also conducted outdoor work. Only a small portion of the ruin has been excavated (fig. 5-9) including one rectangular kiva with southern ventilator inside the plaza, while visible depressions indicate the presence of two or three additional ones.

Two phases of occupation have been identified at Puerco Pueblo, one from 1100 to 1200 and the second from 1300 to 1380. By 1380, the pueblo had been abandoned.

The village occupies a low mesa with the Little Colorado River on the north side and escarpments on the east and south sides. Here, the inhabitants of Puerco Pueblo had pecked many rock art figures on the flat surfaces of many large sandstone boulders

5-10. A portion of the beautiful and easily viewed Puebloan rock art at the Puerco Pueblo Ruin in Petrified Forest National Park.

5-11. One petroglyph panel of figures pecked through dark desert varnish on the surfaces of large sandstone blocks fallen away from the low cliff edge at Puerco Pueblo Ruin in Petrified Forest National Park shows figures of animals, kachina spirits, clouds, lightning, and geometric forms.

that had broken away from the ledge. These figures fall into two groups, eastern and southern. Individual figures represent a wide variety of motifs from geometrics to ceramic designs that reflect influences from both Zuni and Hopi; different animals such as mountain sheep, birds (one shows a heron holding a frog in its bill), and snakes; humanoid stick figures representing kachinas, kachina masks, and faces; human feet; and many abstract designs (figs. 5-10 and 5-11). This site offers a feast for rock art lovers because most of the figures can be readily recognized by their lighter color against the darker desert varnish through which they have been pecked.

A remarkable collection of pecked rock art figures may be seen at the so-called **Newspaper Rock** about a mile to the south of the Puerco Ruin. Numerous images pecked onto the faces of several large, detached sandstone boulders probably mark a prehistoric shrine where the ancient peoples recorded significant events and sightings in a multitude of different figures (fig. 5-12). The meandering line probably represents part of a migration past a host of animal and humanoid "clan" symbols. Footprints could either be

5-12. The concentration of rock art at Newspaper Rock in Petrified Forest National Park probably represents a shrine where the stories of past migrations have been recounted in one continuous line meandering among various symbols of clans and spiritual figures.

5-13. Agate House, near the south end of Petrified Forest National Park, has been partially restored as a small building where Puebloan people collected suitable stone materials (agatized wood) and chipped them into a variety of useful tools such as arrow points, knife blades, drills, and scrapers.

5-14. The building blocks used to construct Agate House consisted of chunks of agatized (petrified) wood. The stone masons set the varicolored pieces of petrified wood, so plentiful in the immediate surroundings, in mud mortar to raise the walls of this temporary shelter at a place where they could gather excellent raw material for manufacturing stone tools.

the tracks of the migrants or bear paws. The site can be viewed from an overlook near the parking area, but it cannot be directly accessed.

Another Puebloan ruin can be visited in the far south part of the Petrified Forest National Park. **Agate House** rests on a promontory with views in all directions (fig. 5-13). This small eight-room hamlet was built entirely out of blocks of agatized wood (fig. 5-14), hence its name. Archaeologist C. B. Cosgrove excavated this site and restored two of its rooms in 1934. He found no kiva and very little refuse (fig. 5-15). However, the host of chips and flakes of agate scattered about the site suggest it probably served as a quarry and chipping station for the manufacture of stone tools rather than as a residence.

Tusayán (Hopi) Subregion

The lower drainage of the Little Colorado River and its tributaries from around Holbrook to Cameron, Arizona, and from the Mogollon Rim to and including

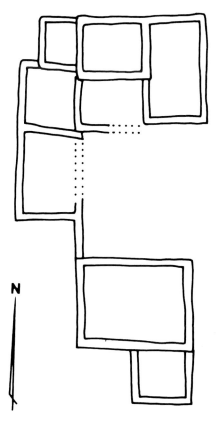

5-15. Ground plan of Agate House.

the southern half of Black Mesa, comprise the ancestral lands of the Hopi. The name "Tusayán" derives from documents of the Coronado expedition in 1540, although he himself did not travel there. Instead he dispatched one of his lieutenants. Sites from Basket Maker III through Pueblo IV have been found scattered throughout Hopi country, while the Hopi themselves have carried the Puebloan cultural tradition into the present.

During Pueblo IV, Tusayán potters began to employ locally derived coal to fire their pottery. This new fuel allowed the potters to achieve high firing temperatures that turned the base colors to orange or yellow. The resulting black-on-orange, black-on-yellow, and polychrome ceramics thus became the finest handmade (not wheel-made) pottery made anywhere in the world, and they also became the distinctive hallmark of historic Hopi craftsmanship.

Several of the Pueblo IV settlements appear to have been quite large. The Chavez Pass Ruin lies toward the Mogollon Rim to the southwest of Winslow, and seven pueblos in the Homol'ovi Settlement Cluster straddle the Little Colorado River to the north and east of Winslow. On the Hopi Mesas, Awatovi, Kawaika-a, Sikyatki, and others preceded the modern Hopi towns. We will only discuss a few of these, but we will also include several of the Puebloan sites from Wupatki National Monument north of Flagstaff, where considerable Kayenta/Tusayán influence can be seen.

Homol'ovi Settlement Cluster

Seven major pueblo ruins make up the Homol'ovi Settlement Cluster, which stretches approximately twenty miles along the Little Colorado River around Winslow, Arizona, at around 4,900 feet in elevation. Jackrabbit, Chevelon, and Cottonwood Creek range to the east, and the four ruins bearing the name Homol'ovi lie on both sides of the Little Colorado

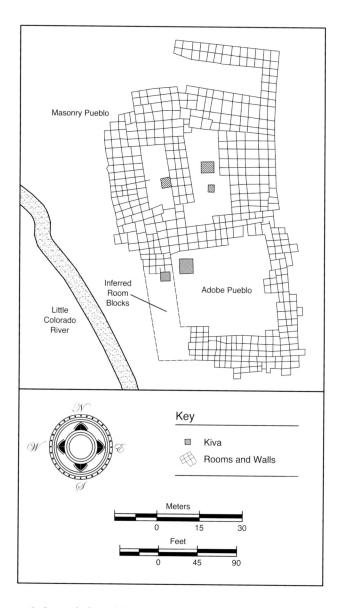

5-16. Ground plan of the Homol'ovi I Ruin at Homolovi State Park, Arizona. The four pueblo ruins of Homol'ovi I, II, III, and IV, plus three others, make up the cluster of Pueblo IV (1300–1540) villages along the Little Colorado River near Winslow, Arizona. (Drawing after Walker 1996.)

5-17. This aerial view of Homol'ovi II shows the layout of the village around two large plazas with rectangular kivas in them. It also shows the extent of illicit digging by relic hunters, who have destroyed many pages of the history of these Hopi ancestors.

5-18. This excavated and stabilized rectangular kiva in Homol'ovi II typifies the ceremonial architecture of these Pueblo IV peoples. In addition to the shape, measuring roughly thirty-three by twenty feet and six feet deep, it has low benches on all four sides, and a stone-lined hearth against the east wall where a ventilator apparently entered. The historic Hopi Pueblos still employ rectangular kivas during their religious practices.

River just north of Winslow. Two spring-fed streams—Clear Creek and Chevelon Creek—flow into the Little Colorado River from the south within this cluster.

Following many years of pothunting by nonarchaeologists, the Arizona State Museum instituted a multiyear investigation of these sites in 1984 under the direction of E. Charles Adams. Then, with the support of the Hopi people, the four ruins bearing the name Homol'ovi became the core of Homolovi Ruins State Park in 1986 to provide for their protection, management, and interpretation. The park opened for visitors in 1993.

Homol'ovi IV, on the west side of the river, seems to be the oldest of the ruins, dating from 1260 to 1280. It contained two hundred or more rooms built partly atop a crude sandstone butte and cascading in steps down the southern and southeastern talus slopes. A short distance to the south, Homol'ovi III was constructed in the river's floodplain between 1280 and 1300. It contained only about fifty rooms and a probable rectangular great kiva.

Homol'ovi I now lies directly on the river's northeastern bank, although only recently, in 1993, the river relocated from an earlier channel farther to the west. Its northern tier of rooms reached three stories in height. Some one thousand to fifteen hundred rooms were laid out around three rectangular plazas in which one large kiva and several smaller kivas existed (fig. 5-16). The builders employed stone masonry for the older rooms in the northern two-thirds of the pueblo but shifted to adobe brick construction for the rooms bounding the east and south sides of the south plaza. The floodplain of the adjacent river provided excellent farmland next to a permanent stream of water as well as fine habitat for birds and animals. Dates for this pueblo range from 1280 to 1390. The position next to the river's floodplain made Homol'ovi I susceptible to flooding that ultimately caused its occupants to relocate to Homol'ovi II.

5-19. Ancient Awatovi, a historic Hopi pueblo located on the south rim of Antelope Mesa and occupied as early as the late 1200s, was probably the first Hopi town to be visited by Spaniards in 1540, and the first Hopi town to accept Christianity in 1629. Following the Pueblo Revolt of 1680, it alone welcomed the missionaries back. The resulting dissension in the pueblo led to total destruction of the town and its inhabitants by other Hopi in 1700–1701, actually at the request of Awatovi's leaders.

Accessible by a foot trail to the north from the visitor center, the largest and latest of the four ruins, Homol'ovi II, had an estimated fifteen hundred to two thousand rooms and possibly forty kivas, all arranged around several plazas (fig. 5-17). Here, too, some room blocks once stood three stories high. One excavated and stabilized kiva has a rectangular shape, almost thirty-three feet long by twenty feet wide and over six feet deep. It has low benches on all four sides, the widest one on the east end, and a stone-lined fire pit against the east wall (fig. 5-18). Apparently all the kivas in the Homol'ovi Settlement Cluster were also rectangular with stone slab–lined hearths and ventilators oriented toward the southeast. Present-day Hopi also use rectangular kivas. Occupation of Homol'ovi II extends from about 1330 to 1400.

Adams's Homol'ovi Research Program has turned up many interesting discoveries. Apparently the Homol'ovi peoples took advantage of favorable growing conditions to raise large quantities of cotton for trade to more northerly Puebloan peoples. They seem to have relied heavily on driftwood brought down the

river by floods for construction timbers and firewood. The middens yielded plentiful remains of rabbits, birds, and even fish. And, an unusually large proportion of the estimated five hundred rooms in Chevelon Pueblo showed signs of burning, as yet unexplained.

According to Hopi oral history, following the abandonment of the Homol'ovi pueblos, the people moved to the Hopi Mesa villages to join other people already living there. A nearby rock art panel displays Hopi symbols for the antelope, spider, water, bluebird, and snake clans.

Awatovi

The ruins of Awatovi lie along the southern edge of Antelope Mesa (fig. 5-19) overlooking the Jeddito Valley to the south. Antelope Mesa represents one of four finger mesas, including First Mesa, Second Mesa, and Third Mesa from east to west, projecting southward from the southern end of Black Mesa, on and around which the ancestral Hopi had settled. The Awatovi Expedition, led by J. O. Brew of Harvard University, conducted five seasons of archaeological

5-20. During the 1930s, J. O. Brew from Harvard University led a multidisciplinary team of specialists in excavating, analyzing, and interpreting significant portions of Awatovi, including the Franciscan churches, and in studying the surrounding geographic setting in which the site stood. These studies established a landmark in Southwestern archaeology.

research in the Jeddito Valley and on the adjacent Antelope Mesa from 1935 through 1939. This expedition excavated parts or all of twenty-one separate sites ranging in occupation age from Basket Maker III through Pueblo IV and into the historic Pueblo V.

The story of Awatovi itself spans the Pueblo III, Pueblo IV, and early historic Pueblo V stages of Hopi history. The town covered twenty-three acres, although no more than one-third of that space may have been inhabited at any one time. Excavations focused on the large western mound where the earliest remains appeared and on the structures surrounding the Franciscan mission (fig. 5-20).

Although one of Coronado's lieutenants visited the Hopi towns in 1540, the Spanish did not establish a permanent presence. Only in 1629 did the Spaniards return to set up permanent missions among the Hopi. Three Franciscan friars established the mission San Bernardo de Aguatubi (Awatovi) (fig. 5-21), while others founded missions on both Second and Third Mesa. However, the uniquely coordinated Pueblo Revolt of 1680 killed all resident friars in Hopiland and drove out the Spaniards from all the pueblos. Such unity of action had never before occurred among the Pueblos, and it never occurred again. Hence, when the Spanish returned in greater force in 1692, they easily reconquered the Rio Grande Pueblos and Zuni. But, the Hopi had now relocated their villages into more defensive settings on the narrow mesa tops, discouraging any serious attacks. Yet, much to the consternation of their neighbors, Awatovi received the Franciscan friars and helped them to build a new church near the ruins of the old one. This action enraged the other Hopi and, coupled with internal dissension, led to the complete destruction of Awatovi Pueblo by the Hopi themselves during the winter of 1700–1701. The Hopi have never again been conquered militarily.

Among the remarkable finds from Awatovi and its sister town of Kawaika-a were major remnants of mural paintings found on the walls of several of the kivas (figs. 5-22 and 5-23). These murals beautifully depict the cosmology of the Hopi before they succumbed under duress to the Franciscan version of Christianity.

5-21. Artist's reconstruction drawing of the Franciscan church and mission at Awatovi.

5-22. Mural painting from a kiva in Awatovi illustrating many of the spiritual concepts in Hopi religion.

5-23. Mural painting from a kiva in Kawaika-a, another Pueblo IV town to the east of Awatovi on Antelope Mesa.

5-24. Oraibi, on Hopi Third Mesa, began at least in the early 1300s, and thus it has become the oldest continuously occupied town in the United States. Parts of the town have begun to fall into ruin as residents have steadily moved out to surrounding homes over the past eighty years. However, Old Oraibi still serves as the place where a great many important ceremonies take place, and to which most Third Mesa Hopi return every year.

5-25. Walpi on Hopi First Mesa has been continuously inhabited since the Pueblo Revolt of 1680. Prior to then Walpi stood on a lower terrace of First Mesa, closer to the valley bottom farmlands. The prehistoric Puebloans of the Kayenta, Canyon de Chelly, and many Little Colorado River valley villages moved into the Hopi Mesas after 1300.

Hopi Villages

The currently occupied village of Old Oraibi on the tip of Third Mesa (fig. 5-24) represents perhaps the oldest continuously inhabited community in the United States. Tree-ring samples taken from roof beams in several of the oldest houses have yielded dates in the 1300s. Most of the other Hopi villages only relocated to the mesa tops from the talus slopes following the successful Pueblo Revolt of 1680. The most defensive situation may be seen at Walpi on First Mesa (fig. 5-25). The arrival of electricity and running water have now caused another relocation back to the valley bottoms for many Hopi, although they retain houses in the mesa-top pueblos for ceremonial occasions.

Wupatki

A number of Puebloan-influenced sites lie beyond the southwestern border of Pueblo-land, several of them located in Wupatki National Monument, northeast of the San Francisco Peaks about twenty miles from Flagstaff. This territory had been relatively sparsely inhabited prior to the eruption of Sunset Crater (variously dated around 1065 to 1067), which spread a blanket of cinders and ash over the Wupatki Basin. This covering helped the soil to retain ground moisture, enhancing dryland farming. The native Sinagua Indians quickly returned to this ash-covered zone, soon to be followed by immigrants from the Kayenta Region, perhaps as part of their contemporaneous expansion westward into the Grand Canyon, and by others from Mogollon and Hohokam regions to the south.

These easily accessible ruins may be reached via a loop road that winds through ponderosa pines, past Sunset Crater, then northward and eastward through the lava beds onto a spectacular tableland covered with multicolored sage growing out of a bed of black cinders and volcanic ash. In the process, this road descends from 7,000 to 5,000 feet in elevation. Along

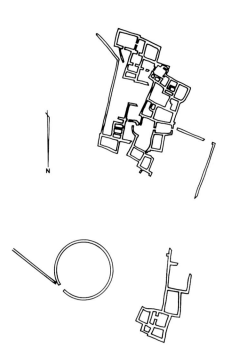

5-26. Wupatki, an essentially Sinagua village in Wupatki National Monument occupied from about 1120 to 1210, exhibits considerable Puebloan influence in its construction. The large circular "amphitheater," or dance plaza, in the foreground may have had a function somewhat analogous to that of great kivas.

5-27. Ground plan of Wupatki Pueblo, north of Flagstaff, Arizona.

the road, the visitor will have beautiful vistas of the Painted Desert and the Little Colorado River valley.

More than two thousand individual sites have been recorded in the basin. These include Wupatki, Wukoki, the Citadel, and Lomaki pueblos plus many small one-, two-, and three-room masonry units that probably served as field houses for outlying farms. Many masonry walls (sandstone blocks, sometimes three stones thick, set in mud mortar), a few kivas, and much Kayenta-style pottery reflect Puebloan influence.

Wupatki Pueblo, with more than one hundred rooms partially excavated (fig. 5-26), can be reached by trail a short distance from the monument headquarters and visitor center. Two separate multistoried room blocks stand on a rock promontory at the head of the canyon. Neither include kivas. These room blocks overlook a large, open structure enclosed by a circular masonry wall with a low interior bench and an opening

toward the northeast (figs. 5-26 and 5-27). Apparently it never had a roof. Archaeologists speculate that this structure may have served the same function as the Puebloan great kivas—as a community gathering place—hence the label "amphitheater."

Well to the north of the pueblo stands an ovoid masonry ballcourt (fig. 5-28) in the style of similar earthen courts found at Hohokam settlements in the Phoenix Basin to the south. Despite these influences from the Puebloans (masonry pueblo) and Hohokam (ballcourt) plus ample quantities of Kayenta pottery as trade wares, the residents of Wupatki seem to have been predominantly Sinagua.

The **Citadel Ruin**, west of the visitor center, resembles a medieval fortress on a steep-sided butte (fig. 5-29). A circular wall circumscribes the top of the volcanic butte and encloses some thirty ground-floor rooms. A narrow opening in the wall on the

5-28. Wupatki lies eighteen miles north of Sunset Crater, a volcano that erupted around 1065–1067, spewing black ash over the entire landscape and creating a moisture-retaining mulch that made the ground very productive agriculturally. The large oval structure in the lower right is a partially restored ballcourt reflecting Hohokam influence from the south.

5-29. The Citadel Ruin crowns a circular, steep-sided butte above the pueblo of Nalakihu. This multistoried pueblo of about thirty ground-floor rooms has an encircling wall through which a single opening provides access, creating a strong defensive posture. Ancient farming terraces can still be seen around the base of the butte.

5-30. Citadel Ruin and Nalakihu formed the core of a small Puebloan-influenced Sinagua settlement occupied during the 1100s and 1200s northwest of Wupatki. The Citadel Sink, a natural trap for water, lies to the south of the Citadel with the San Francisco Peaks on the horizon.

5-31. Lomaki, a short distance north of the Citadel and part of the same settlement, sits on the edge of a jagged crack in the earth. Some of its nine rooms, built during the 1190s, stood two stories tall. The Little Colorado River, about ten miles to the east, provided the only permanent source of water.

5-32. Wukoki perches atop a sandstone erosional remnant about three miles east of Wupatki. Outlines of an ancient field can be seen across the wash in the background.

south provided the only entrance. The Citadel Ruin overlooks a large and deep depression in the ground, called a "sink," beyond which on the horizon rise the San Francisco Peaks (fig. 5-30). The ruins of **Nalakihu**, a one-story ten-room pueblo, lie on the flat below the Citadel. Several individual, small rooms stand on stone-walled agricultural terraces on the slopes surrounding the butte. Their function is unknown, although they look like field houses.

From the Citadel eight other small pueblos can be seen. These and other nearby habitations constituted a village occupied during the twelfth and thirteenth centuries.

To the north of this settlement, a short spur off the loop road leads to a parking area near Box Canyon. A hiking trail from here passes three small pueblos. One of them, **Lomaki**, is a beautiful little building almost hanging over the upper end of the canyon (fig. 5-31). To the east of the visitor center, yet another small fortresslike pueblo, **Wukoki**, has been constructed on top of a rock (fig. 5-32) across a shallow canyon from an ancient field. A large amount of Kayenta-style pottery has been found here.

Down the valley to the east, the Little Colorado River winds through the Painted Desert, flowing toward the Grand Canyon. It provided the ultimate source of water for people in the Wupatki district if the impounded runoff water in the smaller canyons should dry up.

About the middle of the 1200s these Sinagua peoples left the Wupatki region and moved southward below the Mogollon Rim to the valley of the Verde River, where they constructed pueblos such as Tuzigoot and Montezuma Castle.

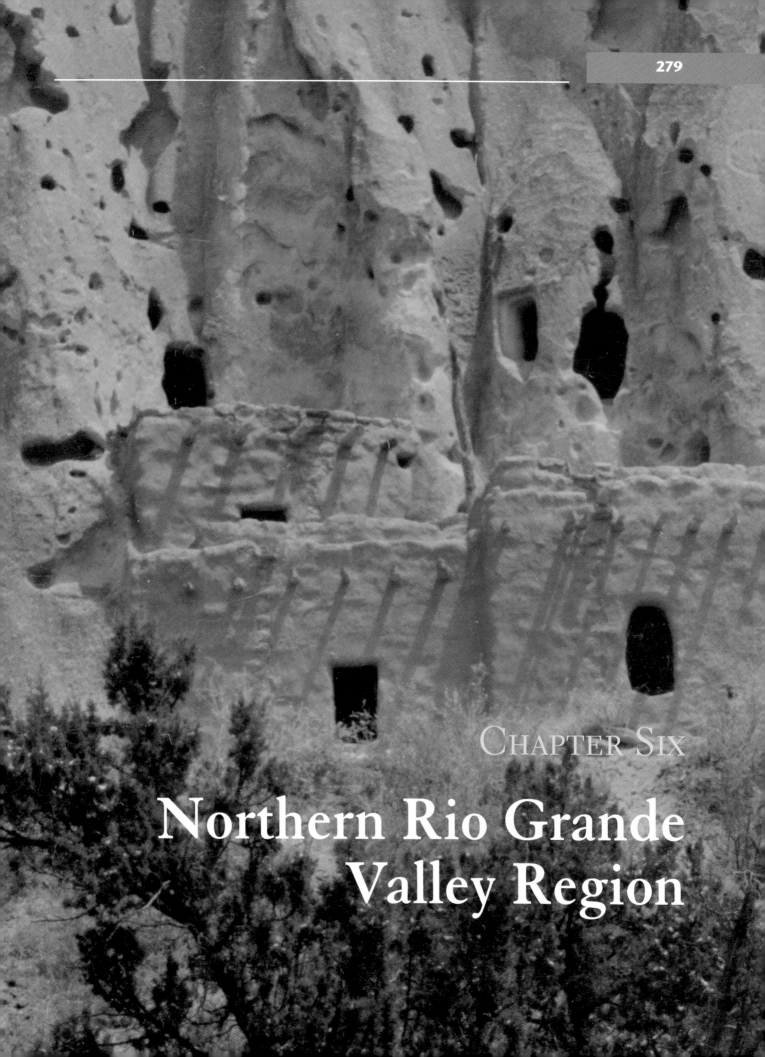

CHAPTER SIX

Northern Rio Grande Valley Region

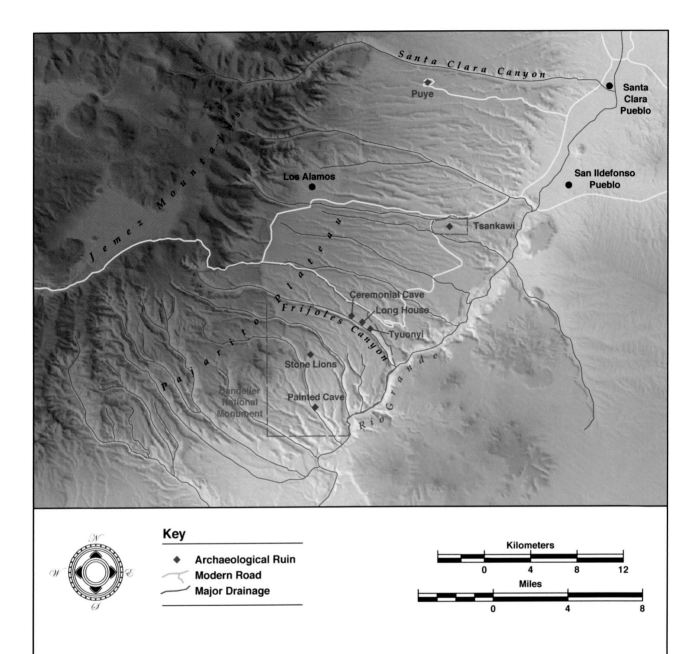

Key

◆ Archaeological Ruin

Modern Road

Major Drainage

Kilometers
0   4   8   12

Miles
0   4   8

6-1. The Pajarito Plateau consists of a flat-topped mass of volcanic tuff (solidified ash) extending between the Jemez Mountains, an ancient volcanic caldera, and the deeply incised canyons of the Rio Grande. The many deep canyons that run into the Rio Grande offered the Pueblo IV people a suitable environment in which to build their pueblos and to raise their crops. Puyé and Bandelier National Monument encompass some of these pueblos on the Pajarito Plateau.

The Rio Grande originates high in the San Juan Mountains west of Creede, Colorado, just across the Continental Divide from the headwaters of the San Juan River. It winds eastward out of the mountains to Alamosa, Colorado, where it bends southward to flow past Taos, Española, Bernalillo, and Albuquerque, New Mexico. This region, north of Albuquerque and south to Los Lunas, constitutes the northern Rio Grande Valley.

This region encompasses Taos Pueblo, San Juan, Santa Clara, San Ildefonso, Cochiti, Santo Domingo, Jemez, Zia, Isleta, and a number of other modern pueblos, plus several excavated and partially restored Pueblo IV ruins such as Puyé, Tsankawi, Bandelier (Frijoles Canyon ruins), Kuaua, and Pecos. Pueblo IV has often been referred to as the Rio Grande Classic, for it was here, as well as in the Little Colorado River regions to the west, between about 1300 and the arrival of the Spaniards in 1540, where the ancient Puebloans reconstituted their culture and carried it into historic times.

A few Puebloan people had lived in the northern Rio Grande Valley during Pueblo II and Pueblo III, but toward the end of Pueblo III, Puebloan populations began to move into the region from the Chaco Basin and the Northern San Juan. None of the resulting sites actually reflects an assemblage of either Chaco or Northern San Juan features. However, these migrants brought with them all the ingredients of Pueblo III culture: masonry-walled pueblos, cliff-dwelling settlements, kin-group kivas, great kivas, decorated ceramics, and an egalitarian social organization with a duality of ceremonial and leadership obligations.

Pueblo IV did not mark a regression of Puebloan culture, but rather it saw a reconstitution of it in somewhat different surroundings following the Great Migrations. Pueblo IV culture continued to evolve and flower in both the Rio Grande Valley and in the Little Colorado River valley to the west. Populations clustered together into increasingly larger pueblos such as Puyé, Pecos, Kuaua, Atsinna, and the Homol'ovi pueblos with multistoried room blocks built around large plazas. These plazas became the focus of community-wide ceremonial functions, partially replacing the older great kivas. Membership in the former kin-group kivas devolved into ceremonial societies that shouldered specific ritual responsibilities. Thus, the numbers of kivas declined considerably during Pueblo IV.

While Tusayán potters in the west started firing their fine ceramics with coal as a fuel, producing a distinctive yellow ware, Rio Grande potters adopted from the Cibola (Zuni) Subregion a technique of decorating their earthenware vessels with various glaze paints. At first they lacked good control, but through time they developed a variety of glaze polychromes. But unlike the Hopi yellow ware, glaze-painted pottery did not last long following the arrival of the Spanish conquistadors. The Spaniards introduced foreign majolica ware that replaced the native-made ceramics.

Unfortunately, none of the prehistoric sites in the Rio Grande Valley have been well dated, except through ceramic styles. Those on the Pajarito Plateau west of Santa Fe were excavated by the School of American Research under the direction of Edgar L. Hewett during the early part of the twentieth century before tree-ring dating had been developed for that region. Alfred V. Kidder excavated at Pecos Pueblo over ten seasons from 1915 through 1929, also ahead of the development of absolute dating techniques.

Only those ruins that can be readily accessed by visitors will be discussed here. Puyé, Tsankawi, and the Frijoles Canyon ruins lie on the Pajarito Plateau (fig. 6-1), all but Puyé encompassed within the boundaries of Bandelier National Monument. Pecos Pueblo forms the focus of Pecos National Monument, and Coronado State Monument near Bernalillo contains Kuaua.

6-2. Puyé ruins combine both cliff dwellings and a mesa-top pueblo built during Pueblo IV (1300–1540) by Puebloans who apparently migrated from the Northern San Juan. These people constructed houses both on top of the mesa in multistoried room blocks surrounding a rectangular plaza and along the south-facing cliffs immediately below. The more than one thousand rooms could have housed around two thousand people. The ruins sit on land in the Santa Clara Indian Reservation near Española, New Mexico. (Photograph taken with the assistance of John Q. Royce.)

Puyé

The Puyé ruins, on the Santa Clara Indian Reservation, located west of Española, New Mexico, combine a series of cliff dwellings with a large mesa-top pueblo (fig. 6-2). The cliff dwellings extend for more than a mile on two levels down the north face of Santa Clara Canyon. Unlike the cliff dwellings in the Four Corners where masonry buildings had simply been built beneath rock overhangs, those on the Pajarito Plateau consisted of masonry buildings constructed against the vertical cliff faces with additional cavate rooms carved out of the soft volcanic tuff of the cliffs themselves. Because of the slopes below

each cliff, the finished buildings assumed a stair-step appearance reaching up to three stories high.

The masonry for the front rooms employed loaf-sized, irregular-shaped blocks of porous volcanic rock set in mud mortar. Consequently few of these walls have survived to any significant height. Hewett actually restored a small room block to show how the buildings once looked (fig. 6-3). Otherwise, the visitor must use his/her imagination to mentally reconstruct the former extent of the buildings from the surviving rows of roof beam sockets cut into the cliff face and from the well-preserved cavate rooms that originally rested behind the now fallen buildings.

6-3. A section of the cliff at Puyé, where cliff dwellings once stood, with several restored two-story rooms to show what the original buildings looked like. The horizontal rows of holes in the cliff on both sides of the restored unit indicate sockets for roof beams where other ancient buildings have collapsed.

6-4. Edgar L. Hewett excavated about half of Puyé's mesa-top pueblo many years ago. The green sage-covered zone to the right of the plaza conceals unexcavated room blocks. Note the large kiva at the near end of the pueblo. (Photograph taken with the assistance of John Q. Royce.)

6-5. A two-story building in the Puyé mesa-top pueblo restored by Edgar L. Hewett.

The ruins of a large rectangular pueblo lie on the mesa top directly above the cliff ruins. Multistoried, masonry-walled room blocks enclose an open plaza (fig. 6-4). A circular kiva lies outside the pueblo on its east side. The pueblo contains approximately one thousand rooms, which housed perhaps 350 families. The masonry also used rough volcanic blocks set in mud mortar. Here, too, Hewett reconstructed one building to aid in interpretation (fig. 6-5). Most rooms were arranged in tiers from front (on the plaza) to back, interconnected by doorways, to make up suites of rooms that would have been inhabited by individual households.

Unfortunately, full archaeological data are sparse. Puyé was one of the first Rio Grande sites to be excavated, and Hewett never published a detailed excavation report. Thus we cannot say with certainty whether or not the cliff dwellings and the mesa-top pueblo had been occupied contemporaneously. Construction of both probably took place no earlier than the late 1300s, and their inhabitants had moved out before the Spaniards had arrived in the mid-1500s.

This apparently contemporaneous habitation of cliff dwellings and mesa-top pueblo also occurred at Frijoles Canyon, Tsankawi, and other Pajarito Plateau locations.

The evidence is circumstantial, yet it points to the conclusion that these towns combined both cliff-dwelling and mesa-top pueblo aspects of Puebloan settlement. The open pueblo–cliff dwelling dichotomy of residence may reflect the duality of sociopolitical organization (Summer and Winter People) found among the modern Pueblos and during Pueblo III in the Northern San Juan and Chaco Canyon. The Tewa-speaking Santa Clara Pueblo Indians claim descent from the prehistoric inhabitants of Puyé.

Tsankawi

The ruins of Tsankawi occupy a nearly detached finger of the Pajarito Plateau jutting out into the Rio Grande Valley. The ruins belong to a detached portion of Bandelier National Monument. As at Puyé, a large rectangular pueblo, with masonry room blocks

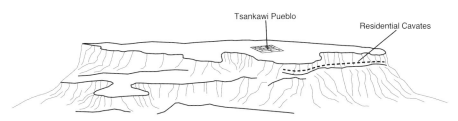

6-6. Simple sketch of Tsankawi, an unexcavated Pueblo IV town on the Pajarito Plateau east of Los Alamos, New Mexico, showing the mesa-top pueblo above and the south cliff and talus slopes where cavates extend. (Sketch by Michael Brack, adapted from original by Cynthia Orr.)

6-7. Frijoles Canyon in Bandelier National Monument showing the visitor center (lower foreground) and the Frijoles Canyon ruins (center) with the Jemez Mountains in the background.

surrounding an open plaza, had been built on the mesa top (fig. 6-6). Two depressions in the plaza surface and several outside appear to indicate the presence of kivas. Little or no excavation has been carried out at Tsankawi, so visitors can see only mounds of rubble where buildings once stood.

Additional buildings, with cavate rooms, have been tucked against the low cliff face to the south and among large boulders strewn about on the long slopes. Cynthia Orr, who wrote her MA thesis on the *Rock Art of Tsankawi*, identified many specific contexts where the rock art figures occurred. Some marked trails as if guarding them; some indicated ritual zones; others identified specific lineages or clans; some denoted natural resources; and some marked community boundaries. The most prominent of the latter consisted of a coiled rattlesnake sculpted on two adjacent boulders. One huge (up to twenty-five feet tall) figure, probably representing a kachina, seems to have greeted people coming into the town along the access trail from the west.

"Tsankawi" is a Tewa word that translates to "gap of the sharp, round cactus." The nearby San Ildefonso Pueblo Indians claim it to be one of their ancestral villages. We have no accurate dating here, but people may have lived on the mesa as early as 1150, while occupation of the pueblo and adjoining cliff dwellings continued into very early historic times.

Frijoles Canyon, Bandelier

The most frequently visited Puebloan ruins in Bandelier National Monument lie in Frijoles Canyon near the monument headquarters (fig. 6-7). The ruins here fall into two major categories—those situated on the valley floor, such as Rainbow House and Tyuonyi, and those built along the base of the cliff on the north side of the canyon (fig. 6-8). Both the valley-floor pueblos and the cliff dwellings date to Pueblo IV, having been built following the Great Migrations of the

1200s. The canyon had been abandoned prior to the arrival of the Spaniards in the mid-1500s, for the journals of Coronado's expedition of 1540–1542 make no mention of it. Edgar L. Hewett excavated most of these ruins from 1908 through 1910 under the auspices of the Museum of New Mexico and the School of American Research, both in Santa Fe.

While Tyuonyi stands apart as the largest pueblo on the canyon floor, several smaller sites also occur there. Most have not been excavated and appear only as low rubble mounds. One such site that the National Park Service has excavated and stabilized for visitors in 1948–1950, **Rainbow House**, lies east of the visitor center and just south of the park entrance road. This small pueblo contains about fifty-five rooms arranged in two room blocks surrounding an open plaza that contains a circular kiva. Excavation yielded eighteen tree-ring dates that place construction between 1408 and 1458.

The foot trail that leads to the major ruins also passes the large, excavated, and stabilized **Great Kiva**. Excavation by Edgar Hewett exposed a circular floor plan approximately forty-two feet in diameter and eight feet deep with an encircling irregular banquette inside the lining wall (see fig. 6-8, lower right). Presumably layers of painted plaster once covered the interior face of this stone masonry wall. The structure's roof rested on six wooden posts set in the floor, and it probably mounded slightly upward above ground surface in order to shed rainwater. It would have been necessary to enter the kiva via a ladder through a hatchway in the roof. Other features include a fire pit near the east side of the room in front of the ventilator tunnel opening that brought in fresh air from the outside; two shallow, masonry-lined boxes in the floor; and a narrow masonry-lined tunnel through the west wall opposite the ventilator. This tunnel seems to have been rather small for use by humans, but spirits could have used it without any difficulty. The size, general

6-8. The major ruins in Frijoles Canyon, Bandelier National Monument, include a large kiva (lower right), the nearly circular Tyuonyi Pueblo (center), Sun House and Snake Village at the base of the cliff to the upper right of Tyuonyi, and Long House at the base of the cliff (upper). These buildings comprised a Pueblo IV town built after 1300 by Puebloan people who migrated here from the Northern San Juan and Chaco regions. (Photograph taken with the assistance of John Q. Royce.)

6-9. Tyuonyi Pueblo, with three hundred ground-floor rooms arranged around a plaza in tiers three to eight deep and two to three stories in height, housed approximately five hundred residents during Pueblo IV (1300–1540). The pueblo had three kivas arrayed along the north side of the plaza. (Photograph taken with the assistance of John Q. Royce.)

6-10. This model shows how Tyuonyi might have appeared when occupied during the fourteenth and fifteenth centuries. A single narrow passageway allowed entrance to the inner plaza, where three subterranean kivas lay beneath its north side.

appearance, and various features are quite reminiscent of great kivas from the Four Corners regions during Pueblo III. Fifteen tree-ring dates from this building suggest its construction during the 1520s.

Tyuonyi, the largest of the valley-floor pueblos, contains more than three hundred ground-floor rooms arranged in a near circle around a central plaza (fig. 6-9). The tiers of rooms range from three to eight rooms deep with plaza-to-exterior rows, like the spokes of a wheel, apparently representing suites of rooms, each of which would have been occupied by a household. Additional second- and third-story rooms would have brought the total room count to between 450 and 500, providing housing for up to five hundred people. The arrangement of these rooms follows the standard Pueblo pattern, although the rounded exterior corners of the pueblo required creation of some pie-shaped room rows. The builders

6-11. This reconstructed room block at Sun House cliff dwelling, a part of the Talus House Ruin above Tyuonyi, illustrates the original appearance of all the Pajarito Plateau cliff-based buildings when occupied during Pueblo IV.

used rough blocks of volcanic lava and tuff laid in abundant mud mortar to construct these buildings. Three circular, underground kivas lay beneath the north end of the plaza. Only one has been excavated, but clearly visible depressions mark the other two.

People could enter the plaza only through a narrow passageway penetrating the tiers of rooms on the east side. Provisions even existed to constrict this passageway if necessary. Since all the suites of rooms opened onto the plaza, with the higher stories of rooms presenting a solid wall on the exterior (fig. 6-10), the residents of Tyuonyi protected themselves against unwanted visitors.

The name "Tyuonyi" means "olla" in the Keresan Pueblo language. The residents of Cochiti Pueblo, who speak Keresan, have applied this name to what they consider to be their ancestral town, now the ruins in Frijoles Canyon, including both the valley-floor pueblo and more than two miles of ruins along the north cliffs.

The cliffs in Frijoles Canyon consist of massive deposits of volcanic tuff, a relatively soft compacted ash spewed forth during numerous volcanic eruptions out of the massive caldera that now forms the Jemez Mountains at the western edge of the Pajarito Plateau. The Puebloan builders used blocks of this tuff to erect masonry walls both at Tyuonyi and along the cliffs. The Pueblo IV peoples built houses against the north cliff face and even burrowed into the soft tuff to create additional rooms. Consequently, visitors can see the bases of masonry-walled rooms that once stood in front of the cliff, as well as rectangular doorways opening into rooms carved wholly out of the tuff.

Paved trails guide visitors past eight of some thirteen housing units stretching along more than two miles of the north cliff face. Directly up behind Tyuonyi are the ruins labeled Sun House and Snake Village by Edgar L. Hewett, who excavated them around 1910. He named **Sun House** after the sun symbol pecked onto the rock face near the top of the cliff above it. The ruin comprises twenty-eight known rooms plus maybe half again as many that have completely collapsed. A low terrace wall in front of the rooms created a flat space that probably served as a dance plaza in lieu of a kiva. One small block of rooms has been restored by the National Park Service (fig. 6-11).

6-12. Long House, against the north cliff in Frijoles Canyon, has 356 rooms divided into five distinct room clusters. The residents of this pueblo built rooms from 1 to 4 deep in front of the cliff and three to four stories high.

6-13. A sketch of the cliff wall and a portion of Long House in Frijoles Canyon shows the outlines of now collapsed rooms with attendant roof beam sockets, niches, rock art, plus doorways and smoke holes into rooms carved wholly within the cliff face. (Drawing by Lisa Ferguson.)

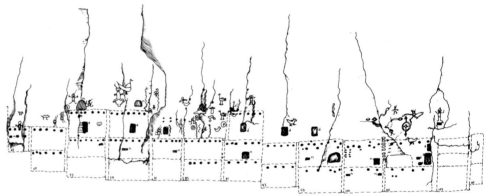

6-14. At Long House in Frijoles Canyon, the flat, contiguous roofs over many second-story rooms provided an open space suitable for conducting ceremonies in front of a major panel of rock art figures. Perhaps such elevated decorated plazas in the Pueblo IV communities of the Pajarito Plateau had begun to replace the older kin-group kivas. (Drawing by Lisa Ferguson.)

6-16. This pecked figure of a macaw, a bird imported from subtropical Mexico, appears on the sheltered cliff face above a small talus house just to the west of Long House in Frijoles Canyon. The figure demonstrates Puebloan contacts with neighboring peoples and trade covering considerable distances.

6-15. Some of the Long House rooms had been carved partially into the soft volcanic tuff of the cliff face. These partial cavate rooms show evidence of painted interior walls and ceilings blackened with soot from ancient fires.

Snake Village took its name from the figure of a feathered serpent that had been painted on the plastered wall of a kiva hollowed out of the cliff. It was considerably larger than Sun House, with many rooms carved into the cliff face. One series of seven such rooms all interconnected with one another inside the rock itself. Some cavate rooms had been finished by constructing a masonry wall across the opening, leaving a small rectangular doorway with a smoke hole above it.

The largest contiguous talus ruin has been named **Long House** (fig. 6-12). In reality its 356 rooms belong to five distinct room clusters (e.g., fig. 6-13). One cluster has a kiva, but the other four each had a second-story dance plaza formed on the roofs of the rooms below. Each cluster exhibited distinctive rock art motifs. The rooms stood 1 to 4 deep in front of the cliff in terraces up to three levels high (fig. 6-14). One set of rooms had even been stacked four high. Even though most of the walls have collapsed, visitors can still see the masonry wall bases and the many marks on the cliff face left from the houses. Horizontal rows of small holes mark where roof beams had been set into the very cliff face. In other instances, the builders had smoothed the cliff face inside a room, sometimes even plastering the cliff face (fig. 6-15).

Most of the rock art figures pecked into the cliff face require the right lighting conditions to be seen. They include faces or masks, humanoid (kachina) figures, animals, birds (fig. 6-16), serpents, shields, and some geometric forms (see also figs. 6-13 and 6-14).

A so-called **Ceremonial Cave** occurs near the west end of the talus ruins. This impressive cave is situated 150 feet above the Rito de los Frijoles and can be reached by a complicated trail involving 90 feet of ladders (fig. 6-17). The cave itself contains a well-preserved kiva, the roof of which has been restored, plus evidence for more than twenty-two masonry-walled

6-17. Ceremonial Cave, actually a residential site in Frijoles Canyon, contains a small, restored kin-group kiva and numerous living rooms. Its perch 150 feet above the canyon floor requires 90 feet of ladders to reach it.

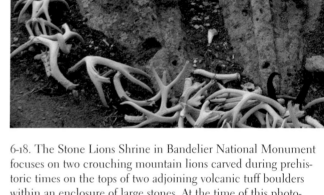

6-18. The Stone Lions Shrine in Bandelier National Monument focuses on two crouching mountain lions carved during prehistoric times on the tops of two adjoining volcanic tuff boulders within an enclosure of large stones. At the time of this photograph, whitened deer and elk antlers encircled the crouching lions, which still serve as a living shrine for the people of Cochiti Pueblo.

rooms. The name "Ceremonial Cave" would appear to be a misnomer since the many rooms suggest that Pueblo IV people lived in the cave and simply used the kiva for their kin-group rituals.

Bandelier's Living Shrines

Two sites within Bandelier National Monument take on a very special interest for students of archaeology and anthropology. The two sites not only represent excellent examples of prehistoric Puebloan shrines, but they both also continue in use as active shrines today. Both are maintained by the inhabitants of Cochiti Pueblo, which helps to confirm the inferred cultural continuity from the pre-Spanish Puebloan culture to the culture of the historic Pueblo Indians of New Mexico and Arizona.

One of these shrines, the **Stone Lions Shrine**, lies on the mesa top three miles southwest of Tyuonyi. Here, the figures of two crouching mountain lions (pumas) have been carved into the tops of

two adjacent volcanic tuff boulders protruding slightly out of the ground (fig. 6-18). This gives the appearance of the lions crouching on the ground surface. Each animal measures about six feet long, including two feet of tail. The lions face southeastward in the southwest portion of a stone enclosure formed with large volcanic tuff blocks, many of them standing up to five feet tall (fig. 6-19). The enclosure forms a rounded pentagon approximately twenty feet across. A similarly stone-lined passageway leads directly southward for sixteen feet from the southeast corner of the enclosure, providing proper ritual access.

Old photographs show traces of vandalism, but the shrine has survived such mistreatment and continues in use. Our photographs, taken in 1983, show an oval ring of antlers encircling the crouching lions (see fig. 6-18). Most represented deer, but a few elk antlers appeared among them. Within the circle of antlers and between the two lions lay a concentration of pottery fragments, obsidian and chert flakes, lumps

6-19. An enclosure of large tuff boulders surrounds the Stone Lions Shrine, but it leaves a stone-lined passageway leading southward out of the enclosure's southeast corner (extreme left of the photograph). Modern-day offerings have also been placed around the trunk and in the branches of the tree growing out of the southwest corner of the enclosure.

6-20. Painted Cave in Capulin Canyon of Bandelier National Monument displays on its back wall many figures painted in a variety of colors by Pueblo peoples from late prehistoric times to the present day. Like many prehistoric rock art panels, this cliff recess represents an important shrine, still in use.

of volcanic basalt, several crow feathers, and a fragment of cotton cloth. A bovine leg bone and a limpet shell with a feather occupied a central position between the lions, while the remains of a dance headdress made from the skull and antlers of a pronghorn antelope sat between the ends of the tails. Twenty-six tiny pouches of cloth in four colors—red, black, white, and yellow—had been tied on a string around the trunk of a piñon tree growing out of the stone enclosure's southwest corner. This same tree's overhanging branches supported two feather prayer plumes above the lions.

Proximity of the Stone Lions Shrine to the pre-Spanish village of Yapashe argues for the first use of the shrine while that village was still inhabited. The crouching lions actually face toward Yapashe. Most of the pottery sherds represent Pueblo IV styles, although they could have been picked up much later. The name "Yapashe" refers specifically to the shrine enclosure.

In Pueblo religion, the mountain lion spirit provides important assistance to hunters and represents the direction north. The Stone Lions Shrine lies less than one-half mile northwest of Yapashe, where the historic Cochiti say their ancestors once lived. During historic times, residents from many pueblos in the Rio Grande Valley and from as far away as Zuni have visited this shrine.

The second shrine comprises many figures painted on the back wall of an arched symmetrical rock shelter or cave (fig. 6-20) situated in the north cliff of Capulin Canyon about three miles south of Yapashe and the Stone Lions Shrine. The floor of **Painted Cave** stands roughly thirty feet above the base of the volcanic tuff cliff, which must have been climbed by supplicants using a series of hand- and toeholds. The route enters the cave at its west end through a small room that had been partially carved into the cliff and decorated with layered rows of red

6-21. This small partial cavate room in Painted Cave displays rows of red geometric figures that may have been painted by prehistoric Puebloans.

dots, diamonds, triangles, and zigzags with a star near the center (fig. 6-21).

Within the cave itself, most of which can be seen from the valley floor below, appear numerous painted figures rendered in red, white, and black paints. The paintings include many recognizable kachina figures and kachina masks, humanlike figures behind large shields, cloud and lightening symbols, various animals such as wolves and a snail, some Christian symbolism, several monsterlike figures, men on horseback, and many others whose meaning is less apparent (figs. 6-22 and 6-23). Many of the figures such as a church, a bell, humans on horseback, and an elk drawn in perspective clearly have a post-Spanish origin, but others quite probably predate the Spaniards' arrival. They at least reflect pre-Hispanic motifs and ideas. The floor of the cave reveals several pecked depressions from three to nine inches in diameter plus engraved outlines of both moccasins and shoes and the tracks of turkeys. A room cut into the base of the cliff below

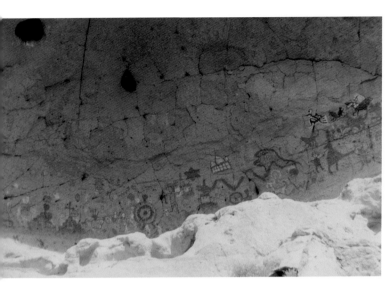

6-22. Painted figures in Painted Cave include kachina figures and masks, humanoid figures, animals, Christian symbols, and monster figures, all of which form part of a living shrine that has been added to and embellished from Pueblo IV into recent times.

6-23. Detail in Painted Cave of a monster figure, humanoids, kachina figures and masks, and a line of Spanish war dogs in red toward the upper right.

the Painted Cave contains a number of stone grinding slabs and hand stones.

Since both these shrines are still used by modern Pueblo peoples, they should be treated as sacred places. Visitors should not enter the sacred portions nor remove any objects from the shrines. The National Park Service preserves the natural context for these shrines, both of which serve as more than religious places. They also provide direct links to a long history reaching far beyond the beginning of written records in the Puebloan Southwest.

Pecos

The ruins of Pecos Pueblo form the central attraction at Pecos National Monument located about twenty-five miles southeast of Santa Fe, New Mexico. Puebloan people had lived in the Pecos River valley in scattered settlements as early as 1100. By 1300 room blocks of one or two stories had been built at Pecos, and by 1450 Pecos Pueblo had reached its maximum size as a large, quadrangular, multistoried town. The pueblo probably housed some twenty-five hundred

residents. In 1591 Castaño de Sosa described the pueblo in his journal as follows:

> The houses in this pueblo are in the manner of house blocks. They have doors on the outside all around, and the houses are back to back. The houses are four and five stories. In the galleries there are no doors to the streets. They go up little ladders that can be pulled up by hand through the hatchways. Every house has three or four apartments so that from top to bottom each house has fifteen or sixteen rooms. The rooms are worthy of note, being well whitewashed.

Alfred V. Kidder excavated the south pueblo, the mission churches, and the *convento* between 1915 and 1929. As Richard B. Woodbury observes: "The Pecos excavations started a new era in American archaeology by showing the importance of stratigraphic information for reconstructing cultural history and by emphasizing the recovery of data over the collection of

6-24. The ruins of the stabilized Pecos South Pueblo (center right) lie on the south end of a low ridge between the unexcavated mounds (upper right) of the much larger North Pueblo of Cicuye and ruins of the church and convento (out of the picture to lower left). Pecos Pueblo began around 1300 and reached its full size by 1450 as a Towa-speaking town surrounded by a low defensive wall (center right to lower left). The arrival of the Spaniards, who brought with them diseases such as smallpox, coupled with devastating raids by the Plains Comanche, whose military capabilities increased dramatically with their acquisition of horses, finally caused complete abandonment of the town in 1838 by its seventeen survivors. (Photograph taken with the assistance of John Q. Royce.)

objects for museums" (Woodbury 1981:15). Here, too, at the invitation of Kidder in 1927, the first Pecos Conference of Southwestern archaeologists established the Pecos Classification of Puebloan stages—Basket Maker I, II, and III followed by Pueblo I through V to cover Pueblo Indian history until 1870.

Little excavation has been done on the original north room block, but four kivas have been partially restored. This unit sits at the north end of a low ridge. Between the north pueblo and the excavated and stabilized mission church and convento, the south pueblo forms a linear block of rooms that have been mostly excavated (fig. 6-24). The south pueblo may have been constructed after the arrival of the Spaniards. Between the two pueblos lies a restored kiva. A low wall, hardly tall enough to function as a major defensive structure, encircles the ridge. The residents dumped their trash down the east slope of the ridge, and as the rubbish pile grew, it became necessary to extend the wall eastward from time to time to make certain it stood on the edge of the ridge.

Pecos Pueblo occupied a strategic spot between the Pueblo villages in the northern Rio Grande Valley and the hunting tribes of the Great Plains. The Pecos people traded grain to the Plains Indians for meat, hides, and animal bones from which to manufacture tools. This trade brought a mixed blessing, however, because continuous raids by the Comanche, with whom they rarely traded, steadily decimated the strength of the pueblo. Coupled with smallpox, unwittingly introduced by the Spaniards, these depredations finally forced the few remaining Pecos Indians to abandon the pueblo by 1838 and join their fellow Towa-speaking compatriots at Jemez Pueblo in the Rio Grande Valley to the west.

After the Spaniards arrived and before 1625, the Franciscan order of monks established the first of four mission churches at Pecos under the name Nuestra Señora de los Angeles de Porciuncula. They had completed and furnished the convento in 1663 (fig. 6-25). The Pueblos burned this early church during the Pueblo Revolt of 1680, and then built a large kiva in what had been the convento courtyard. When the Spaniards reconquered the Pueblos in the early 1690s, they quickly built a new mission church to replace the one destroyed in the rebellion.

Pecos is a beautiful and easily visited site just off I-25 east of Santa Fe. The kiva in the convento courtyard (fig. 6-26) has been restored, and one can climb down into it. A trail leads from the visitor center through the remains of at least two churches and the convento past the south pueblo. The boundary wall for the pueblo has been partially restored along the east side. A second restored kiva may be seen between the south and north pueblos. Finally, the

6-25. Ruins of the mission churches and convento at Pecos National Monument. Franciscan friars established the first of four mission churches, Nuestra Señora de los Angeles de Porciuncula, at Pecos sometime before 1625. They built and furnished the convento around 1663. The first church was burned during the Pueblo Revolt of 1680, but the Spaniards soon returned and constructed a new mission. (Photograph taken with the assistance of John Q. Royce.)

6-26. At the time of the Pueblo Revolt in 1680, the Pecos people burned the church and constructed a kiva in the convento plaza. The restored top of this kiva sits in the foreground in front of ruins of a later church.

6-27. Kuaua Pueblo ruin, in Coronado State Monument near Bernalillo, New Mexico, began around 1300 as a block of about forty rooms around a plaza (to the right of the visitor center) built by immigrants from the Northern San Juan Region. It then grew northward (toward the left) to enclose the north and east plazas, ultimately reaching its currently visible size of more than twelve hundred rooms surrounding three plazas and five courtyard kivas. One rectangular kiva, now restored, contained spectacular murals on its inner walls. People still lived here when the Spaniards first arrived in 1540, but when they returned in 1581, the pueblo had been totally abandoned. (Photograph taken with the assistance of John Q. Royce.)

trail leads around the unexcavated mounds of the north pueblo and back to the visitor center.

Kuaua

Kuaua, a Tiwa word for "evergreen," has been preserved as the core of Coronado State Monument at Bernalillo, New Mexico. It belonged to a group of towns in the region near Albuquerque the Spaniards called Tiguex (Tiwa). The town grew from south to north, ultimately creating a large rectangular pueblo surrounding three plazas and containing a total of more than twelve hundred rooms and five courtyard kivas (fig. 6-27). The room blocks were constructed of adobe bricks laid in courses producing housing units several stories in height.

The oldest section of the pueblo, called the Lummis section, began around 1300. These forty rooms included the plaza to the south with two round

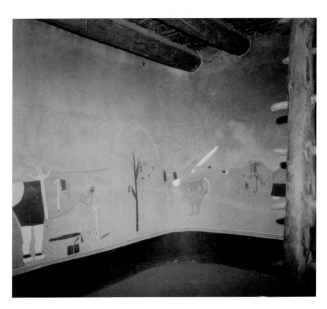

6-28. Pueblo IV in the Rio Grande Valley saw a burgeoning of artistic expressions on the interior walls of Puebloan kivas such as this one at Kuaua in Coronado State Monument. A Zuni interpretation of the figures identifies these (from right to left) as Paiyatuma with a rabbit stick under his wing, a goose, and Ka'nashkule (a priest-clown) with a rain altar above his head. Visitors may view both this restored kiva with restorations of its murals as well as the original murals in the museum next to the visitor center.

6-29. Based upon a Zuni interpretation of the iconography, Bertha P. Dutton describes these figures in her book *Sun Father's Way* (from right to left) as the great spirit surrounded by falling rain (behind the ladder), yellow deer or Maawi, and a stalk of black corn, all recorded on the forty-sixth layer of painted plaster recovered from the walls of Kuaua's restored kiva.

kivas and the square Kiva III, which contained a remarkable series of painted murals. The round kivas and the pottery found here indicate that Puebloan immigrants from the Northern San Juan may have constructed this section. The section burned around 1350, but it had been rebuilt before its abandonment from about 1400 to 1475. Evidence suggests that the burning resulted from warfare or a destructive raid.

The north and east buildings and plazas were completed during the late 1400s. Glaze-painted pottery and the square kivas suggest that newer immigrants from the Little Colorado River Cibola Subregion and possibly from Mogollon regions to the south helped to swell Kuaua's population. Coronado and his army found Kuaua still occupied when they arrived in New Mexico in 1540, but it had been abandoned by the time of the second Spanish expedition in 1581.

Gordon Vivian directed the excavation, stabilization, and kiva restoration at Kuaua with support from the School of American Research, the Museum of New Mexico, and the University of New Mexico. During the 1934 to 1939 investigation, archaeologists discovered eighty-seven layers of plaster in Kiva III with multicolored murals on some of the layers. Kiva III had been plastered, painted, replastered, and painted again over a period covering more than two hundred years. The most significant part of the project, however, involved the transfer of the many plaster layers from Kiva III to the laboratory at the University of New Mexico, where each layer had to be peeled off and preserved. During restoration of the kiva, experts reproduced the murals from Layer N-41 (the forty-sixth layer) on portions of the west, south, and east walls, and the murals from Layer G-26 (the

6-30. This portion of mural seems to depict spirits planting crops, weather, and hunting, showing (from right to left) rain jar and bat, Shulawitsi the fire spirit, rattlesnake and eagle, and Yellow Corn Maiden.

6-31. Yellow Corn Maiden (right) and Blue Corn Maiden (left), with cloud, lightning, and rain symbols between them, as depicted on the sixty-first layer of plaster in the restored kiva at Kuaua.

sixty-first layer) on portions of the east, north, and west walls. The original murals now reside in the museum at Coronado State Monument.

A Zuni interpretation of the iconography of the Kuaua kiva murals suggests the identifications and interpretations for some of them. For example, the Layer N-41 mural begins on the west wall just to the right of the ingress ladder and represents a winter ceremony including, counterclockwise, a duck or Eya; Paiyatuma with a rabbit stick under his wing; a goose or Owa; Ka'nashkule (a priest-clown) with a rain altar above his head (fig. 6-28); Grey Newekwe with jimson weed; Ko'kothlanna, the great spirit, surrounded by falling rain; yellow deer or Maawi; and a stalk of black corn (fig. 6-29).

Layer G-26 depicts the universe with major spirits symbolizing planting, weather control, and hunting. Counterclockwise from the east wall can be seen a deer without its head, a rain jar and bat, Shulawitsi the fire spirit, and a rattlesnake and eagle (fig. 6-30); Yellow Corn Maiden and Blue Corn Maiden (fig. 6-31); an eagle spewing seeds and Lightening Man (fig. 6-32).

The dazzling murals at Kuaua and those we have mentioned from kivas at Awatovi and Kawaika-a on the

6-32. Eagle spewing seeds and Lightning Man flank a corner in the restored mural section of the sixty-first layer of the eighty-seven layers of painted plaster recorded on the interior walls of the restored kiva at Kuaua.

Hopi Mesas, plus Hopi-like paintings at the Pueblo IV site of Pottery Mound on the Puerco River of the east, may as Richard B. Woodbury suggests be only the lucky survivors of a great flowering of Puebloan art during Pueblo IV times. The similarity of style and subject matter in the paintings at these sites may indicate a shared religious pattern employing a symbolism of birds, serpents, animals, and spirits all drawn from nature.

Salinas

The salt flats east of Mountainair, New Mexico, near Willard, represent the remnants of a huge lake that had filled the Estancia Basin twenty thousand years ago. The salt left behind as the lake dried up became a valued trade commodity both for the prehistoric peoples and for the Spaniards who gave this region the name Las Salinas. The Puebloan ruins in this region include three with Spanish mission churches—Gran Quivira, Abó, and Quarai—which make up the Salinas Pueblo Missions National Monument.

The Estancia Valley contains evidence of prehistoric occupation as far back as ten thousand to twelve thousand years ago. Mogollon-style pottery, jacal walls, and pithouses lead us to believe that Mogollon peoples inhabited the region from about A.D. 500 through 1000. Puebloan people and additional Mogollon folk arrived sometime during the late 1200s or early 1300s when they built Gran Quivira, Quarai, Abó, and other pueblos. They probably came from the northern Rio Grande Valley and perhaps from the Cibola Subregion.

The residents of Quarai Pueblo spoke the southern Tiwa language, while those living in Abó and Gran Quivira both spoke the Tompiro language. Both languages belong to the Tanoan language family. These settlements appear to have been typical Pueblo IV towns with stone masonry walls and contiguous residential rooms arranged around plazas in which kivas were situated. Gran Quivira grew to become the largest of these towns, as large as Pecos, housing perhaps as many as three thousand persons during Pueblo IV times.

The Salinas Pueblos formed the southeastern frontier of the Pueblo IV Puebloan distribution. Pecos Pueblo and Taos Pueblo to the north completed this eastern frontier. The residents of the Salinas Pueblos regularly traded salt, corn, and cotton cloth to the nomadic Plains Indians to the east, whom the Spaniards called Jumanos, in return for buffalo meat and hides. Because these nomadic traders frequently appeared at Gran Quivira, the Spaniards came to refer to the town as the "Pueblo de Las Humanas."

Coronado and his army initially bypassed the Salinas Pueblos, but the Spanish incursion had a secondary effect. It may have precipitated the movements of other peoples from the Zuni region and other regions to the south and west of Zuni into the Salinas Region during the middle 1540s. These newcomers apparently influenced the development of Tabirá pottery and brought in the practice of cremation.

After the Spanish had subjugated the Indians by force, Franciscan friars, subsidized by the viceroy of New Spain to Christianize the Indians of New Mexico, arrived in the 1620s and began to build mission churches within or next to existing pueblos. Dry weather, white man's diseases, demands of the missionaries, a feudal system based on *encomiendas* requiring the Indians to pay an annual tribute of cotton cloth or corn, and raids by Apaches brought about the gradual abandonment of the Salinas Pueblos during the 1670s. Many people died of starvation and disease. Those who survived either joined other Pueblos along the Rio Grande or migrated southward to the El Paso region. The Salinas Pueblos were never reoccupied after the Pueblo Revolt of 1680.

Gran Quivira

The Gran Quivira ruins occupy a dry limestone hill about twenty-six miles south of Mountainair, New Mexico, at an elevation of 6,600 feet between Chupadero Mesa to the west and the Gallinas Mountains to the east. By some quirk of fate, this impoverished village where some 450 people died of starvation in 1668 acquired the name "Quivira," the name of the legendary city of gold in Kansas that Coronado's expedition had sought in the 1540s.

6-33. The Buenaventura Mission church and convento (foreground) at Gran Quivira in the Salinas Pueblo Missions National Monument. Puebloans moved into Las Salinas province, named by the Spanish after the many salt basins there, around 1300 and began establishing sizeable Pueblo IV towns including this one, Abó, and Quarai. Spanish friars came to the towns during the 1620s and directed the local people to erect mission churches. San Isidro chapel, in the center beyond San Buenaventura church, was built between 1629 and 1631. Both the mission and the pueblo had been abandoned prior to the Pueblo Revolt of 1680. (Photograph taken with the assistance of John Q. Royce.)

The site comprises seventeen house mounds, nine kivas, the ruins of the historic chapel of San Isidro, built between 1629 and 1631, and the San Buenaventura Mission church and convento (fig. 6-33). In general the stone masonry used to construct room walls was relatively poor, with haphazard coursing and weak mortar. Because of this poor construction, maximum height of the room blocks could not have exceeded two stories.

The room blocks lay scattered around the hillside with plaza areas containing detached circular kivas between them (fig. 6-34). These kivas probably did not serve as kin-group kivas like those built during Pueblo III in the Four Corners regions, but they more likely resembled the ceremonial society kivas found in the modern pueblos. Five interior rooms in Mound 7 show some ceremonial characteristics with plugged doorways and walls covered by several coats

6-34. Gran Quivira, or "Pueblo de Las Humanas," comprised seventeen house mounds, only two of which have been excavated, with at least nine kivas. Mound 7, shown here, has received the most attention from archaeologists, who found that most of the household suites consisted of three rooms in a row facing a plaza. The kivas in the foreground probably served pueblo-wide kiva societies rather than primarily the more localized kin groups of earlier times. (Photograph taken with the assistance of John Q. Royce.)

of plaster. The courtyard kivas appear to have been destroyed some years before final abandonment. This suggests that the missionaries had forced the Indians to fill in their old kivas, so they apparently adapted some interior rooms to serve as kivas. In this way, unknown to the friars, the Indians could secretly perform their traditional rituals.

Excavated House A, just east of San Buenaventura Mission, had been built over the remains of older buildings. Gordon Vivian feels the other mounds probably also represent at least two phases of construction, some of which may have occurred during historic times. More likely the earlier construction took place in Pueblo IV during the 1300s, while the latter dated to Pueblo V after the Spaniards had arrived. The general plan arranged room blocks in a rectangular shape facing a plaza. Most of the ground-floor suites or apartments consisted of three rooms, paralleling the pattern found at most Puebloan sites from Pueblo I through Pueblo IV.

6-35. Only the mission church and convento at Abó in Salinas Pueblo Missions National Monument have been excavated. The unexcavated Pueblo V ruin lies in the background extending to the arroyo, while earlier Pueblo IV mounds lie to the right of the arroyo beyond the picture.

Beneath the center of the excavated rectangular room blocks of Mound 7, archaeologists encountered a circular pueblo of over two hundred rooms with a kiva (Kiva C) in its center. Although smaller, this pueblo had been constructed along the same plan as other circular pueblos at Tyuonyi at Bandelier and Peñasco Blanco at Chaco Canyon. This older pueblo, dating to the 1300s, exhibited substantially better-quality stone masonry than did the later structure on top of it.

Kiva D in the plaza south of Mound 7 has been excavated and stabilized. This circular kiva measures seventeen feet in diameter with its floor dug to a depth of eight or nine feet. Four upright poles supported its roof. The fire pit lay in the center, with an above-floor ventilator tunnel installed on the east side. This east-west axis typifies kivas at Gran Quivira and resembles the Mogollon orientation rather than the Puebloan southern one. The use of this style of kiva through Pueblo IV may indicate a continuity of, or influence by, Mogollon peoples, or it could reflect a mixed population that assembled following the Great

Migrations. Kiva F in the East Plaza approaches a great kiva in size—more than thirty-five feet in diameter—with a low wide bench around the interior walls.

Abó

The Pueblo IV–V ruins of Abó, a Tompiro-speaking pueblo, also comes under the management of Salinas Pueblo Missions National Monument. It lies north of the highway about nine miles west of Mountainair, New Mexico.

It required a six-day battle in 1601 for the Spaniards, under the command of Vicente de Zaldívar, to overcome the resistance of the Indians from Abó, Quarai, and perhaps other pueblos. Less than thirty years later, the Franciscan missionaries oversaw construction by the Indians of San Gregorio de Abó Mission next to the northeast side of the pueblo (fig. 6-35). The inhabitants of Abó apparently got along well with the Franciscans, for many of the Tompiros retreated with the Spaniards to settlements near El Paso, Texas, when the Salinas Pueblos began to decline in the 1670s from the effects of diseases

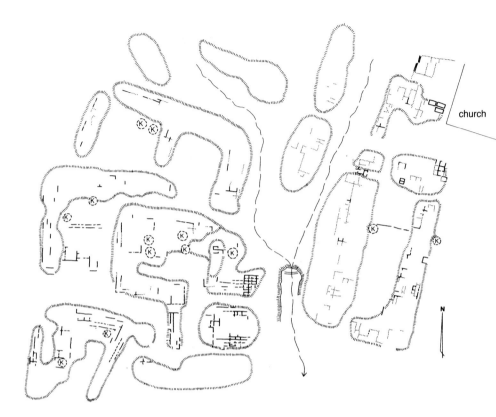

6-36. Ground plan of the rubble house mounds of Abó Pueblo in the Salinas district where the Spanish established a mission church. Those mounds lying east of the arroyo and nearest the church represent the historic Tompiro-speaking pueblo arranged in a large rectangle around a central plaza. Many house mounds of the earlier pre-Spanish pueblo extend west of the wash.

introduced by the Spanish, raiding by Apaches from the Plains, and droughts. By the time of the Pueblo Revolt of 1680, Abó along with all the Salinas Pueblos had been abandoned.

J. H. Toulouse excavated the mission church and attached convento during the 1930s, but he left the pueblo ruins virtually untouched. He did find a kiva in the courtyard of the mission, which had been built about the same time as the church.

The excavated mission complex has been fenced by the National Park Service and may be visited by the public. To the west and southwest of the mission and straddling a small arroyo lie the rubble mounds of a sizeable pueblo (fig. 6-36). Local residents told Adolf Bandelier in the late 1800s that portions of three-story buildings once stood in parts of the historic pueblo. Two- and three-story room blocks surrounding a long rectangular plaza along the east side of the arroyo mark the houses of the Abó residents during Spanish

colonial times. Two rooms, excavated in 1981–1982, may be seen on the south side of the northern mound in this complex. Several kivas lay within the plaza and along the east side of the pueblo. Sometime during the 1800s, Spanish colonists constructed several houses— one on the west side of the plaza and another on the southeastern mound—using stones gathered from ruins of the Indian pueblo.

The numerous low rubble mounds across the arroyo to the west represent the prehistoric Abó Pueblo, first established around 1300. Most of these buildings stood only one story high. The room blocks were arranged around small plazas and courtyards containing kiva depressions. None have been excavated. Artificial catchments along the arroyo and intermittent springs in the canyon to the south provided water to the inhabitants of both pueblos.

Abó's location served as a hub for trails connecting with the other Salinas Pueblos, with the Rio

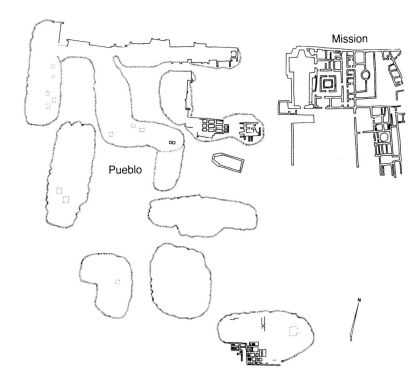

Mission

Pueblo

6-37. Ground plan of the collapsed rubble house mounds of Quarai Pueblo in the Salinas district of New Mexico. This southern Tiwa pueblo had been flourishing from trade with the Indians on the Great Plains to the east when the Spaniards established a mission here. The residents had arranged their housing blocks around numerous plazas where some kivas could be found. Only a few rooms in two of the mounds have been excavated.

Grande Valley to the west, and with the Great Plains to the east. Consequently, Abó became a trading center for products from all three regions, exchanging locally produced pottery, salt, and piñon nuts for such items as obsidian and chalcedony to make tools, buffalo meat and hides, and turquoise, shell, macaw feathers, and copper bells for personal adornment and ritual needs. The Spaniards exploited this same trade network to amass these same items, including buffalo tallow, for shipment southward into Spanish Mexico. They may have built the complex of rooms around the walled yard attached to the west side of the church in which to store and load the goods on ox-cart trains.

Quarai

Located a few miles north of Mountainair, Quarai Pueblo and Mission occupies one of the most picturesque settings in the Southwest. The Indian pueblo

began during very late Pueblo III and saw continuous occupation throughout Pueblo IV and V until general abandonment of the Salinas Region in the 1670s. At its peak, masonry room blocks enclosed at least six plazas with kivas (fig. 6-37). The inhabitants constructed the rooms up to three stories in height using the bright red Abó Sandstone. A few of the later rooms, located just north of the small church, have been excavated.

Adolf Bandelier estimated that some six hundred people lived in Quarai Pueblo. They probably farmed in the broad valley to the west and on terraced hillsides to the north and south. Permanent springs in the wash provided water and may have irrigated terraces on the floodplain downstream to the east. Residents of Quarai imported obsidian and chalcedony from the Rio Grande Valley to manufacture a wide variety of tools. Styles of arrowpoints and bone hide scrapers indicate strong influences from the Plains.

6-38. Quarai Mission and Pueblo, part of the Salinas Pueblo Missions National Monument, located north of Mountainair, New Mexico, had La Purísima Concepción church built there starting in 1628. A large native pueblo, laid out around at least six plazas with kivas and housing around six hundred people, extended to the west and southwest of the mission.

Fray Estévan de Perea began construction of La Purísima Concepción church in 1628. Together with the convento or friar house, storerooms, workshops, and other buildings, the church constituted the mission at Quarai (fig. 6-38). The ruins of the mission have been excavated and may be visited as a part of Salinas Pueblo Missions National Monument.

The Franciscan mission functioned for only about forty-five years. Quarai's Tiwa-speaking inhabitants abandoned the pueblo in 1674. They first went to Tajique Pueblo twelve miles to the north, and shortly afterward to Isleta Pueblo south of Albuquerque.

Living Descendants of the Puebloans

The Pueblo Indians of the existing twenty-nine pueblos of the Rio Grande Valley, the Acoma-Zuni regions of New Mexico, and the Hopi Mesas of Arizona represent the living descendants of the prehistoric Puebloan peoples who once occupied much of the Colorado Plateau in southwestern Colorado, southern Utah, northeastern Arizona, and northwestern New Mexico from the first millennium B.C. through the Great Migrations of the 1200s to the coming of the Spanish conquistadors. The modern Pueblo Indians may include a partial admixture of some ancient Mogollon peoples as well, but today's Pueblo culture derives primarily from the prehistoric Puebloans.

The Great Migrations marked the end of the Pueblo III Puebloans, when they completely abandoned the Northern San Juan, Chaco Basin, and Kayenta regions to resettle in the valleys of the Rio Grande and Little Colorado River to begin the Pueblo IV stage that extended to historic times. When Juan de Oñate began full colonization of the Pueblos in 1598, the Spanish records indicate as many as 134 pueblos with population estimates ranging from 16,000 to 248,000. These figures, particularly the number of

Indians, must be treated with suspicion. We do know that during historic times, 61 pueblos were abandoned, including Gran Quivira, Abó, Quarai, Pecos, Puyé, Awatovi, Hawikuh, and Kuaua.

The Spanish friars attempted to foster Catholicism and to eliminate all aspects of Pueblo religion and customs that did not fit with Christianity. On their part, the Indians resented the Spanish incursion into the pueblos, especially the whippings, torture, and public executions. In a unique cooperative effort, the Pueblos rebelled in 1680 and drove the Spaniards out of northern Arizona and New Mexico, for a few years at least. However, Diego de Vargas finally carried out an often bloody reconquest by 1692.

During the Spanish colonization, Plains Indian tribes increasingly raided the easternmost Pueblo settlements. The Spaniards had introduced horses into North America, and the Indians, both in the Southwest and on the Plains, began to acquire those animals that "escaped" captivity. The Plains Comanche and Apaches quickly used horses in their raids, enabling them to devastate the easternmost pueblos such as Pecos and Gran Quivira. Following the successful Mexican revolt against Spain, New Mexico became a part of the Republic of Mexico in 1821. For twenty-five years the Mexicans substantially ignored the Pueblos and left them unprotected against Plains Indian raids. A United States victory in the Mexican War required Mexico to cede most of New Mexico and Arizona to the United States in 1846. This soon brought an end to the warfare and raids as well as to the unchallenged power of the Catholic Church over the Pueblos.

The prehistoric-historic Puebloan continuum represents one of the very few cultures in the world that can be traced unbroken from early prehistory into modern times. Puebloan culture history exhibits a continuity and homogeneity of evolving culture from roughly 700 B.C. (early Basket Maker II) to the

6-39.

PUEBLO LANGUAGES

LANGUAGE FAMILY	LANGUAGE	PUEBLO
Tanoan	Northern Tiwa	Taos
		Picuris
	Southern Tiwa	Isleta
		Sandia
		[Kuaua]*
		[Quarai]
	Tewa	San Juan
		Santa Clara
		San Ildefonso
		Nambé
		Pojoaque
		Tesuque
		[Puyé]
		[Tsankawi]
	Towa	Jemez
		[Pecos]
	[Tano]	Hopi-Tewa (Hano)
		[Galisteo Basin pueblos]
	[Tompiro]	[Abó]
		[Gran Quivira]
Keresan	Keresan	Cochiti
		Santo Domingo
		San Felipe
		Santa Ana
		Zia
		Laguna
		Acoma
		[Tyuonyi]
		[Yapashe]
Zunian	Zunian	Zuni
		[Halona]
		[Hawikuh]
		[Atsinna]
Shoshonean	Hopi	Walpi
		Sichomovi
		Mishongnovi
		Shipaulovi
		Shungopovi
		Oraibi
		Hotevilla
		Bacabi
		Moencopi
		[Awatovi]
		[Sikyatki]
		[Kawaikaa]
		[Kokopnyama]
		[Homol'ovi]

* [] indicates an abandoned pueblo or a dead language.

6-40. Present-day Acoma Pueblo, appropriately nicknamed "Sky City" because of its location atop a steep-sided mesa, lies about twenty-five miles southeast of Grants, New Mexico. Its Keresan-speaking inhabitants, together with the other modern Pueblo peoples, constitute the living descendants of a more than twenty-five-hundred-year-long Puebloan cultural history. Acoma Pueblo preserves the traditional feeling of its heritage, including the heavy-walled mission church that evidences the coming of Spanish missionaries and colonists. (Photograph taken with the assistance of John Q. Royce.)

present day with a remarkably consistent cultural pattern from Pueblo III (1100 to 1300) into the twentieth century. Puebloan culture has, of course, been influenced during historic times by the Spaniards, Mexicans, and Anglo-Americans. Yet despite these influences, the religious ceremonies, marriage customs, duality of religious ritual and leadership, and languages have remained remarkably constant even since Coronado's incursion in 1540. Even diet and housing did not begin to change radically until well into the twentieth century.

Despite the continuity in Puebloan culture, regional variations reach back into prehistoric times.

Puebloan languages fall into four language families (fig. 6-39). The Tanoan family in the Rio Grande Valley includes four living languages—Northern Tiwa, Southern Tiwa, Tewa, and Towa—plus two languages no longer spoken—Tano and Tompiro. Tanoan has a linguistic relationship to the language of the Kiowa, a Plains Indian tribe. The inhabitants of seven pueblos around Albuquerque speak the Keresan language, which bears no known relationship to any other language in the world. Similarly, the Zuni speak Zunian, also totally unrelated to any other known language. The Hopi villagers speak a Shoshonean language that is related to Numic languages of the Great

Basin and belongs to the Uto-Aztecan language stock, which also includes the Nahuatl tongue of the Aztecs in Mexico. Together, the Uto-Aztecan and Kiowa-Tanoan stocks form a superstock called Aztec-Tanoan.

Anyone who has seen the Puebloan ruins of Mesa Verde, Chaco Canyon, or Kayenta can see the close resemblance to the modern pueblos, especially Taos, Acoma (fig. 6-40), Zuni, or the Hopi towns. Pueblos constructed with room blocks of masonry, from one to three stories high, with room access by ladders, facing a plaza with subterranean kivas were still common at the beginning of the twentieth century. Once small doorways and roof entries to living rooms have given way to full-sized doors, glass-paned windows have appeared, and most pueblos have admitted electricity and running water. Nevertheless, the traditional Pueblo housing patterns remain little changed during historic times.

A more significant continuity may be seen in the survival of the egalitarian society, in which the members of the Pueblo community enforce adherence to custom through general approval or disapproval. Hence, any overt reach for political power becomes effectively thwarted. Although marriage customs vary among the Pueblos, the kinship groups or clans govern marriage relationships so as to protect the integrity of the Pueblo community. Responsibilities for the conduct of ceremonial activities still fall on kin groups or kiva societies with larger responsibilities alternating between Summer People and Winter People.

Perhaps the most remarkable quality of the Puebloans' twenty-seven-hundred-year cultural history (700 B.C. to the present) may be seen in their tremendous achievements in architecture, crafts, water and soil management, and communications networks without surrendering their egalitarian values. So many other human societies readily accepted direction for public works and government from a privileged elite class for the supposed security of a larger urban civilization. Yet, the prehistoric Puebloans and their modern-day Pueblo Indian descendants have shown dramatically how a social system based on equality and cooperation can survive changes in technology and growing population. Pueblo culture has even survived quite successfully the powerful impact of Spanish conquerors and Christian missionaries, both of whom tried to replace traditional Pueblo beliefs and practices with their own. The vitality in living Pueblo culture allows us to breathe life into the ancient pithouse, kiva, great kiva, pueblo, and cliff dwelling ruins of the American Southwest.

Select Bibliography

Adams, Richard E. W.
1977 *Prehistoric America*. Boston: Little, Brown.
Anyon, Roger, and T. J. Ferguson
1983 Settlement Patterns and Changing Adaptations in the Zuni Area After A.D. 1000. Paper presented at the Anasazi Symposium, San Juan Archaeological Research Center and Library, Bloomfield, New Mexico.
Barnes, F. A.
1982 *Canyon Country Prehistoric Rock Art*. Salt Lake City, Utah: Wasatch Publishers.
Breternitz, David A., Arthur H. Rohn, and Elizabeth A. Morris
1974 *Prehistoric Ceramics of the Mesa Verde Region*. Museum of Northern Arizona Ceramic Series, no. 5. Edited by Watson Smith. Flagstaff: Northern Arizona Society of Science and Art.
Brew, J. O.
1946 *Archaeology of Alkali Ridge, Southeastern Utah, with a Review of the Prehistory of the Mesa Verde Division of the San Juan and Some Observations on Archaeological Systematics*. Papers of the Peabody Museum of American Archaeology and Ethnology, vol. 21. Cambridge, Mass.: Harvard University Press.
1979 Hopi Prehistory and History to 1850. In *Handbook of North American Indians, Southwest*, vol. 9. Edited by William C. Sturtevant. Washington, D.C.: Smithsonian Institution Press.
Brody, J. J.
1984 Chacoan Art and the Chaco Phenomenon. In *New Light on Chaco Canyon*. Edited by David Grant Noble. Santa Fe, N.Mex.: School of American Research Press.
Canby, Thomas Y.
1982 The Anasazi, Riddles in the Ruins. *National Geographic* 162(5):554–92.
Cattanach, George S., Jr.
1980 *Long House, Mesa Verde National Park, Colorado*. Publications in Archeology 7-H. Washington, D.C.: National Park Service.
Cole, Sally J.
1990 *Legacy on Stone: Rock Art of the Colorado Plateau and Four Corners Region*. Boulder, Colo.: Johnson Books.
Cordell, Linda S.
1979 Prehistory: Eastern Anasazi. In *Handbook of North American Indians, Southwest*, vol. 9. Edited by William C. Sturtevant. Washington, D.C.: Smithsonian Institution Press.
1984 *Prehistory of the Southwest*. Orlando, Fla.: Academic Press.
Dean, Jeffrey S.
1969 *Chronological Analysis of Tsegi Phase Sites in Northeastern Arizona*. Papers of the Laboratory of Tree-Ring Research, no. 3. Tucson, Ariz.: Laboratory of Tree-Ring Research.
Dozier, Edward P.
1970 *The Pueblo Indians of North America*. New York: Holt, Rinehart and Winston.

Dutton, Bertha P.
1963 *Sun Father's Way; The Kiva Murals of Kuaua; A Pueblo Ruin, Coronado State Monument, New Mexico*. Albuquerque: University of New Mexico Press.
1983 *American Indians of the Southwest*. Albuquerque: University of New Mexico Press.
Eddy, Frank W.
1977 *Archaeological Investigations at Chimney Rock Mesa: 1970–1972*. Memoirs of the Colorado Archaeological Society, no. 1. Boulder: Colorado Archaeological Society.
1981 Upland Anasazi Settlement Adaptations at Chimney Rock Mesa. In *Proceedings of the Anasazi Symposium 1981*. Edited by Jack E. Smith. Mesa Verde, Colo.: Mesa Verde Museum Association.
Euler, Robert C., George J. Gumerman, Thor N. V. Karlstrom, Jeffery S. Dean, and Richard H. Hevly
1979 Colorado Plateaus: Cultural Dynamics and Paleoenvironment. *Science* 205:1089–1101.
Euler, Robert C., and George J. Gumerman, eds.
1978 *Investigations of the Southwest Anthropological Research Group*. Proceedings of the 1976 Conference. Flagstaff: Museum of Northern Arizona.
Grant, Campbell
1978 *Canyon de Chelly, Its People and Rock Art*. Tucson: University of Arizona Press.
Gumerman, George, and Linda S. Cordell, eds.
1990 *Dynamics of Southwestern Prehistory*. Washington, D.C.: Smithsonian Institution Press.
Hargrave, Lyndon L.
1970 *Mexican Macaws: Comparative Osteology and Survey of Remains from the Southwest*. Anthropological Papers of the University of Arizona, no. 20. Tucson: University of Arizona Press.
Haury, Emil W.
1974 The Problem of Contacts between the Southwestern United States and Mexico. In *The Mesoamerican Southwest*. Edited by Basil C. Hedrick, J. Charles Kelley, and Carroll L. Riley. Carbondale: Southern Illinois University Press.
Hayes, Alden C.
1974 *The Four Churches of Pecos*. Albuquerque: University of New Mexico Press.
Hayes, Alden C., D. Brugge, and W. J. Judge
1981 *Archeological Surveys of Chaco Canyon, New Mexico*. Publications in Archeology 18A. Washington, D.C.: National Park Service.
Hewett, Edgar L.
1938 *Pajarito Plateau and Its Ancient People*. Albuquerque: University of New Mexico Press.
Hibben, Frank C.
1975 *Kiva Art of the Anasazi at Pottery Mound*. Las Vegas, Nev.: KC Publications.
Irwin-Williams, Cynthia, ed.
1972 *The Structure of Chacoan Society in the Northern Southwest:*

Investigations at the Salmon Site 1972. Contributions in Anthropology, vol. 4, no. 3. Portales: Eastern New Mexico University.

1973 *The Oshara Tradition: Origins of Anasazi Culture.* Contributions in Anthropology, vol. 5, no. 1. Portales: Eastern New Mexico University.

Jennings, Jesse D.

1956 The American Southwest: A Problem in Cultural Isolation. In *Seminars in Archaeology, 1955.* Edited by Robert Wauchope. Memoirs of the Society for American Archaeology 11. Salt Lake City, Utah: Society for American Archaeology.

1966 *Glen Canyon: A Summary.* Anthropological Paper 81. Salt Lake City: University of Utah Press.

1978 *Ancient Native Americans.* San Francisco: W. H. Freeman.

Jernigan, E. Wesley

1978 *Jewelry of the Prehistoric Southwest.* Albuquerque: University of New Mexico Press.

Judd, Neil M.

1954 *The Material Culture of Pueblo Bonito.* Smithsonian Miscellaneous Collections, vol. 124. Washington, D.C.: Smithsonian Institution Press.

1964 *The Architecture of Pueblo Bonito.* Smithsonian Miscellaneous Collections, vol. 147, no. 1. Washington, D.C.: Smithsonian Institution Press.

Judge, W. James

1984 New Light on Chaco Canyon. In *New Light on Chaco Canyon.* Edited by David Grant Noble. Santa Fe, N.Mex.: School of American Research Press.

Judge, W. James, W. B. Gillespie, Stephen H. Lekson, and H. W. Toll

1981 *Tenth Century Developments in Chaco Canyon.* Archaeological Society of New Mexico Anthropological Papers 6. Santa Fe: Archaeological Society of New Mexico.

Kidder, Alfred V.

1924 *An Introduction to the Study of Southwestern Archaeology, with a Preliminary Account of the Excavations at Pecos.* Papers of the Southwestern Expedition, vol. 1, no. 9. New Haven, Conn.: Yale University Press.

1958 *Pecos, New Mexico: Archaeological Notes.* Papers of the Robert S. Peabody Foundation for Archaeology 5. Andover, Mass.: Phillips Academy.

Kubler, George

1978 *The Religious Architecture of New Mexico.* Albuquerque: University of New Mexico Press.

Lindsay, Alexander J., and Jeffery S. Dean

1981 *The Kayenta Anasazi at A.D. 1250: Prelude to a Migration.* Proceedings of the Anasazi Symposium 1981. Edited by Jack E. Smith. Mesa Verde, Colo.: Mesa Verde Museum Association.

Lister, Robert H., and Florence C. Lister

1978 *Anasazi Pottery.* Albuquerque: University of New Mexico Press.

1981 *Chaco Canyon Archaeology and Archaeologists.* Albuquerque: University of New Mexico Press.

1983 *Those Who Came Before.* Tucson: University of Arizona Press.

1987 *Aztec Ruins on the Animas.* Albuquerque: University of New Mexico Press.

Lyons, Thomas R., and Robert K. Hitchcock

1977 Remote Sensing Interpretation of Anasazi Land Route System. In *Aerial Remote Sensing Techniques in Archeology.* Edited by Thomas R. Lyons and Robert K. Hitchcock. Reports of the Chaco Center 2. Albuquerque: U.S. National Park Service and University of New Mexico Press.

Marshall, Michael P., John R. Stein, Richard W. Loose, and Judith E. Novotny

1979 *Anasazi Communities of the San Juan Basin.* Santa Fe: Public Service Co. of New Mexico and New Mexico Historic Preservation Bureau.

Martin, Paul S., Lawrence Roys, and Gerhardt von Bonin

1936 *Lowry Ruin in Southwestern Colorado.* Publication 356, Anthropological Series, vol. 23, no. 1. Chicago: Field Museum of Natural History.

McGregor, John C.

1982 *Southwestern Archaeology.* 2nd ed. Urbana: University of Illinois Press.

Montgomery, Ross Gordon, Watson Smith, and J. O. Brew

1949 *Franciscan Awatovi.* Papers of the Peabody Museum of American Archaeology and Ethnology, vol. 36. Cambridge, Mass.: Harvard University Press.

Morris, Earl H.

1921 *The House of the Great Kiva at the Aztec Ruin.* Anthropological Papers of the American Museum of Natural History, vol. 26, no. 2. New York: American Museum of Natural History.

1925 Exploring the Canyon of Death: Remains of a People Who Dwelt in Our Southwest at Least 4,000 Years Ago Are Revealed. *National Geographic* 48(3):263–300.

1938 Mummy Cave. *Natural History* 4(2):127–38.

Nickens, Paul R.

1981 *Pueblo III Communities in Transition: Environment Adaptation in Johnson Canyon.* Memoirs of the Colorado Archaeological Society, no. 2. Boulder: Colorado Archaeological Society.

Noble, David Grant

1981 *Ancient Ruins of the Southwest.* Flagstaff, Ariz.: Northland Press.

2004 *In Search of Chaco: New Approaches to an Archaeological Enigma.* Santa Fe, N.Mex.: School of American Research Press.

Nordenskiöld, Gustaf

1893 *The Cliff Dwellers of the Mesa Verde, Southwestern Colorado: Their Pottery and Implements.* Translated by D. Lloyd Morgan. Chicago: P. A. Norsted and Söner.

Olsen, Nancy H.

1981 *Mesa Verde Anasazi Rock Art: A Visual Communication System?* Proceedings of the Anasazi Symposium 1981. Edited by Jack E. Smith. Mesa Verde, Colo.: Mesa Verde Museum Association.

Osborne, Douglas

1964 Solving the Riddles of Wetherill Mesa. *National Geographic* 125(2):155–211.

Parsons, Elsie Clews

1939 *Pueblo Indian Religion.* 2 vols. Chicago: University of Chicago Press.

Peckham, Stewart

1977 *Prehistoric Weapons in the Southwest.* Popular Series Pamphlet, no. 3. Santa Fe: Museum of New Mexico Press.

Pike, Donald G.

1974 *Anasazi, Ancient People of the Rock*. New York: Crown.

Plog, Fred

1979 Prehistory: Western Anasazi. In *Handbook of North American Indians, Southwest*, vol. 9. Edited by William C. Sturtevant. Washington, D.C.: Smithsonian Institution Press.

Powers, Robert P., William B. Gillespie, and Stephen H. Lekson

1983 *The Outlier Survey*. Reports of the Chaco Center, no. 3. Albuquerque, N.Mex.: Division of Cultural Research, U.S. National Park Service.

Powers, Robert P.

1984 Outliers and Roads in the Chaco System. In *New Light on Chaco Canyon*. Edited by David Grant Noble. Santa Fe, N.Mex.: School of American Research Press.

Reed, Erik K.

1964 The Greater Southwest. In *Prehistoric Man in the New World*. Edited by Jesse D. Jennings and Edward Norbeck. Chicago: University of Chicago Press.

Reed, Paul F., ed.

2000 *Foundations of Anasazi Culture: The Basketmaker–Pueblo Transition*. Salt Lake City: University of Utah Press.

Roberts, David

2004 *The Pueblo Revolt: The Secret Rebellion That Drove the Spaniards Out of the Southwest*. New York: Simon and Schuster.

Rohn, Arthur H.

1971 *Mug House, Mesa Verde National Park, Colorado*. Archeological Research Series 7-D. Washington, D.C.: National Park Service.

1977 *Cultural Change and Continuity on Chapin Mesa*. Lawrence: Regents Press of Kansas.

1981 *Budding Urban Settlements in the Northern San Juan*. Proceedings of the Anasazi Symposium 1981. Edited by Jack E. Smith. Mesa Verde, Colo.: Mesa Verde Museum Association.

Schaafsma, Polly

1980 *Indian Rock Art of the Southwest*. Albuquerque: University of New Mexico Press.

Schroeder, Albert H.

1979 Pueblos Abandoned in Historic Times. In *Handbook of North American Indians, Southwest*, vol. 9. Edited by William C. Sturtevant. Washington, D.C.: Smithsonian Institution Press.

Sebastian, Lynne

1992 *The Chaco Anasazi: Sociopolitical Evolution in the Prehistoric Southwest*. London: Cambridge University Press.

Smith, Watson, R. B. Woodbury, and N. F. D. Woodbury, eds.

1966 *The Excavations of Hawikuh by Frederick Webb Hodge*. New York: Museum of the American Indian Press.

Steen, Charles R.

1977 *Pajarito Plateau Archaeological Survey and Excavation*. Los Alamos, N.Mex.: Los Alamos Scientific Laboratories.

Strutin, Michele

1994 *Chaco, A Cultural Legacy*. Tucson, Ariz.: Southwest Parks and Monuments Association.

Stuart, David

2000 *Anasazi America*. Albuquerque: University of New Mexico Press.

Stuart, David E., and Rory P. Gauthier

1981 *Prehistoric New Mexico, Background for Survey*. Edited by Thomas W. Merlan. Santa Fe, N.Mex.: Historic Preservation Bureau.

Tanner, Clara Lee

1976 *Prehistoric Southwestern Craft Arts*. Tucson: University of Arizona Press.

Viele, Catherine W.

1980 *Voices in the Canyon*. Globe, Ariz.: Southwest Parks and Monuments Association.

Vivian, Gordon

1979 *Excavations in a Seventeenth-Century Pueblo, Gran Quivira*. Archeological Research Series, no. 8. Washington, D.C.: National Park Service.

Vivian, Gordon, and Paul Reiter

1960 *The Great Kivas of Chaco Canyon and Their Relationships*. Monographs of the School of American Research 22. Santa Fe, N.Mex.: School of American Research.

Vivian, R. Gwinn

1990 *The Chacoan Prehistory of the San Juan Basin*. New York: Academic Press.

Waters, Frank

1963 *Book of the Hopi*. New York: Penguin Books.

Watson, Don

1961 *Indians of the Mesa Verde*. Mesa Verde, Colo.: Mesa Verde Museum Association.

Wendorf, Fred, and Erik K. Reed

1955 An Alternative Reconstruction of Northern Rio Grande Prehistory. *El Palacio* 62(5–6):131–73.

Wenger, Gilbert R.

1980 *The Story of Mesa Verde National Park*. Mesa Verde, Colo.: Mesa Verde Museum Association.

Willey, Gordon R.

1966 *An Introduction to American Archaeology*. Vol. 1, *North and Middle America*. Englewood Cliffs, N.J.: Prentice-Hall.

Williamson, Ray A., Howard H. Fisher, and Donnel O'Flynn

1977 Anasazi Solar Observations. In *Native American Astronomy*. Edited by Anthony F. Aveni. Austin: University of Texas Press.

Woodbury, Richard B.

1979a Prehistory Introduction. In *Handbook of North American Indians, Southwest*, vol. 9. Edited by William C. Sturtevant. Washington, D.C.: Smithsonian Institution Press.

1979b Zuni Prehistory and History to 1850. In *Handbook of North American Indians, Southwest*, vol. 9. Edited by William C. Sturtevant. Washington, D.C.: Smithsonian Institution Press.

1981 Chaos to Order: A. V. Kidder at Pecos. In *Pecos Ruins*. Edited by David Grant Noble. Santa Fe, N.Mex.: School of American Research Press.

Woodbury, Richard B., and Ezra B. W. Zubrow

1979 Agricultural Beginnings, 2000 B.C.–A.D. 500. In *Handbook of North American Indians, Southwest*, vol. 9. Edited by William C. Sturtevant. Washington, D.C.: Smithsonian Institution Press.

Wormington, H. M.

1969 *Prehistoric Indians of the Southwest*. Denver Museum of Natural History, Popular Series, no. 7. 2nd ed. Denver, Colo.: Denver Museum of Natural History.

Index